Management
and the Arts

Management
and the Arts

Second Edition

William J. Byrnes

**Focal
Press**

Boston   Auckland   Oxford
Johannesburg   Melbourne   New Delhi

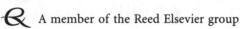

Focal Press is an imprint of Butterworth–Heinemann.

Copyright © 1999 by Butterworth–Heinemann

 A member of the Reed Elsevier group

 Recognizing the importance of preserving what has been written, Butterworth–Heinemann prints its books on acid-free paper whenever possible.

AMERICAN FORESTS
GLOBAL
RELEAF
2000
Butterworth–Heinemann supports the efforts of American Forests and the Global ReLeaf program in its campaign for the betterment of trees, forests, and our environment.

Library of Congress Cataloging-in-Publication Data

Byrnes, William J.
    Management and the arts / William J. Byrnes.–2nd ed.
        p.   cm.
    Includes bibliographical references and index.
    ISBN 0-240-80334-5 (alk. paper)
    1. Arts–United States–Management.   I. Title.
    NX765.B87   1999
    700'.68–dc21   98-31726
                                                          CIP

British Library Cataloguing-in-Publication Data
A catalogue record for this book is available from the British Library.

The publisher offers special discounts on bulk orders of this book.
For information, please contact:
Manager of Special Sales
Butterworth–Heinemann
225 Wildwood Avenue
Woburn, MA 01801-2041
Tel: 781-904-2500
Fax: 781-904-2620

For information on all Butterworth-Heinemann publications available, contact our World Wide Web home page at: http://www.bh.com

10   9   8   7   6   5   4   3   2

Printed in the United States of America

Contents

3 Evolution of Management   37

4 Arts Organizations and Multiple Environments   52

5 Strategic Planning and Decision Making   76

6 Fundamentals of Organizing and Organizational Design   98

9   Control: Management Information Systems and Budgeting   178

10   Economics and the Arts   200

11 Financial Management   222

Foreword

The process commonly thought of as "arts management" is, in essence, bringing artists and audiences together in as effective and efficient a manner as possible. As arts managers, we hope to provide opportunities for our artists to develop their work and flourish in a supportive and productive environment. We present the results of these labors to what we hope will be an audience eager and prepared for the experiences.

It's not getting any easier. And more and more we need to eliminate the "hoped for" above and to produce results on a consistent basis.

As arts organizations face ever-increasing competition for attention, participation and support on all fronts, arts managers are called upon to perform their roles at extraordinarily high levels of competence and to execute them as flawlessly as possible. The challenge can be overwhelming to ill-prepared or inexperienced managers. Today's best managers know not only the "nuts and bolts" of getting a performance onstage or an exhibition mounted; they also understand theories and practicalities of the management process, the external and internal environmental challenges, the effect of organizational culture on operations, the challenge of change, and the opportunities and realities of strategic choices (as well as the consequences that come from *not* making choices). Oh how many of us wish it were as simple as "Hey, Spanky, let's put on a show in the barn."

Management and the Arts is an important resource for today's arts managers, both inquisitive students of the field and seasoned managers. In this book, William Byrnes does more than simply introduce the fundamentals of management as they are applied to the arts and entertainment fields. He provides us with a context for the management process and helps us understand the implications of our actions as managers — the ripple effect on our institutions, our partners, and our stakeholders. As we have learned from other industries and our ever more connected and interdependent world, actions have impact far beyond the visible landscape and with more than the expected collaborators. This is no less true in the arts. And in his book Mr. Byrnes provides a well-constructed map for navigating through the intersecting, interwoven and sometimes conflicting issues, strategies and opportunities. Those interested in beginning a career in arts management could not ask for a better introduction to the field. Working professionals will develop additional confidence in their skills as they come to understand more of the theoretical underpinnings of their work.

As the struggle to fulfill our artistic missions without weakening the institutional foundations intensifies, arts managers need every advantage they can get. *Management and the Arts* is a vital tool in confronting those challenges.

Dan J. Martin
Associate Professor of Arts Management, Carnegie Mellon University
Director, Master of Arts Management Program
Director, Center for Arts Management and Technology

Preface

When I first began teaching arts management, I had to use several textbooks to build the kind of interdisciplinary approach to the field I wanted. I set about writing this text with the goal of blending management theory and practice, economics, personnel management, marketing, and fund raising with the performing and visual arts. The focus of the book is on the process of managing an arts organization through integrating many different disciplines. After covering a brief historical perspective, we examine all the functional and operational areas involved in operating an arts organization. Our study focuses on performing arts organizations in theater, dance, music, and opera and on museums.

This is an introductory text, intended for use in an arts or theater management course. It is designed to give the student an overview of the evolving field of arts management while providing an overview of key concepts in management, marketing, and fundraising. I have assumed that the student has had some course work in the arts, even if only at the introductory level. Although every topic may not receive all of the attention it deserves, I hope that the reader's interest in a specific topic will lead to an exploration of the other resources suggested at the end of most chapters. In the process of writing the second edition, I found it necessary to revise and update all the illustrations. Each chapter has questions that I hope will lead to more in-depth discussion on the material. I also have tried to find case studies that offer thoughtful application of the material in many of the chapters.

Finally, this text was written with the underlying belief that it is important to develop managers in the arts who have sensitivity, use common sense, and apply skills from disciplines such as business, finance, economics, and psychology. The central premise of this text is that an arts manager's specific purpose is to help an organization and its artists fulfill their mission and attain the articulated goals and objectives. This lofty-sounding purpose is grounded in the assumption that an effective arts manager helps bring to audiences or members the unique benefits of the arts experience. There are different ways to describe this experience. For example, when a note is sung or played perfectly or a movement seems to defy gravity or triggers an emotion or creates a realization, we experience something unique. Sometimes a painting, sculpture, or photograph provides an indescribable pleasure as we stand there viewing it. When we witness a scene in the theater that is acted with such power and conviction that it gives us chills, we are enriched.

Working to bring these experiences to others is a worthwhile endeavor. Although this book makes no pretense of having all the answers about how best to go about maximizing the arts experience or operating the perfect organization, I hoped it will provide information and guidance about how an arts manager can be as effective as possible given the resources available. The information and ideas contained in this text are intended to be a springboard for developing your own schematic for leading and managing in the arts.

Organization of the Text

Chapter 1 provides an overview of types and levels of management found in arts organizations. The management process also is discussed.

Chapter 2 examines the historical origins of arts organization as well as profiling the evolution of arts management.

Chapter 3 introduces the reader to the evolution of management theory from ancient times to the present. The basic concepts of systems and contingency management are introduced.

Chapter 4 discusses the relationship of the arts organization to the many external forces that shape how our society functions today.

Chapter 5 begins the examination of the process of management by explaining strategic planning and the decision-making process.

Chapter 6 analyzes the principles of organizing and how organizations are designed. The concept of organizations as complex cultures is discussed.

Chapter 7 integrates strategic planning with organizational design to show various methods for designing jobs, recruiting employees, selecting staff members, and providing job enrichment.

Chapter 8 outlines the major concepts of leadership theory. Trait, behavior, and contingency leadership approaches; group dynamics; and behavior are discussed.

Chapter 9 integrates leadership, planning, and organizing with the management information systems required to effectively operate an arts organization. Concepts of control and resource allocation are introduced.

Chapter 10 examines basic economic theory as it applies to the arts. Concepts in the areas of supply and demand are related to arts organizations. Current and classic studies of performing arts economics also are highlighted.

Chapter 11 relates the economic environment directly to how an organization must organize itself to manage its finances. Such concepts as the balance sheet, the income statement, budgeting, cash flow, and financial planning are reviewed.

Chapter 12 reviews the basic principles of marketing. Marketing is related to the financial planning system and the overall strategic planning process of the organization. The concepts of a marketing audit, marketing management, segmentation, and audience development are discussed.

Chapter 13 focuses on ways that an organization can increase revenues to meet its mission. The fund-raising audit, strategic planning, working with different categories of fund donors, and the techniques of fund raising are discussed.

Chapter 14 develops approaches to integrating management styles, theories, and operations. Dysfunctional, rational, humanistic, and scientific management techniques are discussed.

Chapter 15 asks the arts manager to look to the future and consider where the arts will be in 20 years.

Most chapters conclude with a list of terms and concepts, questions, a case study, and a list of references for further reading in related topics. Where possible, I have tried to create illustrations that provide a visual map to the reader of the concepts discussed in the chapter.

A detailed course syllabus with additional project assignments is available by contacting me at bbyrnes@mailer.fsu.edu. The answer sheet for the case study in Chapter 11 is also available for instructors. Please contact me via e-mail or by writing to School of Theatre, Florida State University, Tallahassee, FL 32306-1160.

Acknowledgments

First Edition

I would like to thank some of the people who assisted with this project. First, I owe much to my wife Christine for the many long hours she spent proofing my drafts and for her suggestions. My student assistant Stephanie Goss also was tremendously helpful in pulling together many of the sources used in this text and in handling the permissions. The ideas and suggestions of Steve Roth and Claudia Chouinard were a big help in the early stages of planning this book. I would also like to thank Professor James Zinser of the Oberlin College Department of Economics for his insightful advice; my daughter Alison for her help at the copying machine; Oberlin College for its help and resources; William Patterson and James Schempp for their many helpful comments on the early drafts; and last but not least, Sharon Falter, Kris Smead, and Pat McLaughlin and the staff at LeGwin Associates for their excellent work in producing this book.

Second Edition

First, I would like to thank the instructors and readers of the first edition for their feedback. I have tried to incorporate your many good suggestions in this new edition. The support of Florida State University and the School of Theatre has also been invaluable. Since arriving at FSU I have been fortunate to have had the opportunity to become director of the MFA Theatre Management Program and to work with many fine faculty and students in the Schools of Music and Visual Arts and Dance. The chance to teach graduate courses covering all aspects of operating an arts organization has proven very helpful in providing more depth to this edition. The assistance of the following FSU staff members and students is deeply appreciated: Patricia Marshall, Dr. Deborah Martin, Dafna Kapshud, Randi Goldstein, Jean Simpson, and Hannah Fuquay. The United Stated Institute for Theatre Technology (USITT), one of the most successful not-for-profit arts-related organizations in North America, also has provided a practical laboratory for applying the principles of managing an organization discussed in this book. In particular, I want to acknowledge Christine Kaiser and Leon Brauner for their help as colleagues in what continues to prove to be a very intense volunteer management experience. I also thank Marie Lee, Theresa Jadick, and Susan Prusak at Focal Press and Matthew Bowditch, the compositor for their guidance and assistance in navigating through the shoals of this edition.

Management
and the Arts

The Entertainment Business

By a unique combination of historical circumstances and the existence of what often is referred to as a market-driven or consumer-driven economy, the United States has created a multibillion dollar entertainment industry that is a mix of for-profit and not-for-profit businesses. Unlike many other nations, the federal government minimally supports the arts and entertainment industry in the United States. Some museums and many performing arts centers are owned by cities or states, but the vast majority of performing arts organizations, media companies, and sports teams are privately owned businesses, public companies with stockholders, or tax-exempt not-for-profit corporations.

Both popular entertainment and not-for-profit businesses depend on admission sales and other investments for income and tax benefits. For-profit arts organizations can take advantage of numerous laws that allow them legally to minimize their tax liability. Not-for-profit organizations enjoy the additional benefits of being exempt from paying taxes and being permitted to raise money through the solicitation of tax-deductible contributions.

The roots of the current system of for-profit and not-for-profit arts businesses were established around the beginning of the twentieth century as advances in technology began to change the way people experienced entertainment. The new technologies created what later would be dubbed the *mass media audience*. People tuned in to the radio, went to the movies, and eventually stayed home to watch television or videotapes. The concept of home entertainment centers built around the ever-advancing computer technology further allows people to choose their entertainment options. In addition, family-oriented theme parks provide active entertainment experiences to millions yearly with events and rides tied directly to film and television industry products. The profits attained by being able to package and distribute entertainment to millions of people led to the creation of an industry based on appealing to the broadest possible audience. Meanwhile, the live performing arts groups continued to face the inherent limitation of seating capacity and the rising costs of delivering the product. Fortunately, the rising levels of education, population, and income fed by unprecedented growth after World War II, along with contributions by individuals, foundations, corporations, and state and federal arts agencies helped support the art forms abandoned by audiences for the mass media.

On paper, the future looks bright. For example, recent surveys by the National Endowment for the Arts (NEA), which has been responsible for helping to stimulate growth in the arts since its inception in 1965, found more than 12,000 performing arts organizations operating in America.[1] As recently as 1996, consumers spent more than $9.1 billion on admissions to performing arts events, $6 billion on tickets to motion pictures, and $6.2 billion on spectator sports in America.[2] More than 1.9 million people were employed in 11 artist job categories according to the NEA in 1997.[3]

Management in Practice

The typical production process for a performing arts event provides a good example of management in practice. For example, a director working to prepare a production draws on many of the same techniques and principles applied every day in the highly competitive world of business. Practices such as teamwork, project management, and performance appraisal are fundamental ingredients in a show. The leadership skills of a director determine how well the entire production will go. Preparing a theatrical production is a group management effort and therefore requires careful attention to the changing, complex dynamics of the cast, designers, and production staff. Motivation levels must be maintained, conflicts must be resolved, and effective time-management skills are required if the show is to open on time and be of a highly quality.

Growing Businesses

With the new ways of experiencing live and prerecorded entertainment and the increase in wealth among the general population came the proliferation of both for-profit and not-for-profit businesses designed to meet the rising demand for entertainment. New jobs for managers were created by the thousands as companies expanded their operations. Each of these enterprises needed people with special skills and knowledge to ensure that the product was created and distributed in a way that realized the organization's goals, as stated by the owners or boards of directors.

For-profit theater, film, television, videos, nightclubs, popular music, radio, and spectator sports are big businesses employing highly visible "stars" and hundreds of thousands of support people. The 1990 book *Jobs in Arts and Media Management* by Stephen Langley and James Abruzzo estimated that there are 77,655 businesses in the entertainment industry.[4] Their total includes theaters, opera companies, musical theater groups, music groups of all types, dance companies, performing arts-presenting organizations, arts councils, broadcasting and cable companies, film companies, museums, unions, and recording companies. Figure 1–1 provides an overview of the various types of organizations where one may find employment in arts management.

Not-for-profit arts organizations in theater, music, dance, and opera and not-for-profit museums make up a great many of these organizations and provide year-round employment at all levels of management. As was noted, these two sectors of the entertainment market account for more than 1.9 million workers. These people in turn contribute to the national economic system with their purchases of goods and services. The arts help to foster economic growth in communities across America. Chapter 10 will elaborate on the economic impact of the arts.

An Uncertain Future

Despite a history of the growth and development, many people in the arts are anxious about the future. Some of these concerns stem from the changing demographics in America, which lead to questions about the source of the future audiences. Others see the political pressure at the state and federal levels to limit or reduce taxes only further increasing the demand on limited resources. Government policy has become more focused on delivering essential services at the expense of what often is perceived as more marginal activities, such a supporting arts and cultural groups. Issues relating to censorship, sexual orientation, and conservative views about funding (see "Other Viewpoints"), all continue to have an impact on art groups. The commercial entertainment industry also is concerned about the plethora of entertainment opportunities available to consumers. In addition, rising production and salary costs are driving up ticket prices to levels that exceed all expectations.

Figure 1-1

Arts Managers and Administrators at Work

Music
Symphony Orchestras
Choral Groups
Music Festivals
Chamber Groups
College/University
Community Groups

Presenting
Booking Agencies
Regional and Local Arts
Presenters
Colleges/Universities

Theater
Broadway
Off & Off-Off Broadway
Touring
Regional
Dinner Theater
Children's Theater
College/University
Community

Service Organizations
Representing and providing support
Performing Arts Groups
(Symphonies, Theater,
Dance, Opera, etc.)
Museums
Arts Agencies
Arts Presenters

Opera
Major Companies
Regional Companies
Touring
College/University
Community

Themed Entertainment
Theme Parks Worldwide
Regional and Local Theme
Parks

Dance
Major Ballet Companies
Regional Dance Companies
Modern Dance Companies
Ethinic Dance Companies
College/University
Community

Broadcast & Cable TV
Major Companies and
National Public TV and
Radio
Local Stations
College/University Stations

Museums
Art/Science/History/Health/
Children, etc.
Galleries
College/University

Film Industry
Major and Independent
Companies
Movie Theaters
Distribution Companies
Music Video Companies

Arts/Humanties Councils
National
State
Regional
Local

Recording Industry
Major Labels
Independent Companies
Recording Studios

These areas offer job opportunities for lower, middle, and upper level managers

Other Viewpoints: The Arts Subsidy Challenged

As the following excerpt demonstrates, arts managers should not assume that everyone agrees that state, local, or federal governments should subsidize the arts. Dr. van den Haag has been a long-time critic of any subsidy for the arts.

Involuntary Patrons: Taxpayers' Rights versus Government Art
Dr. Ernest van den Haag

European governments have traditionally subsidized art and religion because both glorified God, king and country and helped governance: Art and religion were the principle means of indoctrination in social values before TV, radio and print. They were quite indispensable in forging the social bond that makes a nation. Subsidies have continued in Europe, although art and religion have become marginalized. It would be hard to imagine Italy without its cathedrals or its operatic performances. They require subsidies; but they also bring in tourist dollars. In the United States art, mostly imported, never has become a central part of our social bond. Baseball is more like it—and does well without a federal subsidy.

Consider opera. (Exhibitions of paintings would do as well as an example.) Only a small proportion of Americans enjoy it. I do. Yet all taxpayers are forced to subsidize performances. I feel guilty every time I attend, thinking of the people whose taxes are used for my enjoyment, although they would rather use their money for their own enjoyment—perhaps to attend a Madonna concert (unsubsidized). Why is money taken from (low income) taxpayers to benefit (middle class) opera lovers? Congress forces taxpayers to subsidize my aesthetic preferences, because Congress thinks opera is good for taxpayers (or paintings are) even if they don't attend (luckily they are not forced to).

Taxes are often spent on things individual taxpayers do not want. But defense, or police forces, unlike art, cannot be bought individually. They protect people whether they pay or not. To avoid "free riders" everyone must pay through taxes. However opera, concerts, paintings or poetry do not benefit those who do not attend, view, or listen. Why, then, should the voluntary non-beneficiaries be compelled to pay for those who benefit from art (or at least enjoy it)? Why should the non-beneficiaries, or non-enjoyers, not be allowed to spend their money on what they prefer?

SOURCE: Ernest van den Haag, "Involuntary Patrons," *Vantage Point* [the magazine of the Americans for the Arts] (Spring 1990), p. 6. Excerpted with permission.

New technology has permitted entertainment to become more personalized and miniaturized. The change from mass media to individual entertainment systems, coupled with the decreasing resources for arts in the schools, is creating an audience with different attitudes about what they see and hear. Arts administrators often note that people do not know how to "behave" at a concert, theater, dance, or opera. The training of audiences now is an essential part of many arts organizations arsenal of activities.

The often-predicted dramatic increase in leisure time has failed to materialize. With less leisure time available, consumers are making careful choices about how they spend their entertainment dollars. Many organizations also fear that too many arts groups are chasing too few patrons.

In Chapter 4, we delve into a more detailed examination of the forces and trends that affect arts organizations. The development of trend analysis skills can prove to be very useful in plotting the future of an arts organization.

Managers and Organizations

This book will examine how the manager of the arts can use the processes of *planning, organizing, leading,* and *controlling* to solve an organization's problems and fulfill its mission in these uncertain times. These *four functions of management* are the basis for the working relationship between the artist and the manager. Because most of the activity associated with the performing arts and with museums occurs through some type of organization, this text concentrates on management in a group environment.

Let us look now at a brief overview of the manager, the organization, and the process of organizing.

The Manager

In any organization, a *manager* is "a person who is responsible for the work performance of one or more people."[5] The manager's basic job is to organize human and material resources to help the organization achieve its stated goals and objectives. With this definition, a director, a stage manager, a lighting designer, and a curator all are managers. The details of their job descriptions may differ, but the responsibility of getting others to do something is the same. Leadership skills are needed to effectively direct others to accomplish the work that must be done.

The Organization

Managers function within an *organization*, which has been defined as "a collection of people working together in a division of labor to achieve a common purpose."[6] For example, the Hubbard Street Dance Chicago has defined its mission to be "To perform classic, contemporary, and cutting-edge dance with virtuosity, energy, and artistic excellence to local, domestic and international audiences . . ."[7] Other arts groups share equally lofty aims. However, these groups are only as effective as the managers and artists they hire to carry out the mission.

Figure 1–2 shows how organizations interact with many external environments in a process of transforming their resources (inputs) to products or services. The output of an arts enterprise may be a performance or an exhibition. This *Open System Model*, as it is called, is a graphic representation of how organizations interact with the world around them. The primary environments that affect all organizations are economic, political, cultural, demographic, and technological. Chapter 4 examines the impact of each of these environments on organizations. As we will see, the survival and growth of an organization depends on it being able to adapt as these environments change. Managers of organizations must use all the skills and knowledge at their disposal because these environments are always presenting new opportunities and threats.

The Process of Organizing

As we will see in Chapter 5, the process of achieving the organization's goals and objectives requires that the manager actively engage in the process of *organizing*, which has been defined as "dividing work into manageable components."[8] Typical examples of organizing in the arts include a director working with a stage manager to develop a rehearsal schedule for a production and a box office manager designing a staff schedule to cover the upcoming performances.

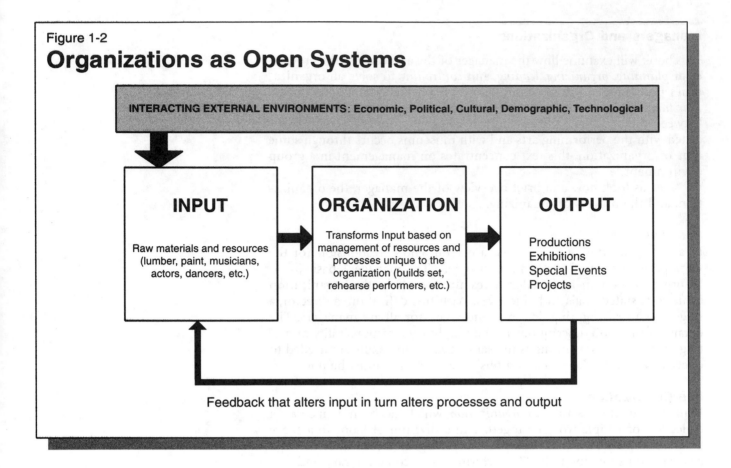

Figure 1-2

Organizations as Open Systems

INTERACTING EXTERNAL ENVIRONMENTS: Economic, Political, Cultural, Demographic, Technological

INPUT

Raw materials and resources
(lumber, paint, musicians,
actors, dancers, etc.)

ORGANIZATION

Transforms Input based on
management of resources and
processes unique to the
organization (builds set,
rehearse performers, etc.)

OUTPUT

Productions
Exhibitions
Special Events
Projects

Feedback that alters input in turn alters processes and output

Levels of Management and Types of Managers

In any organization, there are different levels of management and different types of managers. Typically, organizations have operational, managerial, and strategic levels of management[9] and line, staff, functional, and general managers or administrators[10] (see Figure 1–3).

Levels of management The *operational level* of management is concerned with the day-to-day process of getting the work done. The sets must be built, the museum guards must assume their posts, the rehearsal schedule must be posted, the membership renewals must be mailed, and the box office must sell tickets. The operations level is central to the realization of the organization's goals and objectives. Without the efficient and productive management of its operations, the organization faces extinction.

The *managerial level* often is called *middle management*, because it coordinates the operations and acts as a bridge between the operational and strategic levels of management. For example, the board of directors and the artistic director of a theater company ask the production manager to evaluate the impact of adding a touring season to the company's schedule. If the plan is feasible, the production manager will have the task of coordinating the schedules, materials, and people required to initiate this program of activity. The managerial level usually functions in a one- to two-year planning cycle in the organization.

The *strategic level* of management, on the other hand, watches the overall operation of the organization with an eye toward constantly ad-

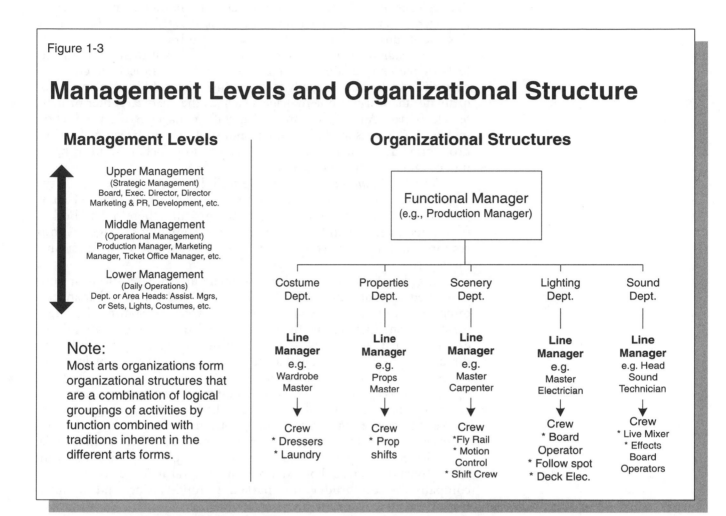

Figure 1-3

Management Levels and Organizational Structure

Management Levels

Upper Management
(Strategic Management)
Board, Exec. Director, Director
Marketing & PR, Development, etc.

Middle Management
(Operational Management)
Production Manager, Marketing
Manager, Ticket Office Manager, etc.

Lower Management
(Daily Operations)
Dept. or Area Heads: Assist. Mgrs,
or Sets, Lights, Costumes, etc.

Note:
Most arts organizations form
organizational structures that
are a combination of logical
groupings of activities by
function combined with
traditions inherent in the
different arts forms.

Organizational Structures

Functional Manager
(e.g., Production Manager)

Costume Dept.	Properties Dept.	Scenery Dept.	Lighting Dept.	Sound Dept.
Line Manager e.g. Wardrobe Master	**Line Manager** e.g. Props Master	**Line Manager** e.g. Master Carpenter	**Line Manager** e.g. Master Electrician	**Line Manager** e.g. Head Sound Technician
Crew * Dressers * Laundry	Crew * Prop shifts	Crew *Fly Rail * Motion Control * Shift Crew	Crew * Board Operator * Follow spot * Deck Elec.	Crew * Live Mixer * Effects Board Operators

justing and adapting to the changing environments that affect the future of the organization while staying true to the mission. The goals and objectives typically are assessed in a three- to five-year time frame. In addition, strategic managers are responsible for looking as far ahead as ten years in an effort to chart a path for the organization. The artistic director, general manager, general director, managing director, marketing director, or other similar senior-level person is associated with this role. In addition, strategic managers typically present these long-range plans to a board of directors. The board ultimately oversees the organization's mission and purpose.

Types of managers   The arts have evolved unique types of managers to make the organizations work. The types of managers listed in this section are found in different combinations in arts organizations depending on the purpose and design of the organization. Each art form has specialized job titles and responsibilities.

The first type of manager is the *line manager*. This person is directly responsible for getting the product or service completed. The head carpenter, who supervises a stage crew, is a good example of such a manager. The head carpenter's job is to get the set onstage and ready for the performance. The ticket office manager is another example of a line manager. This job typically entails supervising a staff responsible for the ticket and subscriptions sales for an arts organization.

Staff managers "use their special technical skill to support the efforts of the line personnel."[11] For example, the technical director in a performing arts group usually is given this responsibility. He or she coordinates the work of line managers such as the head carpenter or master electrician. Another example of a staff manager is the production manager. This person is given the responsibility of overseeing all of the production departments in an arts organization, such as scenery, lighting, costumes, props, and sound.

The *functional manager* has responsibility over a single area in the organization. For example, the production manager in a theater company oversees the production departments and therefore is both a functional manager and a staff manager. A company manager, who is responsible for the performers, is another example of a functional manager.

It is worth noting that, because many arts organizations are understaffed, the roles played by the line, staff, and functional managers often are very blurry. As you will see in Chapter 7, "Staffing the Organization," job titles frequently are combined in arts organizations. For example, a manager may have the title of marketing and public relations director. These two functional areas usually are full-time jobs in themselves, but the lack of funds for managerial positions requires doubling up on work assignments. The lack of staff funding also may mean there are no line managers or staff to work for the functional manager. For example, the marketing director and public relations director may find themselves typing their own press releases and faxing them to the media.

General managers are found in more complex organizations with many functional areas. For example, the general manager of an opera company oversees production, marketing, fund raising, and administration for the organization.

Another managerial title often found in organizations is the *administrator*. Although the administrator is really a manager, based on the definition of being responsible for the work efforts of one or more people, the title may be used in not-for-profit organizations to refer to someone empowered only to carry out functional tasks defined by others. Like the general manager, the administrator does not make plans or policies but is responsible for their implementation.

Common Elements in an Organization

Chapter 3 examines the history and early management theories that influenced much of today's thinking about how to accomplish the objectives of an organization. Some of these theories apply to fundamental issues of organizational design and structure and are applicable to art organizations.

A division of labor and some type of hierarchy exist in most organizations. The *division of labor* usually takes a form that matches the organization's function. A dance company has a different division of labor than an opera company for the simple reason that the processes and techniques used in preparing a performance are different. For example, many opera companies have a small permanent administrative and fund-raising staff. The singers, orchestra, director, stage crew, and designers are hired for short periods of time to do a single show. Ballet companies, on the other hand, often have 30 or 40 dancers under a 40-

week contract each year. They therefore require a different division of labor to meet the needs of a resident company of performers.

The *hierarchy of authority* in an organization is designed to ensure that the work efforts of the different members of the organization come together as a whole.[12] The typical hierarchy involves a vertical reporting, communication, and supervision system. Chapter 6 details various methods for organizing management systems.

In most arts organizations, which are small- to medium-size businesses, the levels of management and the formality of the hierarchy usually are limited. However, as an organization grows in size and more staff members are added, the levels of management increase and the hierarchy tends to become more formal. A good arts manager is watchful of this development, especially if overly complex divisions of labor or a burdensome hierarchy begins to impede the accomplishment of the organization's goals and objectives.

An *informal structure* also exists in all organizations. No organizational chart or detailed plan of staff responsibilities is able to take into account all of the ways people find to work with each other. Employees often find new combinations of people to accomplish tasks that do not fit into the existing hierarchy or organizational design. Some organizations thrive on this sort of internal innovation; others become chaotic. Arts organizations—which tend to cluster toward the rigid, rather than the innovative, end of the structure continuum—often develop organizational designs aligned with functional areas. For example, the production staff, office staff, performers, and upper management develop structures to operate their own areas. The result is four organizations instead of one. At the same time, organizations, like people, can lapse into habitual behavior patterns. Tradition becomes the norm, and innovation is resisted. Again, the arts manager must keep an eye on the organization's formal and informal structure. Careful intercession can correct unproductive structures that develop.

Organizations are not neutral entities. They are microcosms of the society at large. Organizations are collections of individuals with beliefs, biases, and values. Unique myths and rituals are part of what is called the organization's *corporate culture* (see Chapter 6). Simply described, the corporate culture is the way things are done in the organization. For example, the culture of the organization usually establishes values on such things as the quality and quantity of work expected. Some organizations have a positive culture that is communicated to employees. For example, managers might say, "Our stage crew is here to make things work, and their contribution is valued and recognized." In this situation, the overall culture of the organization values the labor of its employees. Other organizations have weak or destructive cultures. Phrases such as "The crew around here is always looking for a way to get out of work, and they are not to be trusted" signal a culture based on distrust and conflict.

The founder-director organization, a model quite prevalent in the arts, can help establish a strong culture imbued with the beliefs and values of one individual. Unfortunately, the departure of this person often leaves the organization adrift.

Any arts organization, no matter how small, ultimately is a complex mixture of behaviors, attitudes, and beliefs of the people who work there. Because people are the major resource used in creating its products, an organization will continue to be influenced and changed in ways that no one can predict. Interaction with external environments

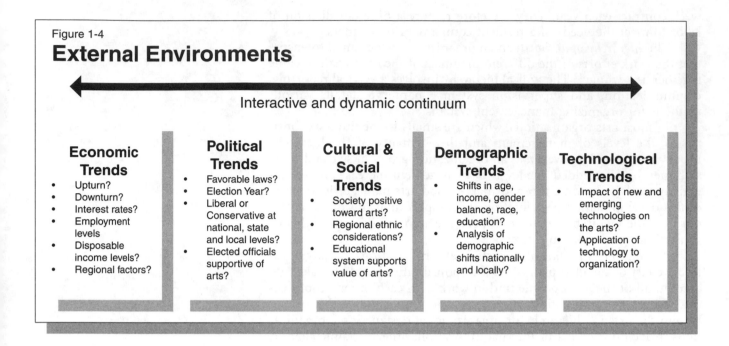

Figure 1-4

External Environments

Interactive and dynamic continuum

Economic Trends
- Upturn?
- Downturn?
- Interest rates?
- Employment levels
- Disposable income levels?
- Regional factors?

Political Trends
- Favorable laws?
- Election Year?
- Liberal or Conservative at national, state and local levels?
- Elected officials supportive of arts?

Cultural & Social Trends
- Society positive toward arts?
- Regional ethnic considerations?
- Educational system supports value of arts?

Demographic Trends
- Shifts in age, income, gender balance, race, education?
- Analysis of demographic shifts nationally and locally?

Technological Trends
- Impact of new and emerging technologies on the arts?
- Application of technology to organization?

also affects the way people inside the organization think, feel, and behave. For example, changes in laws and the social system have led to the addition of multicultural programming and the hiring of more minority-group members in many arts organizations (see Figure 1–4).

An Effective Model?

Arts organizations are learning to effectively integrate long-term strategic thinking while developing a sensitivity to the changing environments that shape the beliefs and values of the entire culture. Because the performing and visual arts depend on the creative explorations of the individual for the new material they present, the design and function of these institutions should be focused on looking to what will be and not at what was. However, many artists perceive of arts organizations as institutions that are more comfortable with the past. The creation of organizations in the performing and visual arts that look like imitations of corporations with executive directors, vice-presidents, and associate directors is not seen universally as a good sign. Many artists are asking organizations to examine such fundamental questions as "What is our mission?" "Just what is it we are doing?" "What things are essential to our mission?" "Who do we serve?" "What do people think we do?" and "What are we really contributing to the community and our culture?" In some cases, artists are seeking a more entrepreneurial environment in which to work. They are finding that rigid structures and corporate models are not the most effective way to bring the audience and artist together.

The continual seeking of answers to these artistic questions needs to be factored into the design and operation of the arts organization. The unique pursuit of an artistic vision and the successful presentation of that vision to the public need as much attention and thought as any commercial business enterprise in the world.

The Management Process

The organization and systems described thus far are predicated on the assumption that there is an artistic product to manage. How does this product come into being? In many cases, an individual or a small group of people have the drive and energy to create something from nothing. For example, a playwright and director may team up to interest other people in a script. If people with money can be found to back the show, they hire performers and designers to bring the work to life. Sometimes, much less often than anyone cares to consider, the show is a hit. A long-standing love for opera may drive someone to start a regional opera company. Two dancers may decide that it is time to start their own company. They are tired of dancing someone else's choreography, and they have some ideas of their own that they would like to see performed. A group of visual artists may start a cooperative exhibition gallery and operate it themselves.

Whatever the circumstances, the success or failure of these artistic ambitions in part will be related directly to how well the four functions of management are fulfilled. Without proper planning, good organization, creative leadership, and some control over the enterprise, the chance of success is greatly diminished. Obviously, projects and programs succeed in this world that do not master these four functions. Poorly planned, badly organized, weakly led, and inadequately controlled events happen all the time. The events that suffer from various forms of dysfunctional management make for great stories, but the human toll taken by such examples of bad management is precisely why good managers are needed in the arts. There is no benefit to the art form or the community if the very people who love the arts are destroyed by it.

It is important to remember, however, that a bad play, opera, musical, ballet, symphony, or exhibition cannot be made good by excellent management. If people do not respond to a work after all the rewrites and extra rehearsals, it does not matter how well it was managed. Ultimately, if no artistic vision lies behind the enterprise the chances for long-term success are greatly diminished.

We take more time to examine the evolution of the arts and how arts managers fit into the entire process in Chapter 2. For now, we consider the four functions and relate each of them to an arts application.

Planning

This first function of management is the hardest. Deciding exactly what we want to do, setting realistic goals (what the organization wants to accomplish), and then determining the objectives (the specific steps to take and the timetable for completing the tasks) to be used in meeting the goals is hard work.

There are various sorts of plans. Some are short-range plans: What am I going to do tomorrow? These plans usually present little challenge. On the other hand, planning five years ahead can be an intimidating, if not impossible, task.

Organizations and people must plan because the world is constantly changing. Audience tastes and values change over time. The arts manager's job is to recognize the elements in the world around the organization that may pose new opportunities or may be a threat. Then the manager must work with the board and the artistic leadership to chart a course of action designed to guide the organization into the future.

The Four Functions of Management

- *Planning* is deciding what is to be done.
- *Organizing* is deciding how it is to be done and who is to do it.
- *Leading* is deciding how other people are to get it done.
- *Controlling* is deciding if it is or is not getting done and what to do if it is not.

For example, the artistic director of the ABC Opera Company reads in the newspaper that state funds for opera companies and music groups that visit schools soon will be available. A goal is established to seek the funding and then implement a touring program in the next year because it relates directly to the organization's mission of bringing opera to the widest possible audience. The staff researches costs and benefits. The plan and the goals are drawn up and reviewed with the board. The board approves the idea and the company established a pilot program.

Organizing

Organizing is the process of converting the plans into a course of action. Getting the people and resources together, defining the details, creating a schedule and budget, estimating the number of people needed, and assigning them their jobs is all part of organizing.

Continuing the example, the ABC Opera Company sets up a special touring department. The company hires a director of touring and puts into place the details of the plan. For the first year, the company will have a small group of six actors tour 20 schools to perform scenes and hold theater workshops. Detailed schedules, contracts, and evaluation methods are established.

Leading

The third function of management requires getting everyone in the organization to share a vision of what can be accomplished if everyone works together. Leadership skill and effectiveness are highly prized attributes in any situation. For the arts manager, working with the highly self-motivated, independent-minded people often found in the arts offers a unique leadership opportunity.

After the ABC Opera Company touring staff is hired, the artistic director meets with everyone to clarify the project's purposes and goals. The director provides an overall timetable and explains where this new operation fits into the organization. The company's mission is recalled, and a challenge is issued to make this a high-quality touring program. The leader of the tour group provides the day-to-day guidance needed to make the project a success.

Controlling

The fourth function of management is concerned with monitoring the work process, checking the results against the objectives, and taking corrective action when required.

After six months, the artistic director reviews the activities of the touring company and finds that bookings are down, cast turnover is high, and the budget for the year is almost gone. Meetings are held to pinpoint problems and consider solutions. Staffing changes are made, and the project is monitored on a weekly basis. After a year, many of the problems have lessened and the touring project is having a positive impact on the community.

Functional Areas

When engaged in planning, organizing, leading, and controlling an arts organization there are seven basic functions an arts manager fulfills:[13]

1. Planning and development,
2. Marketing and public relations,
3. Personnel management,
4. Fiscal management,

Sample Core Values, Purpose, Mission, Goals and Strategies Statements

The Alliance Theatre Company, a profession resident theater organization located in Atlanta Georgia, provides one example of an arts organization attempting to communicate to the world who it is, what it does, and what it wants to do.

Alliance Theatre Company Long Range Plan
Core Values
Excellence, Creativity, Integrity, Diversity, Responsibility

Core Purpose
Connecting human beings through the live theatrical experience.

Mission Statement
The Alliance Theatre is dedicated to celebrating our diversity by building bridges, which can connect us as human beings through the development and production of exciting, entertaining and stimulating plays, nurturing and enriching both the art, artists and audience.

Goals
1. Artistic
   • Present a mix of classic and contemporary plays which speak to the heart and illuminate the human condition
   • Create an artistic environment that is rich, challenging and alive through the research and development of new works
   • Provide opportunities for individual artistic growth

2. Audience
   • Increase paid attendance for all performances to 400,000
   • Develop our core audience to consistently reflect the diverse multi-cultural profile of Metro Atlanta's five core counties (Fulton & contiguous counties)
   • Build a loyal and diverse subscriber base of 20,000 with an annual renewal rate of at least 75%

3. Financial
   • Generate an annual operating surplus equal to at least 2% of total operating revenues
   • Build our cash reserves up to $1.5 million by the end of FY03
   • Add to our endowment funds an amount equal to the Robert W. Woodruff endowment gift by the end of FY03

Strategies
   • Produce and develop plays of consistently high artistic quality that attract our targeted audiences
   • Use the income from the Robert W. Woodruff Foundation endowment gift and the additional funds raised to exclusively support our artistic product
   • Provide maximum financial resources to develop "best-in-class" marketing and development activities
   • Attract and develop competent, well-trained artists and professional staff, an active board and a strong corps of volunteers that reflect the diverse, multi-cultural profile of Metro Atlanta's five counties
   • Continue to develop strong education, outreach and training programs that support and feed the company's overall programming
   • Through Theatre for Young Audiences (TYA) identify, attract and build a young, diverse, multi-cultural audience that is our audience of tomorrow

Source: Alliance Theatre Company, May 28, 1998, used with permission.

---

5. Board relations,
6. Labor relations,
7. Government relations.

Planning and development are linked because arts organizations always are seeking ways to increase revenue to fund new programs and to pay for the inevitable increases in operating costs. Marketing and public relations provide the organization's most visible link to the community. Without a strong connection to the community, the arts organization will find it difficult to attract an audience and donors. Good personnel management and labor relations are essential if the organization is to be productive. Neglect or abuse of the human resources available to a manager can disrupt the entire enterprise. Good fiscal management is critical if the organization's planning, marketing, and fund-raising efforts are to succeed. In addition, donors prefer to contribute to organizations that show they know how to manage their financial resources. As with personnel relations, an arts manager must effectively work with and report to a board of directors. The board and the management sometimes have different sets of priorities. Until the differences are resolved, the organization will find it difficult to meet its goals and objectives. Finally, government relations, at the local, state, and national levels, grows more complex each year. New laws are passed or court rulings are enforced that change the way an organization does business. These types of changes typically add to the expenses of the organization.

Throughout this text, we examine how external environments and internal organizational dynamics make the task of being a manager in the arts a challenging and demanding job. The almost endless variety and changing circumstances in the world around the arts organization keep the manager's job from ever getting too dull or routine.

Key Terms and Concepts

Review these terms from the chapter and begin to incorporate them into your day-to-day thinking about management and the arts.

Manager
Organization
Organizing
Open system model
Levels of management: operational, managerial, strategic
Types of managers: line, staff, functional, general, administrative
Division of labor
Hierarchy of authority
Formal and informal structures
Corporate culture
Functions of management: planning, organizing, leading, controlling
Functional areas of work for an arts manager: planning and development, marketing and public relations, personnel management, fiscal management, board relations, labor relations, government relations

Questions

1. Are you aware of any arts organizations that have been particularly successful or have faced difficulty in your community? Outline the situation, and explain why you think the organization did well or faltered.

2. Can you recall a particular work situation you have been in that was either positive or negative as a direct result of the manager in charge? What type of manager was this person (line, staff, functional)? What made this manager effective or ineffective?

3. What are some recent changes in the five environments cited in the open system model (economic, political, cultural, demographic, technological) that may have an impact on arts organizations?

4. Do you agree or disagree with the author of the "Involuntary Patrons" article? Why? Do you agree that art "never has become a central part of our social bond" in America? The author argues that because the arts are not available to everyone, subsidies are inappropriate. What is your opinion?

5. List some examples of how you "manage" your life. Have you used any combinations of the management functions of planning, organizing, leading, or controlling to achieve objectives you have set for yourself?

6. The mission statement provided by the Alliance Theatre Company seems to describe a series of activities. What do you think is the mission of the Alliance Theatre? Attempt to condense the concepts expressed into a more concise mission statement. Compare and discuss your efforts.

Project Organization

Over the course of the semester, select an arts organization and request (or download) a copy of its mission statement, bylaws, and other relevant planning documents (for example, a five-year plan) for a discussion by the class. Based on some of the topics covered in this chapter, answer the following questions:

1. Is the organization fulfilling its stated mission. If yes, how? If no, why not?

2. Is the organization facing financial problems? Did it have a deficit or surplus in the last budget year?

3. Based on the information gathered, is it possible to ascertain if this is a well-managed organization? If yes, what evidence supports this position? If no, what are the management areas that need improvement (planning and development, marketing and public relations, personnel management, fiscal management, board relations, labor relations, government relations)?

References

1. Research Division Note #62, NEA (Washington, DC, 1998).
2. Research Division Note #59, NEA (Washington, DC, 1997).
3. Research Division Note #61, NEA (Washington, DC, 1997).
4. Stephen Langley and James Abruzzo, *Jobs in Arts and Media Management* (New York: American Council for the Arts, 1990), pp. 10–11.
5. John R. Schermerhorn, Jr., *Management for Productivity*, 2d ed. (New York: John Wiley and Sons, 1986), p. 7.
6. Ibid., p. 8.
7. Philip Kotler and Joanne Scheff, *Standing Room Only* (Boston: Harvard Business School Press, 1997), p. 53.
8. Schermerhorn, *Management for Productivity*, p. 161.
9. James H. Donnelly, Jr., James L. Gibson, and John M. Ivancevich, *Fundamentals of Management*, 7th ed. (Homewood, IL: BPI-Irwin, 1990), pp. 28–29.
10. Schermerhorn, *Management for Productivity*, pp. 13–15.
11. Ibid., p. 13.
12. Ibid., p. 12.
13. Paul DiMaggio, *Managers of the Arts*, Research Division Report #20, NEA (Washington, DC: Seven Locks Press, 1987).

2

□ □ □ □ □

The Evolution of Arts Organizations and Arts Management

In this chapter, we review the evolution of the job of arts manager. We explore how the responsibilities have changed to meet the increasingly complex demands placed on arts organizations and artists. We also touch on the impact the National Endowment for the Arts has had on the arts scene in the United States. The chapter concludes with an examination of the national network of performing arts centers in communities and on university campuses in the United States.

The Artist-Manager

For more than 2,000 years, the artist-manager has been the person who created and arranged the meeting of artist and public. Creative drive, leadership, and the ability to organize a group of people around a common goal remain the foundation on which all arts management is built. The traditional role of the artist-manager has been split into separate jobs to better cope with the increasingly complex demands placed on managers. However, this split does not mean that a division or barrier must be erected between these two roles. Instead, the separation should be viewed in much the same way as the human brain functions: The two hemispheres are linked and communicate with each other while each side continues to do what it does best.

The Arts as Institutions

One result of the political and social upheaval of the last 400 years has been the establishment of institutions designed to provide continuing support and recognition for the artist and the arts. In much of the world, the performing arts are part of a state-supported system, operated by resident managers with extensive administrative staffs. Performing and visual arts centers for opera, dance, theater, and music as well as museums reserved exclusively for art, history, and science are integral parts of many communities in the world.

In the United States, token government backing for the arts is a recent phenomenon. Fund-matching grants, special project support, and a taxation system designed to promote deductible donations by individuals and corporations continue to be the extent of government involvement in the arts. More recently, in the last hundred years, the U.S. government opted for an alternative system that encouraged the creation of tax-exempt, nonprofit corporations to supply and distribute the arts and culture in society.

The increasing complexity of an industrially based society hastened the shift from the artist-manager as the dominant approach to organizing and presenting the arts. As many communities began to establish arts institutions late in the nineteenth century (museums, symphony orchestras), year-round management experts began to emerge. Many arts institutions now appear to be organized along patterns similar to large business corporations.

Today, the role of the artist and the manager and the degree of control each has over his or her respective domain vary from art form to art form. Many small arts organizations still are created and managed by artist-managers. However, the norm is a corporate structure with a board of directors and multiple levels of staff arranged in a hierarchy.

A Brief Historical Overview

Let us examine some selected points in Western history to trace the development of the management function in the arts. As has been noted, the artist-manager is a well-established figure in the arts. Although this pattern of management has not changed much in the last 2,000 years, the demands placed on this individual have increased to the point where the artist-manager format is now only one of many ways to organize the presentation of arts events.

Ancient Times

As the centers of civilization grew, so did those functions we associate with the arts. The first examples of performance management were the public assemblies associated with religious rites in early societies. These "performances" were "managed" by the priest and enmeshed in the fabric of a society. The theatrical trappings of costumes, dramatic settings, music, movement, and so on all supported and heightened the event. Ultimately though, these events were not an expression of the creative drive of a people but rather a way of controlling and molding a culture. However, these staged events did provide a model for organizing large-scale public gatherings.

The beginnings of a system of state-sponsored play festivals can be traced to the Greeks around 534 B.C. These festivals required the management skills of planning, organizing, leading, and controlling, much as they do today. Typically, a principal magistrate, the *archon eponymous*, supervised the production of the play festivals sponsored in Athens. Financial support came from the richer citizens (*choregoi*), and the cities provided the facilities. The playwright functioned as the director and had something akin to total artistic control over the show.[1]

The Romans also produced state-sponsored arts festivals as part of an overall cycle of public events throughout the year. City magistrates were responsible for screening and coordinating the entertainment for their communities. The managers (*domini*) acted as producers, bringing the play and the performers to the festivals. These early managers arranged all the elements needed for the production with the financial support of the local magistrate. According to research in theater history, as many as 100 days a year were committed to the various theater festivals of ancient Rome. If this schedule indeed is true, a great deal of managerial skill must have been required to coordinate and produce these events.[2]

With the decline of Rome came the dissolution of the state-sponsored festivals. The breakup of the empire did not mean that all artistic activity came to a halt. However, the transition into the Dark Ages left society without a developing dramatic literature generating works to perform. The disappearance of organized financing and facilities also made it impossible to sustain an ongoing arts community. Performance groups therefore resorted to touring as a means of survival. The management of the troupe was done by a member of the performing group. Smaller-scale community festivals helped provide opportunities for the itinerant artists to eke out a living. On the whole, Western history has not provided much evidence of significant artistic activity in Europe during this time.

Other cultures of course were developing indigenous forms of music, dance, and theater. The arts were very much a part of Byzantium, India, and China. While Europe was struggling, other cultures were establishing forms of dance, theater, music, and visual arts that are with us today. Varying degrees of state and private sponsorship were involved. The role of the manager did not differ radically in these cultures because the functions required to organize and coordinate arts events were the same.

The Middle Ages

The Church was the producer of many sanctioned performances during the Middle Ages. The performance of liturgical drama, which served as a type of religious instruction, originally resided within the management structure of the Church. As communities developed and the overall economic environment improved, this drama moved outdoors and became part of public pageants (using stages mounted on portable wagons) and festivals. Nonliturgical drama and various forms of popular entertainment, such as jugglers and mimes, were part of a rebirth of performance.

By the fourteenth century, the Church had little control over the proliferating performances. A system of patronage and sponsorship by the trade guilds led to an expanding role for the manager-director. Historian Oscar Brockett notes that, during the fifteenth and sixteenth centuries,

> complex productions required careful organization, for the handling of casts that sometimes included as many as 300 actors, of complex special effects, and large sums of money could not be left to chance. Consequently, the director (or stage manager, or pageant master) was of considerable importance. Often this position was given to a member of the guild, but in some instances a "pageant master" was put under contract for a number of years at an annual salary. The pageant master secured actors, arranged rehearsals, and took charge of every phase of production.[3]

The Renaissance

The continuing surge of the arts was dramatic throughout the Renaissance. The social, political, economic, and cultural environments were undergoing changes that fundamentally altered people's perceptions of the world. The rediscovery of the Greeks opened up the creative spirit of the times. During the fourteenth to sixteenth centuries, neoclassical theater began to flourish, opera and ballet were born, and the role of the arts manager burgeoned.

In theater, the expansion of literature was accompanied by the construction of performance spaces that took advantage of the new stage technology of the time. This in turn led to the rise of stage crew specialists in such areas as rigging, lighting, special effects, and costumes. The coordination required of the increasingly complex productions helped solidify many of the traditional roles in backstage operations and management.

In the late sixteenth century, opera was born in Italy out of the *intermezzi*, which was a form of entertainment that occurred between the five-act dramas of the time. In 1594, the first opera, *Dafne*, premiered and laid the foundation for an entire art form.[4]

The court dance of the thirteenth and fourteenth centuries helped forge a path for the creation of ballet. The court "dance masters of the [fourteenth and fifteenth centuries] began to develop a theory of dance instruction that systematized its various movements and styles."[5] The first ballet, *Ballet Comique de la Reine*, was performed in 1581 in the court of Henry III of France.[6] As with opera, specialized production and management techniques evolved over the centuries to support the art form.

Like today, finding financial support was an ongoing activity of the early artist-managers. Church support, royal patronage, and shareholder arrangements were the chief means of financing work. The shares sold to people helped provide the resources needed to pay for salaries and production support. Management functions were expanded to include overseeing the distribution of any profits to the shareholders.

The other major problem managers and artists grappled with was censorship. Throughout history, the performing and visual arts have had to contend with varying degrees of control from both the Church and the State. The selection of plays, the access to performance spaces, and sometimes even the selection of performers have been subject to very severe constraints. The arts manager often is placed in the middle of the battle between an artist seeking an avenue of expression and a state or religious group attempting to suppress the work. We see the legacy of the sometimes uneasy relationship between the arts and society in the continuing controversy over the reauthorization of the National Endowment for the Arts.

The Seventeenth through Nineteenth Centuries

In many European countries during this time, the arts continued to grow and flourish. Playwrights, directors, composers, musicians, dancers, and singers found work in newly created companies and institutions. In France, the theater, opera, and ballet companies were being organized in state-run facilities, and the performers received salaries and pensions. Germany established a state theater by 1767. It became the foundation for a national network of subsidized arts institutions. England also had a thriving performing arts community. The Education Act of 1870 and the Local Governments Act of 1888 helped promote the growth of museums and performing arts facilities throughout Great Britain.[7] British support for museums was well rooted in the nineteenth century. However, the first Arts Council in England was not created until 1945.[8] Throughout the seventeenth to nineteenth centuries, especially on the Continent, the formalization of management structures and systems to operate the state theaters solidified the role of the arts manager.

In the United States, theatrical presentations were made up of touring groups performing varied programs in cities across the nation. The development of the railroad system in America assisted with the spread of touring groups and artists in the eighteenth and nineteenth centuries. The local theater venue often contained stock sets that were used by the performers, who brought their own costumes. The spreading rail system of the mid-nineteenth century helped support an extensive touring network of performing groups. Companies were formed and disbanded almost constantly, and no permanent theater companies were established. The management structure was dominated by the producers and booking agents who arranged the tours. The control of most theaters eventually fell into the hands of these booking agents. A monopoly known as *The Syndicate* controlled what was available for viewing around the country. This monopoly was supplanted by another group of theater owners, the Shuberts. The Shubert brothers created a management dynasty that lasts to this day.[9]

Unlike the impermanent theater, symphony orchestras and opera companies began to secure a more stable place in the larger metropolitan areas in the United States. For example, the support of wealthy patrons made it possible to establish symphony orchestras in New York City (1842) and Boston (1881). Opera, which had been performed in the United States since early in the eighteenth century, found its first home in the Metropolitan Opera in 1883.[10] Dance often was included in touring theatrical productions in the eighteenth and nineteenth centuries. European dance stars also regularly toured the country. However, permanent resident dance companies were not a regular part of the arts scene until the twentieth century.[11]

The Twentieth Century

The role of management increased as the continued growth of the arts accelerated. Despite two world wars, European arts institutions expanded into smaller communities, developing national networks of performing spaces and providing jobs for managers and artists. Seasons expanded, repertories grew, and new facilities were constructed—especially after World War II—in an overall environment of support from the government. As noted, England eventually established a state-supported system for the arts after the war.

In Europe and the United States, the new technologies of radio and film significantly changed attendance patterns at live performance events. The theater in the United States, for example, saw a rapid decline in attendance by the 1920s.[12] Because there were no resident theater companies, it was difficult to keep a loyal audience base such as existed for the few opera and symphony groups in the country.

The rise of the Off Broadway and regional theater system helped renew the theater and, at the same time, helped build a base for what were to become established organizations. The more experimental but still profit-driven Off-Broadway system was born in the early 1950s. The not-for-profit regional theater network was built from the Barter Theater in Virginia (1932), Alley Theatre in Houston (1947), Arena Stage in Washington, D.C. (1950), and the Actor's Workshop in San Francisco (1952). These theaters formed the nucleus of the new distribution system for theater in America.[13] The need for good managers escalated in the professional world, and because of the unprecedented baby boom after the war, the educational system—especially colleges and universities—expanded offerings in the arts. Community and campus performing arts centers helped establish a new network for touring and provided local groups with venues to use. Managers were needed to operate the new multimillion dollar complexes and book events throughout the year.

Opera first spread beyond New York into the major metropolitan areas of Chicago, San Francisco, Philadelphia, St. Louis, and New Orleans. However, after the Great Depression, only New York and San Francisco were able to hold onto their companies.[14] The support in the 1950s by the Ford Foundation helped bring opera to the American arts scene. By the early 1970s, 27 opera companies were in operation.[15] Today, the Central Opera Service reports over 110 major opera companies. Part of this growth was due to the NEA matching grant programs, which enabled many companies to professionalize their management.

Until the early 1960s, dance companies were in limited supply in the United States. The American Ballet Theatre, the New York City Ballet, and the San Francisco Ballet topped the list of professional companies. Ballet West in Utah and Ruth Page's dancers, who were associated with the Chicago Lyric Opera, offered regular programs with their semi-professional companies.[16] At the same time, modern dance companies were being operated on very tight budgets by such pioneers as Martha Graham, Alvin Ailey, Merce Cunningham, José Limon, and Paul Taylor. Their staff resources and their seasons were very limited.

The Ford Foundation in the 1960s and the NEA in the 1970s helped create a new national support system for ballet and later for modem dance. Although these groups still struggle, now more than 400 dance groups operate, according to data collected by the NEA in 1992.[17]

Symphony orchestras also have grown in number over the last 30 years. According to the NEA, in 1992 there were 349 symphony orchestras and 130 chamber music organizations in the United States[18] It is estimated that the United States has 3,105 museums and art galleries, 2,749 of which are tax exempt.[19]

The expansion period in the arts seems to be slowing now that most communities have established visual and performing arts institutions. The long-term struggle for operating funds accelerated in recent years as competition for support has increased. Additional funding from the state and federal governments appears to be an unrealistic expectation. Demand is increasing for resources to assist with social programs, medical research, and education. Foundation, corporate, and individual support is being tapped by increasingly sophisticated fund raisers from hospitals to day-care centers. Meanwhile, in Europe, the government subsidy is being reevaluated. Ironically, the model being adopted is the U.S. approach of private and public support for the arts. Performing and visual arts organizations are scrambling to develop the expertise to become successful fund raisers to maintain their current levels of operation. In England, for example, bitter battles have been fought with the conservative government over the level of support for the arts. Recently, England shifted to funding the arts from lottery sales. In some cases, this has proven a boon to arts organizations. Lottery funding also has gone to support projects that extend beyond the traditional scope of the fine and performing arts.

Profile of the Arts Manager

The growth in the arts over the last 30 years has created a tremendous demand for managers at all levels and in all disciplines. However, arts managers are not clearly identified as a work group when counting the over 1.9 million people employed in the arts. The Census Bureau counts performers, architects, composers, printmakers, and instructors in the arts but does not include people in arts management, sales, consulting, or promotion or public television employees.[20] It is not clear whether the people who do not directly make art were counted in the census data, but they are obviously a central part of the culture industry in the United States.

One source that provides substantial information on the arts manager is Paul DiMaggio's 1987 book, *Managers of the Arts*. Originally created for the NEA under the official title *Research Division Report #20*, the book outlines the background, training, salaries, and attitudes of arts managers in theater, orchestra, and museum management and community arts associations.

Unfortunately, DiMaggio includes no data about opera or dance managers. In addition, the survey was conducted in 1981, which may make the data somewhat irrelevant to today's market. DiMaggio's book only samples a limited number of people. With these limitations in mind, let us take a look at some of the highlights of this report.

DiMaggio's book revealed the following profile of arts managers: upper-middle class, highly educated individuals who either majored in the subject they were managing or were humanities majors in English, history, or foreign languages. DiMaggio found that a limited number of managers had management or arts management degrees. The upper management jobs tended to be held by men in museums (85 percent), theater companies (66 percent), and orchestras (66 percent), but women held the majority of positions in community arts associations (55 percent).[21] The data also indicated that there were a wide variety of ways to enter the career path in arts management, thus making it a fairly open system.

The section of DiMaggio's report on training offers some interesting insights into the opinions of those surveyed regarding their preparation for their jobs. Figure 2–1 shows the results of a survey that asked how well prepared participants felt to handle various aspects of the job, including fiscal and personnel management, planning, and board, labor, and government relations. The data indicates that "few managers felt they were well prepared to assume many of [the] functions" required for their jobs.[22] Labor relations consistently stands out as an area for which respondents felt poorly prepared. The survey results show that, in many areas, less than 40 percent felt they had "good preparation" for budgeting and finance, planning and development, personnel management, and government relations.

DiMaggio also asked arts managers how they learned to do their jobs. An overwhelming number of the respondents indicated that they learned how to manage while on the job. These managers included 95 percent in theater and orchestra management, 90 percent in museum management, and 86 percent in community arts agency (CAA) management.[23] Typically, around 20 percent said they had learned through university arts administration courses.

Updating the Profile

A recent survey of 641 professional managed performing arts organizations, examined the role of education in arts administrative training.[24] The survey identified 26 management skills, ranging from accounting to trustee/volunteer relations. Respondents provided their ratings of the skills needed to be an effective arts manager (see Figure 2–2). The top skills, not surprisingly, included leadership, fund raising, communication

Figure 2-1

Self-Evaluation of Preparedness at the Time of First Managership by Function (in percent)

	Fiscal Management	Personnel Management	Board Relations	Planning and Development	Marketing and Public Relations	Labor Relations	Government Relations
THEATERS							
Had good preparation	27.45%	42.57%	30.69%	37.62%	39.60%	20.00%	NA
Had poor preparation	25.49	13.86	29.70	23.76	16.83	16.83	
(Respondents)	(102)	(101)	(101)	(101)	(101)	(95)	
ART MUSEUMS							
Had good preparation	25.60	30.40	45.83	32.52	29.27	15.25	21.95
Had poor preparation	40.80	24.00	14.17	23.58	30.89	55.00	43.09
(Respondents)	(125)	(125)	(120)	(123)	(123)	(118)	(123)
ORCHESTRAS							
Had good preparation	26.42	36.89	43.14	33.33	47.06	22.00	NA
Had poor preparation	23.58	15.53	23.53	19.61	20.59	49.00	
(Respondents)	(106)	(103)	(102)	(102)	(102)	(100)	
ARTS ASSOCIATIONS							
Had good preparation	29.46	39.84	42.64	52.71	53.13	11.02	37.01
Had poor preparation	20.16	13.28	17.83	14.73	11.72	50.85	25.20
(Respondents)	(129)	(128)	(129)	(129)	(128)	(118)	(127)

NOTE: NA = Not asked/not applicable

Source: Paul DiMaggio, *Managers of the Arts,* 1987, Research Division Report #20, National Endowment for the Arts , Santa Ana, CA: Seven Locks Press).

and writing, marketing and audience development, and budgeting. The survey also identified skills employers thought best learned on the classroom versus those learned on the job. Interestingly the respondents could not seem to agree about whether classroom or on the job training was better. For example, the report noted the following:

- Arts managers want more training in marketing and fund raising (executive education).
- Arts managers prefer to hire marketing and development directors with formal arts administration training.
- They believe that marketing and fund raising is, by and large, best learned "on the job."[25]

In the 1990s, the diversification of arts institutions continued to increase the opportunities for women and minority-group members in the field of arts management. As a result, the profile of today's arts manager is more representative of our society. In the 1990s, the diversification

Figure 2-2

Critical Value of Management Skills

NOTE: 10 being the highest	Median	Mean	High	Low
Leadership	10	9.12	10	1
Budgeting	9	8.82	10	4
Team Building	9	8.82	10	1
Fundraising	9	8.79	10	1
Communication Skills/Writing	9	8.76	10	3
Marketing/Audience Development	9	8.49	10	4
Financial Management	9	8.41	10	3
Aesthetics/Artistic Sense	9	8.23	10	1
Trustee/Volunteer Relations	9	8.12	10	1
Strategic Management	8	8.18	10	3
Grantsmanship	8	8.01	10	1
Public Relations/Press Relations	8	7.89	10	3
Organizational Behavior	8	7.69	10	1
Public Speaking	8	7.66	10	1
Etiquette/Socal Grace	8	7.62	10	1
Information Management	8	7.52	10	1
Community Outreach/Education	8	7.41	10	1
Accounting	7	7.10	10	1
Expertise in One Arts Discipline	7	6.91	10	1
Political Understanding	7	6.50	10	1
Knowledge of Many Arts Disciplines	7	6.48	10	1
Personnel Relations/Unions	7	6.26	10	1
Contract Law	6	5.61	10	1
Statistical Analysis	6	5.38	10	1
Collective Bargaining	5	5.39	10	1
Computer Programming	5	5.08	10	1

Source: J. Dennis Rich and Dan J. Martin, "The Role of Formal Education in Arts Administration Training," from *The Guide to Arts Administration Training and Research 1997-99*, 1997, Association of Arts Administration Educators (AAAE), Washington, DC. Used with permission.

of arts institutions continued to increase the opportunities for women and minorities in the field of arts management. As a result, today's arts manager profile is somewhat more representative of our society. The National Study of Arts Managers (NSAM) conducted in 1996 found that "67 percent of the upper-level (management) positions are held by males, whereas 33 percent of upper-level positions are held by females."[26] The percentage of males to females in middle management positions was quite different at the middle-management level: 24 percent male and 76 percent female. The survey also found significant differences in salaries. "The average salary for a male arts manager is $56,936; however, the average salary for a female arts manager is $41, 368." [27]

Jobs for Arts Managers Today

When scanning a publication like *ArtSEARCH*, an employment service bulletin issued 23 times a year by the Theatre Communications Group (TCG),[28] it is possible to gain an overview of the job market for arts managers. The job listings also reveal organizations' expectations about staff qualifications for an arts manager in today's workplace. For example, a typical issue of *ArtSEARCH* will list openings for executive directors, managing directors, administrative assistants, box office managers, development directors, education directors, general managers, public relations mangers, and telemarketing managers.[29] The qualifications often noted for executive directors, for example, include skills in areas such as administration, communication, planning supervision, fund raising, and fiscal management. Obviously, executive director positions require previous experience or, as it is often indicated in a job posting, "a proven track record."

Depending on what part of the United States the job is in and the overall operating budget of the organization, the salaries for beginning level assistants may range (in thousands per year) from the high teens to the low twenties. Middle management positions may start in the low twenties and range to the high forties and upper management could start in the low thirties and go to the sixties and beyond. The benefits will vary with the resources of the organization. Most offer health insurance through a group policy and may require the employee to pay a percentage of the benefit costs. Larger organizations and institutions (such colleges and universities) offer more comprehensive benefit packages. The reality about employment opportunities in the area of arts management is that jobs are available. However, many of the smaller not-for-profit arts and culture organizations simply lack the resources to offer salaries competitive with the private sector.

The Manager's Personal Mission

An essential ingredient in the mix of knowledge, skills, and abilities a person brings to any arts management job must include a passion for what he or she is doing and a strong sense of purpose. The challenges a person will face in this field will be many. Therefore, a strong personal mission and sense of purpose is an important part of the profile of an arts manager. While it is difficult to quantify and list often-intangible attributes, nonetheless, one must be prepared to offer a clear point of view about the value and contribution the arts make to a community. As you will see in Chapter 7, on staffing, and Chapter 8, on leadership, a successful arts manager must tackle many related issues.

The National Endowment for the Arts

The role of the arts manager in the United States was further defined by the passage of legislation establishing the National Endowment for the Arts and Humanities on September 16, 1965.[30] The struggle to create a modest system for promoting growth and excellence in the arts took several years, numerous congressional hearings, and incredible dedication by a few people. Since its establishment, the NEA has helped shape the arts scene in the United States by organizing an identifiable arts constituency, stimulating donations through matching grants, and providing guidance to arts groups on ways to manage their limited resources effectively. Although the NEA budget was only $99.4 million in 1997, or roughly $0.38 per person in the United States,[31] the endowment regularly generates millions more through various matching grants.

The NEA's revised mission statement is worth noting because it helps shape the numerous grant categories created to support the arts. The following is from the NEA's current Web site:

The mission of the National Endowment for the Arts is:

To foster the excellence, diversity and vitality of the arts in the United States, and
To broaden public access to the arts.

Goals

To fulfill its mission, the Arts Endowment has established the following goals:
To encourage the development, availability, and preservation of America's artistic resources.
To foster opportunities for the creation and presentation of artistic work.
To strengthen the role of the arts in enriching educational experiences, enhancing the vitality of communities, and promoting individual growth and well-being.
To enhance the quality of service and efficiency of the agency's operations.[32]

The creation of the NEA led to the development of a support system for performers, performing arts organizations, museums, and film, design, and humanities projects over the last 30-plus years. Currently the NEA grants funds to individuals in the form of fellowships in literature and national heritage as well as sponsoring grants for an American jazz masters program and the national Medal of Arts. Grants to organizations fall under four categories: Heritage and Preservation, Education and Access, Creation and Presentation, and Planning and Stabilization.[33] In addition, the NEA provides funds to seven regional arts agencies, who in turn, distribute funds regionally and locally.

The typical application process moves through a system of staff screening, review by a committee of peers in the discipline, review of the peer group recommendation by the National Council on the Arts, and final decision by the chair of the endowment. Applications can take from six months to a year to work their way through the system. The chance of receiving funding is dependent to a large degree on how well the proposed project matches the criteria the NEA has set for the funding area. Chapter 13 provides more information about the overall process.

Government Support

The pros and cons of government support for the arts have not changed significantly since the inception of the NEA (see "Involuntary Patrons" in Chapter 1). The supporters of the legislation that led to the creation of the NEA saw it as an opportunity to make the arts more available to people throughout the United States and to enrich the nation's cultural life. Programs were designed to promote a type of cultural democracy through very modest grants to a wide range of projects and institutions. It was deemed important to support the creative spirit and at the same time promote new work. The preservation of a cultural heritage was a high priority, and the support of work that might not otherwise exist in a market-driven economic system was thought to benefit everyone.

The critics of the legislation believed that the establishment of a government subsidy system eventually would result in a general mediocrity creeping into the arts. There was fear that centralizing the power of the subsidy in the hands of a few would lead to less, not more, creative work in the country. Others believed that it was wrong to give the taxpayers' money to projects and programs with no appeal beyond a limited number of people. Some people argued that a type of cultural dictatorship would result from the peer review system. Still others argued that, if the government started subsidizing the arts, private and corporate philanthropy would dry up.

Budget Battles and Censorship

In the end, the astute shepherding of the legislation through the House and Senate by Livingston Biddle and others helped neutralize critics in the early days of the endowment. The NEA flourished and survived the annual congressional budget hearing process until 1981. Under the budget planning guidance of David Stockman, the Reagan administration proposed a 50 percent cut in the NEA budget for 1982 and additional cuts in 1983–1986.[34] The new administration saw in the NEA an example of the government creating a disincentive for private support for the arts. When confronted with the increase in private giving that had been generated by the endowment, the Reagan administration backed away from massive budget cutting, and reductions of 6 percent were adopted by Congress. The political spotlight shifted off the NEA and the budget actually continued to increase up until 1992 (see Figure 2–3 and "In the News").

The budget battles of the early 1980s were minor in comparison with the firestorm that erupted with the reauthorization legislation in 1989 and 1990. The reauthorization of the NEA became the focal point for a political struggle over censorship and the whole concept of funding for the arts. In the fall of 1990, arts lobby groups pleaded with arts groups across the country to support the NEA's reauthorization. Telegrams and letters were sent to Washington to show the members of Congress that there were constituents who supported the arts.

The compromise legislation eventually enacted required grant recipients to return the grant if the work they produced was found to be obscene by the courts. This compromise did not sit well with the artistic community. Controversy continued to follow the NEA as artists and organizations sued over the obscenity pledge. Several organizations, among them the Public Theater in New York City, turned down substantial grants rather than agree to the terms that the NEA established.

Censorship charges continued to be leveled at the NEA when grant recommendations by the National Council on the Arts were overturned by the acting director of the endowment in the spring of 1992. The resignation of peer review panels and key staff members have disrupted the operations of the NEA.

The remainder of the 1990s saw more trouble for the NEA as it went through further reauthorization hearings. The shift to a Republican-controlled House and Senate kept the NEA on the budget hot seat. Proposals to shut down the NEA completely found favor in the House and the eventual budget compromise process lead to the agency being funded at $98 million in 1998.[35] A casualty of the political struggles of the NEA has been funding for individual artists. In 1996, the NEA revised many of its grant categories and limited individual grants to fellowships for the most part. The hard work of Clinton-appointee Jane Alexander, chairing the NEA from 1993 to 1997, helped keep the agency alive.

For Further Consideration

Livingston Biddle's comprehensive personal history of the NEA, *Our Government and the Arts: A Perspective from the Inside*, is filled with hundreds of anecdotes about the struggle to establish and maintain what may be one of the most cost-effective organizations in government. In addition to telling interesting stories, the author takes the reader inside the legislative system as well as the management structure of the NEA. The book was published in 1988 by the Americans for the Arts, 1 East 53rd St., New York, NY 10022.

In the News

In what has become an annual rite of passage, a subcommittee of the House of Representatives voted Thursday to eliminate federal funds for the National Endowment for the Arts in the next fiscal year. But the panel's chairman conceded that the agency probably had enough support elsewhere in Congress to survive.

Source: Friday, 19 June 1998 08:00:00 EDT, news@chronicle.com, Daily Report from *Academe Today*.

Note: In July of that same year, Congress changed its mind and approved a budget for the NEA of $98 million.

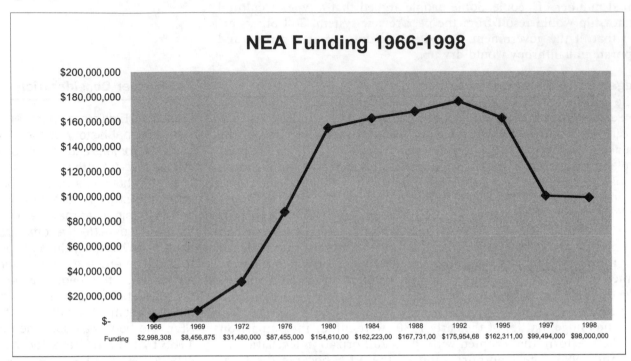

Figure 2-3

NEA Funding 1966-1998

	1966	1969	1972	1976	1980	1984	1988	1992	1995	1997	1998
Funding	$2,998,308	$8,456,875	$31,480,000	$87,455,000	$154,610,00	$162,223,00	$167,731,00	$175,954,68	$162,311,00	$99,494,000	$98,000,000

Source: Summary of Appropriated Funds 1966-1998, National Endowment for the Arts, May 1998. Not adjusted for inflation.

The NEA and the Arts Manager

The granting process implemented by the NEA in the late 1960s helped to stimulate the growth of many careers in arts management and hasten the professionalization of the field. The specialized skills required to seek out grants were in great demand. Because all organizational grants were at least a one-to-one match, meaning that for every federal dollar of a grant a matching dollar of other money must be found, fund-raising staffs and development experts began to be hired. Typically, grants to large organizations required three dollars of private money for every dollar of federal money over a three-year period. This further necessitated establishing a staff support system to run the initial campaign and to continue bringing the money in after the grant expired.

The development of the now-common board of directors and management staff structure was a product of the new accountability that arts organizations faced. Organizations had to prove that they could manage responsibly the funds they were given. Annual reports, financial statements, and five-year plans became standard operating procedures for organizations that wanted to be considered by the federal, corporate, and foundation funders. The result was an increase in staff openings, which provided jobs for the baby boomers graduating from the colleges and universities across America in the 1970s and 1980s.

State Agencies

The original NEA legislation provided funds for the creation of state agencies to distribute 20 percent of the endowment's overall budget.

The state and local arts agencies created another network of funding opportunities for artists and arts groups and created staff positions for arts managers. Today, the NEA is mandated to provide 40 percent of its budget to the new partnerships funding program with the states.[36]

The Education Revolution

Arts managers became an integral part of the unprecedented growth in the higher education industry. The baby boom and the resulting expansion programs undertaken by many schools to accommodate the incoming students led to the creation of numerous fine arts programs integrated into the overall mission of the institution.

There are more than 1,800 administrative heads of university or college theater programs in the United States today.[37] In 1990, Langley and Abruzzo listed 961 music programs, 409 opera programs or workshops, 1,622 visual arts programs, and 266 dance programs graduating future artists each year.[38] The Association of Arts Administration Educators (AAAE) listed over 30 graduate degree programs in arts and theater management around the world.[39]

In many larger university graduate programs, the performing arts evolved into preprofessional training programs in the late 1960s and 1970s. The number of management jobs grew as fine arts centers were built to house the visual and performing arts programs across the country. In many cases, at least one large facility was constructed to serve the dual purposes of supporting the academic programs and providing a venue for community events. Subscriptions to various arts series were offered to the community and students and provided the performance experience that arts students needed. Even small college and university programs adopted more professional approaches to producing shows due, in part, to the influx of faculty trained in the graduate programs of the large universities. The late 1970s and early 1980s were a period of tremendous growth in the smaller performing arts programs.

Educators within the arts community began to recognize the need to develop trained managers as well as performers, designers, and technicians. Several schools, such as Yale, Northwestern, University of Wisconsin, and University of California at Los Angeles, created training programs that became models for developing art managers.

By the early 1970s, the network of facilities managers had developed into an organization now known as the Association of Performing Arts Presenters (APAP). APAP sponsors an annual conference that is an important booking opportunity for theater groups, dance companies, music ensembles, and soloists. Student associations also hold annual meetings to book acts on campuses around the country.

The Slowdown in Growth

The educational boom began to slow at the end of the 1980s as the number of college-age students dropped. The consolidation of arts programs and the outright elimination of arts departments began to be discussed. By the early 1990s, the talk had turned to action. Budget cutting, little or no facility maintenance, and staff reductions began to sweep across the U.S. campuses. Many programs experienced difficulty filling their graduate classes even when they offered full scholarship support. As the 1990s progressed, the pressure of rising tuition costs and the increasing overhead costs of operating colleges and universities brought issues of resource redistribution to the forefront. Arts programs are particular costly to support. The need for small classes and one-on-one instruction makes the unit cost per student very high in comparison to departments than can delivery their subject matter in large lecture classes. The issues efficiency and maximizing resources will continue as the next wave of college student come in to the system after the turn of the century.

Conclusion

The evolution of the role of the arts manager continues as thousands of arts organizations undergo the arduous process of adapting to the changing cultural environment. As we will see in Chapter 4, arts groups constantly must assess the opportunities and threats that present themselves in the world around them. In theory at least, an arts manager should be trained to serve the needs of his or her particular discipline by effectively solving the problems of today and anticipating the significant changes of tomorrow. Unfortunately, the day-to-day struggle for financial survival that goes on in most organizations leaves little time for planning for the future.

Whatever changes take place in the next 20 years, arts managers working with artists, boards, and staffs will play a central role in the future of the arts in the United States. Dynamic vision and articulate leadership will be required if the arts are to build on the growth of the last 50 years.

Summary

Over the last 2,000 years, the basic functions of the artist-manager have remained the same. Bringing the art and the public together is the continuing objective.

In ancient times, simple religious ceremonies evolved into full-scale state-sponsored arts events that lasted from several days to a few weeks. The functions of management (planning, organizing, leading, and controlling) were distributed between artist-managers and the public officials who acted as arts managers. The rise of the Church and the decline of Rome created a shift away from State-sponsored events.

The late Middle Ages produced an economic growth that allowed the expansion of population centers. The rise of guilds and community-sponsored celebrations helped fuel changes in the overall arts climate. Complex pageants often needed people with management expertise to organize the large casts and the various sets associated with the productions.

Continued changes in society and the birth of more democratic forms of government eventually led to changes that became the foundation of many modern organizations. The Renaissance fostered the rebirth of drama and contributed to the development of the first operas and ballets. Problems with financing, patronage, and censorship also accompanied the growth in the arts. The additional art forms created additional jobs for arts managers.

In the seventeenth and eighteenth centuries, some countries began to establish national dance, opera, music, and theater companies. Permanent staff members and performers received salaries and pension benefits. By the nineteenth century in Europe and the United States, the arts had expanded into smaller population centers. However, there were no State-recognized arts institutions in the United States comparable to those of Europe. As communities became cities, orchestras, opera companies, and museums became permanent institutions. Most were supported by a small group of philanthropists. The role of the arts manager in the United States expanded with the continued development of touring, which was made possible by an extensive rail system. Monopolistic enterprises took control of many of the theaters at the end of the nineteenth century. The invention of movies and radio contributed to a decline in attendance at arts events by the 1920s.

The last 90 years have been shaped by major wars, slowly improving economic conditions; the new technologies of television, videotape, computers; and a population boom. As a profession and a recognized field of work, arts management is a product of changes in United States national policy since the 1950s. Ford Foundation funding and, beginning in the late 1960s, the National Endowment for the Arts helped make private and public support for the arts a high priority. The expanding arts market resulting from the population increase and the education boom also contributed to the creation of thousands of new jobs in the arts.

The profile of a typical arts manager in the 1980s was of a highly educated, upper-middle-class person with a background in the humanities. A limited number had done course work in management while in school. Survey results show that many arts managers had to learn the functions of their positions on the job and that a gender wage gap exists in arts management jobs. The growth in training programs in the 1980s and 1990s created a more diversified group of arts managers.

The NEA was created in 1965 to promote excellence, broaden the availability of the arts, and preserve work identified as part of the United States national heritage. The political environment has reshaped the NEA, and the resulting changes have reduced its budget by nearly 50 percent since 1992. The NEA has assisted many groups in organizing and professionalizing their staffs. In addition to promoting the growth of the arts at a national level, the NEA also supports numerous state and local arts agencies.

The field of arts management also has grown as a result of the boom in arts programs at colleges and universities across the United States. Degree programs, new facilities, and often extensive staffs have created a national network of arts centers with jobs for arts managers. Recent shifts in demographics have placed more pressure on the higher education field to deliver its product more efficiently.

Key Terms and Concepts

Artist-manager
Archon eponymous
Choregoi
Domini
The Syndicate
The NEA, its mission

Questions

1. Summarize the major arts management activity associated with the following time periods:
   a. Ancient Greece
   b. Ancient Rome
   c. Middle Ages

 d. Renaissance
 e. Seventeenth through nineteenth centuries
 f. Twentieth century
 2. What changes have taken place in the job market that might alter DiMaggio's profile of the arts manager?
 3. How much control should management have over the artistic product of an organization? For example, how much input should management have when it comes time to select the season's titles? Can you think of a situation in which too much or too little control was exercised by the management of an arts organization? What were the results?

Case Study

The following article from the early 1990s presents a model for change in the world of museum management. As you will see, not everyone agrees that this change is good.

Wanted: Art Scholar, M.B.A. Required
Alexander Stille

When Jack Lane took over as director of the San Francisco Museum of Modern Art three years ago, one of the first things he did was shut his office door. "The previous director's door was open to everyone who wanted to talk to him," Mr. Lane explains. "That just seemed unworkable. I wanted to clarify the chain of command, so we divided the museum into four major areas, and the heads of those areas report directly to me."

It was that kind of tough-minded decision the museum's trustees had hired Mr. Lane, who holds a master's degree in business from the University of Chicago as well as a Ph.D. from Harvard, to make. They wanted a director with a degree in business as well as art to lead the museum through a period of major expansion.

Their choice is representative of a growing perception that leadership at museums requires business acumen as well as connoisseurship. Although business management techniques have been used in museums for at least two decades, in the last few years those skills have been more heavily emphasized—to the dismay of some in the art world.

While many cultural institutions have long had business departments to take care of marketing, public relations and accounting functions, the emphasis at the top had been on scholarship. But now, at some major museums, even directors are being chosen for their business training as well as for their fine arts backgrounds.

Perhaps the most conspicuous and controversial appointment has been that of Thomas Krens at the Guggenheim Museum in New York. The 43-year-old director, who has a master's degree from the Yale School of Management, has come under criticism for his plans to create a multinational museum with branches in this Country and abroad, and for selling paintings from the museum's permanent collection to buy newer works.

Museums run by art historians are also making increasing use of modern management techniques. "You have to know how to negotiate with Unions, hire contractors, run a restaurant and a bookstore," says Patterson Sims, associate director of the Seattle Art Museum, who does not hold an M.B.A. "Those are not issues that connoisseurship prepares you for."

To help meet the demand, several of the country's best business schools—Harvard, Yale, Stanford, and the University of California at Los Angeles—offer courses in arts management. And the American Federation of Arts, a New York-based service organization that offers both exhibitions and professional training to 600 member museums, runs a summer program to train museum curators in business administration.

Perhaps not surprisingly, this mingling of art and business tends to polarize the museum world. "Administrative imperatives are taking precedence over artistic judgments," says Hilton Kramer, art critic and editor of *The New Criterion*, a magazine of cultural criticism. Others disagree. "A well-run operation should free the curator," counters Graham W. J. Beal, director of the Joslyn Art Museum in Omaha, who made the jump from curator to administrator after participating in the American Federation of Arts' training program.

Whether they see it as a blessing or a curse, there is widespread agreement that a business orientation in a museum is here to stay. "It's not a question of whether it will happen," says Roger M. Berkowitz, deputy director of the Toledo Museum of Art. "It is happening."

The Changing Profile of the Curator

According to museum professionals, the trend is linked to the increased size and complexity of many arts institutions.

"Museums are demonstrably more complex," says J. Carter Brown, director of the National Gallery in Washington and perhaps the first museum head to combine a joint M.B.A.–art history track as a calculated career strategy. He decided to take a business degree from Harvard while pursuing a master's degree in art history at the Institute of Fine Arts in New York. "When I became director in 1970," says Mr. Brown, "we had 350 employees. Now we have 1,000. Back then the museum was all in one building; we have doubled the space. Our budget was $5.9 million in 1970; today it's $53.9 million.

"My predecessor's fund-raising activities were simple," he continued. "He had lunch with Ailsa Mellon, and if he needed a Leonardo she would write a check." During Mr. Brown's tenure, the National Gallery has raised $40 million from 92 corporations.

As a result of such changes, the profile of the typical museum director has changed since the mid-70s. Directors of the old school tended to be socially prominent connoisseurs, as knowledgeable in wooing wealthy collectors as in evaluating art. "It was a hobby," says Thomas Hoving, director of the Metropolitan Museum from 1966 to 1977 and now editor in chief of Connoisseur magazine. "When I first got out of graduate school, people told me that the biggest prerequisite for becoming a curator was an outside income."

Although Mr. Hoving has no degree in business (nor does his successor, Philippe de Montebello), many credit—or blame— him for starting the focus on business in museums. "It was during Hoving's tenure at the Met that museums became broad, popular institutions, with blockbuster shows, expanded education programs, gift shops, bookstores and restaurants maximizing income," says Mr. Lane, who has raised more than $65 million for the San Francisco museum and will double its exhibition space with a new building.

Last year the Minneapolis Institute of Art hired Daniel E. O'Leary as deputy director, in part because of his experience turning around a financially troubled museum. After earning a joint Ph.D. and M.B.A. at the University of Michigan, Mr. O'Leary became director of Artrain, a Michigan-based regional museum that presents traveling exhibitions in a railroad car. "I applied classical business school analysis," he says. "We booked exhibitions of greater appeal, extended the touring schedule to create a greater economy of scale. We managed to more than double the revenues and cut expenses by a third, and audiences went from 40,000 annually to 130,000."

One of the first things he did at Minneapolis was to conduct a market survey. "We live in a competitive world. We have to justify ourselves to government, to foundations, to corporations."

Some critics of the trend toward a business mentality fear that museums' preoccupation with attendance is inimical to their artistic purpose. "Museums are market-driven," says Hilton Kramer. "Museum directors have become salesmen."

Others insist that ignoring the bottom line can jeopardize a museum's artistic mission.

"A number of museums have become more or less insolvent," says Myrna Smoot, director of the American Federation of Arts. "They reduce their hours, they don't change their collections, they reduce maintenance and security, stop paying to conserve the collection, in order to keep the doors open."

Does "Thank You" Mean Forever?

The problem of continual growth is one that preoccupies Mr. Krens at the Guggenheim, the most outspoken advocate of the so-called M.B.A. revolution, who has sought to challenge the assumptions on which museums have traditionally operated. "It's increasingly expensive to store and preserve works of art," he says. "When you accept an object into your collection, do you take on an obligation to preserve the work forever?" Older museums, he says, are at a critical juncture; they cannot continue indefinitely as both custodians of the past and purveyors of the new. Do you go on collecting forever? And if not, where do you stop?"

Mr. Krens clearly answered his own question with his decision to sell a Kandinski, a Modigliani and a Klee last year to pay for a major collection of Minimalist art from the Italian Count Giuseppe Panza.

Most M.B.A. curators warn against taking this trend too far. "If M.B.A.'s are running museums without an art history background, we're in for a grim future," says Mr. Nash.

For the moment, anyway, the low wage scale of the not-for-profit world ensures to some degree that the M.B.A.'s entering the museum world will have to be passionate about more than money.

SOURCE: Alexander Stille, "Wanted: Art Scholar. M.B.A. Required," *New York Times* (January 19, 1991). Copyright @1991 by the New York Times Company. Reprinted with permission.

FYI: In the spring and summer of 1998 the Guggenhiem hosted an exhibition of motorcycles that attracted thousands of new visitors to the museum.

Thomas Krens, the Guggenhiems director, was the show's curator. Bikers and motorcycle club members from across the country flocked to see the exhibition. Some of the critics of Mr. Krens doubted the audience attracted to BMW and Harley-Davidson classic motorcycles would be coming back to the museum on a regular basis.

Note: A related article about Thomas Krens may be found in *The New York Times*, April 19, 1998, Section 2, Arts and Leisure. "The Global Straddler of the Art World" provides an interesting profile about Mr. Krens, who celebrated his tenth year as the Guggenheim's director on July 1, 1998.

Case Study Questions

1. List at least two reasons why a museum curator needs business management skills.

2. Do you agree or disagree with Hilton Kramer's judgment that museums have become "market driven" and museum directors have become "salesmen"? Explain.

3. What alternatives can museums pursue to increase membership other than high-visibility exhibitions?

4. Do you agree with the notion of selling off museum holdings to raise money for other works? What should museums do about preserving their holdings?

References

1. Oscar G. Brockett, *History of the Theatre*, 3d ed. (Boston: Allyn and Bacon, 1977), pp. 15–47.
2. Ibid., pp. 51–73.
3. Ibid., p. 105.
4. Ibid., p. 136.
5. Richard Kraus and Sarah Alberti Chapman, *History of the Dance in Art and Education*, 2d ed. (Englewood Cliffs, NJ: Prentice-Hall, 1981), p. 62.
6. Ibid., p. 67.
7. John Pick, *Managing the Arts? The British Experience* (London: Rhinegold, 1986), p. 23.
8. Ibid., p. 45.
9. William J. Baumol and William G. Bowen, *Performing Arts: The Economic Dilemma* (Cambridge, MA: MIT Press, 1966), p. 20.
10. Ibid., p. 29.
11. Kraus and Chapman, *History of the Dance*, pp. 93–95.
12. Baumol and Bowen, *Performing Art*, p. 29.
13. Ibid., pp. 27–28.
14. Martin Mayer, "The Opera," in *The Performing Arts and American Society*, ed. W. McNeil Lowry (Englewood Cliffs, NJ: Prentice-Hall, Spectrum Books, 1977), p. 45.
15. W. McNeil Lowry, ed., *The Performing Arts and American Society* (Englewood Cliffs, NJ: Prentice-Hall, Spectrum Books, 1977), p. 14.
16. Ibid., p. 11.
17. NEA Research Division, Note # 67, May 1998: "Dance Organizations Report 43% Growth in Economic Census: 1987–1992"
18. NEA Research Division, Note # 68, May, 1998: "Classical Music Groups Report 22% Growth in Economic Census: 1987–1992."
19. NEA Research Division, Note # 64, May 1998: "Museums, Arboreta, Botanical Gardens and Zoos Report 18% Growth, 1987–1992."

20. John Naisbitt and Patricia Aburdene, *Megatrends 2000* (New York: Avon, 1990), p. 67.
21. Paul DiMaggio, *Managers of the Arts*, Research Division Report #20, NEA (Washington, DC.: Seven Locks Press, 1987), p. 12.
22. Ibid., p. 42.
23. Ibid., p. 46.
24. Dennis Rich and Dan J. Martin, *Guide to Arts Administration Training and Research 1997–1999* (Washington, DC: Association of Arts Administration Educators, 1997), pp. 69–73.
25. Ibid., p. 72.
26. Donna G. Herron, Tamara S. Hubbard, Amy E. Kirner, Lynn Newcomb, Michelle Reisner-Memmer, Michael E. Robertson II, Matthew W. Smith, Leslie A. Tullo, and Jennifer S. Young, "The Effect of Gender on the Career Advancement of Arts Managers," *Journal of Arts Management, Law and Society*, Volume 28, Number 1, Spring 1998, p. 30.
27. Ibid.
28. *ArtSEARCH* is published by the Theatre Communications Group, Inc., 355 Lexington Ave., New York, NY 10017.
29. *ArtSEARCH* (May 1, 1998), pp. 1–11.
30. Livingston Biddle, *Our Government and the Arts* (New York: American Council for the Arts, 1988), p. 180.
31. The per person cost was calculated by dividing the current budget for the NEA (fiscal year 1997) by the total population according to the 1995 U.S. Department of Commerce current population reports, publication #P25-1130.
32. Guide to the NEA, Washington, DC, http://arts.endow.gov/Guide/NewLook/Overview.html, p. 1.
33. Ibid., . . ./Organizations.html, p. 1.
34. Biddle, *Our Government and the Arts*, p. 492.
35. National Endowment for the Arts, Summary of Appropriated Funds 1966 to 1998, http://arts.endow.gov/Guide/Facts/Appropriations.html, p. 2.
36. Guide to the NEA, Washington, DC, http://arts.endow.gov/Guide/NewLook/Overview.html.
37. According to the Association of Theatre in Higher Education (ATHE) Membership Directory 1997.
38. Stephen Langley and James Abruzzo, *Jobs in Arts and Media Management* (New York: American Council for the Arts, 1990), pp. 10–11.
39. Rich and Martin, *Guide to Arts Administration Training and Research 1997–1999*.

Additional Resources

The Journal of Arts Management and Law, volume 13, number 1 (Spring 1983), is devoted to the arts and public policy. The topics covered in this issue give the reader a good sense of today's important topics in arts management. This journal frequently covers issues related to the arts and public policy.

The New York Times covered the NEA extensively in "Washington's Stake in the Arts," (April 12, 1998), Arts and Leisure, Section 2. The article offers a great deal of useful background on the current state of affairs of the NEA and is recommended reading for arts managers.

Evolution of Management

3
□ □ □ □ □

In this chapter, we scan the evolution of management thought. We review early management practices and then examine the management concepts that grew out of the shift to mass production during the Industrial Revolution. Finally, we look at the impact of scientific management and the application of psychological theories on the workplace.

Little mention is made of arts organizations in this chapter because the primary objective is to provide a general historical background on management. Many of the terms and concepts noted in Chapters 1 and 2 developed from classic and contemporary management theory and practice. If you have taken college courses in business or management, the terms, concepts, and people noted in this chapter should not be new to you. Before moving into the specific areas of the external environments, planning, organizational design, and human resource management, it seems appropriate to explore the source of the current management systems used to operate all organizations.

Management as an Art and a Science

A basic assumption of this text is that management is an art. In this case, an *art* is defined as *an ability or special skill that someone develops and applies.* Studying the theories of management, synthesizing the application of these theories to a practical work environment, and then creating a workable system for a specific organization requires a tremendous amount of thought and effort. It often is a lifetime job.

Management also can be considered a science. While the idea of science in the workplace may not be very appealing to an aspiring arts manager, the reality is that applying some of the techniques noted in the chapter may help make a stronger arts organization. As we will see, the general concept of *scientific management* is not universally welcomed in the workplace. The term describes a particular approach to maximizing productivity by applying research and quantitative analysis to the work process. The creation of general and specific management theories to explain and predict how organizations and people behave also is integral to thinking of management as a science.

At the center of any theory is the ability to predict an outcome if given a specific set of circumstances. A scientist develops a theory, conducts experiments, establishes an outcome that can be repeated by others, and provides proof of the theory. Management theory tries to achieve the same goal: predictable outcomes given specific inputs. Unfortunately, the science of management, as with any social science, sometimes is subject to unanticipated outcomes. In management science, numerous other variables, including the behavior of employees in the work environment, can quickly undermine a theory.

7

On-the-Job Management Theory

When studying management theory and practice, which frequently are examined by using case studies, it becomes apparent that managers often enter into the practice of managing with virtually no theoretical background. For example, Katherine Graham, who once owned the *Washington Post*, had no formal training in business management. The sudden death of her husband thrust her into the role of chief executive officer. Nonetheless, she was able to successfully operate a major newspaper using her personal ability and adaptability. She was able to learn on the job and further develop her own operating theories and practices to maintain a successful business. For every Katherine Graham many other people in the workplace are less successful at playing the role of manager. Your local bookstores are stocked with readings about how employees should deal with the boss or supervisor who does not seem to have mastered the art of managing.

In Paul DiMaggio's 1987 study for the National Endowment for the Arts, more than 85 percent of the arts managers in theaters, art museums, orchestras, and arts associations said that they learned from on-the-job training.[1] The university-trained arts managers surveyed claimed that their schooling did not adequately prepare them for many of the demands of running an organization. While the numbers of university-trained arts managers has increased in the last few years, it still is safe to say that the experience in the workplace is required to complete the education of any arts manager.

Regardless of how an individual learns the art and science of management, an effective manager eventually must be able to analyze variables and predict outcomes based on experience. In other words, the manager must find a set of operating principles that can be used. For example, an arts manager might have to say to the board, "If we raise prices, ticket orders will decline, based on the discretionary spending patterns of our audience. If we change our subscription plans, fewer people will order because any change creates confusion. If we perform nothing but concerts of avant-garde music, a significant portion of our subscribers will stay home." It may be perfectly appropriate, given the mission, for an organization to make a decision that will produce a negative outcome. A good manager should be able to articulate his or her expectations of outcomes based on an understanding of the effects of variables on particular decisions. Obviously experience is, and always will be, a great teacher.

To be an effective arts manager one should have an awareness and appreciation of the overall field of management. The rest of this chapter focuses on some of the major theories and principles that shape management today.

Evolution of Management Thought

Preindustrialization

For the last several thousand years, organized social systems have managed the resources needed to feed, house, and protect people. The evolution of management is intertwined with the development of the social, religious, and economic systems needed to support cities, states, and countries. The Church and State provided the first systems for planning, organizing, leading, and controlling. These management systems were predicated on philosophies that placed people within complex hierarchies.

History provides many examples of management systems established by the Egyptians, Romans, and Chinese. Many basic principles of supervision and control evolved from the projects undertaken by these societies. Building temples, pyramids, and other massive structures required extensive management and organizational skill. Modern management concepts expanded on the skill needed to implement public works projects as the world shifted from an agrarian to an industrial base.

A Change in Philosophies

The decline of the Catholic superstate in the fourteenth and fifteenth centuries and the subsequent religious struggles created by the rise of Protestantism slowly changed the fundamental relationship of people to their government and religious systems. The seeds of the Protestant work ethic were planted in the new order. The expansion of trade and the creation of a permanent middle class grew out of the changes brought about by the national and international economic systems. The effects of the Renaissance and the Reformation extended far beyond rediscovering the thoughts and philosophies of antiquity. The development of new political and social theories of government and management by such theorists as Niccolò Machiavelli, Thomas Hobbes, John Locke, and Adam Smith led to crucial changes in thinking about the individual and the society at large. For example, Adam Smith's *Wealth of Nations*, published in 1776, moved economic theory beyond the mercantile system with Smith's now-famous economic principles. The "invisible hand" of the marketplace is the core concept of the system of economic self-regulation that survives today.

The Industrial Revolution and Early Pioneers of Management

Four principal changes in the management of the workplace are often attributed to the Industrial Revolution:

1. Mechanization of work,
2. Centralization of production,
3. Creation of the labor class,
4. Creation of the job of manager.

The elements of science and technology, changes in government policies, population growth, improved health conditions, and the more productive use of farmland were all part of the changes that occurred during the seventeenth, eighteenth, and nineteenth centuries. The early entrepreneurs who established manufacturing businesses using the new technologies of the time (e.g., the steam engine) needed others to supervise the laborers hired to operate the equipment. Essentially, the industrial manager was created to watch over the laborers. The problem of treating people as nothing more than extensions of machines and the subsequent abuses of labor—long hours, low pay, no job security, health and safety hazards, child labor, and so on—has left a legacy we still grapple with today. For example, the concept of "the carrot and the stick," which was used as a motivational management method in the factories, survives in the minds of many managers today. The positive inducement (the carrot) to earn more by working harder and faster was set off against a punishment (the stick), which included such things as a cut in wages or a more dangerous task, as a method of motivating people. However, not all owners and managers approached labor and production with the same attitude.

One of the early pioneers of a more enlightened approach to management was Robert Owen (1771–1858). At age 18, Owen operated and supervised a cotton mill, where he observed problems occurring in the manufacturing process. He tried to improve overall working conditions and changed the equipment to reduce the hazards to workers. However, due to a shortage of labor, he too hired children to work 13 hours a day.[2]

Charles Babbage (1792–1871), often cited as the inventor of the world's first computer (a counting machine actually), in 1822, also is credited with creating the first research techniques to study work.[3] His early work was the forerunner of what is now called scientific management. In *The Evolution of Management Thought*, Daniel Wren notes that Babbage attempted to establish salary systems that showed the mutual interest labor and management shared in the process of production. "Babbage's profit-sharing scheme had two facets: one, that a portion of wages would depend on factory profits; and two, that the worker should derive more advantage from applying any improvement he might discover, that is, a bonus for suggestions."[4]

Figure 3–1 provides a visual depiction of the major movements and the people involved in evolution of management theory.

Changes in America

The early stages of the Industrial Revolution in the United States depended on borrowing management and organizational techniques from England and Scotland. However, by the middle nineteenth century, U.S. manufacturers began to show the world how to mass-produce interchangeable parts for a variety of equipment.[5] Late-nineteenth century America's management system development, in large part, was due to the engineer. Mechanical, industrial, and civil engineers were the primary force behind the development of "systems" for doing work.

The railroads and the new technology of the telegraph created a climate for rapid business expansion in America. Daniel Craig McCallum (1815–1878), a manager for the Erie railroad, is credited with such things as creating a formal organization chart (it was shaped like a tree), matching authority with responsibility, and using the telegraph system to provide feedback about the location of trains.[6]

Henry Varnum Poor (1812–1905), the editor of the *American Railroad Journal*, wrote extensively about management organization and systems. Wren describes Poor's three-part philosophy as follows:

> [First,] organization was basic to all management; there must be a clear division of labor from the president down to the common laborer, each with specific duties and responsibilities. Second, communication was devising a method of reporting throughout the organization to give top management a continuous and accurate accounting of operations. Finally, information was "recorded communication," Poor saw the need for a set of operating reports to be compiled for costs, revenues, and rate making.[7]

As noted in Chapter 2, the railroads played an important part in changing how entertainment was distributed in the United States. As we saw, the railroad brought to the arts the need for a specialist to manage the logistics of moving the company from city to city. The complexity of railroad schedules (time zones as we know them today were not in place until the late 1880s) also demanded a large portion of a manager's time.

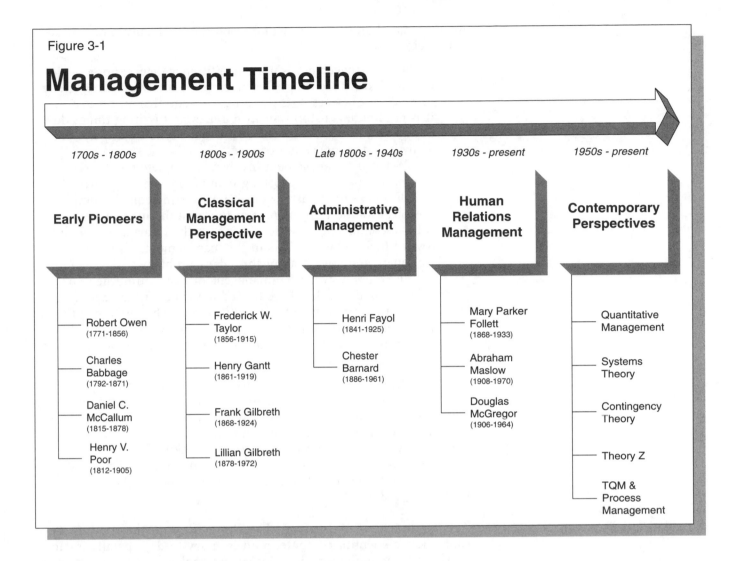

Figure 3-1

Management Timeline

1700s - 1800s	1800s - 1900s	Late 1800s - 1940s	1930s - present	1950s - present
Early Pioneers	**Classical Management Perspective**	**Administrative Management**	**Human Relations Management**	**Contemporary Perspectives**
Robert Owen (1771-1856)	Frederick W. Taylor (1856-1915)	Henri Fayol (1841-1925)	Mary Parker Follett (1868-1933)	Quantitative Management
Charles Babbage (1792-1871)	Henry Gantt (1861-1919)	Chester Barnard (1886-1961)	Abraham Maslow (1908-1970)	Systems Theory
Daniel C. McCallum (1815-1878)	Frank Gilbreth (1868-1924)		Douglas McGregor (1906-1964)	Contingency Theory
Henry V. Poor (1812-1905)	Lillian Gilbreth (1878-1972)			Theory Z
				TQM & Process Management

Although management concepts may have been growing in sophistication and depth during this period, the treatment of employees lagged behind. The safety and well-being of workers were not high priorities. Child labor, extremely low wages, and the lack of job security helped create powerful labor unions later in the nineteenth and early twentieth centuries.

Management Trends to the Present

Classical Management Perspectives

One founder of modern management is Frederick W. Taylor (1856–1915). Taylor is credited as the founder of scientific management. His efforts to change the workplace often faced bitter opposition. In 1912, Taylor stated his principles before a special congressional committee created to investigate the effects of scientific management on the worker. His words speak clearly of a management theory that is far different from the highly efficient assembly line many people imagine as the realization of his principles. Taylor's ultimate goal was to use his methods to achieve a "great mental revolution."[8] His testimony makes a convincing case:

> Scientific management is not any efficiency device, not a device of any kind for securing efficiency; nor is it any bunch or group of efficiency devices. It is not a new system of figuring costs; . . . it is not holding a stop watch on a man and writing things down about him; it is not time study; it is not motion study nor an analysis of the movement of men. . . .
>
> Scientific management involves a complete mental revolution on the part of the working man engaged in any particular establishment or industry. And it involves the equally complete mental revolution on the part of those on the management's side—a complete mental revolution on their part as to the duties toward their fellow workers in the management, toward their workmen, and toward all of their daily problems.
>
> Frequently, when the management have found the selling price going down they have turned toward a cut in wages . . . as a way of . . . preserving their profits intact. Thus it is over the division of the surplus [or profits] that most of the troubles have arisen; in the extreme cases this has been the cause of serious disagreements and strikes.[9]

The drive toward making the workplace and the work process as efficient as possible by careful analysis of all phases of manufacturing continues to the present. Taylor's early time and motion studies, for example, are now regular fixtures in examining how an organization is accomplishing its tasks, from building cars to making hamburgers.

Some of the other pioneers of the scientific management field were Henry L. Gantt (1861–1919), Frank Gilbreth (1868–1924), and Lillian Gilbreth (1878–1972).[10]

Arts applications   Arts groups have limited use in the application of sophisticated scientific computer models in day-to-day operations. However, whatever limited gains in organizational productivity are to be achieved will result from integrating specific quantitative techniques in the organization. As you will see in Chapter 10, the basic economics of the arts mitigates against productivity increases. However, some components of arts organizations lend themselves to quantitative applications rooted in scientific management. For example, inventory and accounting systems easily can be computerized and linked to networked office computer systems. The process of assembling sets may be streamlined if time is spent analyzing how the work is being done. Often the way a task is done is based more on tradition than a detailed process analysis of the work. In fact, almost any routine procedure is worth examining. Often almost any work can be done in a more efficient way, whether it is counting ticket stubs, building platforms, sorting color media, or hanging lights.

Administrative Management (1916 to Present)

Henri Fayol (1841–1925), a mine engineer, was a pioneer in the field of modern *administrative management*. The basic idea of this approach is that it focuses on principles that can be used to coordinate the work in an organization. Fayol's Fourteen Principles (Figure 3–2) helped form the first comprehensive approach to management theory. Although many of Fayol's Fourteen Principles seem straightforward today, they

Figure 3-2

Fayol's Fourteen Principles of Management

1. **DIVISION OF LABOR**
Work specializations can result in efficiencies in both managerial and technical functions. However, there are limits to how much work specializations can be divided.
2. **AUTHORITY**
Managers have the right to give orders and exact obedience. With authority comes responsibility.
3. **DISCIPLINE**
Discipline is necessary to develop obedience, diligence, energy, and respect.
4. **UNITY OF COMMAND**
An employee should receive orders from one supervisor only.
5. **UNITY OF DIRECTION**
All operations with the same objective should have one manager and one plan.
6. **SUBORDINATION OF INDIVIDUAL INTERESTS TO GENERAL INTERESTS**
The interests of one employee or group of employees should not take precedence over the interests and goals of the organization.
7. **REMUNERATION**
Compensation should be fair for employee and employer.
8. **CENTRALIZATION**
The proper amount of centralization or decentralization should depend on the situation.
9. **SCALAR CHAIN (Hierarchical)**
A clear line of authority should extend from the highest to lowest levels in the organization. Horizontal communication is encouraged as long as the employees in the chain are informed.
10. **ORDER**
Materials should be kept in well-chosen places to facilitate activities.
11. **EQUITY**
Employees should be treated with kindness and justice.
12. **STABILITY OF PERSONNEL TENURE**
Because time is required to become effective in a new jobs, high turnover should be prevented.
13. **INITIATIVE**
Managers should encourage and develop employee initiative to the fullest.
14. **ESPRIT DE CORPS**
Harmony and union build organization strength.

Source: Adapted from Henri Fayol, *General and Industrial Management*, trans., Constance Stoors, (London: Pitman & Sons, London, 1949) pp. 19-42.

broke new ground in 1917 by helping to establish a basis for administrative management.

Fayol also postulated that an individual with more skill in management than in technical expertise would not necessarily be bad for a company. In fact, he believed that an engineer with no aptitude for management would do more harm than good in an organization.[11] He also saw that management could be studied separately from engineering, and he noted that every organization required management: "Be it a case of commerce, industry, politics, religion, war, or philanthropy, in every concern there is a management function to be performed."[12]

Chester Barnard (1886–1961) frequently is cited as another contributor to the field of administrative management theory. In 1938 he wrote *The Functions of Management*, which brought forward the notion of *acceptance theory of authority*.[13] Acceptance theory postulates that authority is derived from the acceptance of authority by the people being managed. The efficient day-to-day administration of an organization depends on the willingness of the employees to comply with directives given them by managers. As long as these directives generally fit within the realm of the possible from the employees perspective, they accept the control of the management structure. The successful Dilbert cartoon series often utilizes acceptance theory situations from the workplace. Humor is found as the hapless employees receive directives from the manager that often are at odds with common sense. We will discuss importance of acceptance theory in more detail in Chapter 8.

Arts application   Many typical work situations in the arts can be identified by a quick review of Fayol's principles (Figure 3–2). For example, labor onstage is divided into specialized departments for carpentry, props, lighting, and sound. A gap in authority and responsibility (Principle 2) may be found in some arts settings. An example would be the university student stage manager with a great deal of responsibility but very little authority in the organization. The idea of unity of direction comes in to play with the director or conductor leading the ensemble. A good example of Barnard's theory of acceptance of authority often is seen in the process managing of volunteers. Typically, the volunteers in the organization respond to the leadership of a manager based on the acceptance they have of the directives they are given.

Human Relations Management (1927 to Present)

The behavioral approach   The major failure of the classic approaches to management mentioned thus far was their lack of understanding of the human factor in work. The most efficient way of accomplishing a task often was thwarted by what the scientific management theorists thought was stubborn resistance of employees to change. The researchers began to apply principles and concepts from the new field of psychology in an effort to understand workers better and to make organizations and people more productive. The basic assumptions behind much of this research were that (1) people desire satisfying social relationships and derive satisfaction from accomplishing specific tasks, (2) they respond to group and peer pressure in their work output, and (3) they search for individual fulfillment in their work.

Mary Parker Follett (1868–1933), a Radcliff graduate and social worker in the Boston area, articulated several ideas about group dynamics in the workplace. Follett noted that people working in organizations are continually influenced by each other and are very capable of accomplishing work in groups. In fact, her ideas are in use today as many organizations develop "teams" to accomplish tasks. Follett argued for a workplace in which management shared power with, not over, employees. She also developed the concept of *integrative unity* to describe how organizations could better reach their goals by coordinating group activities.[14]

A valuable piece of research involving people in the workplace, and a classic example of an unintended consequence, can be found in a project undertaken at the Hawthorne Wire Works in Illinois in the 1920s.

The Hawthorne effect   In 1924, Vannevar Bush of MIT undertook a study of worker productivity at the Hawthorne Wire Works. The employees wound wires on motor coils or inspected small parts. Bush and his colleagues experimented with different lighting conditions on the assumption that different intensities of light would affect worker output. They found that the lighting level had no effect. Worker output increased despite wide variations in brightness.

Elton Mayo and Fritz Roethlisberger, professors at Harvard, began the second phase of the study in 1927. A group of workers were carefully monitored for five years using a special test facility built for the experiment. The researchers gave the workers physicals every six weeks, monitored their blood pressure, recorded weather conditions, noted their eating and sleeping habits, and so forth. No matter what changes were instituted, worker productivity kept increasing. It became clear to the researchers that other factors were influencing the employees work behavior. Mayo and Roethlisberger surmised that the extra attention being paid to the experimental group combined with such things as changes in the supervision system, the creation of a small social system in the work groups, and the creation of a type of esprit de corps among the workers contributed to the increased output.[15] The Hawthorne effect, as it is now called, stresses the importance of human interaction in the workplace.

Maslow's hierarchy of needs   Another theory that helped shape the human relations approach to management was Abraham Maslow's hierarchy of needs. Maslow's 1943 paper, "A Theory of Human Motivation," was quickly incorporated into management theory and practice. Chapter 8 discusses ways to apply his approach in the work setting from the leadership perspective. In summary, the theory suggests that part of the manager's job is to provide avenues leading to employee satisfaction and that managers must work to remove obstacles that prevent employees from accomplishing their jobs. According to Maslow, the various needs people have (lowest to highest: physiological, safety, belongingness, esteem, and self-actualization) can never be fully met nor can they be ignored in designing the workplace.

McGregor's Theory X and Theory Y   Douglas McGregor gave a speech in 1957 at the Sloan School of Management called "The Human Side of Enterprise." His presentation included an idea about work that changed the relationship of manager to employee. McGregor's theory is based on the concept that managers develop "self-fulfilling prophecies" about people that affect all of their interactions with employees.[16] He identified two major perspectives held by managers: Theory X and Theory Y. Theory X assumes that (1) people generally dislike work and avoid it when possible; (2) they must be coerced, controlled, and threatened with punishment to get them to work; and (3) they want to be directed and avoid taking responsibility. On the other hand, Theory Y assumes that (1) people are generally willing to work, (2) they are willing to accept responsibility, (3) they are capable of self-direction, and (4) they have creative and imaginative resources that are not effectively utilized in the work environment. The Theory Y approach to management has become a part of current trends toward what is called *participative management*. Companies are now beginning to ask employees what they think, rather than treating them simply as labor. McGregor believed that any enterprise can flourish if there is a partnership between the workers and the managers.[17]

Arts application   The very process of rehearsal in the arts is central to improving a person's eventual "performance." Therefore, the success of an artist-manager often is tied to how well he or she can motivate the people in the company. When we say the performance was "excellent" we are really responding to how the people were managed and prepared for the performance. Follett's integrative unity is seen in the bringing together of cast and crew in the group effort of producing a live performance, special event, or exhibition. It is easy to see how McGregor's description of a Theory X manager might apply to directors, choreographers, conductors, or designers who work with their cast, dancers, musicians, or crew from the point of view that assumes people need to be coerced, controlled, and threatened in order to produce good work. It is also possible to find artistic leaders who work with people from the Theory Y point of view. They see their job as carefully directing self-motivated people to even higher levels of achievement.

Modern Management

Scientific Management Today—Quantitative Approaches

The rise of research universities and graduate schools of business and management and the increased application of scientific management to the workplace have come together in the last 50 years to form a strong theoretical base for the study of management. Wharton was the first undergraduate school to offer a degree in business (1881), and Dartmouth (1900) and Harvard (1909) were the first universities to offer graduate programs in management.[18]

Scientific management techniques have undergone further refinement with the assistance of computer models to help design the most efficient and productive workplace. The worldwide application of these techniques is well documented. Terms such as *operations research* (OR), the application of quantitative analysis to all parts of a business operation, are common.[19] The critical path method (CPM), for scheduling and controlling work on projects, is part of standard operating procedures in many businesses. Scientific management techniques have been applied by the Japanese in much of their manufacturing, and the resulting gains in productivity have advanced them to the forefront of world competition. Ironically, the processes to achieve this productivity was the result of the work of American quality expert W. Edwards Deming. Such concepts as "just-in-time inventory" (or Kanban), computer-aided design (CAD), computer-assisted manufacturing (CAM), and computer-integrated manufacturing (CIM) are natural extensions of the work started by Taylor 100 years ago.

Systems Theory

Systems theory assumes that organizations are composed of interrelated parts and activities that are arranged by design to produce goods or services. The open system model, which was briefly noted in Chapter 1, is an example of applying systems theory to an organization. It assumes that an organization functions in a complex world influenced by multiple environments as it goes about gathering inputs and transforming them into outputs in the form of goods or services. The "inputs" are the people who work for the organization and the materials, equipment, and money required to produce the organization's goods or services. The "output," or performance of the organization, is not the sum of its parts but rather the result of the interaction of the parts. The process of management transforms the inputs into the output. Ideally, an organizational *synergy* results from the process and the whole becomes greater than the sum of its parts.[20]

Contingency Approaches

The contingency approach to managing an organization works on the assumption that no one way works best in all circumstances facing an organization. The management therefore must be adaptable and capable of understanding the different mixes of management techniques that may be required at different times. This approach also recognizes that the people who make up the organization have differing styles of work and management. The top management therefore must expect that different work groups will have alternative ways of achieving the stated objectives. Rather than seeing this as a threat, diversity must be perceived as a strength. Synergy once again can be achieved if the management is capable of effectively coordinating the different work groups.[21]

Arts Applications

One assumption this text makes is that arts organizations are open systems subject to internal and external forces that shape and change how they operate. The next chapter specifically discusses the larger world in which the arts organization must function. The system model allows a manager to create, revise, or remove subsystems that do not effectively support the mission. For example, a subsystem within an arts organization might be volunteer support. As a subsystem, it may have goals, specific objectives, a staff member assigned to coordinate work, and budget resources allocated. However, poor turnout by volunteers or low-quality work can prevent this subsystem from effectively adding to the overall productivity of the organization. The manager then would step in, analyze the problems, and attempt to put in place changes that would help make the volunteer system work better.

The contingency theory assumes that the appropriate action to take by management should be driven by a careful analysis of the problem and situation. One assumes no one universal set of principles will work for all organizations. Situational factors should determine the best application of management solutions. For example, the solution to the volunteer problem may be a simple change in venue. Perhaps there is no problem with volunteer leadership but rather a lack of space big enough to have the group gather to work on its projects. So rather than delve into applying human relations theory solutions to the problem, a manager might apply a quantitative approach by studying the work processes of the volunteers and improving the work space to facilitate what they do for the organization.

Emerging Views

It remains to be seen if one theory ever can be applied to best establish and operate an organization. The basis for effectively managing most organizations in the current world in which we live recognizes that a contingency approach makes the most sense. Flexibility and adjusting to pressures applied to the organization from the outside, while carefully monitoring the inside processes of the organization, is paramount. Theories will continue to evolve. For example, we have *Theory Z* proposed by William G. Ouchi and Alfred M. Jaeger, which attempts to take positive management techniques from the American and Japanese manufacturing and integrate them in to a new system.[22] *Total quality management* (TQM), embraced by companies producing goods and services, is based on the assumption that an organization can better satisfy its customers if it is dedicated to continuously improving its product or service. The management and improvement of all of the processes an organization undertakes to accomplish its mission is very much a part of the contemporary thinking about how to better manage organizations.

The management theorists often speak of major *paradigm shifts* and the *reengineering*[23] of corporations today. Let us briefly focus on the first term. A current definition of a *paradigm* is "A set of rules and regulations (written and unwritten) that does two things; (1) establishes or defines boundaries, and (2) tells you how to behave inside the boundaries in order to be successful."[24] For example, we accept as a paradigm that a college education is best administered by gathering people together in large buildings, setting them down in neat rows of chairs, and imparting information from 9 to 9:50 A.M. Monday, Wednesday, and Friday for 15 weeks, over a four-year period. The emergence of long-distance learning is good example of a paradigm shift. In a larger sense, the shift really is about the way in which information is imparted to people and who controls the classroom. The nineteenth century paradigm of the schoolroom and all it involves is undergoing change. Arts organizations face similar challenges with shifting paradigms, as you will see in Chapter 4.

What does the future hold for management theories? One place to look is the business section of any bookstore. There, you will find the latest trends in management thinking. So many good books are published each year, it is difficult to keep up with the output. Another good source is *The Manager's Bookshelf* by Jon L. Pierce and John W. Newstrom,[25] which covers a wide range of topics from management paradigms to ethics and management.

University business schools also are a source of ideas about future directions in management. The major research universities support faculty in the development of refined and new theories of management and organizational design. Many of the journals found in college and university libraries provide an academic view of all of the major fields of management. Specialty journals are published regularly on such topics as operations, systems analysis, human resources, organizational psychology, and marketing.

Conclusion

Several thousand years in the evolution of management theory have led to the open system and contingency approaches to organizational management. During this time, societies have created organizations capable of accomplishing an incredible range of activities. Cities, roads, dams, hospitals, schools, and churches have been built by organized groups of individuals using the techniques and theories of management. At the same time, it is important to remember management techniques have been and continue to be used to organize and implement unimaginable amounts of destruction and suffering.

Organizations and systems of management are still evolving. The nineteenth century organizational model, with its rigid hierarchy and complex chains of command, has proven to be incapable of responding quickly enough to change. Newer, information-based organizational models with fewer levels of management are forming. As we enter the twenty-first century, political and economic upheaval will continue in ways we cannot foresee. Change seems to be the only constant on which organizations and individuals can count. If change is managed wisely as part of the planning process, the resources needed to provide for the future of the organization will be available. However, it also is possible to envision a world overwhelmed by the problems of population, pollution, and hunger. The images of an unmanageable world that come to us from both science and fiction writers may provide the incentive people need to solve the problems around us. Ultimately, the people who make up the organizations will determine the type of future we all share. Co-operation and collective action among these people and organizations hold the key to the future.

In the next chapter, we examine how all organizations are affected by the social and political systems within which they must function. These and other external environments shape how the organization defines its mission and what the people in the organization believe.

Summary

Management is an integral part of all social systems, from a family to a multinational corporation. Whether the objective is gathering food or taking over another corporation, managers are required to coordinate the interactions of people carrying out designated tasks. Although many people have learned to manage while on the job, a body of knowledge accumulated over the last 2,000 years constitutes management theory and practice.

Preindustrial societies developed laws, rules, myths, and rituals to control and direct people. The Renaissance and the Reformation created many new dynamics in the Western world. The opening of trade, the expansion of city centers, the rise of the middle class, and the major changes in political and social philosophy led to the formation of more sophisticated concepts of managing.

The Industrial Revolution produced fundamental changes in the nature of work and production, and it transformed Western societies. The mechanization of work in factories created the need for managers to supervise the activities of the factory workers.

The railroads, telegraph communication, the ability to manufacture precise interchangeable parts, and other new inventions and advances in technology radically altered the workplace in the nineteenth century. As new production methods were devised, techniques for managing employees and organizing work began to be documented. The early systems of organizational design, production supervision, and data recording that were used in the railroads and factories became the basis of modern systems of scientific management.

Frederick Taylor was the first to document techniques for improving work output and streamlining antiquated manufacturing techniques. Scientific research was quickly adopted by the business world. Computer models and simulations now are used regularly to improve productivity and output in factories.

Other major management practices focused on organizational design and optimal ways to structure the operation. The basic principles expressed by Henri Fayol and others about such things as chain of command, lines of authority, and rules and policies in business were thought to be applicable to any organization.

Another branch of management theory falls under the heading of human relations management, The premise underlying this research is that people want socially satisfying work situations. The Hawthorne studies verified that work output increases if employees are given more control over their jobs. Mary Parker Follett's integrative unity, Abraham Maslow's hierarchy of needs, and Douglas McGregor's Theory X and Theory Y articulated many of the complex needs and interrelationships people bring to the workplace.

Contemporary management practices are based on integration models. One model assumes that organizations are open systems affected by external environments in the process of transforming inputs into outputs. The other model, the contingency approach, assumes that there is no one best way to operate an organization; managers therefore must be flexible and find the best match between the resources available and the problems to be solved.

Key People, Terms, and Concepts

Robert Owen
Charles Babbage
Daniel Craig McCallum
Henry Varnum Poor
Frederick W. Taylor
Scientific management
Henri Fayol's Fourteen Principles
Human relations management
Mary Parker Follett's integrative unity
The Hawthorne effect
Elton Mayo
Fritz Roethlisberger
Abraham Maslow's hierarchy of needs
Douglas McGregor's Theory X and Theory Y
Operations research
Critical path method
Computer-aided design, computer-assisted manufacturing, and computer-implemented manufacturing
Systems theory
Synergy
Contingency theory
Paradigms

Questions

1. Describe examples from antiquity that demonstrate the use of the basic management functions of planning, organizing, leading, and controlling.

2. Describe some of the legacies of the Industrial Revolution in manufacturing today.

3. Which of Fayol's Fourteen Principles can be applied most easily in an arts organization? Which principles seem inappropriate?

4. Have you ever worked for a Theory X or Theory Y manager? To which theory do you subscribe?

5. How does a college or university fit into the open system model? What are the inputs? What happens in the transformation process? What are the typical outputs?

6. Do you think government, business, and social service organizations in the United States are capable of solving the problems facing society? If not, what changes must be made in these organizations to meet the demands?

References

1. Paul DiMaggio, *Managers of the Arts*, Research Division Report #20, NEA (Washington, DC: Seven Locks Press, 1987), p. 46.
2. Daniel Wren, *The Evolution of Management Thought*, 3d ed. (New York: John Wiley and Sons, 1987), p. 56.
3. Ibid., pp. 58–62.
4. Ibid., p. 61.
5. Ibid., pp. 68–72.
6. Ibid., pp. 74–76.
7. Ibid., p. 78.
8. Michael T. Matteson and John M. Ivancevich, eds., *Management and Organizational Behavior Classics*, 4th ed. (Homewood, IL: Richard D. Irwin, 1989), p. 4.
9. Ibid., pp. 3–5.
10. Wren, *Evolution of Management Thought*, p. 132.
11. Ibid., p. 180
12. Henri Fayol, *General and Industrial Management*, trans. Constance Storrs (London: Pitman and Sons, 1949), p. 15.
13. Kathryn M. Bartol and David C. Martin, *Management*, 3d ed. (Boston: McGraw-Hill, 1998), p. 46.
14. Ibid., pp. 47–48.
15. Wren, *Evolution of Management Thought*, p. 240.
16. Warren Bemis, Foreword to Douglas McGregor, *The Human Side of Management* (New York: McGraw-Hill, 1960), pp. iv–viii.
17. McGregor, *The Human Side of Management*, pp. 33–57.
18. Wren, *Evolution of Management Thought*, p. 199.
19. Ibid., p. 397.
20. Bartol and Martin, *Management*, pp. 54–57.
21. Ibid., p. 58.
22. Ibid., pp. 58–60.
23. Michael Hammer and James Champy, *Reengineering the Corporation* (New York: Harper Business, 1993).
24. Joel A. Barker, *Paradigms: The Business of Discovering the Future* (New York: Harper Collins, 1993), p. 32.
25. Jon L. Pierce and John W. Newstrom, *The Manager's Bookshelf: A Mosaic of Contemporary Views*, 4th ed. (New York: HarperCollins College Publishers, 1996).

4

□ □ □ □ □

Arts Organizations and Multiple Environments

In the eight months since the Metropolitan Opera announced that it was working on an experimental titling system that would provide translations of operas on computer screens mounted on the backs of seats, the company has kept its progress shrouded in secrecy. But late last month the Met invited its board to look at a working prototype of the system, which was designed and largely built by the house's technical staff.
The New York Times (February 7, 1994)

Orchestras Experiment with Video-Projection Screens
Listeners will be able to get a big-screen view of cellist Yo Yo Ma when he plays with the Philadelphia Orchestra Jan. 4.
Philadelphia Inquirer (December 24, 1995)

The preceding news highlights are good examples of organizations experimenting with ways of responding to trend shifts in opera and music. Rather than resort to a projection screen above the stage, which often may distract from the action onstage, the Met opted for a less intrusive approach and the Philadelphia Orchestra borrowed a projection technique used at popular music concerts for years. The Met and the Philadelphia Orchestra experiments also illustrate the ways that an organization exploits an opportunity made available by the changing technological environment in which it functions. This Met solution was estimated to cost $1.25 million. However, the option of making opera sung in a foreign language more accessible to American audiences may have a longer-term payoff for the opera company. The Philadelphia Orchestra solution used existing technology to transform the traditional audience-performer relationship at classical music concerts. As we will see in this chapter, arts organizations must adapt to the changes in many other areas of society if they are to survive in an increasingly competitive marketplace.

An arts organization, like any business, must work within changing environments. The term *environment* is used throughout this text to denote external forces that interact with organizations. We examine six environments: economic, political and legal, cultural and social, demographic, technological, and educational. We assess the impact of each of these environments on arts organizations and, later in the chapter, examine some trends that may reshape the arts in the near future. In addition, we study how arts organizations interact with these environments based on the information received from six major sources: audiences,

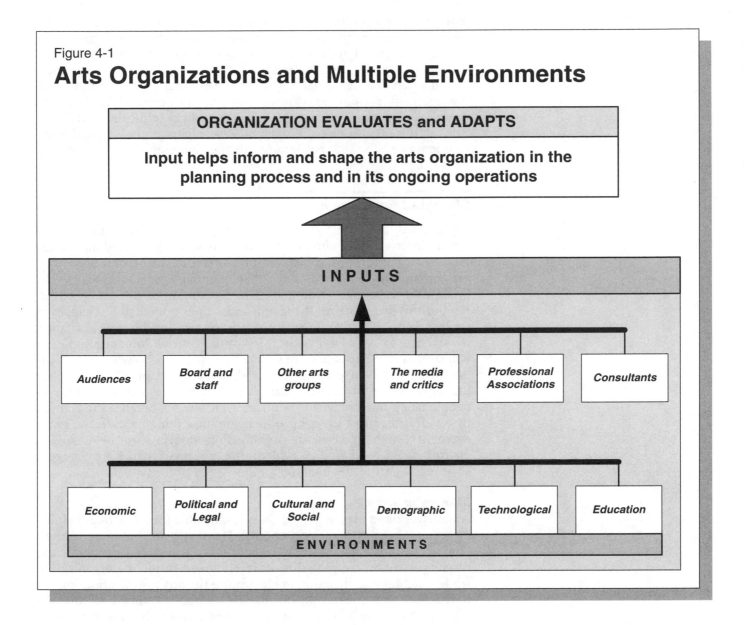

Figure 4-1

Arts Organizations and Multiple Environments

ORGANIZATION EVALUATES and ADAPTS

Input helps inform and shape the arts organization in the planning process and in its ongoing operations

INPUTS

| Audiences | Board and staff | Other arts groups | The media and critics | Professional Associations | Consultants |

| Economic | Political and Legal | Cultural and Social | Demographic | Technological | Education |

ENVIRONMENTS

other arts groups, board and staff members, the media, professional meetings and associations, and consultants.

Figure 4–1 provides a graphic representation of the organization, the information sources (inputs), and the environments. The relationship to the information sources and the different environments may vary from organization to organization. Some organizations are more responsive to audiences and patrons; others are more responsive to their boards or staff members. The process used in evaluating input from various sources and external environments therefore will vary with the predominant operating approach of the organization.

The information provided by external environments and obtained from the major source areas helps the organization in the vital process of strategic planning, which is covered in Chapter 5. In addition, how an organization is designed relies on the input received from these sources. The areas of hiring, leadership, economics and financial management, marketing, and fund raising use input from the environments and information sources to help shape decisions made about programming, advertising campaigns, and fund raising strategies. Nearly all of the activities that an arts organization undertakes can be related to the interaction between external environments and the functions of management: planning, organizing, leading, and controlling. Based on these relationships, the manager's goal is to help fulfill the stated mission of the organization by dynamically balancing the external environments and the internal input with the changing opportunities and threats posed by each.

Changing Environments

As depicted in Figure 1–2, organizations are open systems that receive inputs from various sources: The inputs then are processed and transformed to output. This process applies whether the organization is an arts organization or a company that manufactures automobiles. The mission of the organization and its interpretation of the data may differ, but this fact remains: If the enterprise does not adapt to changes in environments, it is likely to suffer. If it is too rigid or too slow to change, it will cease to exist. Ultimately, it is not the abstract "organization" that will suffer if the business is shut down. The people who work within the organization will pay the price for the lack of adaptability and poor management decisions. For example, when you read of thousands of people being unemployed by a business, it often is because the company was slow to adapt to new processes and new thinking. Effective management can help keep an organization thriving in the changing environments. As should be evident, the process of managing change is an integral part of the manager's job.

Managing Change

A manager of an arts organization is responsible for more than helping to get the show or exhibition opened. He or she must manage change. One of the most challenging aspects of management is keeping a sense of perspective on the growth and development inside the organization while watching the changing world around the arts organization for opportunities and threats. Unfortunately, change is difficult to monitor accurately because, like the hands of a clock, you notice the movement only after the fact.

In addition to navigating the organization through uncertain external circumstances, the manager must attend to its internal needs. For example, in most organizations, people feel comfortable with a certain degree of routine or predictability. For this reason, the enterprise establishes specific rules of operation and detailed procedures for getting the work done. For example, payroll procedures and basic work conditions are established as a routine part of the organization. People cannot function anywhere near their potential if they are worrying about whether they will be paid or about other conditions of their employment. Once conditions are stabilized, these same people will tend to be bored if their jobs begin to take on a routine that seldom varies. Subtle changes in work patterns can be just as important to the long-term health of an organization as major shifts to new programs. An important part of the manager's job is to remain aware of the overall direction and mood of the organization while helping people do their day-to-day jobs.

Growing into Change

As we saw in Chapter 2, arts organizations often are the result of a person or a small group of people willing to commit themselves to the task of bringing an idea to life. The same could be said for many of the major corporations in existence today. It is possible to trace the founding of many companies to one or two people with the drive and the ambition to make it happen. Many arts organizations are a product of the post-World War II boom in births coupled with increased access to education and financial support from foundations and the government. An unplanned mix of circumstances from the 1950s to the 1980s supported the unprecedented growth in performing and visual arts organizations across the nation. New theater, dance, and opera companies were founded; symphony orchestras spread throughout the nation; and museums opened in large and small cities. Once established, the arduous task of maintaining arts institutions began to take center stage.

Let us examine a hypothetical example. A small opera company, founded by its director, with an annual budget of $35,000 in the early 1970s grows to become an arts institution in its community with a budget of $4.5 million in the late 1990s. As the organization evolves, a board of directors is added, and new staff members are hired to do what the original founder and one or two other people were doing. The tiny storefront office becomes a large storefront office, and when that space is suddenly too small, a suite of offices is found in a high-rise. Slowly, but inevitably, the small opera company begins to function on a scale that requires longer-term planning and careful analysis of its future. In other words, the company begins to move from a year-to-year planning cycle to a three- to five-year planning cycle. The original founder-director no doubt had a vision of what the opera company could become, but now that it has grown into a full-fledged business and nearly 20 years have passed, the world around the organization has changed.

As an organization matures, it begins to take on characteristics that make it less responsive to change. After all, when a company finds something that works, it continues making more and more of the product. The opera company finds that a particular pattern of performances (two grand operas, two operettas, one musical) sells well, and so it repeats that cycle with different works every year. Suppose now that the same community also becomes home to a theater company, a ballet company, and a symphony orchestra. The creation of each new organization will have an impact on the opera company. It will compete for arts revenues because audiences have more choices. The theater company, for example, may decide to do two or three musicals or operettas each season. The change in the cultural environment of the community requires that the opera company's decisions about programming be made in the context of three other groups struggling for entertainment dollars.

To better adapt to its new circumstances, a process of continual evaluation should become the company's operating norm. Asking questions about where the opera company stands with respect to the six environments and the other arts groups and sifting through the feedback from its information sources becomes as critical as mounting a season of high-quality productions. Does adopting this process offer any guarantee that the opera company will fare better than a business that doesn't? Unfortunately no, but it can give the opera company an edge if the management and artistic teams cooperate.

It is important to remember that the process of continual evaluation is nothing more than a tool for survival and that it will be only as effective as the managers and artists who use it. If the managers are not skilled at using the process, they may chart a course for the organization that leads to ruin. On the other hand, successful assessment and planning should lead the opera company to develop at a pace that fits well within the parameters of the community and the six environments.

Organizations discover that a process of ongoing assessment requires the development of techniques for gathering and analyzing information. Technique, as any performer will tell you, is acquired through long hours of rehearsal. Just as dancers, singers, and actors learn to master their art through developing techniques for approaching a role, analyzing a musical score, or examining a play text, so too can an arts manager master the art of organizational evaluation. Once mastered, this technique can be applied to the four functions of management. For example, consultation with the theater company on upcoming works and dates would become a routine part of the opera company's planning procedures to avoid duplication or conflict. This may seem obvious, but many organizations do not think of their work as part of a larger cultural context in their community.

Before discussing techniques for exploring individual environments, let us examine a general approach to organizational evaluation and assessment. As we will see, the biggest problem in assessing the opportunities and threats to an organization is the conflicting input facing a manager.

Content Analysis

An arts manager can start gathering vital information from books, newspapers, magazines, and the broadcast media. The basic methodology, called *content analysis*, simply involves identifying sources for clues about current practices and possible future trends. Gathering input from sources external to the organization is complicated by the cyclical patterns of the print and electronic media. Topics come and go from the front page and evening news with incredible speed. The key component in an arts manager's quest for information through content analysis therefore is sufficient variety. However, the manager must differentiate between trends and fads. For example, shifts in population growth establish trends that ripple through a society for years: more people, more services, more houses, more apartments, and so forth. Fads, on the other hand, tend to die out more quickly. Arts organizations that react to fads sometimes find themselves scheduling programming that is out of step with current topical stories. In the time between the decision to produce a particular program and its actual production, a new hot issue may arise to take its place.

The arts manager therefore must use caution when trying to sort through what the future may bring. For example, it is not unusual to find contradictory opinions expressed about a particular topic. Let us compare two distinctly different views of how the arts will fare in the future. While reading the extracts that follow, consider the different directions that an organization might follow in its planning if it subscribed to one speculation or the other. After presenting these two views from the early 1990s we will assess their relevancy at the end of the decade.

In the final years before the millennium there will be a fundamental and revolutionary shift in leisure time and spending priorities. During the 1990's the arts will gradually replace sports as society's primary leisure activity. This extraordinary megatrend is already visible in an explosion in the visual and performing arts that is already well under way:

- Since 1965 American museum attendance has increased from 200 million to 500 million annually.
- The 1988–89 season on Broadway broke every record in history.
- Membership in the leading chamber music associations grew from 20 ensembles in 1979 to 578 in 1989.
- Since 1970 U.S. opera audiences nearly tripled.

From the United States and Europe to the Pacific Rim, wherever the affluent information economy has spread, the need to reexamine the meaning of life through the arts has followed.[1]

When John Naisbitt and Patricia Aburdene offered this and other equally optimistic assessments about the future of the arts in the United States in *Megatrends 2000*, people struggling in the trenches of many arts organizations were stunned. Were the authors talking about the same country where many arts groups were grappling with insolvency on a daily basis? Because the economy lingered in recession in the early 1990s, state and local governments were slashing their support for the arts, and corporations were putting thousands of white and blue collar workers out of jobs. The glowing picture painted by Naisbitt and Aburdene seemed a cruel hoax to many in the arts industry. Yet, the authors reached this prediction by using many of the same sources that any inquisitive arts manager would use in his or her content analysis: *Variety, Opera News, American Theatre, Dance News, The Chronicle of Philanthropy*, NEA Research Reports, or standbys such as the *Wall Street Journal, The New York Times, Business Week.* In fact, Naisbitt and Aburdene's research found enough positive signs to lead them to title their chapter "Renaissance in the Arts." They discuss one art form after another and conclude that things are only going to get better. The art market, museums, opera companies, and so on are all headed for a future filled with patrons resulting from the strong support of corporate America.

Meanwhile, in other quarters, a different picture of the future was painted.

Whatever the balance of this decade holds, our assumptions about the role of the arts in the complex and contradictory scheme of American life have begun to unravel. And, our assumptions about the strength, endurance and resilience of our arts institutions have been challenged by the hard economic realities of the Reagan/Bush era. While we will ultimately view this period in the light of many economic, social, environmental and political events, the situation for the arts has been, and still is, defined by two crises.

The crisis that has most captured our attention has been the attack on the National Endowment for the Arts led by Jesse Helms and Donald Wildman. It began with seemingly isolated cases of criticism of certain NEA-supported arts projects by certain conservative members of Congress. Today, it has become a major debate over government funding in the arts and over freedom of expression.

Update

The follow up to *The Quiet Crisis, Towards a New Arts Order*, was published in 1993 and gives the manager of the arts organization a blueprint for reconceptualization. McDaniel and Thorn go on to note:

> The most frequent question posed to us as we travel around the country is, "Is the quiet crisis over yet?" First, we have to agree that this crisis is not a quiet one any longer, as conference themes, workshop agendas, and private conversations show. Secondly, some serious challenges remain:
>
> • *Although we have a new president (Clinton), eco-nomic conditions have not changed dramatically.* [Au-thor's note—The economy steadily improved through the middle to late 1990s.] *The religious right lost ground in the White House, but made gains elsewhere.*
>
> • *Most arts organizations continue to operate 30 to 50 percent above the real-istic floor of available and achievable human and fi-nancial resources, which has resulted in mounting human and financial deficits.*
>
> • *Growth is still the primary measure of success in the field.*
>
> • *Fraying relationships and the breakdown of trust, cooperation, and partner-ship between profession-als and board leaders still prevail.*
>
> • *Exhausted professionals are giving up and leaving the field, thereby depleting the pool of valuable re-sources.*
>
> • *Organizational behavior pat-terns have not changed, and old solutions are inap-propriately applied to new problems and conditions.*

SOURCE: Nello McDaniel and George Thorn, *Toward a New Arts Order* (New York: ARTS Action Issues, 1993), pp. 12, 13. Used with permission.

The second crisis afflicting the arts is much harder to see or understand, but it is at least as threatening as the first. The quiet crisis is about mounting debt and organizational dysfunction.

A confluence of factors, financial and otherwise, that have developed during the last 10 to 15 years has changed the world by happenstance and by careful, calculated design. The three most dramatic factors are (1) financial shifts and the debt cul-ture; (2) the shrinking human capital pool, and (3) over-regula-tion and stagnation in the arts structure and community.[2]

Nello McDaniel and George Thorn's book *Workpapers: A Special Report—The Quiet Crisis in the Arts* depicts a very different world from *Megatrends 2000*. McDaniel and Thorn predict that, unless organizations face the fact that debt financing, a shrinking labor pool, and unrealistic fund raising expectations have become the distorted norm, the trickle of bankrupt arts groups will increase to a flood. They point out that arts organizations acquired debt by expanding beyond a reasonable funding base. They stress that organizations are extended beyond the means of their supporters and staffs. They counsel a complete reevaluation of revenue and expense patterns and urge organizations to seek a balance between what they realistically can do with the resources they have and the programs and projects they undertake.

As you can see from these contrasting perspectives, arts organiza-tions face continual challenges. McDaniel and Thorn are much closer to the pulse of the arts organizations through their consulting work. Their thoughtful analysis of course was based on circumstances in the late 1980s and early 1990s. As we will see in the rest of this chapter, the changes in many of the environments reshaped the way arts organization behaved.

Ultimately these examples are not about who were right or wrong in their predictions. Our objective in the rest of this chapter is to piece together a composite of the forces that shape the arts organization. At the same time, we establish a process you may use for your own analysis of arts organizations.

Environments

To effectively manage change, the arts manager must identify the environments that will have the most direct impact on the organization. Let us review some of the environments that interact with the organization and try to establish some basic guidelines about what constitutes significant input.

Economic

Arts organizations, as part of a national economic system, experience the effects of expansions and contractions in the national economy. In addition, regions, states, and cities exhibit different reactions to changes in the national economic environment. Some of the factors that may have an impact on an arts organization include the federal banking system (raising and lowering interest rates), new tax increases or cuts, revisions in existing tax legislation (which may promote or hinder donations), and inflation (price increases). This last factor can be the most destructive to an arts organization in the long run. When the cost of doing business continues to escalate, the organization faces tremendous pressure to increase revenue from either more sales or more donations. Chapter 10 reviews some basic principles of economics and explores the unique economic dilemma that increasing costs and limits on productivity impose on arts groups.

The process of evaluating the economic environment often is subject to contradictory reports by experts in the field. One expert may issue a news release announcing that the recession is over while another says it will continue for six more months. If a manager is trying to plan a budget based on projections of income and expenses in uncertain economic times, the most practical approach is to plan contingency budgets. In other words, the organization's budget would be subject to constant revision depending on whether the economy is growing, stable, or slowing down.

A myth of the entertainment industry is that, when times are tough, people seek escape by spending what they have on entertainment. The facts indicate that when the economy goes into a recession, people in the middle-income levels reduce their spending, people in the upper income levels do not radically change their spending, and people in the lower income levels curtail what little spending they do on the arts.[3] Donation frequency seems to follow similar patterns. If a recession extends beyond a year, arts organizations generally will see a slowdown in ticket purchases and donations from upper-income patrons as well. In more severe economic conditions, such as a depression, spending and donation activity at all levels will slow dramatically. Knowing this, arts organizations can plan for reduced revenues, plan to increase fund raising activity, or both. The key to working with the economic environment is to always have alternative budgets ready to implement should conditions change.

Political and Legal

The arts in the United States today are very much a part of the political scene. However, with the heightened visibility of the arts has come the added responsibility for artists and arts organizations to lobby continually to protect the support gained over the last 30 years. Up until the creation of the NEA in the mid-1960s, the arts were involved only minimally with the political system. The only other time that the government and the arts had joined forces was during the 1930s, when work projects that employed actors, singers, dancers, painters, and so on became part of the U.S. economic recovery plan. The Federal Theatre Project, for example, burst on the scene in 1935; by 1939, it was gone in a maelstrom of political struggle. The fear of Communist infiltration of the theater groups sent the whole program into budgetary limbo. The productions produced by the Theatre Project often challenged the mainstream political environment to the point that it lost its base of support in Congress.[4]

The input from such sources as professional associations, consultants, board members, and the media can help shape how an organization will adjust to changes in the political and legal environment. For example, the quote from *The Quiet Crisis in the Arts* given earlier in this chapter spoke of the issue of conservative political and religious movements bringing pressure to bear on funding sources and influencing the freedom of expression. The board and staff of an arts organization, whether they like it or not, face increasing scrutiny when they receive public funds. It is unlikely that the next few years will lessen the pressure on arts groups to justify their needs against the needs of the poor, the ill, and the homeless. The current trend at state and local levels is to cut support for the arts and allocate the funds to other needs. This trend is driven by local governments seeking nongovernment agencies to provide services. The concept is that more efficient and cost-effective private sector firms can do such jobs as run prisons, issue licenses, and so forth. The savings then can be passed along to the public in the form of either no tax increases or lowered tax rates. The goal of lower taxes while delivering the same services typically can be met only by cutting funds for what are termed "nonessential" activities. Supporting a Shakespeare or music festival unfortunately often falls under this category.

Changes in the legal environment are carried out through federal, state, and local enforcement agencies. For example, the Occupational Safety and Health Administration (OSHA) and similar state agencies issue regulations that have a direct impact on the operation of the technical production shops and museum laboratories in the United States. Employees sometimes have reported unsafe conditions and practices to these agencies as a way to force unresponsive arts managers to make the workplace safer. The impact of laws that affect the design of public spaces and the workplace by mandating access for people with disabilities must be taken into account. Issues relating to smoking, sexual harassment, medical and retirement benefits, maternity leave, and the like have had an impact on arts organizations over the last ten years. In most cases, changes in the legal environment have a price tag attached, and the implementation of new laws translates into expense items that appear in the operating budget.

More arts organizations are adopting an active rather than a reactive approach to coping with changes in the political and legal environment. In fact the word *proactive* has replaced *active* and has become a part of the arts managers vocabulary. For example, arts organizations ex-

---

In the News 1

Outlining Arguments for "Rent" Trial

William Grimes

The battle lines are drawn in the "Rent" war. Late last week, lawyers submitted pretrial memorandums outlying their arguments in the lawsuit that pits Lynn M. Thompson, the dramaturge who worked on "Rent" when it was being developed at the New York Theater Workshop, against the family of the writer and composer Jonathan Larson. The trial, which begins in the United States District Court in Manhattan on July 21, will determine whether Ms. Thompson should be named a co-author of the musical and receive the 16 percent of the author's royalties earned by the show that she is demanding.

Laws and the Arts

This 1991 article illustrates how changes in laws can have a direct effect on arts organizations. In this case, political lobbying by unions influenced the legislative system, and now arts organizations are attempting to exert their own influence to change the regulations. The implementation of the legislation was delayed in the fall of 1991 by last-minute lobbying by arts-presenting groups and universities.

Law That Would Limit Artists Causes Uproar
John Bennett

WASHINGTON—They are stacked by the hundreds in cardboard boxes—angry letters attacking new restrictions on the number of foreign artists who can enter this country.

The Immigration Act of 1990 caused the outrage by limiting to 25,000 the number of foreign artists who may enter the country each year. The law, to become effective on October 1 after the Immigration and Naturalization Service publishes the regulations, has drawn opposition as the deadline nears.

The letters arrive from opera houses, symphony orchestras and ballet centers in New York City, Boston, Houston, Los Angeles, Denver, Cleveland and Santa Fe, N.M.

Universities from Michigan to Florida have joined the chorus, arguing their stakes in artistic campus tours arriving from Europe.

The law further requires an artist to be affiliated with the institution or performing group for more than a year before applying to come to the United States.

Further, it bars an application for a visa until 90 days before a scheduled arrival and requires those presenting the tour to explain how the event would benefit the U.S.

Then, in a requirement that annoys U.S. cultural centers, labor unions would have to be consulted before bringing the artists into the country.

Lawmakers feeling the heat from across the Country are rushing to amend the law. Many of those who backed the idea have switched sides.

"It will all probably be cured in a few months," said an INS official.

The AFL-CIO lobbied for the alien restrictions on ground that the non-immigrant visas threatened the jobs of U.S. workers.

Congress approved the limitations after a report noted that temporary non-immigrant visas issued to entertainers had been climbing rapidly, creating controversy.

tend to politicians personal invitations to arts events that are accompanied by high-visibility social activity. Trips to Washington, D.C., the state house, or city hall for one-on-one discussions with the legislators, governor, or mayor have become mandatory. In their regular communication with lawmakers, arts managers stress that the people who attend the arts are voters. In addition, lobbyists representing arts organizations now are a regular fixture on the national scene. One job of a lobbyist is to keep abreast of pending legislation that may have an effect on the arts.

Cultural and Social
The United States' cultural and social environment in the late twentieth century is heavily influenced by the economic, technological, and political environments. The traditional social structures (family, schools, and religious organizations), though undergoing change, still play major roles in the transmission of social values and beliefs.

Some of the changes affecting the cultural and social environment include two-income households, single-parent households, and attitudes about gender roles and race, health care, and leisure time. The potential impact of these changes on arts organizations is far too complex to predict accurately.

The other major force in the socialization process in U.S. society is the broadcast media. Television and radio are the major sources of information and entertainment for millions of people. Unfortunately, the broadcast media focus little attention on the fine arts. An interest in opera, the symphony, or the fine arts often is the source of humor, if it is mentioned at all, in the shows watched by millions every night. In fact, an appreciation for the arts is often depicted as the act of a snob who speaks with an affectation and acts pretentious.

The arts, which are a leisure time activity for most people, face difficult times ahead as the cultural and social environment of the United States continues to diversify. The generation that created the baby boom and contributed greatly to the growth of the arts has not been replaced in equally large numbers. In fact, the trend seems to be toward a generally lower standard of living for Americans under 30. A recent article in *Business Week* pointed out that in a typical American family, heads of household who are under 30 are making less money today than their counterparts made in 1973. Families headed by college graduates are the only segment making more money than in 1973. The education level, which consistently correlates with attendance at arts events, also correlates with the income level. In all cases, families headed by individuals with some or no college were making less than their peers made in 1973. The same applies to African-Americans and Hispanics.[5] These lower numbers may make it harder for arts groups to diversify their audiences because these groups will probably spend any extra money on less expensive entertainment options.

The arts manager also must recognize that alternative living arrangements have created new definitions of "families" and have led to new arts consumption patterns. The high cost of housing has meant that many young people have not moved out of their family homes and established their own independent living arrangements. Single-parent families are common today. In many communities, a greater number of people are living alone. Career pursuits also contribute to fewer leisure hours for a large segment of the highly educated population. Finding creative ways to reach these potential audiences with special discount ticket plans or through the type of programs offered will mean rethinking marketing and fund raising strategies for many organizations.

Peer group influence is another social factor identified in research about potential audiences. The Ziff Marketing, Inc., survey undertaken for the Cleveland Foundation in 1985 found a strong correlation between arts attendance, education, and peer attendance. People often try attending an arts event because a friend invites them. They may find they like the experience of attending the arts and become a regular consumer of the arts form they enjoy the most.

The arts manager's energies probably are best directed toward developing, maintaining, and increasing a positive public awareness of and interest in the performing and visual arts. These objectives can be met best by working with artists to shape the audience of the future.

Artists often are at the leading edge of change in a society. For example, much of the content of the traditional and, of course, popular works in the repertories of theater and opera companies reflects gender roles that were much different than they are today. Increasingly, the dominant culture is changing to reflect more diverse points of view as directors and producers seek out other perspectives. Women, African-American, Hispanic-American, and Asian-American artists are seeking to change cultural values to reflect a broader vision than that of the white Euro-centric worldview (see Chapter 7's "In the News 1," which covers a debate on cultural power, and that chapter's case study). Many arts organizations are proud of the programs they do for Black History Month. However, for many African-Americans, this special month of programming begs the question, "What about the other 11 months of the year?" In addition, contemporary marketing techniques focus on the segmentation of audiences as a way to reach new people. This approach may only further divide the audience into smaller and less cohesive supporters of the arts. Ultimately, arts organization have to address the issue whether it is worth trying to be all things to all people in their quest for an audience and donors.

Changes in the cultural and social environment will continue to present major challenges to arts organization in the future. As the society becomes more diverse, audience tastes and preferences will continue to increase to the point where arts groups need to reexamine their mission and fundamental choices in works and programming options.

Demographic

The arts manager must closely monitor the demographic environment, which comprises the vital statistics of a society. Factors such as gender, age, race, income level, occupation, education, birth and death rate, and geographic distribution influence organizations. The more that is known about a community and the surrounding region, the better able the organization's ongoing assessment process will be to address community needs. For example, the baby boom generation will create a large number of elderly after the turn of the century. Together, the boomers and the current elderly population account for a significant portion of today's arts consumers. Trying to anticipate the changing taste and attendance patterns of the aging boomers will be a high priority for arts managers over the next 20 years.

The arts manager also must be concerned about the low birth rate since the 1970s. Arts attendance may drop in direct proportion to the population base. This will have devastating consequences for organizations facing what no doubt will be greater financial pressures in the next 30 years.

It probably is safe to assume that with an aging population health care costs will continue to take up a greater portion of the financial resources of society. This demographic trend already is being noticed by arts organizations as state funding for the arts is cut due to the pressure of financing federally mandated health care support.

The AIDS epidemic has had an impact on arts organizations as well as on society as a whole. Sadly, many talented artists have been lost to future generations. Arts managers have had to become more informed about the complex legal and ethical issues of HIV and AIDS in the workplace. In addition, artists and arts organizations have faced the ever-increasing medical insurance costs and the shift to HMOs as the administrative system.

Demographic trends in the next 25 years will require arts organizations to adapt to a more ethnically diverse audience that spans a greater age range. One strategy that arts groups can take is to adjust programming choices to the audience, rather than expecting the audience to adjust to the program. For example, the older crowd might have its own special symphony series, while the younger audience might have a series tailored to its tastes. This is the equivalent of the "narrowcasting" of cable television companies.

Research Tool

In Chapter 12, we briefly examine the results of NEA Research Division Report #34, *Age and Arts Participation with a Focus on the Baby Boom Cohort.* The findings of this report raise questions about the attendance patterns of what is called the *baby boom generation.* At issue is the lower attendance percentage of this generation at many performing arts events. Despite being highly educated the many of the baby boomers seem to seeking their entertainment from electronic and not live events. This report, published by Seven Locks Press of Santa Ana, California, is worth adding to your management library.

In the News 2—Technology Enters the Orchestra Pit

This article from the early 1990s illustrates the economic and technological environments converging on the musicians in the Broadway orchestra pit. The desire to keep costs down will put further pressure on the union to fight the advance of a technology that will put members out of work. In fact, as the technology has improved in the 1990s, the ability to more accurately create an orchestra sound without an orchestra has accelerated. Digital sound, sampling techniques, increasing computer capabilities, and lower cost for technology will no doubt lead to fewer jobs for pit musicians.

At Issue: A Synthesizer in the Pit
Glenn Collings

Can "Grand Hotel" replace the string section of its orchestra with an electronic synthesizer? Local 802 of the American Federation of Musicians contends that the musical is letting go eight string players to do just that. Marvin Krauss, a "Hotel" co-producer, says that only four musicians are at issue, that the synthesizer—played by a union member—is already being used in the show, and that "it's all a tempest in a teapot."

"We're not arguing that he can't use a synthesizer, we're saying it can't play the same parts our musicians used to play," said 802's lawyer, Leonard Leibowitz. The complex contractual dispute will be decided by an arbitrator before September.

SOURCE: Glenn Collings, "At Issue: A Synthesizer in the Pit," *New York Times* (July 26, 1991). Copyright © 1991 by the New York Times Company. Used with permission.

According to the Bureau of the Census, population growth will be slow over the next few decades. The baby boomers, of course, will continue to influence the statistics for the next 30 to 40 years. In fact, one set of projections includes a fivefold increase in the 85+ population by 2050. Current projections are that by 2030 the non-Hispanic white population will be less than half the U.S. population under age 18.[6]

Technological

As noted in Chapter 2, the invention and distribution of film, radio, and television had a profound effect on the arts around the world. In the United States, the new technologies were quickly adopted for commercial profit-making purposes. The displacement of live performers with film, for example, put thousands of actors, dancers, singers, musicians, and technicians out of work in the 1920s and 1930s. New jobs were created, of course, but many of the older performers in the larger metropolitan areas were put out of work permanently by the movie screen and the soundtrack. As the job market adjusted to the new technology, the live performing arts have adapted and grown since the end of World War II.

As we have seen, the arts boom was due in large part to the combination of the birth rate, economic growth, and increased levels of education. Through the 1960s and 1970s, arts centers and performing arts groups came into existence even though television sets and movie screens could be found nearly everywhere. By the 1980s, the home videotape recorder (VCR), video laser disc, and compact disc player created a new demand for program material. Home computers further expanded the market for entertainment in the 1990s. The VCR, laser discs, and DVD provided more opportunities for the distribution of films worldwide. It also allowed viewers to rent or purchase programs of opera, theater, and dance performances or museum collections. The issuance of thousands of classical titles on compact discs, coupled with improved sound quality, has helped keep the limited classical music industry alive. On the whole, then, the new technologies seem to present opportunities rather than threats to arts organizations. However, the birth rate may have more to say about the future than technological advancements. It is possible that attendance will decline as the aging baby boomers stay home to be entertained by their own home theaters.

Some of the developments expected in the future offer further opportunities for the arts. For example, high-definition television (HDTV) will make the home entertainment center a reality for millions of consumers. Integrating advanced computer systems with these entertainment centers may make possible home versions of the new technology of virtual reality. Virtual reality (VR) is an interactive computer technology that allows the individual to enter into an electronic world that not only appears real to the viewer but also allows direct interaction in an environment. As the current technology keeps improving and the cost of equipment continues to fall, the application of VR will continue to expand. The technology is moving us toward the point where a person will be able to be part of a performance rather than simply viewing it.

The opportunities for the performing arts and VR are still developing. It seems clear that VR will influence the relationship between the performer and the audience even more profoundly than film, radio, and television. For example, Mark Reaney, at the University of Kansas, has demonstrated interesting possibilities for VR on stage in recent productions of the *Adding Machine* and *Tesla Electric*.[7] Another interesting source of VR information may be found at the Human Interface Technology Laboratory Web site entitled "Virtual Reality Online.[8] This site lists a wide range of projects, publications, and people engaged in VR activities around the world.

An article in the February 1998 *Opera America Newsline* detailed a $1.3 million dollar project to create a Multimedia Modular Stage (MMS) for the Houston Grand Opera. The target for this technology application to an opera presentation is younger audiences. Of course, no amount of technology can substitute for the lack of awareness, appreciation, and understanding of the art form of opera brought about by a deficit arts education.

Educational

Studies show that education is one of the most significant factors in developing an arts consumer. Researcher Lynne Fitzhugh notes, "The socio-economic variable most often and most perfectly associated with cultural attendance is, not surprisingly, education."[9] Many surveys have found that more than half of the people attending arts events have college or graduate degrees. When considering how little focus is given to arts education in the United States, these numbers are all the more startling. One can only guess how much greater the attendance would be at cultural events if the arts were more integrated into the educational environment.

Arts organizations stand to gain the greatest long-term benefit from working in cooperation with the local school systems. However, because the schools seldom have the resources to pay for the services of arts organizations, outside funding is required. Foundation and corporate grants to improve the quality of education may provide opportunities for arts groups to establish good community relations and build future audiences.

The most effective methods for making the arts a significant part of the educational environment usually combine visits to the schools with planned lessons throughout the year. Transporting busloads of kids to an auditorium and putting on a show only offers a superficial connection to the arts event, and in many cases, it only further alienates young audiences from the arts. Without a context for the experience, the concert, play, or opera is an isolated incident at best and boring at worst.

In the decades to come, schools will be the focus of much political attention. Performance standards, national testing, increasing budgetary pressures, and parental choice in selecting schools will be among the issues facing the 15,000 school districts across the United States. Arts organizations will have to take aggressive action to positively position themselves in this environment.

There are signs of improvement in the status of arts education. An article in *The New York Times* (May 1998), "An Arts Revival Grows in New York Schools," noted 500 art and music teachers had been hired and 400 more were being recruited for the next schoolyear. (See the "In the News 3" regarding the Los Angeles schools.) The recognition that the arts are a valuable tool for increasing student skill, commitment, and discipline has begun to surface as a motivating factor in increased support for new positions and courses. The *Times* article points out the current lack of a citywide curriculum in the arts as there is math and science in the New York City schools. Since the funding per pupil varies so widely in the school system, the positive effects of this trend were not

---

In the News 3

As this excerpt from the *Los Angeles Times* points out, not only will Los Angeles lead the curve on arts education, but the issue of finding enough qualified instructors will offer a huge challenge to realizing the mission.

Arts Instruction to Make Comeback in Schools
Doug Smith

After decades of drift in teaching of the arts, Los Angeles schools at last have been given a clear mission to imbue every student with the knowledge of music, dance, drama and visual expression.

Riding a nationwide wave of renewed interest in arts instruction, the Board of Education adopted standards last week that will incorporate the arts at all grade levels with testing to ensure that students learn.

As a condition of graduation, every student—including those who are not artistically inclined—would have to demonstrate an ability to interpret art and create it.

Adoption of the new standards places Los Angeles Unified ahead of the curve in California, which will soon have statewide guidelines on what public school students should learn about art.

Because of the dearth of qualified instructors after two decades of neglect, the most difficult hurdle will be training teachers in all the district's 660 schools. . . .

being felt evenly. One could project the same funding issue to schools across America. The disparity between rich and poor schools typically equates to whether arts instruction is offered.

Information Sources

To effectively manage change and operate a useful evaluation and assessment system, arts managers must identify the sources they will use for gathering information and develop an ongoing process for evaluating the opportunities and threats facing the organization. Let us examine the type of information each source generates.

Audiences

Smart arts managers want to know as much as possible about the individual who expends the effort to go to a show or an exhibition or who gives an organization money in exchange for a ticket, subscription, or membership. Why? Simply because the organization's survival depends on establishing a long-term relationship with this person. Within the bounds of an ethical system of gathering data, a manager would want to know (1) why this person made the purchase, (2) what he or she liked about the product, (3) what he or she did not like, and (4) what other related products this person would be interested in purchasing. Members of the audience, patrons, donors, members—whatever they are called—are tremendous resources usually waiting to be asked what they think and feel. Exit surveys for museums, program insert surveys, phone surveys, or small discussion groups of randomly selected arts consumers are viable techniques for gathering information. Some techniques will be more effective than others, but regardless of the method, the arts organization able to provide detailed profiles of the consumers of its products will be better able to predict how a planned change will affect the relationship that exists between the individual and the organization.

Does this data-gathering process imply pandering to the audience's tastes? Hardly. The primary purpose of asking people what they think about a product is to learn how to communicate better with them. Arts organizations forget that their audiences do not use the same vocabulary to describe the product and the process of the arts. In the open system, the arts manager designs the communication devices (brochures, letters, posters, and so on) to the outside world to reflect terms and concepts that effectively translate the organization's mission to the widest possible audience. Ineffective communication only raises barriers between the organization and repeat customers or future customers. (Chapters 12 and 13 discuss this topic in more detail.)

To summarize, then, establishing an ongoing communication process with the users of a product is essential to the long-term health of an organization. The importance of knowing as much as possible about who is interested in what cannot be stressed enough. Feedback from the consumers of the product is a resource that will shape the future of an organization. Unfortunately, providing such data could mean that the consumer or donor is bombarded by requests from similar organizations all over the country.

Other Arts Groups

A community with several arts groups can achieve a synergistic boost from the combination of programs and activities—the whole is greater than the sum of its parts. When the different arts groups recognize that they can benefit from communicating with others about their seasonal or exhibition plans, the local arts scene can flourish.

Strategic thinking and long-term planning should create a mutual understanding among arts groups that there is a complex "arts audience," in addition to individual audiences for ballet, opera, theater, and the like. Research seems to indicate that a segment of the audience can be classified as users of different art forms, while other segments are loyal to one form and seldom go to other events.[10] One strategy that seems to address these differences is the consortium approach. For example, many cities publish a quarterly arts calendar covering different arts groups and museums. These calendars give potential arts consumers an overview of all events happening in their area. Discount coupons and advertisements may be used to highlight special events. Multiple-page flyers can be widely distributed through a Sunday newspaper or a mass mailing. The result can be a piece that enhances awareness of the overall arts scene, recognizes individual audience segments, and promotes cooperation among the arts groups.

In addition to cooperative publications, different arts groups can work together to present new programming combinations that benefit both groups. The symphony and the ballet or the ballet and the opera can pool their resources on occasion to present larger-scale productions than either could mount individually.

If nothing else, a regularly scheduled meeting among the different presenting groups in a community offers an opportunity to share ideas about trends in the different art forms. The sharing of information ultimately helps a manager better understand the overall arts dynamics of the community.

Board and Staff Members

The board of directors and the staff of an arts organization are vital components in the information-gathering process. The key to success is ongoing input via staff meetings, suggestion boxes, retreats, informal social gatherings, and formal planning sessions. When a board member asks about presenting a particular type of program or a staff member suggests a new procedure, the organization must have a mechanism for responding to the input. An open system depends on these suggestions and works from the assumption that there are always alternatives to what is currently being done. An organization that does not allow for input from the board or the staff probably will become stagnant and dysfunctional over time.

The Media

The print and broadcast media provide the arts manager with up-to-the-minute information about many of the external environments that have an impact on the organization. Some insight into the general mood of the country or region also can be gained from polling conducted by the media. Trade publications in the arts as well as national and regional news sources should be part of the arts manager's regular reading list. As noted at the beginning of the chapter, contradictory information frequently is generated by these sources, but that is to be expected.

Cultivating and sustaining a positive working relationship with the press and the broadcast media can be of obvious long-term benefit to arts organizations. However, arts and nonprofit groups are often naive about the realities of media coverage. Column space or on air time is an issue of money. For the print media, advertising sales space and news articles always are in a complex struggle with each other. For the local commercial television or radio station, ratings determine advertising revenue. Therefore, coverage that will generate ratings is the focus of attention. Getting a feature story in the arts section of a newspaper or getting 30 seconds of on-air time at the end of the six o'clock news can be a struggle. Attaining a level of visibility is critical for the arts organization's interactions with the external environments. No matter how good and noble the programs or projects of an organization may be, it is hard to establish credibility in the community without publicity.

One example of the ebb and flow of media coverage was the NEA struggle described in Chapter 2. The media focused on the obscenity issue rather than the larger questions of government support for the arts, because the struggle of Congress with the NEA was simply more interesting than an abstract national policy issue. The result was a great deal of publicity for the NEA, most of which unfortunately cast it in a negative light. Very few stories mentioned the thousands of grants made each year and the millions of people who benefit from grants and endowment services.

Arts organizations are in a very competitive situation when it comes to getting the attention of the media for the good work being done. However, a carefully designed public relations program will keep the arts organization in the news and help create a positive image.

Professional Meetings and Associations
Each of the arts has a professional service organization or trade association that provides regular information about issues of importance to its constituency. Many of the organizations and associations publish newsletters or magazines, and almost all hold annual conferences. The information-exchange process among members often focuses on current operational problems or topics related to new methods for raising money. The benefit for the arts managers of belonging to these associations or attending these conferences lies in expanding their knowledge of how other organizations are adapting to external forces.

Consultants
Consultants are another source for information about methods of keeping an organization functioning effectively. In theory, a consultant gives the organization a needed outside perspective. Of course, arts managers should never assume that consultants always are right any more than they would blindly trust any other source of information. However, because consultants usually deal with several organizations at one time, they can suggest new ideas and approaches that would not occur to the internal management staff. Consultants also can validate the staff members' ideas about how best to manage change in the organization.

Other Sources
Depending on the art form, other input sources may provide valuable information to the manager of an open system. For example, the U.S. government regularly publishes statistical data from the Census Bureau and the Commerce Department that arts managers could apply. This is especially useful when the data profiles a region of the country in which the arts organization resides. Another source of information might be found among the various suppliers of goods and services purchased by the organization. For example, the bank used by the organization could be an excellent source of local economic information. Printers or graph-

ic arts firms could be a source of information about new trends and techniques in advertising. Other useful sources might be the local chamber of commerce. After all, the arts organization is a business in the community, and belonging to local groups that attract other businesses could prove helpful when seeking direct information about the economic health of the area.

The Impact of Future Trends on the Arts

Trying to anticipate change is a difficult task. As we have seen from this brief overview of the major environments affecting arts organizations, complex forces can interact to produce unforeseen results. Some of the issues of today that will continue to have a direct impact on the arts tomorrow include censorship and mounting economic pressures.

Censorship

The choices for programming in U.S. arts centers ultimately will be influenced by the arts organization's perception about the degree of censorship in the community. A fair amount of self-censorship already occurs in many arts organizations. For example, arts organizations that seek corporate funding and a broad base of community support think twice before tackling controversial topics that may turn away donors. Instead, these arts institutions tend to leave the topical work to the fringe arts groups. (See this chapter's case study, "On the Wings of a Storm.")

The typical result when an arts organization begins to move onto a path that the majority of the audience is unwilling to follow is a sudden drop in ticket revenue. The reality of keeping a steady cash flow and meeting the payroll provides another type of censorship that most arts groups face: economic. Once an arts group reaches the level of requiring a staff and an organizational structure to operate, the pressure to take fewer programming risks increases. Unfortunately, the economic pressures on arts groups appear to be increasing.

Economic Pressure

As mentioned earlier in this chapter, the authors of *Megatrends 2000* set an optimistic tone about the future of the arts in the United States. Part of their reason for being so optimistic is their prediction that "as we turn to the next century we will witness the linkup of North America, Europe, and Japan to form a golden triangle of free trade."[11]

Although there is no reason to be overly pessimistic, many people in the arts world are a great deal less hopeful than Naisbitt and Aburdene. The escalating costs of operating an arts organization combined with increased competition for donors and ticket buyers is not a mix that promises much relief in the years to come. The fundamental structural problem may be one of costly operational redundancy. It makes little sense for several small arts groups in one community to have their own staffs and operational overhead. Consolidation of management functions and fund raising and marketing activities through cooperative management firms may become a necessity in the next few years.

In some ways, the growth attributed to the baby boom generation may have led to an oversupply of arts organizations in relationship to the demographic changes currently in progress. Ticket sales and donation levels may have peaked, and the marketplace now may be left with too many arts groups chasing too few dollars. Some combination of regional cooperative productions and cable television distribution may provide the needed revenues to keep the arts an important part of U.S. society. It is possible to envision a whole new subscriber base made up of television viewers watching the show from their home theaters.

Summary

All organizations in an open system interact with changing environments that shape the transformation and output of the product. The economic, political and legal, cultural and social, demographic, technological, and educational environments interact to form a complex set of conditions that influence how well an organization will be able to meet its objectives. The evaluation of the six environments is a function of information gathered from audiences, other arts groups, board and staff members, the media, professional meetings and associations, and consultants. Managers must assume that the environments are constantly changing and therefore develop a process for continually evaluating input.

The economic environment is the most influential external force. General conditions such as inflation or recession, interest rates, and the taxation system determine the financial health of the operation.

The impact of the political and legal environment on an arts organization extends from the international scene to the local level. Cultivating positive communication and stressing the important part the arts play in the lives of voters can help build support from within the political arena.

The cultural and social environment is a combination of the values and beliefs of the society, as communicated through the family, the educational system, religion, and increasingly, the broadcast media. The changing family profile, increased racial diversification, expanding career and work choices for women, and gender role differences in U.S. society are creating a different profile of the potential audience member.

The distribution of the people in the United States is changing in terms of age, sex, race, income level, education, and location. The baby boom generation that fueled much of the growth in the arts is aging, and it is not being replaced in equally large numbers. The birth rate has been dropping since 1970. The impact of these demographic changes will have a profound effect on the arts well into the next century.

Technology, once a major threat to the live performing arts, is now helping artists reach a wider audience than at any time in history. New technologies such as videotape and video laser discs have helped increase the distribution of the arts in the United States. New technologies may make the experience of the live performance available to consumers in their homes.

The U.S. education system is undergoing tremendous pressure to increase its effectiveness. Because education levels are a strong predictor of later attendance at arts events, arts managers would do well to become part of the education revolution by working to incorporate the arts into the changing educational environment.

Issues of censorship and the increasing economic pressures on arts organizations present challenges few organizations have effectively solved. It is clear that new strategies for delivering the product must be developed if the current demographic trends continue.

Key Terms and Concepts

Environments in the open system: economic, political and legal, cultural and social, demographic, technological, educational
Continual evaluation process
Content analysis
Demographic descriptors: sex, age, race, income level, occupation, education, birth and death rates, geographic distribution
Virtual reality
Information sources: audiences, other arts groups, board and staff members, the media professional meetings and associations, consultants

Questions

1. Do the six environments affect the various art forms in different ways? For example, are theater groups more or less influenced by changes in these environments than art museums? Explain.

2. This chapter focused on the influence of the environments on organizations. What influence do these environments have on the individual artist?

3. Do you agree with the views expressed in *Megatrends 2000*, or do is McDaniel and Thorn's assessment of the arts in crisis closer to your view?

4. Although it appears that the ruling to limit the number of artists granted entry visas is headed for revision, can you make an argument for defending such restrictions?

5. What combination of demographic descriptors would you use to outline why you and your family or associates are arts consumers?

6. What opportunities and threats will artists and arts organizations face over the next 20 years?

Case Study

On the Wings of a Storm
Nancianne Pfister

The uproar in North Carolina over the Charlotte Repertory Theatre production of *Angels in America* prompted not only this month's Spotlight, but an entire special section as well.

Why? Because the Charlotte story speaks directly to a central concern shared by theater companies of all sizes and descriptions: What is the role of a theater company in its community? Should it mirror only the majority society around it and downplay or ignore other viewpoints? Should it produce only "safe" plays—however that may be interpreted—or is controversy to be allowed, and even encouraged? And if controversial works are sometimes performed, how does the company deal with the uproar and work to maintain its audiences, funding, and community support?

The Storm

In 1994, Charlotte Repertory Theatre was one of only six regional companies selected by Tony Kushner to receive the rights to produce his Pulitzer Prize-winning play, *Angels in America*. The script is seven hours long and is presented in two parts: *Millennium Approaches* and *Perestroika*.

There was no doubt this was a controversial work. The epic plot involves AIDS, political corruption, religion, betrayal, and the tolerance—if not acceptance—of alternative life choices. All Charlotte Rep publicity, therefore, noted this was a play for mature audiences, which, incidentally, also contained frontal nudity and a simulated sex act.

This cautionary information brought outraged protests from groups of religious and political conservatives. Shortly after; the managers of the city's performing arts center, which houses Charlotte Rep and where *Angels in America* was scheduled to play, claimed CRT—by breaking the state's indecent exposure statute—had violated the terms of its lease by public displays of nudity. On the morning of opening night the performing arts center issued a cease-and-desist order against the production.

CRT fought back. For one thing, *Angels in America* was a $260,000 investment—the most expensive production in the company's history—that could not be abandoned. For another; changing the words or actions of the play would have been a contract violation. Finally, canceling the production would have forfeited both the freedom and the responsibility of artistic expression.

Only hours before curtain, CRT staged what may have been its finest production: a court battle that allowed the show to open on schedule. In response to a lawsuit initiated by Charlotte Rep, a state court issued a temporary restraining order against the facility, its board, and staff—and concurrently, against any other individual or government agency that had the legal authority to shut down the play—enjoining them from "any acts which seek to prevent, hinder; or impair the presentation of the production of *Angels in America. . . .*"

Predictably, opening night patrons shared the sidewalk with picketers. Perhaps not as predictably, there were four times as many picket signs supporting the show as protesting it. In total, 11,000 tickets were sold for the run and the company added 10 performances to meet public demand. Why the overwhelming positive response?

"You can do in-your-face theater; but you can't do in-your-face public relations," managing director Keith Martin told us. "We define theater as a forum for the exchange of ideas among people of good will who happen to disagree." No news there, but community support on the scale enjoyed by CRT does not come overnight. Clearly, the company had established such a strong reputation in Charlotte that when it was besieged, artists from every discipline joined patrons in rallying to its defense.

Triumphs and Trials
The first thing CRT had going for it was stability; a less-rooted company might have caved in under protests. Founded by Steve Umberger in 1976 as Actors Contemporary Ensemble, the group's goal was to offer contemporary drama other than that already available locally. Newer, less mainstream fare was the ideal.

Five years later; ACE established its season of two shows in repertory during the summer months. In 1984, under then-producer Mark Woods, ACE changed its name to Charlotte Repertory Theatre and initiated a full season of performances. Alliance with

Actors Equity, the actors' union, made CRT the first professional theater company in Charlotte.

In 1985 CRT merged with another local group, PlayWorks, which mounted new works and original plays. The merger created harmonious and efficient collaboration among CRT's artists, staff, administration, and board. No small part of that renewal was moving into a new facility, designed to order for CRT. By 1994, when *Angels in America* was contracted, CRT had demonstrated its good judgment for 19 years.

There was one period when that judgment might have been questioned. After expanding from summer-only to a year-long production schedule, CRT lost money almost every season. Additionally, the closing for renovations of the venue where they had performed left the group with no consistent playing space. (It's easy to lose audiences if they can't find you.)

Further complications involved overdue pension and health contributions owed to Equity, a situation that threatened CRT with decertification as a union company. Viewed a poor risk by funding agencies, CRT's losses mounted and grant money was withheld. By 1990, the company's $250,000 debt was more than half its annual budget. In a defining moment, the board was faced a choice between Keith Martin or bankruptcy. The board hired Martin. Mission: save the company.

Less than three years later, Martin retired the debt and now administers a $1.35 million annual budget. How did he do it? The same painful way any company would, by cutting costs—administrative costs are now less than 8 percent of the total budget—and reassigning personnel.

Further steps included collaborating on shows with other troupes in order to save money and enlarge CRT's donor base, pursuing greater corporate underwriting, increasing the number of patron gifts and in-kind donations, and merging with Golden Circle Theatre in order to produce classic works. Since it was no secret that CRT's 1990 cumulative debt was the worst in town, changing its own destiny had to earn community respect.

We've previously noted Keith Martin's use of the bartering system. [*Stage Directions* (June–July 1996), "The Bartering Kind"] Thanks to his skills, one quarter of CRT's budget—approximately $350,000—comes from in-kind donations. It's a simple system, one your company easily can adopt.

Perhaps the most painful revenue-reclaiming act was postponing Umberger's dream of a company that mounted only new or original works. To reach a broader audience, the company needed to produce more shows with greater name recognition: *Beau Jest*, *Breaking Legs*, and *Fences*. Classic works joined contemporary plays to bring more people into the theater. Umberger's dream delayed did not dry up, but lives in CRT's annual Charlotte Festival/New Plays in America series. The week-long event offers six staged readings of unproduced plays and works in progress. The upcoming season includes three world premieres of plays that have graduated from the festival.

Because full-scale theatrical production is a great economic risk, unheralded authors have a difficult time hearing their scripts brought to life. Through CRT staged readings, which include discussions with the audience, the playwrights gain increased understanding of what works or what needs to be clarified. The festival is a bonanza for audiences, too; $25 gains admission to all readings, talk-back sessions, and special events. CRT earns the trust of its patrons by allowing them the chance to influence new works. In quite a different way, CRT established itself as a benefactor of the area's students through its choice of shows.

"We have an entire series of shows chosen from the state education department's required reading list," explained Martin. "It's part of our outreach program. If a specific play isn't on the required list, maybe there is something else by the same author." Once "we've chosen a show, we try to schedule as many school performances as possible."

Pushing the Envelope

Things were going well for CRT: debt-free, a balanced budget, loyal audiences, in-kind donations, and the freedom to do quality work. Why rock the boat? Why even apply for the right to produce *Angels in America*, a show Martin admits is "an equal opportunity offender"?

"This is a landmark production," Martin told us, "perhaps the most important theatrical work of my lifetime because of the issues addressed. Charlotte Rep has always had an affinity for Tony Kushner's writing. Beyond that, we were ready for a *Nicholas Nickleby*-style production. We also needed a cornerstone for our 1995–96 season."

"This was a difficult piece of theater;" adds director Steve Umberger. "We knew we would be incredibly challenged, and we welcomed it."

The other five companies granted rights to *Angels in America* are in major metropolitan areas like Chicago and Los Angeles. CRT anticipated some uproar, even though none had occurred in the five other cities granted performance rights or at the 38 other locations where the national touring production was presented. To keep faith with its audiences, CRT scheduled *Laughter on the 23rd Floor* as the final show of the season and allowed subscribers to exchange their *Angels* tickets for additional tickets to Neil Simon's comedy.

Was it worth it? Should most groups shy away from controversial shows because the cost in money, time, and energy—not to mention risk to your company—would be too great? What was the overall effect on CRT?

"Our subscription revenues grew 20 percent during the next year;" reports Martin. "The artistic freedoms we defended unified the board, the staff, the audience, and the entire arts community. We learned our audiences were much more savvy than we thought. And now we have enhanced name recognition. There are 67 theater groups in a 50-mile radius, many with the word 'Charlotte' in their names. We were just one of many, now people know exactly who we are and the principles on which we stand."

Having conquered its financial problems, CRT now can concentrate on artistic growth. Awards, grants, and enviable reviews suggest not mere abundance, but quality of work. The *Angels in America* episode brought evidence of more loyalty than the company knew it had.

The company seeks to expand its subscriber base to 3,000 households by the year 2000. There's a chance some of them will be offended during 2001. When that happens, CRT will be able to rely on the backing of the community. They've earned it.

SOURCE: Nancianne Pfister, "On the Wings of a Storm," *Stage Directions* 10, no. 6 (June–July 1997. Copyright © 1997 *Stage Directions*, 3101 Poplarwood Court, Suite 310, Raleigh, NC 27604. Used with permission.

FYI: A related story in *The New York Times* (March 22, 1996) pointed out there were 15 people demonstrating against the play and 50 counterdemonstrators. The demonstrators were led by Rev. Joseph Chambers. According to the article, Rev. Chambers orchestrated a letter-writing campaign to elected officials about the play. The mayor of Charlotte was quoted as saying the theater company should "use some common sense" and change the nude scene. The *Times* reported the theater "sold more tickets than on any other day in its 18-year history."

Case Study Questions

1. Cite examples of as many of the six external environments that relate to this article as possible. Which environment predominated?

2. Could the theater have taken to mitigate the "outraged protests from groups of religious and political conservatives?"

3. What are some of the steps you, as an arts manager, could take to ensure a controversial work could be performed in your arts organization?

References

1. John Naisbitt and Patricia Aburdene, *Megatrends 2000* (New York: Avon, 1990), p. 76.
2. Nello McDaniel and George Thorn, *Workpapers: A Special Report— The Quiet Crisis in the Arts* (New York: ARTS Action Issues, 1991), pp. 7–10.
3. Lynne Fitzhugh, "An Analysis of Audience Studies for the Performing Arts in America, Part 2," *Journal of Arts Management and Law* 13 (Fall 1983), p. 7.
4. John O'Connor and Lorraine Brown, eds., *Free, Adult, Uncensored— The Living History of the Federal Theatre Project* (Washington, DC: New Republic, 1978).
5. "What Happened to the American Dream," *Business Week* (August 19, 1991), pp. 80–85.
6. *Population Projections of the United States by Age, Sex, Race, and Hispanic Origin: 1995 to 2050*, U.S. Department of Commerce, Bureau of the Census, http://www.census.gov/, May 1998.
7. Mark Reaney, http://ukanaix.cc.ukans.edu/~mreaney/, 1998.
8. Virtual Reality Online, http://hitl.washington.edu/projects/knowledge_base/onthenet.html, 1998.
9. Lynne Fitzhugh, "An Analysis of Audience Studies for the Performing Arts in America, Part 1," *Journal of Arts Management and Law* 13 (Summer 1983).
10. Ibid., p. 56.
11. Naisbitt and Aburdene, *Megatrends 2000*, p. 5.

5
□ □ □ □ □

Strategic Planning and Decision Making

If you aren't thinking ahead, you'll be left behind.

As noted in Chapter 1, planning is a primary function of management. In this chapter, we define planning and look at strategic and operational planning and the decision-making process. We examine types of plans, the planning process, and the development of a mission statement. The decision-making process is examined as a tool to assist the planning process. This chapter borrows terminology and concepts from the business world and adapts these to the needs of arts organizations.

Before we can delve into the topic of planning, we need to step back for a moment and consider an important question: Why are we doing this concert, play, or exhibition? Are we trying to raise money for a cause? Are we trying to make a profit or generate a surplus in our depleted operating budget? Are we trying to bring something new to the audience—a new play, new choreography, a new composer, a seldom-seen artist? The planning we do must be driven by the answer to this important "why."

As we discovered in Chapter 4, complex forces are at work in the various environments in which an arts organization must function. Artists and organizations, whether they like it or not, have had to adapt to the pressures of the external environments that are an integral part of our society. For example, solo artists unencumbered by a board of directors and an administrative staff may be able to achieve the goal of performing a new work through the sheer force of their energy and drive. A well-established orchestra, on the other hand, may debate for months over the conductor's desire to do a series of modern music concerts. In the latter case, the various and probably differing attitudes of the members of the board enter into determining why an organization selects a new direction.

After answering the hard questions—the whys—the remainder of the planning process may seem simple.

Planning Basics

Planning, Goals, and Objectives Defined

At the most basic level, *planning* is a process of stating objectives and determining what should be done to accomplish them. Planning involves thinking about the future—even if that is only tomorrow. It requires imagination, careful thought, and most important, time. Management textbooks often cite these reasons why planning fails: (1) people do not think beyond the immediate future, (2) they are too impatient to work through the details of a plan, and (3) they think planning is part of someone else's job.[1]

This text will define *goal* as a desired outcome and *objective* as the means to achieve the outcome. For example, "It is our goal for the museum to have the widest possible distribution of members. One of our objectives is to increase minority membership by 10 percent in a new membership recruitment campaign by June 2000."

Types of Plans

A plan is a statement of intended means for accomplishing stated results. A plan should answer five questions: Why? What? When? Where? Who?

Here is an example of this approach: "To fulfill the organizational mission of bringing new music to the community, our marketing and sales staff will expand our subscription audience by 7 percent for next year's concert series in Smedly Hall by contacting corporate personnel departments and offering group discounts." As you can see, we have our *why* (the organization's mission to bring new music to the area), *what* (expand concert subscriptions by 7 percent through group sales), *when* (for next season), *where* (Smedly Hall), and *who* (the marketing and sales staff).

Now we look at the various types of plans before describing the planning process in more detail.

Short-, intermediate-, and long-range plans   A short-range plan covers one year or less, intermediate-range plans cover one to four years, and long-range plans cover five or more years. Generally, long-range plans that exceed five years are of limited value because of too many unforeseen variables.

It is important to consider how people within the organization perceive time as you start the planning process. Research on planning points out that most people are comfortable with thinking three to six months ahead. Once you get past one year, most people are able to think only in general terms. The age of an organization also determines perceptions of time. When you are first getting an organization up and running, four months can seem like a long time. However, if you are part of a long-standing arts organization, three- to five-year plans might not be so difficult to comprehend. A manager must be aware of and sensitive to the organizational (staff and board) perception of time.

Strategic and operational plans   The phrase *strategic planning* has an impressive "corporate" ring to it. The original use of the phrase was to describe the planning and direction of large-scale military operations to maximize forces before engaging the enemy. The business world regularly transposes military concepts into its daily operations. We define *strategic planning* as a set of comprehensive plans designed to marshal all the resources available to the organization to meet the defined goals and objectives derived from the mission statement.

Operational plans usually are more limited in scope. These are the tactics in our military model. In this case, we are talking about marshaling the resources to support the strategic plan. For example, a museum that wants a larger membership base would need an operational plan that might include a specific marketing plan. At the same time, to undertake the strategic plan, the museum might need a personnel plan

Planning Proverb

"Planning is 80% thinking and 20% writing. Then 100% doing!"[2]

that calls for hiring new people with the expertise needed to run an effective marketing campaign.

Single-use and standing-use plans   These plans are often the most common ones found in arts organizations. Examples of *single-use plans* include a budget, a schedule, and a project timeline. Examples of *standing-use plans* include a policy, operating procedures, and rules.[3]

A *budget* is a plan for distributing resources. A budget that allocates more money for costumes than for scenery says something about the idea driving the production. An exhibition budget may allocate 80 percent of the money for a full-color book and only 20 percent for mounting the exhibition. A symphony may decide to focus on national touring and reduce its home schedule by 20 percent. These choices ideally represent a plan agreed to by all the people involved in putting on the show or concert or setting up the exhibition.

Another single-use plan would be a *schedule.* A schedule is a list of deadlines for completing specific tasks designed to meet the overall objective. Most of us in arts organizations work with either list or monthly calendar formats. For example, when an opera company sits down to plan a season, it works from a single-use plan: the season production schedule. A company that knows it will perform *Aida* next season can plan for accommodating the animals for the triumphal march scene. The logistics related to this part of the plan can be arranged far in advance. Budgeting and scheduling are discussed in more depth in Chapter 9.

A *standing-use plan* is designed to be used over and over again. For example, an arts organization should have a standing-use plan dealing specifically with how the administrative offices will operate. A theater box office should have a standing-use plan detailing the day-to-day operational procedures for processing orders and accounting for all revenue. Standing-use plans also are found in policy books, employee regulations, or posted rules.

On the surface, these two planning components may seem less weighty than the grand strategic plans, but they often are critical to the success of an organization. As we will see in Chapter 7, employees depend on well-designed single-use and standing-use plans to do their jobs.

The Planning Process

Most of us use a planning process of one sort or another to get through the day. You start your day by saying, "After class I have to go to the bank, then lunch with Fred, and over to the library at 2 P.M." Let us take a look at a more formal process.

Five Steps in Formal Planning

Assume you manage a small professional chamber music group. Your mission is to broaden the appreciation and understanding of chamber music in the tri-state area and your overall goal is to present high-quality concerts that will reach geographically diverse audiences. To fulfill your mission and realize your goal you have to develop plans to carry out specific activities. Let us walk through the process.

1. Define your objectives   This key first step defines what you want to achieve. For example, "I want to have 40 bookings for my touring concert group by November 1, two weeks before we start our seven month season." You must be specific in this first step. Specifying a quantitative achievement by a fixed date is one way to define your objectives.

2. Assess the current situation in relation to your objectives   You must clearly assess where you are and just how far you have to go. "I have 15 bookings, and it is September 1. I still have 25 to go in two months. It took me four months to book the first 15. I'd better be more aggressive in seeking out bookings, or I'll never make my target."

3. Formulate your options regarding future outcomes   Now you must design specific options from which to choose to reach your objective. "I will need three to four bookings per week over the next eight weeks. I can are devote are two more hours per day to this project after I adjust my schedule. I could hire someone to help me, but I'll have to pay the person. I could lower my target figure to 30 bookings, but our booking income will go down and we will not meet our revenue budget. I could extend the deadline to January 30 in the hope of reaching my original target figure."

4. Identify and choose among the options   After creating and reviewing your options, you must select the option you assess as the most effective. For example, you might decide to hire a temporary assistant to help you secure bookings. Your reason might be driven by financial need or by the fact that your musicians have other commitments and they need to know the final tour schedule by November 1.

5. Implement your decision and evaluate the outcome   If this plan is to work, it will be critical for you to set up short-term measuring points to mark how well you are doing. You may find that you need to implement other options if the outcome still seems questionable. You may establish a weekly review of the bookings totals and further adjust the plans as needed.

These five steps may seem simple and straightforward, but more often than not, people and organizations fail to even make a detailed plan. It takes work and self-discipline to keep on top of this process. One of the most important skills you can develop as a manager is to master the planning process and effectively put it to use.

The business world is filled with different approaches or combinations of approaches to take when planning. Arts organizations usually are not as bureaucratic in the planning process as businesses. However, care must be taken to not fall into the trap of spend more time planning than actually doing the work that needs to be done.

Other Planning Approaches

Top-down and bottom-up planning   *Top-down planning* simply is a process where the upper-level management sets the broad objectives and then middle- and lower-level management work out detailed plans within a limited structure. *Bottom-up planning* begins with lower and middle management setting the objectives; upper management responds with final planning documents that reflect the input. Mixtures of these approaches make sense for most organizations.[4]

Top-down planning can fail if upper management does not consult with middle and lower management and labor when setting objectives. For example, suppose that the board and artistic director of a theater company plan to expand the season of a regional theater company from 24 to 36 weeks. Before trying to implement this plan, they should ask the people in the other levels of management (managing director, production manager, marketing and fund-raising directors) to evaluate the impact of this change. Middle- and lower-level management will be asked to prepare reports showing the increased costs and increased revenue anticipated as a result of this plan. Upper management then will have the information it needs to assess the consequences of expanding the season. Modifications can be made in the plan before final implementation. (Given the number of anecdotal stories by staff people about never being consulted when sweeping changes are being made in their arts organizations, I surmise that an effective top-down planning process is an ideal in some settings.)

Pure bottom-up planning is fairly rare because it usually is a cumbersome process. Too much staff time is spent meeting and reviewing every detail of the planning documents. More typically, the process might begin with upper management requesting that middle and lower management draw up planning documents for their areas or departments. Difficulties may arise when middle and lower management are not well informed about the overall organizational goals and objectives. The fact is, if everyone in the organization does not understand the mission and goals of the organization, a bottom-up planning process actually may be counterproductive.

Contingency planning   As the name implies, the *contingency planning* approach sets alternative courses of action that depend on different conditions. Contingency planning is most effective when trigger points are built into the process. For example, suppose that your season subscription campaign began in March. You expected to have a 70 percent renewal rate by July, but the box office reports only a 40 percent renewal by July 15. You would now activate your contingency plan for another mailing and a media blitz.

Crisis planning   *Crisis planning* is an offshoot of contingency planning. Unfortunately, many arts organizations adopt this planning process as a standard operating procedure or management style. The key reason why many arts organizations operate in a crisis management mode is the poor management skills of the staff. For example, when a ballet company plans a season based on selling 80 percent of capacity and has no formal plan when only 50 percent of the seats are sold, the atmosphere will be one of constant crisis. Crisis management often leads to middle- and lower-level staff members saying, "We seem to be making it up as we go along." The other form of crisis planning is formulating how the organization will respond in time of need.

Plans for dealing with a crisis do have a place in arts organizations. This is especially true when the organization must deal with the media, supporters, subscribers, or the general public. For example, an arts organization should have a plan ready to activate in the event of the death of a key person like a founder-director. It is also a good idea to plan for crisis if an organization decides to tackle a controversial project or play title. Arts organizations all too often go through months and years of chaos because no one took the time to map out a plan before a crisis strikes.

Strategic Planning

To engage in *strategic planning*, which was previously defined as a set of comprehensive plans designed to marshal all the resources available to the organization to meet the defined goals and objectives derived from the mission statement, the management must start at its source: the mission statement.

Figure 5–1 depicts a flowchart for a strategic planning process. The cycle begins with a mission statement that expresses a general approach to solving a problem or meeting a particular need in a society. An analysis of the current status of the organization helps inform the development of a strategy that will help support and enhance the mission. The organization then formulates goals and establishes specific objectives designed to fulfill the mission of the organization. The specific plans are implemented to influence the input environments that created the mission of the organization. Let us look more closely at each phase of this process.

In the News 1—Planning for Success?

As this article for the *Los Angeles Times* indicates, the Getty Museum planners did not predict the public demand to see their new museum.

Public Just Can't Get Enough of the Getty
The arts: As crowds overwhelm the new center in Brentwood, officials rethink the admittance policy.
Suzanne Muchnic

Struggling to cope with the overwhelming popularity of the $1-billion Getty Center in Brentwood— and bracing for an even larger demand during the spring holiday period—the J. Paul Getty Trust has issued a warning that visitors who arrive at the center without parking reservations may encounter long lines and possibly not be admitted.

Before the center's Dec. 16 opening, as an international media frenzy drew attention to the new cultural complex and whetted the public's appetite to see it, the Getty's estimates of inaugural year attendance escalated from 1 million to 1.5 million. But more than 500,000 people have visited during the first three months of operation, so the projected total has jumped to 2 million.

Parking reservations—which are required for all automobiles—are booked until October, except for a few slots late in the day, said Lori Starr, the Getty's director of public affairs. Most public programs are booked through March.

Visitors who couldn't obtain a reservation for one of the center's 1,200 parking spaces have been encouraged to take a bus, shuttle or taxi to the Getty. But those who use such alternative modes of transportation must wait until visitors with parking reservations are admitted. Many drop-in visitors have experienced significant delays, particularly on weekends.

On days when the Getty reaches capacity, public bus, taxi and shuttle companies and hotel concierges will be asked to inform their patrons that no additional visitors can be accommodated, Starr said. Parking is restricted in surrounding neighborhoods, passengers who are dropped off at the center must be driven onto the premises and will be subject to delays.

Public interest in the Getty has so exceeded expectations that trust officials are considering alternative reservation systems to ensure access and reduce waiting periods. Using a major commercial ticketing agency is one possibility, but no decision has been made, Starr said.

The trust is exploring possibilities, and if it instates a new system, will honor all existing reservations.

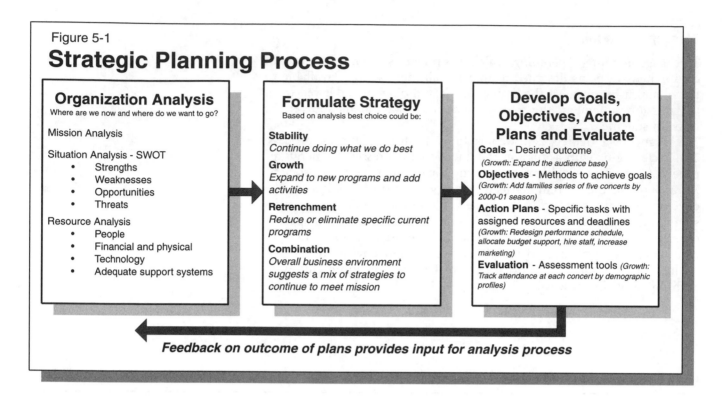

Figure 5-1

Strategic Planning Process

Organization Analysis
Where are we now and where do we want to go?

Mission Analysis

Situation Analysis - SWOT
- Strengths
- Weaknesses
- Opportunities
- Threats

Resource Analysis
- People
- Financial and physical
- Technology
- Adequate support systems

Formulate Strategy
Based on analysis best choice could be:

Stability
Continue doing what we do best

Growth
Expand to new programs and add activities

Retrenchment
Reduce or eliminate specific current programs

Combination
Overall business environment suggests a mix of strategies to continue to meet mission

Develop Goals, Objectives, Action Plans and Evaluate

Goals - Desired outcome
(Growth: Expand the audience base)
Objectives - Methods to achieve goals
(Growth: Add families series of five concerts by 2000-01 season)
Action Plans - Specific tasks with assigned resources and deadlines
(Growth: Redesign performance schedule, allocate budget support, hire staff, increase marketing)
Evaluation - Assessment tools *(Growth: Track attendance at each concert by demographic profiles)*

Feedback on outcome of plans provides input for analysis process

The Mission Statement

A clear mission statement, which defines the organization's "reason to be," is the source from which all plans should spring. It makes no difference whether the organization is a small modern dance company or a large regional arts center. Groups of all sizes need a concise statement that may communicate to the world why they exist.

The Effective Nonprofit Executive Handbook, an excellent resource book published by the Public Management Institute of San Francisco, provides a checklist to help arts managers organize their thoughts about the mission statement. They suggest that arts groups ask these nine questions:

1. Why do we exist as an organization?
2. What "business" are we in?
3. What is our most important product or service?
4. Who are our clients, volunteers, audiences and donors?
5. Why do they come to us?
6. How have we changed in the past five years?
7. What are our organization's unique strengths and major weaknesses?
8. What philosophical issues are most important to us?
9. What would be lost if we ceased to exist?[5]

Another source of a highly systematized information about planning may be found in John M. Bryson's *Strategic Planning for Public and Nonprofit* Organizations.[6] Byron sets a benchmark for organizational planning. His approach is particularly helpful because it recognizes the unique elements of the not-for-profit organization in a planning process. He also articulates a helpful perspective about strategic thinking and acting as it informs strategic planning. Last, he provides concrete examples of successful and unsuccessful planning practices.

Mission Analysis

An organization's mission statement should broadly describe its "reason to be." For example, a theater company might be dedicated to presenting new works, or a ballet company might be committed to performing classical works. The following are some real-life examples:

- Actors' Guild of Lexington Kentucky states its mission is to "create and present compelling, contemporary theatre for the region."[7]
- The Guthrie Theater describes as part of its mission statement that "Its primary task is to celebrate, through theatrical performances, the common humanity binding us all together."[8]
- The San Diego Chamber Orchestra's mission is "To be a world-class ensemble with a local focus; a missionary orchestra serving the people of the region, wherever they may live; an ensemble preserving the quality and tradition of chamber repertoire in perpetuity; and, a vehicle for the artistic expression of the finest conductor musicians."[9]
- Mission Statement: "The Alliance Theatre is dedicated to celebrating our diversity by building bridges, which can connect us as human beings through the development and production of exciting, entertaining and stimulating plays, nurturing and enriching both the art, artists and audience.[10]

The readers of the Actors' Guild mission statement is a succinct phrase that describes who the guild is and what it does where. A first-time reader of the Chamber Orchestra and the Alliance Theater mission statements may come away a bit confused. A wordy mission statement will not be remembered by most people, including your own staff. When communicating to people inside and outside the organization, arts managers most often find themselves in the position of saying "We are the X arts organization and our mission is . . ." In neither case, do these last two mission statements communicate succinctly. In fact, an arts manager would find himself or herself improvising a simpler statement. Ultimately, this should not be the way a mission is communicated. The crafting of a short, distinctive mission statement is much harder than people realize. However, the effort will pay off through clearer communication to people inside the organization and to the wider public.

Analysis of strengths and weaknesses   The process of looking at oneself and frankly assessing one's good points and shortcomings is as difficult for an organization as it is for an individual. The arts consulting business thrives on bringing the outsider's viewpoint into what too often becomes a self-congratulatory process. Organizations, like people, have a hard time seeing their flaws. One approach to organizational self-analysis is to break down the review into an evaluation of the organization's internal human, material, and technological resources and its operating system. Questions such as the following must be posed:

1. Do we have the people with the skills we need to realize the plan?
2. Do we have the facilities, money, equipment, and so on, to make the plan work?
3. To what extent can we apply technology to our plan?
4. Do we have the systems in place for supporting additional programs of activity?

5. Do we have the ability to monitor progress and make corrections as we proceed?

A further technique used in the planning process is to undertake what often is referred to as a *SWOT* (strengths, weaknesses, opportunities, and threats) *analysis*. One creates a detailed inventory of items under each area to develop an overview of the organization in relation to factors that may help or hinder it from realizing its mission. For example, a controversial experimental theater company, with a mission of presenting only new works, may have the strength of very talented writers and an outstanding acting company. Its weakness may be that they lack experience working within the arts community in their area. It may have the opportunity for access to a better venue for its work. Last, it may face the threat that the work produced may be subject to censorship in its community.

How does all of this shape planning for the experimental theater company? First, it may discover that, in doing a rigorous analysis of the situation, the organization may never thrive in this community and it would be best to relocate to a more conducive setting. Or, it may decide that the challenge of presenting controversial new works in this community is worth the effort, even if that means the company never will achieve widespread public and financial support. Or, based on the SWOT analysis, the company could decide to change its mission and produce only hit Broadway musicals.

An organization's entire planning process should be directed at creating objectives and plans of action based on fulfilling its mission statement. This may seem like an obvious starting point for planning, but I have spent many hours in meetings where conflicting views of an organization's mission statement were never resolved. The planning went ahead, but conflicts always came up when the planning process led to the stage of deciding what was most important to the organization. A weak or contradictory mission statement is like an out-of-focus photograph. When people view the picture, they often see different things. They reach conclusions and make assumptions based on imprecise information. Actions are taken and then questions are raised: "How does this project or program serve our mission?" Often it may not, but resources are allocated anyway.

Formulating an Organization's Strategy

Strategy defines the direction in which the whole organization intends to move. It also establishes the framework for the action to be taken to achieve the goals outlined in the strategy. We have noted that the strategy should relate to the environment in which the organization must function. In Chapter 4, six environments were outlined: economic, political and legal, cultural and social, demographic, technological, and educational. Depending on any number of conditions, one or more of these environments could be stable, undergoing change, or even be uncertain.

Strategic planning usually draws on one of the following approaches: stability, growth, retrenchment, or some combination of these.

Stability strategy   The basic thinking behind this strategy is, "We are doing pretty well with our current operation, and there is no reason to make any big changes." This does not mean that the organization is doing nothing to meet its stated goals and objectives. It simply implies there is no reason to move off in new directions. Many arts organizations probably would feel comfortable adopting this strategy. The major arts organizations in a community often are seen as part of the basic fabric of the area. People cannot imagine not having the museum, the symphony, and so on.

Growth strategy   This approach makes sense when expanding operations into new markets. With this strategy, a company may diversify its product line or actively seek a bigger share of the market. Arts organizations may adopt growth as an overall strategy by doing such things as increasing the numbers and types of events that it produces. Another example of a growth strategy is to deliberately push for greater community involvement by adding a ballet school or an art school to the dance company or museum. With growth comes increased costs and, it is hoped, increased income. These elements should be carefully calculated in the overall strategy.

Retrenchment strategy   The third strategy describes a slowdown, cutback, or elimination of some portion of the organization's activity. Because this process often is viewed as retreating, many organizations will go to great lengths to describe it as something else. For example, a music group might say, "We are engaged in a planned phase-out of our Tuesday night concert series." In other words, the group is retrenching and cutting back on its programming to save money. As we saw in Chapter 4, the early 1990s have been marked by a great deal of cutting back and retrenching among many arts organizations.

Combination strategy   An organization might use all three of these strategies at any given time. Again, the influence of the external environments will determine to what degree various strategies must be adopted. If the community is experiencing an economic slump combined with an uncertain political environment, the organization might need to retrench in some areas and expand in others.

To formulate an overall strategy requires an honest appraisal of the organization's mission statement and its strengths, weaknesses, threats, and opportunities. Here, again, the services of an outside consultant can help the board of directors and staff keep a sense of perspective about what the organization really will be able to accomplish through its strategic plan.

The final phase of the planning process results in developing goals, objectives, action plans, and evaluation systems. The goals are shaped by the choice of strategy, and the objectives address the goal with specific targets. Action plans develop concrete steps to be taken through allocating human, financial, and equipment resources to meet the objective. Last, a measurement or assessment process is established to monitor the how well the organization is achieving the goals and objectives it set for itself.

Figure 5–2 demonstrates many component parts make up the overall strategic plan of an organization. It is not usual to find plans for marketing, fund raising, programs, or facilities being driven by the overall strategic plan. The dynamic nature of planning, implementation, and assessment is difficult to impart in a diagram. As you see from the diagram, the flow of the process leads back to analysis and assessment. To have an effectively managed planning process it must be clear to the board, staff, artists, and potential supporters what you are trying to

In the News 2

As this brief new item indicates, arts organizations can change course just like any business.

Opera Housing

The Washington Opera has abandoned plans to convert a former department store into a landmark opera house for the nation's capital. The company's board voted Tuesday to stay at is current home in the Kennedy Center; it signed a 15-year agreement that will allow it to expand its season from 74 to as many as 100. The center agreed to a technical updating and renovation of its opera house in 2001.

Figure 5-2

Operational Plans Related to Strategic Plans

There is a dynamic interaction between overall strategic plan and operational plans in specific areas of the organization.

Overall Strategic Plan
- Mission & Analysis
- Strategies
- Goals
- Objectives
- Action Plans
- Evaluation Systems

OPERATIONAL PLANS

Programming Plans
Example
Goal: Expand audience base
Objective: Add family series of five concerts by 2000-01
Action Plan: New season schedule and coordinate with marketing & fund raising
Evaluate: Track attendance at concerts

Marketing Plans
Example
Goal: Maximize sales & attendance
Objective: Develop marketing approach targeted to families
Action Plan: Survey potential target market to assess interest in family series
Evaluate: Monitor audience with satisfaction survey

Fund Raising Plans
Example
Goal: Identify & cultivate new donors
Objective: Target donors interested in family concert series
Action Plan: Contact business, foundation, & private donors
Evaluate: Query donors on satisfaction with new series

Murphy's Law and Planning: Bachman's Inevitability Theory

"The greater the cost of putting a plan into operation, the less chance there is of abandoning the plan—even if it becomes irrelevant."[12]

---

achieve. In general, plans expressed through diagrams often are easier for everyone to comprehend and implement.

Limits to Planning
A by-product of the growth and development of the arts in the 1960s and 1970s has been the steady increase in organizations developing strategic plans. The NEA helped foster the process of organized planning as part of its funding process. In the 1980s and 1990s, *visioning* became a buzzword. To secure funding arts organizations needed to demonstrate they had a vision, a planning process, and plans in place for the funds they were requesting. While the level of resources allocated to planning never reached the intensity of the corporate world, many arts organizations generated thick tomes of strategic plans that took considerable to time and effort to assemble. Unfortunately, many of these plans went on a shelf in an office because they lacked operational relevance to the organization. The systematic application of these plans often failed to materialize for the simple reason they were never fully integrated into the day-to-day operation of the organization.

In *Management for Productivity*, John Schermerhorn cites seven general reasons why organizational plans fail:[11]

1. The upper management fails to build a formal planning process into the general operating routine.
2. The people involved in planning are not very skilled in the planning process.
3. The data used in making the plans are incorrect.
4. The resources needed are not made available to execute the plans.
5. Circumstances change due to unforeseen events.
6. Staff members do not want to change, and they hold to plans that do not work.
7. Staff members become bogged down in the details and fail to reach the broader objective of the plan.

For many arts organization a combination of these reasons limited the success of the planning process. Often months would be spent developing detailed planning documents with the help of outside consultants, only to have them become irrelevant because of a change in board or artistic leadership. In many cases the planning documents are too complex to implement given the limited staffing resources of the organization. McDaniel and Thorn in *Towards a New Arts Order* point out that planning often "places one more burden and distraction on an already overburdened organization."[13] Another writer in the field of management, Richard Farson, points out in *Management of the Absurd* that, "By and large, organizations are simply not good at changing themselves. They change more often as a result of invasions from the outside or rebellion from the inside, less so as a result of planning."[14]

Another point of view about planning was raised by Henry Mintzberg, respected management author, in *The Rise and Fall of Strategic Planning*. Mintzberg's opinion is that the term *strategic planning* is an oxymoron and that strategy and planning are two different processes that do not work well together. He states:

> An organization can plan (consider its future) without engaging in planning (formal procedure) even if it produces plans (explicit intentions); alternately, an organization can engage in planning (formalized procedure) yet not plan (consider its future) . . .[15]

At the heart of Mintzberg's challenge to some aspects of strategic planning process is the assumption one can predict the future. When we sit down to "plan," do we really know what unforeseen events will occur that will shape how the organization behaves? For example, would anyone have predicted that the federal government would actually balance the budget and show a surplus before the end of the twentieth century? Or, relating unforeseen events in an arts context, could anyone have predicted the impact on arts the community of canceling an exhibit of Robert Maplethorpe's photographs in a gallery in Washington, D.C., in 1990? On the positive side, Mintzberg challenges many planning assumptions and offers good suggestions to all managers on how to develop a realistic planning process that will be more responsive to change.

Relationship of Planning to the Arts

The creation and ongoing use of a strategic plan can be an excellent way to provide the overall framework for keeping an organization headed in a general direction. But in some cases the strategic plan and the mission statement are put away in attractive folders and pulled out only once a year at the annual board meeting. However, for these ideas and plans to be effective, they should be integrated into the daily operation of the organization. Does this ensure that the organization will be a success? No. In fact, many founder-driven arts organizations came to life and struggled to national prominence with none of this documentation. However, it would be more difficult today for an arts organization to get long-term support from foundations, corporations, or government agencies without a published mission statement and strategic plan.

The Necessity of Planning

Over the last 30 years, arts organizations and artists have had to deal with ever-increasing accountability, especially when dealing with donations, public money, corporate donations, and foundation support. It is typical for arts organizations to provide three- to five-year plans in their funding applications. However, the need for arts organizations to remain flexible and open to change is important, too. Planning that locks an arts organization into rigid thinking can be deadly to the whole enterprise.

The management of any arts organization must assume that change is a given. Opportunities and threats to the organization will constantly present themselves. Therefore, there is no choice other than to draw up plans detailing how the organization will respond to change. The key is to develop a planning process and planning implementation system that fits with the scope and scale of the organization.

The Organization's Map and Leadership

Most of us have had to read a map at some point in our lives. In effect, the strategic plan for an organization is the map it plans to use to get to its ultimate destination. Although most of us have read maps, few of us regularly create them. Arts organizations need the skilled assistance of managers who know how to use the techniques of strategic planning to help make these maps. Ultimately, all the planning in the world will not ensure success. Without dynamic and articulate leadership, an organization will suffer and probably fail. Board and management leadership that is not trained in developing and implementing plans must learn these skills if the organization is to remain healthy over the long run.

Decision Making

For any planning process to succeed, the organization must have a well-defined decision-making process in place. A good arts manager (or any manager for that matter) locates problems to be solved, decides on appropriate solutions, and uses organizational resources to implement the solutions. Our discussion of planning was based on the assumption that the ability to make decisions was an integral part of the manager's background. Let us take a closer look at this key part of the entire planning process.

Choices, Decisions, and Problem Solving

You make hundreds of decisions every day. For example, you make a choice to wear the long coat based on a decision arrived at after (1) identifying a problem (it is cold), (2) generating alternatives (wear no coat, wear two sweaters, wear a short coat), and (3) evaluating the alternatives (no coat and freeze, two sweaters and look bulky). This process leads to solving a problem (keeping warm). *Problem solving*, then, is "the process of identifying a discrepancy between an actual and desired state of affairs and then taking action to resolve this discrepancy."[16]

Schermerhorn identifies three types of problem solvers: problem avoiders, problem solvers, and problem seekers.[17] The first two types need little explanation. The third type describes the rare person who actively looks for problems to solve. At any given time, all of us have probably exhibited a little of each type. You should give it some thought if one of these types dominates your problem-solving approach.

When approaching problems, it is helpful to define whether you are dealing with *expected* or *unexpected problems*. For example, you should expect that from time to time an audience member will appear on Saturday night with a ticket for Friday's show. You should have a solution to this problem ready to be activated when the situation arises. An unexpected problem might be smoke pouring into the lobby from an overheated motor in the air circulation system. In this case, you must quickly assess your alternatives without creating a panic.

Steps in Problem Solving

The following steps are one way to proceed through the problem-solving process:

1. Identify the problem   What is the actual situation? What is the desired situation? What is causing the difference? For example, suppose that your interns always are late and you want them to be on time. Try to determine why they are late. Is it inadequate transportation, inappropriate work schedules, an unsafe workplace, a difference between the workload and their expectations, or their supervisor?

2. Generate alternative solutions   This step is critical and often requires some imaginative thinking. Your investigation of the situation should allow you to gather as much information as possible to evaluate various courses of action. For example, you may discover that the interns are late because the supervisor is disorganized and sometimes verbally abusive. Further investigation reveals that one of the interns has an attitude problem. He has been rallying others to stage a work slowdown by showing up late every day.

3. Evaluate alternatives and select a solution   You consider replacing the supervisor, the intern, or both. You also assess the workload expectations and any other relevant information you gathered about the situation. Your solution is to dispense with the assistance of the intern and reassign the supervisor. You also enroll the supervisor in a two-day workshop on human relations skills.

4. Implement the solution   After consulting others within the organization (there could be some legal or interpersonal problems you had not foreseen), implement your solution.

5. Evaluate the results and make adjustments as needed   Monitor the new supervisor and interns on a regular basis, conduct formal and informal talks with all concerned, and monitor the former intern supervisor.

Problem-Solving Techniques

If problem solving were as easy as these five steps imply, then managing would be a much simpler task. In reality, problem solving is a difficult and demanding part of the manager's job.

Defining problems, making hasty decisions, and accepting the risk
One of the many difficulties in problem solving is accurately defining the problem. People often incorrectly identify the symptom as the cause of the problem. For example, the lateness of the interns was the symptom for which we later identified the causes. In the planning process, you may create many extra difficulties if you formulate objectives based on incorrectly identified problems. For example, a drop in subscription sales is a warning symptom of a whole host of possible problems. The ultimate cause may be show titles, prices, schedule, or even sales staff, among other things.

Another difficulty in problem solving is jumping to a solution too quickly. The first solution is not always the best one. This is where trying out ideas on others can be helpful. A group brainstorming session may give you the added dimension you need to solve the problem.

Management texts frequently note that problem solving can take place in environments that are uncertain and risky.[18] The way you implement the five-step problem-solving process depends a great deal on factors over which you may have little control. For example, if the intern supervisor happened to be the spouse of the artistic director of the theater company, your decision would have an added element of risk.

Analyzing alternatives   Probably the best approach to analyzing your alternatives is to write them down. You can make an inventory of alternatives[19] by simply listing all of the those you have and writing out the good and bad points of each choice. Figure 5–3 demonstrates the use of this process to decide on the appropriate action to take in upgrading computer systems. By forcing yourself to write it down, you may see other alternatives or ramifications of a decision.

Making the final choice   Writing out all of the alternatives brings you to the stage of making the decision. After all is said and done, you need to ask yourself, "Is a decision really necessary?" The intern may quit out of frustration or the supervisor may ask for a transfer to some other part of the operation before you have finished gathering all of the evidence you need for a decision.

Decision Theory

In reality, the classic decision theory situation (clear problem, knowledge of possible outcomes, and optimum alternative) seldom exists.[20] Arts managers more commonly find themselves operating in the realm of *behavioral decision theory*. This theory assumes that "people only act in terms of what they perceive about a given situation. Because such perceptions are frequently imperfect, the behavioral decision maker acts with limited information."[21] According to this theory, people reach decisions based on finding a solution they feel comfortable with given limited knowledge about the outcome. For example, when faced with the problem of the difficult intern, you may opt for dismissing the intern and tolerating the obnoxious supervisor. You may assess the risk of transferring the supervisor and in turn alienating the artistic director and find that it is too high.

Figure 5-3

Decision Inventory

Upgrade levels or replace five ticket office computers

ALTERNATIVES	Time Required to Implement	Estimated Cost	PROS	CONS
DECISION 1 Upgrade to improved but lower-level performance machines. Keep existing cases, monitors, keyboards, mouse, and video cards.	3 days down time: Take machines to local vendor for upgrade.	Equipment: $550 per machine = $2,750 Motherboards, RAM, hard drives, modem Labor: 15 hours labor @ $35 per hour: $525 Maintenance contract 2 yrs @$50/yr: $900 **TOTAL COST = $4,175**	A. Will have faster machines B. No staff time spent on equipment-all labor by supplier	A. Upgrade is minimal. B. Limited life of low-end upgrade to 24 months? Costs avg. $162 per month in parts and labor over 2 years.
DECISION 2 Upgrade to improved but middle-level performance machines. Keep cases, keyboards, and mouse.	3 days down time: Take machines to local vendor for upgrade.	Equipment: $1270 per machine = $6,350 Motherboards, RAM, hard drives, monitor, video card, modem Labor: 18 hours labor @ $35 per hour: $630 Maintenance contract 3-1/2 yrs: $1725 **TOTAL COST = $8,705**	A. Will have much faster machines with longer use B. No staff time spent on equipment-all labor by supplier	A. Upgrade is middle range. B. Life of mid-range upgrade-42 months? Costs avg. $207per month in parts and labor for 3-1/2 years.
DECISION 3 Upgrade to highest current level. Keep cases, keyboards, and mouse.	3 days down time: Take machines to local vendor for upgrade.	Equipment: $1750 per machine = $8,750 Motherboards, RAM, hard drives, monitor, video card, modem Labor: 18 hours labor @ $35 per hour: $630 Maintenance contract 5 yrs: $2250 **TOTAL COST = $11,630**	A. Will have much faster machines with longer use B. No staff time spent on equipment-all labor by supplier	A. Labor costs to upgrade are higher B. Life of top of line upgrade-60 months? Costs avg. $194 per month in parts and labor for 5 years.
DECISION 4 Replace current machines with all new equipment that is one level below the top of the line.	1 day down time: Vendor brings new machines and installs them on site.	Equipment: $2,200 per machine = $11,250 New machines with latest hardware and software configuration. Labor: 8 hours labor @ $35 per hour: $280 Maintenance contract 5 yrs: $2250 Less credit for sale of old machines: $750 **TOTAL COST = $13,030**	A. Will have much faster machines with longer use B. No staff time spent on equipment-all labor by supplier C. Faster turn around D. Garage sale of old computers for $150 each?	A. Cost of extra work of selling old system. B. Higer cost per unit during life of near top of range upgrade-60 months? Costs avg. $217 per month in parts and labor for 5 years.

Conclusion

Planning, as described in this chapter, is a series of logical steps that can lead to creative solutions to problems. One of the manager's most important functions is to solve problems. An excellent way of solving problems is to ensure that planning is integrated into all phases of an organization. For an arts manager, the organization's mission statement is a fundamental element in the planning process. The mission statement is not some historical relic to be taken off the shelf once a year for a board meeting. Rather, it is a statement of the purpose of the organization, and at the same time, it is the force behind all decision making. The distribution of resources to performance, production, marketing, fund raising, and administration should be traceable back to the mission statement. When this link is broken, an organization finds itself in a struggle to make sense of why it is doing what it is doing.

Planning is a tool that any organization can put to good use. In his introductory chapter to *No Quick Fix (Planning)*, Robert W. Crawford writes, "Planning is, in reality, a commonsense way of defining what it is that one wants, when one would like to attain it, and how one goes about attaining it."[22] Crawford makes an excellent point about how people misconceive what planning really involves. He observes:

> It is fascinating how difficult it often is for individuals to transfer their understanding of planning in their own lives, and its flexibility, to organizations of which they are a part. More often than not, when organizational planning is brought up or initially discussed, psychological blinders appear. It often is assumed that planning is a restrictive process, that the organization and its creative leadership will be locked into a plan which may well not be good for either; that a plan must be adhered to rigidly once it is formulated and approved; that change is impossible, or at the very best, difficult; that it forces people to do things when they realize from further experience that doing something else would be better; that because one doesn't know what is going to happen in the future, one is precluded by a plan from taking advantage of opportunities which may arise unexpectedly. To put it succinctly, such perceptions of planning are ridiculous.[23]

Later in this text, we will focus on planning as it relates to the areas of finance (Chapter 11), marketing (Chapter 12), and fund raising (Chapter 13). All three areas rely on and should come from the work done in the strategic planning process.

Summary

Planning is a primary function of management. For arts organizations, creating a mission statement that defines its "reason to be" is an important first step in the planning process. A plan is a statement of means to accomplish results. The entire process of planning should clearly state the organization's objectives and help determine what should be done to achieve those objectives. Short-range plans (under one year), intermediate-range plans (one to four years), and long-range plans (five to ten years) are used to reach the stated objectives.

The overall master plan, called a *strategic plan*, supports the mission of the organization. Strategic plans may stress stability, growth, retrenchment, or some combination of these. The strategic planning process analyzes the organization's mission, reviews external environments, and examines the organization's strengths and weaknesses. Within the strategic plan, various operational plans are designed to achieve specific objectives. Operational plans include single-use plans (budgets and schedules) and standing-use plans (policies, rules, and regulations).

Formal planning comprises five steps: defining objectives, assessing the current situation, formulating options, identifying and choosing options, and implementing the decision and evaluating the outcome. Planning approaches include top-down and bottom-up planning, contingency planning, and crisis planning. Organizations can benefit from formulating plans in case a crisis occurs.

Planning can fail if it is not integrated into normal operations, planning skills are poor, inaccurate data are used, resources are scarce, unforeseen events intervene, staff members resist change, or plans become bogged down in excessive detail.

For the planning process to be effective, an organization must have a decision-making system in place. Problem solving is the process of identifying a discrepancy between the actual and desired states of affairs then resolving this discrepancy. Five steps make up the process: identifying the problem, generating alternative solutions, evaluating the alternatives and selecting a solution, implementing the solution, and evaluating the results. You must assess the risks involved in your decision and carefully analyze alternatives.

Key Terms and Concepts

Planning
Goals
Objectives
Short-, intermediate-, and long-range plans
Strategic plans
Operational plans
Single-use and standing-use plans
Top-down and bottom-up planning
Contingency and crisis planning
Mission statement
SWOT analysis
Decision making
Inventory of alternatives
Decision theory

Questions

1. Analyze the mission statement of the project organization you choose from Chapter 1. Is it clear and to the point? How would you change the mission statement to improve its clarity?

2. What would be a good strategy for an arts organization to adopt if the national economy is in a recession?

3. Use the five steps of the formal planning process to plot out your own personal short-range plans (within the next year) and intermediate-range plans (within the next two to three years).

Case Study

Asolo Theatre Strategic Plan
Mission Statement

The Asolo Theatre Company is a not-for-profit corporation whose mission is to produce and present high quality professional theatre in a fiscally responsible manner for its community [Sarasota, Florida]. The Asolo performs primarily in rotating repertory with a resident company to celebrate the actor-artist, to attract regional, national and international audiences and to provide a training ground for FSU [Florida State University] graduate students. The Asolo is dedicated to work which moves, enlightens, entertains, and educates individuals of all ages and backgrounds.

Goals
Produce and Present
To express the artistic conscience of our community through the creation, production, and presentation of live theatre. We belong to the community so our work must express the community's conscience, its values, its beliefs, its concerns, its hopes, and its joys.

Fiscal Responsibility
Our artistic freedom is rooted in our fiscal stability. We intend to achieve the financial and operational capability to support and nurture the people and programs that comprise the institution.

Quality
We will continuously strive for the highest standards of professional theatre in the quality of both our artistry and our administration, for they are interdependent.

Celebrating the Actor-Artist
As an actor-driven theatre, we are dedicated to the nurturing of the American repertory actor.

Professional Training
As a "teaching hospital" for theatre artists, craftspeople, and administrators, it is our goal to provide a professional theatre environment for Florida State University, students and faculty.

Audience Development
We are dedicated to developing, through formal and informal interactions, both the quality and the quantity of our audience. We will strive to communicate our knowledge of and love for live theatre to both children and adults through our work, and through a variety of educational activities to support it.

THE VISION—YEAR 2002

> *"Without a dream there is no reality."*
> —Menachem Begin

The Asolo Theatre Company is fully established as a year-round destination theatre deeply rooted in a home community reaching north to Tampa/St. Petersburg and south to Port Charlotte. Because of the quality of our artistic and administrative work, our relationship with the community, and the richness of the audience experience, we are operating with a cash reserve sufficient to accomplish each season; a replenished and actively growing endowment fund; and the theatre is playing to the maximum earned income potential of its current facility. We are producing in a third Sarasota performance space and we have a "summer home" to which we move our winter repertory. Our conservatory, renowned for producing working actors, is the rival of Yale and Juilliard for attracting talented students.

The Executive Summary
It is the opinion of the planning committee that the Asolo is at a rare intersection of time and opportunity to capitalize on the

positive energy flowing into and out of the organization. In addition, in lieu of the crisis management that has so dominated our existence for the past four years, it's imperative that we define an exciting and positive direction that will galvanize the leadership, management, and staff toward an exciting, compelling future. Therefore, we propose that this organization be pulled into the next millennium by the following events.

Artistic

- Establishment of a summer season in the Conservatory Theatre—There is a summer audience in Sarasota who will come to see our work. And we have a theatre that is currently sitting idle during the summer months. It's our goal to minimize dark time in any theatre.
- Establishment of a "summer home"—Currently, at the end of the season, we have four fully mounted plays. We have a proven ability to attract tourists. Why not take our completed work to another community with either a summer tourism base, or year-round audience to further amortize the expense of rehearsal/production. There is already expressed interest from FSU in helping us find the necessary "seed money" in the state legislature for this initiative.
- A Year 2000 celebration/40th Anniversary—The year 2000 is our 40th anniversary season. We should take the opportunity to make the season a celebration.
- The establishment of a third performance space—All the destination theatres, Oregon, Shaw, and Stratford, have three performance spaces. It is our goal to achieve the maximum income potential of our current facility so there will be an audience demand for more "product." If we achieve our other goals, this is nearly inevitable.

Administrative/Fiscal

- Establishment of a Visitor's Services Department—In order to become a "Destination Theatre," we must focus significant resources on providing services to tourists. We believe its importance to our future warrants its establishment as a separate department.
- Re-establishment of our endowment—Our artistic freedom is rooted in our fiscal stability. The endowment represents that stability.
- Establishment of a sufficient operating reserve—Like the endowment, the operating reserve is a key component of our fiscal stability, freeing us artistically.
- Increase the ratio of earned income to contributed income—Given the predicted difficult giving environment of the future.

The exciting and dramatic growth described above will have a significant impact on our operating budget. However, it is imperative that we build this new growth on the foundation of a viable and significant endowment, and operate with a sufficient cash reserve to smooth the flow of cash. Further, it is our goal to positively impact the ratio of earned income to contributed income by introducing programs that will make us money while moving us along the path to achieving our Vision.

As a result, we foresee the Asolo evolving from its current austere $3.3 million budget to a $6 million plus budget over the five-year plan period, assuming the best of all scenarios. Realizing that events may steer us to a situation that is better than we planned, they may keep us on our plan, or they may force us to perform worse than our plan, we can't overstate the fact that these projects will be implemented on a step-by-step basis, with board involvement and approval at each step, and that each project must respond to the dynamic fiscal and economic realities of their time.

SOURCE: Asolo Theatre Company, Spring 1998. Copyright © Asolo Theatre Company, Inc. I thank Linda DiGabriele, managing director, for her assistance with this document.

Case Study Questions

1. How would you describe the overall strategy of the Asolo Theatre (stability, growth, retrenchment, or a combination)?

2. Summarize the six goals listed. Do these goals seem reasonable given the strategies chosen?

3. The Executive Summary provides a description of a series of "events" that will realize the goals of the theater. Discuss each item under the Artistic and Administrative/Fiscal headings with particular attention to the planning model discussed in this chapter.

References

1. John R. Schermerhorn, Jr., *Management for Productivity*, 2d ed. (New York: John Wiley and Sons, 1986), p. 98.
2. Harold R. McAlindon, *Management Magic* (Lombard, IL: Great Quotations, 1989).
3. Schermerhorn, *Management for Productivity*, p. 100.
4. Ibid., p. 105.
5. *The Effective Nonprofit Executive Handbook* (San Francisco: Public Management Institute, 1982), p. 83.
6. John M. Bryson, *Strategic Planning for Public and Nonprofit Organizations*, rev. ed. (San Francisco: Jossey-Bass, 1995).
7. Actors' Guild of Lexington, source: Dr. Deborah Martin, former Producing and Development Manager, June 1998.
8. Guthrie Theater WWW site at http://www.guthrietheater.org/, August 1998.
9. San Diego Chamber Orchestra home page at http://www.sdco.org/, May 1998.
10. Alliance Theatre Company Long Range Plan, May 28, 1998.
11. Schermerhorn, *Management for Productivity*, p. 114.
12. Arthur Bloch, *The Complete Murphy's Law* (Los Angeles: Price Stern Sloan, 1990), p. 52.
13. Nello McDaniel and George Thorn, *Toward a New Arts Order* (New York: ARTS Action Issues, 1993), p. 44.

14. Richard Farson, *Management of the Absurd* (New York: Touchstone, 1996), p. 122.
15. Henry Mintzberg, *The Rise and Fall of Strategic Planning* (New York: The Free Press, 1994), p. 32.
16. Schermerhorn, *Management for Productivity*, p. 64.
17. Ibid., p. 65.
18. Ibid., p. 76.
19. Ibid., p. 77.
20. Ibid., p. 79.
21. Ibid., p. 80.
22. Robert W. Crawford, "The Overall Structure and Process of Planning," in *No Quick Fix (Planning)*, ed. F. B. Vogel (New York: FEDAPT, 1985), p. 14.
23. Ibid., p. 14.

Additional Resources

The following sources were also used in writing this chapter.

Arthur G. Bedeian. *Management.* New York: Dryden Press, 1986.

James H. Donnelly, Jr., James L. Gibson, and John M. Ivancevich. *Fundamentals of Management*, 8th ed. Homewood, IL: BPI/Irwin, 1992.

Kathryn M. Bartol and David C. Martin. *Management*, 3d ed. Boston: Irwin, McGraw-Hill, 1998.

6
□ □ □ □ □

Fundamentals of Organizing and Organizational Design

Whether we like it not, we spend the greater part of our lives in organizations. Our contact with organizations may start with a day care center, then move to a series of educational organizations, then to a work organization, and finally, we may live out retirement in an organized elder care system. The family, which also is an example of an organizational unit, can be a powerful force in shaping how we interact with others and with organizations. Our ability to relate to the numerous complex organizations in our society determines how successful we are in achieving our personal goals and objectives. The powerful myths of the individual going it alone in society are offset by the reality that we need the support of people in an organization to achieve maximum results. One person can make a difference, but many people working together can create permanent change.

In this chapter, we analyze many of the basic concepts pertaining to organizations and organizational design. Then we apply these theories to arts organizations. We also examine the importance of matching the organization's structure to the task at hand. Finally, we review the phenomenon of organizations as cultures.

The Management Function of Organizing

In the study of management, organizing usually is listed as the second basic function.[1] If you are to implement effectively the strategic plans formulated in Chapter 5, you will need a way to organize your resources to realize your objectives.

A good starting point is to return to our earlier definition of an *organization* as "a collection of people in a division of labor working together to achieve a common purpose."[2] The term *organizing* was defined as "a process of dividing work into manageable components and coordinating results to serve a specific purpose."[3] We previously defined a *manager* as a person in an organization who is responsible for the work performance of one or more other people, and we defined *management* as a process of planning, organizing, leading, and controlling.

Four Benefits of Organizing
No matter what project or production you plan to undertake, four benefits can be derived from organizing:[4]

1. Making clear who is supposed to do what,
2. Establishing who is in charge of whom,
3. Defining the channels of communication,
4. Applying the resources to defined objectives.

Part of the arts manager's job as an organizer is to decide how to divide the workload into manageable tasks, assign people to perform these tasks, give them the resources they need, and coordinate the entire effort to meet the planning objectives.[5]

Organizing for the Arts

The task of organizing to achieve results always should be the arts manager's objective. The underlying assumption of this text is that an effective arts manager functions in a collaborative and cooperative relationship with the artist. People outside the arts sometimes erroneously assume that artists and arts organizations, by their very nature, are less structured than other organizations or that they function best in a disorganized setting. Nothing could be further from the truth. In fact, artists and arts organizations often foster what is popularly known as a workaholic attitude among employees. (See "FYI—A Book of Interest," later in the chapter, for a brief discussion about the addictive organization.)

Although there are different ways to approach the process of putting on an exhibition or presenting a theater, dance, opera, or concert performance, each art form shares an inherent organizational structure that bests suits its function. Each arts form typically faces the pressure of being ready for an audience by a specific date and time. For example, theater is rooted in developing a performance based on many hours of text study, blocking and line rehearsals, technical and dress rehearsals and eventually opening night. The organizational support required to prepare, rehearse, design, produce, and find an audience for the play need not be discovered each time a new show is put before the public. There are standard ways of pulling together a production. When the support system is in place and functioning correctly, it is almost invisible. However, when something goes wrong with this system, it becomes the hot topic of discussion. As we will see in this chapter, there are various ways to organize any enterprise. It is not an issue of a right way or a wrong way. As previously noted, organizational design and organizing should be aimed at achieving the desired results.

Before exploring the structural details of various arts organizations, let us take a look at the overall concept of the organization as an open system.

Organizational Design Approaches

Management theory approaches organizational design by using concepts such as mechanistic versus organic organizations,[6] the relationship to external environments, and the degree of bureaucracy within an organization. The mixture of these concepts may be outlined in a model of an open system. Figure 6–1 depicts how an organization transforms inputs to outputs. Within the overall environment, a constant feedback loop exists back to the input stage. For example, if the output is exhibitions and the stated mission is education, you will want to monitor the input from the people viewing your product to see if you are fulfilling your mission. First, you probably want to define your customers—members of the audience (how many or what percentage) or teachers or educational institutions? To search for data, you need to determine what data are of interest. You then would be sure to design into the organization a way to transform the data you received from the people who viewed your service. This translates into a department that gathers survey data, tabulates the results, and publishes reports informing management of how effectively the mission is being met.

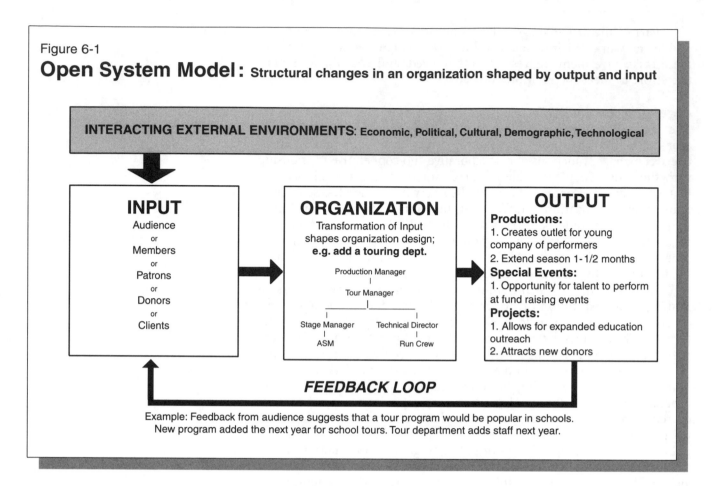

Figure 6-1

Open System Model: Structural changes in an organization shaped by output and input

INTERACTING EXTERNAL ENVIRONMENTS: Economic, Political, Cultural, Demographic, Technological

INPUT
Audience
or
Members
or
Patrons
or
Donors
or
Clients

ORGANIZATION
Transformation of Input
shapes organization design;
e.g. add a touring dept.

Production Manager

Tour Manager

Stage Manager   Technical Director

ASM   Run Crew

OUTPUT
Productions:
1. Creates outlet for young
company of performers
2. Extend season 1-1/2 months
Special Events:
1. Opportunity for talent to perform
at fund raising events
Projects:
1. Allows for expanded education
outreach
2. Attracts new donors

FEEDBACK LOOP

Example: Feedback from audience suggests that a tour program would be popular in schools.
New program added the next year for school tours. Tour department adds staff next year.

Another way to turn this model into a practical tool is to examine how an arts organization might more effectively reach beyond its traditional audience. For example, if an arts organization's objective is to build a larger subscriber or membership base from minority groups in the community, how should the organization's input, transformation, and output stages be designed? One obvious structural element to put in place would be a staff member heading up a minority development project. This position would function with horizontal authority. In other words, the staff member in this area would be given sufficient authority to cut across departments in an attempt to increase the number of minority-group employees within the organization. He or she could work with the board of directors to get board seats for members of minority groups. Over time, the organization's overall output should begin to create a feedback loop that signals to the community (input stage) that this organization is trying to address minority-group concerns.

Mechanistic and Organic Organizational Design

Arts organizations tend to be found at the organic end of the continuum of mechanistic versus organic organizational structure. The distinguishing features of an *organic organization* are a less centralized structure, fewer detailed rules and regulations, often ambiguous divisions of labor, wide spans of control or multiple job titles, and more informal and personal forms of coordination. A *mechanistic organization* tends to have a great deal of centralization, many rules, very precise divisions of labor, narrow spans of control, and formal and impersonal coordination procedures.[7] Of course, organizations vary in degree when it comes to classifying them within this continuum. Some arts organizations may adopt aspects of a mechanistic organization. The size and complexity of the operation usually dictates these attributes. For example, the Metropolitan Opera is more likely to adopt aspects of a mechanistic organization than a smaller organization like the Opera Theatre of St. Louis. Why? The size and scale of the operation play a role in determining the placement of an organization along this continuum.

Bureaucracy

When an organization adopts a mechanistic organizational structure, we often refer to it as a bureaucracy. Ideally, a bureaucratic organization has clear lines of authority, well-trained staff members assigned to their areas of specialization, and a systematic application of rules and regulations in a fair and impersonal manner.[8] This form of organization, originally found in government by bureaus or civil servants, was created to overcome the excesses of nepotistic control of social infrastructures. Today, we tend not to associate bureaucracy with democratic principles. Instead, we have very negative perceptions of bureaucracy. Anecdotes abound regarding bureaucratic structures bringing out the worst in an organization. We all have seen a rigid and unwieldy organization where, like a black hole in space, things are sucked in and never seen again. Government agencies often are cited as prime examples of bureaucracy at its most entrenched. However, James Q. Wilson's insightful book, *Bureaucracy: What Government Agencies Do and Why They Do It*, argues that bureaucracies are not black boxes into which input is converted impersonally to output but rather changing, complex cultures.[9] Wilson also argues that the perceived mission and the people within the government bureaucracies are significant forces in shaping interactions with the society at large.

Modern views of bureaucratic structure suggest that it would be best to adopt a contingency approach in organizational design. In other words, the organization adopts only the amount of bureaucratic structure necessary to accomplish its objectives. Does this mean that an arts organization needs to have some bureaucratic structures? Yes, to some degree. For example, an arts organization must establish ticket refund, crediting, and billing policies and procedures. It needs a consistent structure that handles most, if not all, transactions in the same manner. You cannot operate a box office with every employee setting his or her own rules or procedures for routine tasks. The patron who comes to the ticket office to request a refund or exchange should be given fast and efficient service. Staff members should not have to consult one another on the proper procedure.

Another area in which arts organizations need a great deal of structure is the payroll department. Employees may complain about the bureaucracy, but because the payroll department must interface with local, state, and federal agencies, there is no choice in the matter. Because of the complexity of state payroll and IRS regulations you cannot make it up as you go along.

The idea of a flexible framework of policies, rules, and regulations makes a great deal of sense for an arts organization when it comes to adopting bureaucratic structure. As we have seen, some areas within the organization need more rigid structure than others. The box office and payroll both need a clearly defined framework with rules, regulations, and policies. However, a resident scene designer in a regional theater will not find a highly structured framework very helpful if he or she has to fill out a purchase requisition for every a new pencil.

Probably the most useful tool for an arts manager to use in managing the degree of bureaucracy in the organization is testing; that is, walking through the procedures that are in place. The manager may discover policies, procedures, or rules that are confusing, contradictory, or inessential to the mission of the organization.

Organizational Structure

We now delve now into a more detailed examination of how to structure an arts organization. When we talk about *organizational structure*, we are referring to the "formal system of working relationships among people and the tasks they must do to meet the defined objectives."[10] These relationships and tasks are usually shown in an *organizational chart*, which is "an arrangement of work positions in an organization."[11]

In the business and arts worlds, adherence to the organizational chart must be tempered with a healthy dose of reality. It is important to establish the organizational chart to help clarify how things work and who to contact about getting something done. The organizational chart should help, not hinder, operations. If an organization finds itself unable to accomplish its objectives because the organizational structure frustrates action, it is time to reexamine how it is organized.

Organizational Charts and Formal Structure

A typical organizational chart should clearly show six key elements about the organization: divisions of work, types of work, working relationships, departments or work groups, levels of management, and lines of communication.[12]

Divisions of work   Each box on an organizational chart should represent a work area. Each area should designate an individual or group assigned to complete the organization's objectives. Figure 6–2 shows divisions of work in a hypothetical regional theater company. Under each division are specific workers and crews assigned to complete the task. For example, the production manager is responsible for the production area. The technical director is assigned the specific task of completing the scenery. The technical director in turn has people supporting the work area: the scene shop manager and the construction crew.

Type of work performed   The title you use for the person in charge of an area—for example, marketing director, box office manager, costume shop manager—should help describe the kind of work that person or crew will do. Care should be taken to avoid obscure work area titles. Vague or misleading titles often indicate that an organization is carrying staff positions that serve marginal functions.

Working relationships   The organizational chart should show who reports to whom. The solid line between the production manager and the technical director indicates a supervisor-subordinate relationship. The production manager and director of marketing are on the same level, and a communication line connects them to other supervisors.

Departments or work groups   The grouping of job titles in a work area should be communicated by your organizational chart. A per-

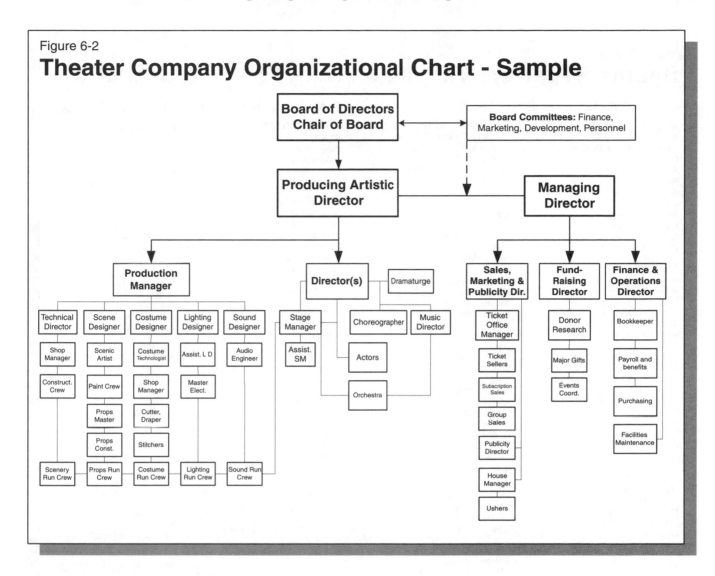

Figure 6-2
Theater Company Organizational Chart - Sample

forming arts organization may be large enough to warrant separate departments for work areas. For example, a well-established organization like the Seattle Repertory Theatre lists 15 different departments in its 1997–98 season program.[13] Six subunits of the production staff can be identified: carpenters, costumes shop, scenic arts, properties, stage crew, stage management. The names of 51 different people are listed in staff positions in the production area. The administrative staff listings included departments in the following areas: communications, box office, front of house, development, finance and administration, and the Professional Arts Training Program. The names of 67 staff members were listed for 47 job titles. See Figure 6–3 for a detailed listing of the job titles and a department breakdown of the organization.

Smaller organizations often combine departments. For example, the box office might include all single and subscription sales. Group sales and telemarketing might be included in this department as well. It is not unusual in a small operation to find one person heading up four or five different subdepartments. As an organization grows, the creation of separate departments usually follows.

Figure 6-3

Seattle Repertory Theatre Staff for 1997 - 98 Season

Sharon Ott, *Artistic Director*

Benjamin Moore, *Managing Director*

ARTISTIC STAFF
Kurt Beattie
Associate Artistic Director
Christine Sumption
Artistic Associate
Peggy Scales
Artistic Administrator
Ted Sod
Artist-in-Residence
Outreach/Education
Andrea L. Allen
Education Coordinator

PRODUCTION STAFF
Ten Eyck Swackhamer
Production Manager
Michal Immerwahr
Technical Director
Kirsten Amos
Assistant Technical Director
Jason Meininger
Lighting Design Associate
Claire Sigman
Assistant Production Manager
Christy Bain
Company Manager
Derek Baylor
Technical Production Assistant
Tonya Derrickson
Company Management
Assistant

CARPENTERS
Michael Boulanger
Scene Shop Foreman
Norbert Herriges
Scenic Coordinator
Ben Bryant
Tony Furr
Denny Hartung
Al Nelson
Jon Zucker
Scenic Carpenters
Colin Buckhurst
Scenic Carpenter Apprentice

STAGE CREW
Bagley Wright Theatre
Ross M. Brown
Master Stage Carpenter
Michael Maag
Master Electrician
Bill Droege
Head Sound Technician
Diana Gervais
Master Properties
B.S. Morningstar
Head Flyman
Laurel Horton
Swingperson
Leo Kreielsheimer Theatre
William Spaulding
Stage Carpenter
Roger Shaffer, Jr.
Master Electrician
Steve Collins
Sound Technician

COSTUME SHOP
Christine Smith-McNamara
Costume Shop Manager
Christine Joly
Assistant Costume Shop
Manager
Margaret Diehl
Wardrobe Master
Camille Benda
Leo K. Wardrobe Master
Marilyn McGuire
Tailor
Valerie Mayse
Draper
Lisa Lockard
Junior Draper
Sarah Gladden
Nancy Keye
Laura M
Janet Edman
1st Hands
Joyce Degenfelder
Wig Master
Kelly J Schmidt
Assistant Wig Master
Martin Lopez
Dyer/Craftsperson
Karen King
Milliner
Paula Bouchart
Stitcher

SCENIC ARTS
Nancy Knott
Scenic Charge Painter
Maurren Christoffel
Sharon McNeil
Scenic Artists

PROPERTIES
Jolene Oberlin
Properties Coordinator
David Logan
Associate Properties
Coordinator
Elizabeth Carpenter
Curtis Coyote
Nicolette Vannais
Properties Artisans
Julia Coyote
Properties Assistant

STAGE MANAGEMENT
Joseph Smelser
Production Stage Manager
Narda Alcorn
Stephanie Hagarty
Jeffrey K Hanson
John Kingsbury
Michael B. Paul
Wendiana Walker
Stage Managers
Gregory Hatch
Mindy Johnson
Laura MacNeil
Madelyn Mackie
Production Assistants

ADMINISTRATIVE STAFF
Sarah Newell
Human Resources Manager
Karen Shoffner
Executive Assistant

COMMUNICATIONS
Alan Harrison
Director of Marketing &
Communications
Jeffery Fickes
Public Relations Manager
Tiffany Diamond
Advertising Manager
Tom Milewski
Marketing Graphic Designer
Beth Anderson
Sales Manager
Sarah Bowes
Publications Manager
Kevin Lynch
Telephone Campaign Manager
Matt Henry
Telephone Room Manager
Sydney Allrud
Tom Barnes
Chris Boscia
Scott Goodrich
Andrew Higgins
Mike Uetz
Telephone Representatives

BOX OFFICE
Tridib Pal
Ticket Services Manager
Robert Lawson
Subscriber Services Supervisor
Robert Knop
Box Office Supervisor
Rosa Alvarez
Becky Kruger
Heather Moore
Erik Rader
Elisabeth Sanborn
Jasson Scully
Stephanie Stroud
Anthony Trunzo
Customer Service Representatives

FRONT OF HOUSE
Reiner Peery
Audience Services Manager
Michael Betts
Torrie McDonald
Assistant Audience Services
Managers
Patty Mondo
Assistant Lobby Manager
Sheryl Kossi
ASL Program Coordinator

DEVELOPMENT
Christine A. Fiedler
Director of Development
Suzanne Fortier
Manager Corporate and
Foundation Relations
Dawn Rains
Major Gifts Manager
Jenny Selby
Grants Manager
Anne Shrauner
Development Operations
Manager
Kimberly Gonzales
Annual Fund Manager
Rachel Whalen
Special Events Manager
Anne Copeland
Development Associate

FINANCE & ADMINISTRATION
Rachel M. Robert. CPA
Director of Finance and
Administration
Jim Neese
Payroll Specialist
Peter Spieker
Accounting Specialist
Randi Rourke
Operations & Events
Manager
Dan Gilbert
Information Systems
Manager
David Gehrman
Inez Lindsey
John R. MeNamara
Receptionists

PROFESSIONAL ARTS TRAINING PROGRAM
Matthew Montelongo
Hedda Sjogren
Acting Interns
Carrie Ryan
Artistic Intern - 5th Avenue
Theatre Fund
Carolyn Casselman
Arts Management Intern
Aimee Fettinger
Kira Knight
Costume Design Interns
Bonnie Hill
Costume Shop Intern
Jana Gollinger
Development Intern
Shannon O'Donnell
Directing Intern
Amy Waschke
Education & Outreach Intern
Kristine Young
Graphic Design Intern
Heather Wood
Production Management Intern
Janelle Baarspul
Properties Intern
Trevaughn Bynum
Owen Collins
Scenic Arts Interns
Lindsay A. Beacham
Heather Beckett
Chenos Torklep
Stage Management Interns
Marc Saunders
Technical Production Intern

Source: Seattle Repertory Theatre 1997-98 Program, Vol 17, No. 6/7. Copyright 1997, Used with permission.

The levels of management   The organizational chart should act like a map in depicting all of the levels of management (upper, middle, and lower). In Figure 6–2, the upper level is represented by the artistic director and the managing director. The production manager and the technical director can be identified as middle management, and the scene shop manager as lower-level management. This hierarchy theoretically reflects how information flows and work objectives are carried out in the organization. For example, one would expect the marketing/PR director to be the person passing along the information about the shows to the press relations and ticket office staff.

As an organization grows, the layers of management also tend to grow. When an arts organization first begins to operate, it usually has three levels of management: upper, middle and lower. Each level is staffed minimally and each person fulfills several major job functions. For example, if you call the artistic director of a new dance company, the phone most probably will be answered by a lower level administrative assistant who will connect you to the director. This administrative assistant most probably provides support for most, if not all, the artistic and management staff. Now assume our dance company is successful and expands its operation. It adds an associate artistic director, establishes a central receptionist to take all calls, and hires an assistant to the artistic director. Your call will now be taken by a receptionist, who in turn transfers you to the assistant to the artistic director, who then connects you to the associate artistic director. The associate artistic director screens the call to see if you really need to speak to the artistic director. By the way, when this type of scenario actually exists, it might be time to reexamine how many levels management the organization really needs.

Lines of communication   Finally, the organizational chart should represent the lines of communication throughout the hierarchy. For example, the scene shop manager tells the technical director that he or she will have to go overbudget to complete the set as designed. The technical director informs the production manager of the situation. The production manager informs the artistic director, who in turn communicates to the managing director. In theory, the upper managers decide what they want to do, and that decision is passed back down through the hierarchy.

Informal Structure

Every organization has an informal organizational structure. Good managers remain aware of this underlying framework and use it to their advantage. At the same time, they must discern when this informal structure is damaging the organization and hindering the achievement of its overall objectives.

One reason why an informal structure exists is to fill in the gaps in the formal structure. Interactions in an organization involve people, and that translates into complexity and a subtlety no chart could capture. Inventive employees will find a way to get things done in the organization with or without using the formal structure. For example, suppose the scene shop manager wants a new table saw, but the technical director has refused to act on the request for months. At a cast party, the shop manager casually lets the production manager know that his department could speed up the set construction process if only it had that new saw. A crafty shop manager who uses this informal communication system properly may end up with a new saw before the technical director knows what has happened. The shop manager also will enhance his or her status with the shop staff because of this ability to get what is needed despite the system. In so doing, he or she unwittingly may send a message to the staff that it is all right to bypass your supervisor to get things done.

Problems inherent in the informal system   This example points out some of the problems with the informal structure. One major fault is that the informal structure diverts efforts from the important objectives of the organization. This shadow organization may be concerned more with personal status.

Another difficulty with the informal organization is its resistance to change. You may define new objectives and marshal your resources to put a new procedure in place, but if the informal organization rallies around the "old way," your efforts may be in vain.

As we saw in the example of the table saw, an alternative communication system usually accompanies the informal structure. One key element of this informal system is the rumor-spreading mechanism. Arts organizations, despite the common perception, are no more and no less prone to rumor spreading than other businesses. The rumor mill usually is a prime source of informal communication in a performing arts setting. Good managers will determine how the informal communication system works in their organization to track what employees really are saying about the workplace. From time to time, it can be useful to feed information into the rumor mill. For example, you might let it leak that upper management is not happy with the lax compliance with the new no-smoking policy. If carefully leaked, the rumor might create greater adherence to the new rule when staff members think there will be consequences if they continue their current behavior.

All organizations have these shadow structures. The sooner managers become informed about them, the better they will be able to monitor and influence them.

Structure from an Arts Manager's Perspective

General Considerations

The complexity of the organizational structure should be directly related to the size and scope of the operation. It is a good practice to keep the structure to a minimum. There are no rules about how much structure is required. If an arts organization's mission is to further its art and serve the public good, creating elaborate organizational charts may be diverting time and energy. To help keep organizational design in perspective, consider the five elements that are often listed as influences on the final design: strategy, people, size, technology, and environment.[14] Of these five influences, strategy, people, and size have the most direct applications to the arts.

Strategy   The organizational structure should be designed to support the organization's overall strategy. For example, if you are starting a new regional opera company, your objective might be to build a subscription base as quickly as possible. Your strategy in building that base might be to select your season around well-known titles with famous guest singers. Your organizational design therefore would stress more staff to take care of the guest artists and carry out the organization's marketing, public and press relations, and ticket sales. To maximize resources, your strategy also would include keeping your operating costs as low as possible. One way to do that would be to rent all the sets and costumes for the season. You therefore would need only a relatively small production department and no resident design staff.

A few years later, you might expand your audience development strategy by adding a community outreach program. Now your objective is to hire a tour director and a small staff to promote and support bringing opera scenes into schools. You might consider reorganizing another area within your existing organization to save on the expense of adding staff. Either way, you must make changes in the organization's design.

One reason why new programs of activity sometimes suffer in an organization is that no one has thought about what was going to be done by whom. Without careful thought about job design, an organization can quickly overload an employee with too many tasks.

People The most important element in any organization is the people who work within the overall structure. Realistically, there must be flexibility between the structure and the person in an arts organization. The military is a prime example of a rigid organizational structure designed to mold its "employees" to the specific jobs at hand. A strict hierarchy and adherence to numerous rules and regulations both are focused toward a set of specific objectives. People usually do not join the staff of an arts organization because they want a rigid, highly controlled work environment. In fact, people who work in arts organizations often are highly self-motivated, and they vigorously resist regimentation.

Care must be taken when applying organizational theory to real organizations. In an arts organization, for example, the degree of structure varies with the type of job. For example, the director of a museum probably would be wise to allow for a degree of creative independence among the department heads of the curatorial staff. The security guards, on the other hand, would have a rigid work schedule with little independence.

Size When an arts organization is first established, no more than three or four people may be doing all the jobs in the organization. The artistic director may direct the operas, write the brochure copy, hire the singers and the artistic staff, and raise all the funds. As the organization grows—a board of directors is added; staff specialists are hired to do the marketing, scheduling, advertising; and so on—the simple organizational chart and lines of communication suddenly become much more complicated. In management theory, the organization would be said to be moving from an *agency form* to a *functional department form*.[15] An *agency form of management* refers to a structure in which everyone reports to one boss, and this boss provides all of the coordination. Each staff member is in effect an extension of the boss. When an arts organization decides to hire a marketing director, it may be because the artistic director no longer can supervise all of these activities. A new department with a specific function and the support staff to do the marketing would be established in this scenario. Problems and conflicts will arise if the artistic director attempts to give direct orders to the staff of the marketing director instead of going through the new structure.

Technology and environment   The other elements that influence organizational design are technology and environment. I did not list these as primary influences because of what I perceive to be the unique place of arts organizations in the overall business world. When speaking of the influence of technology in the business world, it is easier to see how new systems and methods can affect how products are produced. There usually is a direct connection between how an organization is structured and how technology may help it become more productive. For example, a large company may add a whole department to do nothing but assess new technologies and advise about their application to that business. Arts organizations, on the other hand, have used new technologies in office and information management and, in limited ways, applied new approaches to the technical production aspects of their operations. However, the technological changes do not radically transform what the arts organization does or how it goes about preparing or delivering its product. The addition of staff in such areas as computer support probably is the most obvious change found in many arts organizations.

External environments   The political and legal environments may legislate new laws that affect hiring or training in the organization. For example, virtually no affirmative action or health and safety programs could be found in arts organizations 25 years ago. Today, some staff members probably are designated to administer and monitor these areas in the organization. In addition, the ever-increasing complexity of tax laws and compliance with proliferating local, state, and federal regulations no doubt has added to the workload of the finance and accounting departments of many arts organizations.

Departmentalization

To *departmentalize*, or to set up departments in an organization, simply means "grouping people and activities together under the supervision of a manager."[16] Departments may be structured in three ways: by function, by division, and by matrix.

Function   Most arts organizations use a structure defined by functional departments. It makes sense to group people by the specialized functions they perform within the organization. Figure 6–2 shows how the production manager of a theater company supervises the functional departments of scenery, costumes, lighting, and sound.

Divisions   Departments can be organized around a product or a territory. An example on a small scale is a major arts center that not only hosts touring productions but also produces its own shows, runs a gift shop and art gallery, and operates a restaurant. An organization may decide to establish a divisional structure that keeps booking, production, exhibition, and food services separate. The logic behind this choice is that each activity involves very different operating conditions with specialized supervision and staff needs. The division in charge of production might include a marketing person to supervise the subscription series for the regular events. The division in charge of touring might employ another person to market the organization's shows to other arts centers and producers. Both employees are marketing specialists, but they market their products from very different perspectives.

Another divisional structure would be by territory. If a dance company decides to pursue a strategy of dual-city operations, one of the first steps would be to establish an organizational structure to staff two different geographical sites. There would have to be some staff duplication. You cannot expect the city A marketing staff to do the marketing for city B without local staff designated for each campaign.

Matrix   The most complex structure is a matrix organizational structure. The matrix is created by overlaying the departmental and functional organizations in a vertical and horizontal pattern. The matrix system was created in the late 1950s by the cofounder of TRW, Inc., Simon Ramo.[17] The department structure proved to be inadequate when TRW tried to manage several technologically complex projects for the defense industry. Ramo's scheme was to use a department structure for important activities like research and development (R&D) and place the department under the control of a department head. However, within the R&D department were smaller groups of people working on different projects under the supervision of a project manager. The vertical matrix in the structure therefore is the department head to the various R&D groups. The horizontal matrix consists of the individual project managers working with the separate R&D groups.

In an arts organization, a matrix structure often evolves, although no one actually plans a change to this type of structure. For example, suppose that a museum is organized around a department structure. The six departments are responsible for various sections of the collection, and other departments take care of marketing, fund raising, operations, maintenance, accounting, and payroll. The museum's centennial is coming up in three years. A staff member is designated the director of the centennial events. If this project director is to create a successful celebration of all the things the museum has done in the last 100 years, a matrix structure must be created. The project director will require that each department head designate a person to be the centennial coordinator for that department. In addition to their regular duties, members of the marketing staff also will work on this special project.

Arts organizations often find themselves involved in special projects. However, with no recognition of the need to shift to a matrix organizational structure, trouble may occur. For example, if the added staff members required to make a special project work are not hired, the project coordinator will have to work horizontally through the organizational structure. He or she will discover that the overworked staff in the various departments lack the time to give to the project or, worse, the staff members will find the time at the expense of their regular responsibilities and the effectiveness of the entire organization will suffer.

Another example of the matrix organizational structure in an arts organization is shown in Figure 6–4. A matrix working relationship is formed between the resident design staff and the guest directors or choreographers that may come into this regional arts organization. The staff members are hired by the organization and may work within their separate departments. When a guest director or choreographer arrives, this staff now has a new "boss," specifically for a particular show. A good production manager will recognize this matrix structure and establish the needed lines of communication to keep all of these overlapping projects on track.

Figure 6-4

Simplified Matrix Organizational Chart for a Project - or Production-Driven Organization

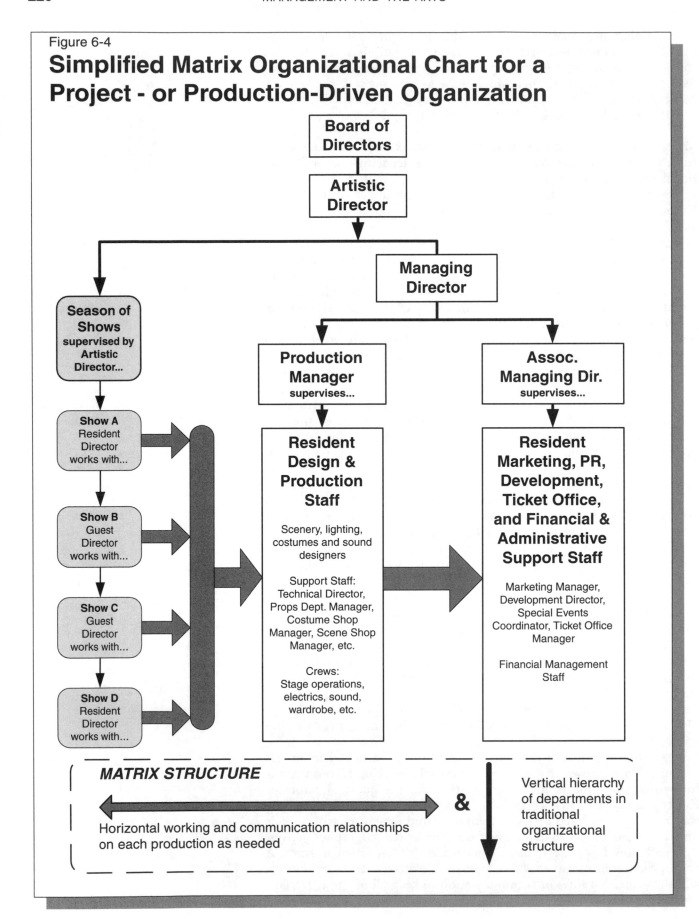

Coordination

A principal concept in organizing any enterprise is coordination. Coordination can be divided into vertical and horizontal components. The first area of concern, *vertical coordination*, is defined as "the process of using a hierarchy of authority to integrate the activities of various departments and projects within an organization."[18] Vertical coordination is split into four areas: chain of command, span of control, delegation, and centralization-decentralization. Each of these has applications to arts groups.

Horizontal coordination simply refers to the process of integrating activities across the organization. Many arts organizations use this structure to promote interdepartmental cooperation.

Vertical Coordination

Chain of command   Classic management theory, as noted in Chapter 3 in Fayol's Fourteen Principles, states that "there should be a clear and unbroken chain of command linking every person in the organization with successively higher levels of authority."[19] This is known as the *scalar principle*. The military is a good example of this concept of chain of command applied completely. Your common sense should tell you that problems will develop in an organization that lacks a clear authority and clear lines of communication. On the other hand, not all situations allow for a clear "unbroken chain of command" within an organization. A small arts organization may hire an administrative assistant to work for several people and departments. On paper, the job description says the "administrative assistant is supervised by the managing director." However, as the organization grows, the assistant is asked to complete work for the artistic director, the new marketing director, the newly formed fund raising department, and others. Unless the staff member is extremely good at time management and setting priorities, work may become backed up or simply not be done. In this example, too many people have authority to ask the secretary to work for them. Ironically, what often happens is that, to survive in the job, the administrative assistant becomes the person determining what work is done for who and when. The administrative assistant becomes a de facto manager of the supervisors.

Span of control   The span of control describes how many people report to one person. There are no fixed rules about how much or how little span of control one person should have in an organization. The factors often cited in determining this are "(1) Similarity of functions supervised, (2) physical proximity of functions supervised, (3) complexity of functions supervised and (4) the required coordination among functions supervised."[20]

If the marketing director is asked to take over supervision of the fund raising and ticket service, there is a reasonable match between functional areas and a limited span of control. However, if the marketing director tries to take over management of the acting company—that is, becomes, in effect, the company manager—there may be problems. The needs of the acting company are not similar to the needs of the marketing department. Also the marketing director's expertise may be exceeded. The marketing director could supervise the company manager—the person responsible for seeing to all of the needs of the acting company—however, the marketing director may lack enough understanding of the job to know if it is being done properly.

An example of physical proximity in span of control occurs when the production manager is asked to supervise the activities in theaters in three different locations in the city. The production manager soon discovers that it is impossible to be in three places at once. Three staff assistants are needed, one for each theater. Similarly, if the functional areas become complex, as in the data-management system for an organization, you may need to reduce the span of control. The staff member in the accounting area, who became the "systems administrator" in the finance department by virtue of his or her knowledge no longer may be able to keep control of the expanded computer systems used in the marketing department, the box office, and fund raising. Either someone must be hired to coordinate the organization's computer needs or the accounting work of the existing staff member must be reduced.

Delegation   As a manager, you must decide how much day-to-day work you should do yourself and how much should be assigned to others. *Delegation* is "a distribution of work to others."[21] The process involves three steps: assigning duties, granting authority, and establishing an obligation. When you assign duties, you must have a solid understanding of the work to be done, and you must spend time in analyzing and communicating what you expect the employee to do.

Problems sometimes arise with the second step: granting authority. If the delegation process is to be effective, you must transfer some of your authority to the employee. If you do not grant that authority, it is difficult to establish an obligation on the part of the employee to assume the responsibility. For example, suppose that you delegate the responsibility of providing daily sales summaries for the organization to your ticket office manager, but you go down to the office the next day and run the numbers yourself. The ticket office manager will wonder what happened to this delegated responsibility if you duplicate his or her work. The employee will assume that you do not trust his or her work. A key principle to remember is that the "authority should equal the responsibility when you delegate work."[22] For example, if you give a staff member responsibility for a budget but then take away the authority to use the funds, you have undermined the delegation process.

No area creates more bad feelings than delegation. Overprotective managers tend to create employees who are bored with their jobs and not particularly committed to meeting the organization's objectives. Because they have not been given any real responsibility, they develop an attitude of "Don't ask me; I just work here." Meanwhile, the whole organization suffers because the manager is doing work that would be more effectively done by others.

Centralization-decentralization   This last area of vertical coordination simply refers to how the organization will concentrate or disperse authority. Colleges and universities are cited as examples of decentralized organizations. The individual departments (history, government, physics, and so on) often have autonomy over personnel and course offerings. The department heads report to a central authority—that is, the dean—but the faculty members of the department exercise a great deal of control over their own day-to-day activities. On the other hand, a large corporation may have a rigidly organized authority structure in which only designated managers have the authority to make decisions. In an arts organization, the degree of centralization or decentralization depends on the functional area. For example, the process of running a subscription or membership campaign requires a centralized authority structure. You cannot have several people autonomously making key decisions about the campaign. To control the look and language of the campaign, one person must make the final decisions. In other areas, it may be more efficient to decentralize the authority. For example, the production manager delegates the purchasing of production supplies (lumber, fabric, steel, paint, and so on) to the technical director. The technical director then delegates the purchasing to the individual department heads.

Horizontal Coordination

Horizontal coordination is a key function in the matrix organizational structure. In the business world, the function of horizontal coordination most often is identified with such areas as personnel and accounting. All the departments in the organization use the personnel department as a resource for hiring, firing, and evaluating employees. Payroll is a good example of another department that has a horizontal relationship to a vertical structure. Everyone in the organization is affected by the payroll department. Organizations could not function effectively if every department handled its own payroll.

In an arts organization, similar personnel and payroll functions may cut across departmental lines. As already noted, the project orientation of many arts organizations creates the need for horizontal coordination. A successful production, concert, or exhibition often requires that different departments cooperate and communicate over an extended period of time. For example, a stage manager must be able to coordinate with what is called *functional authority*. This authority allows the stage manager to cut across the formal chain of command. When a problem backstage needs to be solved instantly, the state manager can issue orders that bypass the traditional crew head hierarchy.

When an event is presented by an organization, horizontal coordination typically is shown through the formation of a production team. The heavy emphasis on team management as an innovative approach to solving problems in the business world over the last 20 years, in fact, is standard operating procedure in the arts. Without effective horizontal coordination, a theater, dance, or concert performance suffers. When the performance style does not match well with the scenery, lighting, and costumes design, the problems most probably can be traced back to a breakdown in the coordination among the designers and the director.

Organizational Growth

Organizations seem to have a way of growing beyond anyone's original expectations. As one sage wit once noted, "The number of people in any working group tends to increase regardless of the amount of work to be done."[23] Almost constant attention must be paid to the proliferation of staff members with each new cycle of strategic planning. As new plans are implemented, the workload seems to increase, so new staff members are hired and more levels of management are put into place. The production manager now has three production assistants. The secretary is now the director of office operations and has three administrative assistants. This growth carries with it increased costs to the organization. The cycle of overloading the current staff, hiring new staff members to help reduce the overload, overloading the budget, laying off the new staff members, thus overloading the original staff, and so on can be avoided if the manager remains in control of the planning function. One element of planning is keeping accurate records of where you have been. Tracking the growth of a department over a period of time can be a helpful way to monitor growth. In my comparison of staff growth in arts organizations over the last 20 years, I found that increases of 25 to 125 percent were not uncommon. This is all the more significant when it is realized that many of these organizations were only doing 5 to 10 percent more programming.

Managers must think of the design of the organization as a creative challenge and not a burden. As we have seen, the manager's job is to anticipate and solve problems. Lack of attention to problems with organizational design can lead to fundamental flaws in the operation of the enterprise, and these flaws could lead to the demise of the organization.

Corporate Culture and the Arts

Theory versus Reality in Organizations

In the last 20 years, management experts have found that organizations behave in ways that the theories cannot always explain. As you would expect, no theory of organizational design can take into account all the variables that affect businesses. One of the more interesting approaches to analyzing how organizations behave may be found in Terrence Deal and Allen Kennedy's *Corporate Cultures: The Rites and Rituals of Corporate Life*.[24] The basic premise of the book is that organizations are social systems, and these social systems are based on the shared values, beliefs, myths, rituals, language, and behavioral patterns of the employees. All these factors are carried on from year to year over the life of the organization. A manager may find comfort in the structure, policies and procedures of the company, but in reality, these things are not necessarily why people choose to work in the organization. Deal and Kennedy list five elements in the corporate culture: (1) the business environment, (2) values, (3) heroes, (4) rites and rituals, and (5) the cultural network. As you will see, this study of corporate for-profit organizations intersects with the arts world at several points.

Application to the Arts

Because many arts organizations are going through the transition from a strong founder-director orientation to a system with professional staff and volunteer board management, it is worthwhile to take a brief look at the cultural aspects of an organization. Also important is to gain insight into the rites and rituals that may affect your ability to function effectively within the formal and informal structure of an organization. Let us look briefly at each element of the corporate culture and examine how arts managers may benefit from a keen awareness of this often-overlooked aspect of organizational life.

Five Elements of Corporate Culture

Business environment   As previously noted, organizations function in relation to various political, educational, technological, cultural, and economic environments. Deal and Kennedy found that "to succeed in the marketplace, each company must carry out certain kinds of activities very well. . . . This business environment is the single greatest influence in shaping a corporate culture."[25]

The authors identify four types of organizational cultures. As with all classification systems, the reader should keep in mind that creative combinations of some or all of the types may exist in complex organizations. Deal and Kennedy note that companies in highly competitive markets tend to develop approaches that stress a *work hard/ play hard culture* to keep the sales force motivated. Companies like McDonalds, Xerox, and Mary Kay Cosmetics are cited as examples. Other cultures present the *tough-guy or macho culture*, which includes people in high-risk businesses who get quick feedback on their decisions. Such businesses include construction, advertising, and entertainment. The *bet-your-company culture* functions in the world of high risk and slow feedback. Large oil companies and the aircraft industry are examples of companies that must wait a long time before their decisions pay off. Finally, there is the *process culture*, a low-risk, slow-feedback business world. Government, heavily regulated industries like utilities, and financial service organizations tend to have this type of culture. The very low level of feedback "forces employees to focus on how they do something, not what they do."[26]

Arts organizations may take on some combination of these cultures, depending on the circumstances. For example, a newly formed dance company may have a driven leader who creates an ongoing culture of risk taking. As the organization establishes itself—a board of directors is formed; foundation, corporate, and public grants are found—another culture with a more process-orientated approach may evolve. The organization shifts from operating on the edge to focus on a more stable and long-term perspective. As a matter of fact, there is an inherent conflict between the risk-taking and process cultures. This may explain why many arts organizations go through a great deal of personnel turmoil between artistic directors and boards. For example, a conservative board may want to move the organization in a different direction than that desired by the adventurous artistic director. Employees within the arts organization become caught in the conflict. A strong artistic director, creating a culture in the organization that stresses taking risks, will want to be surrounded by like-minded people.

Values The values of the organization define the criteria for employee success and tell the employee what is important to the organization. These values usually are communicated through a corporate slogan (Ford Motors: "Quality is job one"; General Electric: "Quality is our most important product") or through glossy annual reports. Arts organizations usually produce annual reports, and the comments by the artistic director or chair of the board illustrate the values stressed by the leadership. For example, a 1989–90 annual report by the American Repertory Theatre in Cambridge, Massachusetts, places a high value on "the presentation of challenging and innovative works."[27]

Although it is important to communicate values to the public, it is more important that the employees of the organization know how their work is guided by these values. A strong culture will reinforce the organization's values at every opportunity. This is not easy in a complex arts organization. For example, the artistic director may not direct every production in a season. Guest directors may bring into the organization values that are at odds with the organization's leadership. This requires that the staff constantly adapt to changing values. The entire strength of the organization's culture can be eroded if the problem is ignored. On the other hand, contrasting cultures could be used to advantage by deliberately creating the value, "We stress diversity."

Strong artistic leadership should bring with it a strong culture with clear values to which everyone in the organization can subscribe. A cutting-edge dance company, led by a true experimenter, that tries successfully to work with a managing director who thinks the sun rises and sets on nineteenth-century story ballets will experience a major conflict of cultures and values. The staff will notice these differences in obvious and subtle ways, and the overall enterprise will be hampered by such extreme contrasts.

Heroes   The expression of the organization's culture most often can be found in the person filling the key leadership role in the corporation or arts organization. For example, Lee Iaccoca functioned as his company's hero-rescuer and used commercials to project Chrysler's corporate culture as an aggressive, quality-orientated, customer-driven business. On the other hand, Ford Motor company used commercials of its employees articulating their commitment to quality in an effort to stress how much the company values its employees and, in a sense, to make them the heroes.

Arts organizations, especially founder-directed groups, look to the artistic director, music director, and so on to set the tone for the organization. This person should be a role model who can articulate the mission and values of the organization. A strong leader sets the standards for performance, motivates employees, and helps to carry on the history of the organization. Unfortunately, the true hero-leader is a rare creature. A hero-leader need not necessarily be loved by all of the employees, but he or she certainly needs to be respected.

Arts organizations often experience a great deal of dislocation when a powerful founder-director leaves the organization. The death of Robert Joffery sent the Joffery Ballet reeling for several seasons. George Szell's death forced the Cleveland Orchestra into a long period of readjustment. The departure of Rudolf Bing from the Metropolitan Opera in 1972 created a significant change in the corporate culture of that organization.

Rites and rituals   Just as the larger culture in a society has various rites and rituals to assimilate its people, organizations have routines and patterns of behavior that they expect their employees to follow. These may be yearly ceremonies or daily activities, but in either case, the objective is to show employees how to behave. In an organization with a strong culture, the message about what is expected of employees is communicated clearly. Observing the way things get done usually is the first contact an employee has with the culture of an organization. The employee's initial orientation sets out the norms of behavior and performance. If carefully orchestrated, Deal and Kennedy point out, organizations will develop symbolic actions to help reinforce the values and beliefs of the company. They cite a number of social and management rituals that organizations adopt to surround employees with the organization, such as company recognition awards, clinics, and company newsletters.

In the arts, rites and rituals extend throughout various organizations. The mere act of giving a public performance or putting on an exhibition connects the organization to the culture at large. Hundreds of different ways of doing things become established routine within the organization. Rehearsal and production schedules, performer warm-ups, backstage behavior, exhibition installation, and recognition of individual excellence all help to shape the culture of the organization. Each art form has its own sets of rites and rituals in addition to those associated with the individual company. Dancers, actors, singers, musicians, directors, designers, technicians, and craftspeople all have ways of doing things that feel comfortable and make sense to them. In fact, these rites and rituals are often so ingrained that people are not aware of them until conflicting cultures are introduced. A company of actors accustomed to working in a general pattern with a resident director may have trouble adapting to a guest director who brings very different values and approaches to the rehearsal process. Being aware of these rites and rituals and carefully channeling them can help build a strong and positive culture in an arts organization. On the other hand, ignoring cultural clashes of rites and rituals can lead to a breakdown of the spirit of an entire group of artists.

The cultural network   The last element that Deal and Kennedy discuss is the internal communication system, which acts as a network to circulate the values of the corporate culture. As noted before, organizations have both formal and informal structures. The "hidden hierarchy" in an organization's culture includes the storytellers, spies, priests, and others who create the overall environment in the organization.[28] The authors accurately identify various characters who play roles in the culture. For example, the storytellers are good at putting incidents in the organization into a reality that others can understand. Storytellers usually add to and embellish the event, and as you would expect, the good ones develop an audience of rapt listeners. Storytellers can help provide a sense of history and perspective for new employees. They also can be conduits for passing along the myths and rituals of the organization. The organization's priests take on the role of confessors, arbitrators of moral dilemmas, and symbols of the mature and serious view of the organization. Spies function as they do in the general society. They look beyond the surface to what is going on behind the scenes. As the authors point out, "Truly effective spies never say a bad word about anybody and are thus much loved as well as much needed. . . . Sharp spies keep their fingers on the pulse of the organization."[29]

Because the cultural network does not appear in the organizational chart or memos or published reports, managers must learn to tap into the network to stay on top of what employees are thinking and feeling about the organization. Deal and Kennedy recommend that managers stay in contact with the storytellers and priests, in particular.

In an arts organization, it is particularly important to remain plugged into the cultural network. The ability to manage and shape this network can be especially important when an arts group finds itself in financial trouble, and people begin to fear for their jobs. In addition, as arts organizations attempt to reach out to diversify their audiences and their staffs, entire new cultural perspectives will enter into the mix. For example, employees from different cultural and ethnic backgrounds will bring values and beliefs that may initially conflict with the prevailing culture of the organization. Managers need to be sensitive to the ethical issues of trying to reprogram staff members to following the company culture at the expense of their belief system. It is important that everyone be aware of and support the organization's goals and objectives. However, care must be taken not to create an organization with

FYI—A Book of Interest

The Addictive Organization, by Anne Wilson Schaef and Diane Fassel, explains "Why we overwork, cover up, pick up the pieces, please the boss and perpetuate sick organizations."

In this chapter, we have been examining the theory and practice of organizational design. Once an organization is in operation, it is important to evaluate constantly its "health." Organizations, like people, can become ill with a variety of "diseases." *The Addictive Organization* is one of the more interesting management and psychology books to be published on the subject of organizational illness. The authors take the perspective that organizations and individuals exhibit addictive behaviors that lead to their own self-destruction. Schaef and Fassel first identify the addictive system and the terms and characteristic behavior of people in the addictive system. Then they look at the four major forms of addiction in organizations. They wrap up their study with a look at the recovery process and the long-term implications of addictive organizations.

Arts organizations suffer from the same pattern of addictive behavior as large corporations. At the heart of the matter is what is best described as the addictive tendency in humans. Research points to the possibility that humans, by their genetic composition, are susceptible to addictive attachments to a variety of substances. When this research is coupled with a larger culture that stresses and rewards certain types of addictive behavior, you have an unhealthy situation. It is not an exaggeration to say that some people "work themselves to death." Arts organizations often are built on a cultural value system that stresses a willingness to sacrifice yourself for the good of the art form: You will work long hours for very little pay, often under hazardous conditions, and say you "love it!"

With the understanding that it can sometimes be misleading to quote out of context, here are two quotes from the section on "The Organization as the Addictive Substance" in *The Addictive Organization*:

Organizations function as the addictive substance in the lives of many people. We recognize that for many people, the workplace, the job, and the organization were the central foci of their lives. Because the organization was so primary in their lives, because they were totally preoccupied with it, they begin to lose touch with other aspects of their lives and gradually gave up what they knew, felt and believed. (p. 119)

The organization becomes the addictive substance for its employees when the employees become hooked on the promise of the mission and choose not to look at how the system is really operating. The organization becomes an addictive substance when its actions are excused because it has a lofty mission. We have found an inverse correlation between the loftiness of the mission and the congruence between stated and unstated goals. (p 123)

SOURCE: Anne Wilson Schaef and Diane Fassel, *The Addictive Organization* (New York: Harper and Row, 1988).

such a rigid corporate culture that it forces people into uncomfortable circumstances.

Corporate Cultures and the Real World

When you start a new job, you are brought into an organization's cultural system. It may be a very strong culture that stresses maximum performance at all times, or it may be a very relaxed culture that stresses slow and steady progress. No matter where the culture fits along this continuum, it will fit somewhere. The sooner you recognize it, the sooner you can adapt to it as needed. For example, if you go to work for a marketing director in an arts organization that prides itself on huge leaps in its subscriber base each season, you had better be ready to adopt the attitudes and beliefs that go along with the job or you will find yourself outside the system and eventually out of a job. On the other hand, once you have established yourself as a manager in the organization and have come to know the culture, you can begin to alter it to better achieve the overall goals and objectives established in your strategic plans. Remember, the culture of an organization is not static. It adapts to changes in the internal and external forces that affect the organization.

Summary

Organizing is the second basic function of management. Organizations are collections of people in a division of labor who work together for a common purpose. Organizing makes clear what everyone is to do, who is in charge, channels of communication, and resource allocation. Managers should organize for results. Organizational charts provide a map of the organization's formal structure. All organizations also have informal structures, which managers should monitor. Organizations can be designed to use functional, divisional, or matrix structures or a combination of these. Organizations use vertical and horizontal structures and coordination to operate effectively. They may take on organic or mechanistic structures, depending on what they do. All organizations have social systems that define a distinctive culture for that organization. Strong leadership helps define the culture. Organizational design is affected by the organization's culture and social systems.

Key Terms and Concepts

Organization
Organizing
Open system model of organizational design
Bureaucracy
Mechanistic versus organic organizations
Organizational structure
Organizational chart
Division of work
Informal organizational structure
Agency form of management
Functional department management
Departmentalization
Division structure
Matrix structure
Vertical coordination
Chain of command, or the scalar principle
Span of control
Delegation
Centralization versus decentralization
Horizontal coordination
Corporate culture

Questions

1. What are the formal and informal organizational structures of the theater, dance, music, or art department at your college or university?

Do these structures effectively support the mission of the department? Explain how. How would you reorganize the department to make it more effectively support the mission of the university?

2. Can you cite examples of breakdowns in the vertical or horizontal coordination on a project or production with which you were recently involved? How would you improve the coordination systems to minimize these problems in the future?

3. Based on your own work experience, identify as many of the values, behavior patterns, language, rites, and rituals that formed the corporate culture of the organization.

Case Study

The following excerpt from a 1991 article in the *Chronicle of Philanthropy* provides a good example of how the concepts from Chapters 5 and 6 can be put to use. Assume that further changes in the Kennedy Center's organization structure have taken place since this was published. You may consult the Web site for the Kennedy Center at http://www.kennedy-center.org/history/kctoday.html.

An Arts Institution's Management Overhaul
Plagued by a persistent deficit, Washington's Kennedy Center turns to techniques used by for-profit companies.
Vince Stehle

WASHINGTON—The John F. Kennedy Center for the Performing Arts here is trying to raise its standards of performance, from backstage to the board room.

After a year-long review, the center is making changes in its fund raising and marketing departments, as well as in other administrative offices, to bring the performance of its management team into line with the quality of its presentations on stage—and to erase a persistent multimillion-dollar deficit.

While many non-profits engage in strategic planning to improve their operations, the Kennedy Center's effort is unusual because of the depth of financial analysis it entailed and because it is based largely in techniques used by for-profit businesses.

The review prompted numerous changes in various departments and has led to more cooperation between divisions to make the center more efficient as a whole. . . .

James D. Wolfensohn, the respected New York investment banker who took over as the Kennedy Center's chairman and chief executive officer 18 months ago, has restructured the senior management team at the institution, delegating day-to-day control to a new official, the chief operating officer.

Many of the changes at the Kennedy Center were suggested by Cannon Devane Associates, a management-consulting firm in Washington. The management-review process began over a year ago, in June, when Mr. Wolfensohn, who works part-time as chairman, accepted an offer from Martin Cannon, the president of the firm, who volunteered to sort out the center's management systems on a pro bono basis. The two men had worked together as advisers in the sale of a major hotel chain.

In analyzing the center's management, says Mr. Cannon, he found that many of the same questions facing for-profit business companies applied to non-profit organizations.

"The reassuring message is that there are capabilities that have been largely devoted to the management of the for-profit business sector that are very relevant to the center's business operations," says Mr. Cannon. "And they should not feel embarrassed to call upon those capabilities. Successful businesses do it all the time. . .."

[The Process]

After several months of analyzing the center's finances and management practices, [Mr. Cannon] says, the management study revealed numerous untapped sources of revenue, including greater potential income from the box office and private fund-raising efforts.

The consultants then began gathering information, including financial data from all the center's departments, data about competing local performing-arts institutions, and demographic information about the Washington metropolitan area. Some of the findings demonstrated that the Kennedy Center had some serious troubles:

- During the late 1980's, more than a third of the center's subscribers had failed to renew their subscriptions, and single-ticket sales had fallen sharply . . .
- Private donations . . . remained virtually flat from 1985 to 1990, while the costs of raising funds jumped from 13 percent to 18 percent of contributions.

In addition to the vast array of facts and figures, the consultants solicited the opinions of any staff member who wanted to be interviewed. Given the understanding that all interviews would be confidential, over 100 members of the 186-member staff agreed to talk to the consultants. . . .

Taking all the evidence together, Mr. Cannon presented two scenarios. In one, the center could continue business as usual, increasing its annual operating deficit from $3.9 million in 1990 to $6.3 million in 1993. In the other, Mr. Cannon showed how, by cutting costs and increasing revenues, the center could actually realize a $9.2 million surplus by 1993.

Cannon Devane projected that, among other things, administrative overhead costs and production costs could be trimmed by about $1.3 million, in part by establishing a single procedure for negotiating contracts that would cover the Kennedy Center employees and outside producers alike. . . .

[Implementation]

Despite the importance of a healthy balance sheet, most people at the Kennedy Center said they believed that financial considerations must be tailored to the center's mission statement, and not the reverse. So, before committing to the new regime, senior staff members created a new "vision" statement for the center. The statement says the center will "embody, stimulate, and transmit the values of freedom, creativity, expression, and joy inherent in the performing arts" and it will present high-quality, diverse performances and try to attract a wide audience.

Once the new mission statement was adopted, each department began drawing up new plans, setting goals and priorities consistent with the statement. Those plans are still under review by the new chief operating officer, Lawrence J. Wilker, former president and chief operating officer of the Playhouse Square Foundation in Cleveland. Even though Mr. Wilker hasn't made final decisions about the changes that will be made, some new programs and policies have already begun. . . .

New Fund-Raising Efforts Begun
Special Festivals
The center sponsored a "Texas Festival," which was the first Kennedy Center festival to focus on the arts of a single state. The event, which included performances by the Houston Ballet, the Texas Boys Choir, and the Dallas Symphony Orchestra, as well as a popular music program known as the Roadhouse Cafe, helped raise $2.4 million in contributions from corporations, foundations, and individuals, which more than paid for the additional costs associated with the festival.

New Policy for Board Members
The center's Board of Trustees agreed to form a fund-raising committee and approved a resolution suggesting, but not requiring, that all trustees either give, or obtain from others, commitments each year to give $100,000, payable over three years.

Giving Clubs
Two new giving clubs for donors have been set up: the "100 Club," for companies that give at least $100,000 over three years, and "The Trustees' Circle," for individual donors who do the same. The club has attracted 61 members so far.

The center's marketing department has adopted new policies and programs designed to attract new subscribers and, in some cases, to assist fund raisers. For example, last season the marketing department designed a deeply discounted subscription package—three concerts at half price—at the request of the development department. . . .

Another of the management review's findings involved the high cost of attracting new subscribers. . . . The expense of promoting the institution to new customers prompted the management consultants to suggest that subscribing should be made easier, and that complaints be dealt with long before a customer became disillusioned.

A Window into What Didn't Work
In response, the center has made numerous changes to make it easier for subscribers to exchange tickets and make sure that patrons will have no difficulty finding their way to the six different theaters in the complex or getting something to eat in a hurry before performances.

Still, it's difficult for the administrative staff, most of whom work during the day, to know what's happening in the evening, when most of the center's performances take place.

"We'd get in the office, and the first phone call at 10 o'-clock was from an irate patron, and that was your window into what didn't work the night before," says Geraldine Ottremba, director of government relations.

"The obvious solution is to train people to solve problems as they happen."

In addition, she says, when customers now call to complain, the call is not passed around, "in what we affectionately called 'Kennedy Center roulette.'" Instead, all complaints are now routed to a central customer-service office. "Now you have a fairly accurate picture of what your complaint level is, and you have people who are trained to make reparations, whose goal is to recover that patron immediately, and not let them off the phone until they are satisfied. . . ."

Source: Vince Stehle, "An Arts Institution's Management Overhaul," *The Chronicle of Philanthropy* (September 24, 1991). Copyright © 1991, The Chronicle of Philanthropy. Used with permission.

Case Study Questions

1. Summarize the main changes made in the Kennedy Center's management structure, as noted in the article.
2. Based on the information in the article, how would you characterize the management structure of the center? For example, is it hierarchical, divisional, or a matrix?
3. What changes in the corporate culture of the center are implied in the reorganization plans?

References

1. John R. Schermerhorn, Jr., *Management for Productivity*, 2d ed. (New York: John Wiley and Sons, 1986), p. 20.
2. Ibid., p. 161.
3. Ibid.
4. Ibid., p. 162.
5. Ibid., p. 163.
6. Ibid., p. 190.
7. Ibid., p. 191.
8. Ibid., p. 188.
9. James Q. Wilson, *Bureaucracy: What Government Agencies Do and Why They Do It* (New York: Basic Books, 1989), p. x.
10. Schermerhorn, *Management for Productivity*, p. 163.
11. Ibid., p. 164.
12. Ibid.
13. 1997–98 Seattle Repertory Theatre season program, vol. 17, nos. 6–7, p. 23.
14. Schermerhorn, *Management for Productivity*, p. 167.
15. Arthur G. Bedeian, *Management* (New York: Dryden Press, 1986), p. 258.
16. Schermerhorn, *Management for Productivity*, p. 169.
17. Bedeian, *Management*, p. 265.
18. Schermerhorn, *Management for Productivity*, p. 173.
19. Ibid., p. 174.

20. Ibid.
21. Ibid., p. 176.
22. Ibid., p. 177.
23. Arthur Bloch, *The Complete Murphy's Law* (Los Angeles: Price-Stern-Sloan, 1990), p. 62.
24. Terrence E. Deal and Allen A. Kennedy, *Corporate Cultures: The Rites and Rituals of Corporate Life* (Reading, MA: Addison-Wesley, 1982).
25. Ibid., pp. 13, 14.
26. Ibid., p. 119.
27. Barbara W. Grossman, *Annual Report 1989–90 of the American Repertory Theatre* (Seattle: American Repertory Theatre, 1990), p. 2.
28. Deal and Kennedy, *Corporate Cultures*, p. 85.
29. Ibid., p. 94.

Staffing the Organization

7

◻ ◻ ◻ ◻ ◻

The last two chapters covered the areas of planning and organizational design. We saw how the mission of an organization becomes the foundation on which the strategic and operational plans are built. Specific goals and objectives then are established. The plans also details how human and financial resources are to be used to meet the organization's goals and objectives. The organizing process is designed to move plans from an idea to a reality. The manager designs the organization to fulfill the plans. The structure of the organization, the lines of communication, and the combinations of vertical, horizontal, and matrix relationships are established among the departments and projects. Departments and other subunits are created to support the plan effectively.

The next stage in the process of creating an organization is staffing it. The human resources required to fulfill the mission and support the strategic and operational plans of the organization become the key element in the success or failure of an enterprise. The organization's strategic and operational plans also must provide staffing objectives. Descriptions of jobs and the complex working relationships among employees must be carefully factored into the organization.

Arts organizations face numerous challenges when it comes to staffing. An arts manager must be aware of the laws regulating employment and versed in the art of negotiation. Several unions may represent employee groups throughout the organization, and they may have different contract periods. The task of finding the right people for the jobs, keeping them, and developing them is a never-ending process.

The Staffing Process

All organizations want to fill their jobs with the best people available. Finding the most talented, qualified, and motivated people to work with you is much harder than it sounds. To make the overall system clear, we break down the staffing process into six basic parts: planning, recruiting, selecting, orienting, training, and replacing.[1] We also look at how this process varies across the fields of theater, dance, opera, music, and museums. Figure 7–1 provides an overview of the entire human resource management staffing process. As you might expect, there are variations between and within various art forms.

In the business world, the somewhat imposing-sounding phrase *human resources planning* simply translates into analyzing your staffing needs and then identifying the various activities you need to undertake to make the organization function effectively. In many large corporations, a manager identifies specific staffing needs to determine where human resources are required. The manager then works with the human

125

Figure 7-1

Human Resource Management Staffing Process

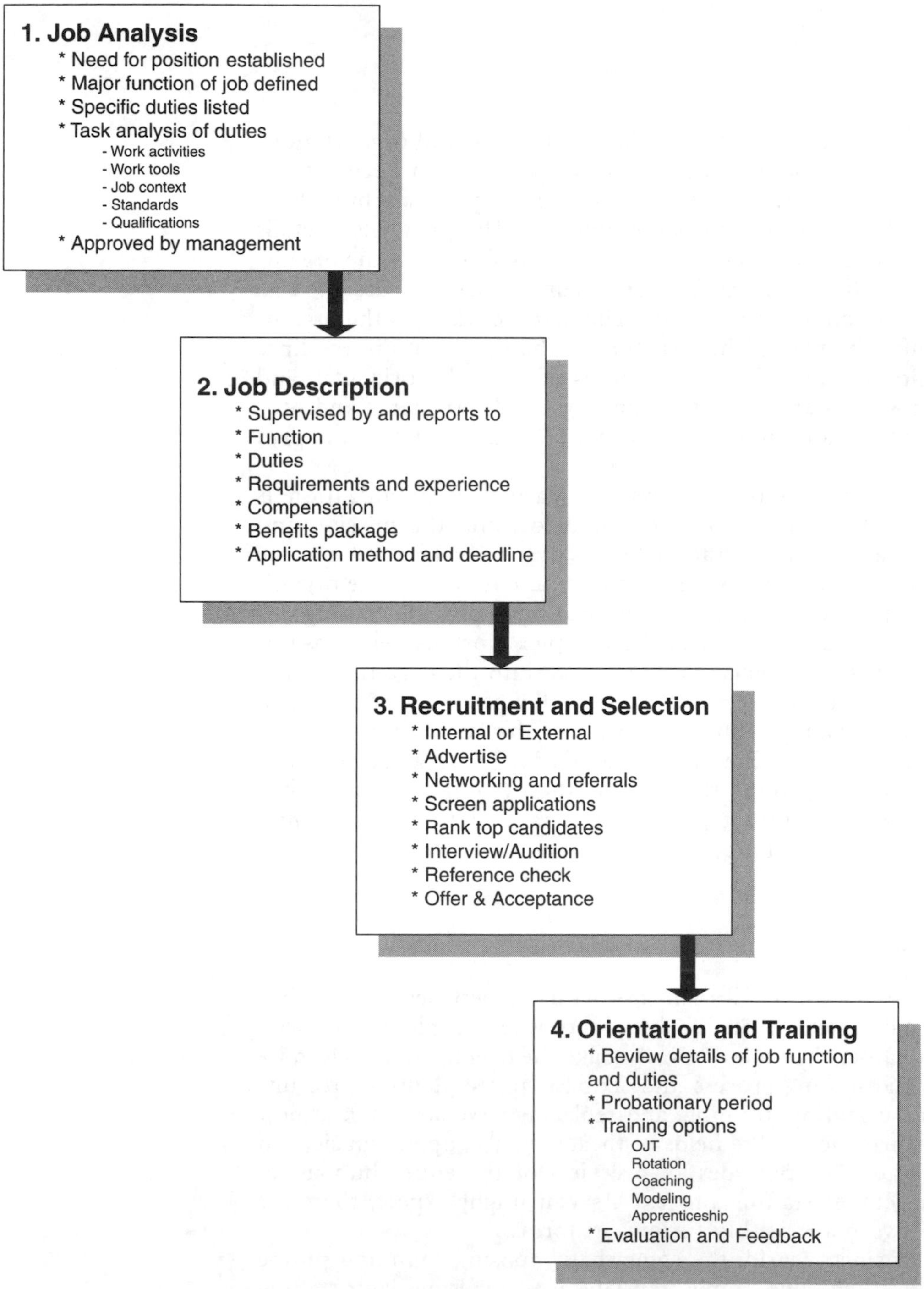

1. Job Analysis
 * Need for position established
 * Major function of job defined
 * Specific duties listed
 * Task analysis of duties
    - Work activities
    - Work tools
    - Job context
    - Standards
    - Qualifications
 * Approved by management

2. Job Description
 * Supervised by and reports to
 * Function
 * Duties
 * Requirements and experience
 * Compensation
 * Benefits package
 * Application method and deadline

3. Recruitment and Selection
 * Internal or External
 * Advertise
 * Networking and referrals
 * Screen applications
 * Rank top candidates
 * Interview/Audition
 * Reference check
 * Offer & Acceptance

4. Orientation and Training
 * Review details of job function and duties
 * Probationary period
 * Training options
    OJT
    Rotation
    Coaching
    Modeling
    Apprenticeship
 * Evaluation and Feedback

resources or personnel department to find the required staff. Because most arts organizations have no human resources department, it becomes all the more important for the manager to have an excellent grasp of the rules and regulations controlling the hiring and firing of employees. Mistakes in these areas can be very costly. More and more organizations face lawsuits because of badly handled personnel decisions. Given the often informal circumstances surrounding the hiring of people in the arts, it is surprising that lawsuits are not more frequent. Let us look at the steps involved in planning for the people needed to make the performance or exhibition possible.

Job Analysis

The process of finding out who you need must be based on careful thought. What are the planning objectives of the organization? Everyone would agree an arts organization would want to hire the most talented artists. However, how are you going to judge the quality of your artists? What screening process will ensure you have the best people your organization can afford? Your organization may have larger goals about the composition of the total staff for the organization. Do you have a commitment to diversity in the workplace? How can you ensure that minority-group applicants apply for the openings you advertise? Will your workplace accommodate individuals with disabilities? Whatever the circumstances, the planning phase requires that you review five key areas for all of the jobs in the organization: work activities, work tools, job context, standards, and personnel qualifications?

Work activities　What is to be done? A performing arts organization obviously will need actors, singers, dancers, or musicians. Plans for the season often dictate the range of performers the organization will need.

Based on your organization's design (as illustrated in its organizational chart), you should be able to create a clear distribution for the rest of the staff you need. In arts organizations, where staff resources usually are very limited, it is critical that the manager carefully analyze how to combine the work activities to get the most productivity from each person.

Work tools　Some employees will need specific tools to do their jobs. For example, a regional ballet company that decides to set up its own scenery and costume shop will need thousands of dollars for equipment and space rental. An organization that hires a marketing director had better be ready to provide the computer equipment and software he or she will need to do the job.

Job context　Each employee will have an overall context in which he or she will function. Performers have a set rehearsal and performance schedule, office personnel work within a daily schedule, and all employees work within an overall package that includes contracts, compensation, and benefits.

Standards　The manager of an organization must set clear standards for work output and quality. The manager of an arts organization may have various degrees of control, depending on contracts and agreements. The music director of the symphony and possibly a select group from the ensemble may be responsible for maintaining the performance standards at the highest level. On the other hand, complex negotiated agreements may limit the actions that the management may take to dismiss a musician who is not performing up to the standard.

Personnel qualifications   The level of education and experience required for each position may vary widely in an organization. The process used to select performers requires different personnel qualifications than that used to hire ticket office salespeople.

Job Description
From this analysis, the manager will be able to create a job description for the new position. The description, which is widely distributed to the labor market, usually covers six areas: general description, responsibilities, specific duties, requirements for employment, compensation, and application method.[2]

The "Sample Job Description" shows how a report of a staff opening might be worded. A shortened version of this description normally appears in a newspaper or job placement listing service such as *Art-SEARCH*. Let us look briefly at each section of this description.

General description   The opening paragraph describes who is looking for someone to fill what position and for what length of employment. The opening also clarifies to whom the employee reports and is supervised by. Regardless of the exact wording chosen, these basic ingredients can be used in any job description.

Responsibilities   The next section of the description lists the employee's general responsibilities in the job. This example clarifies the scope of the job, the types of events done, and the departments producing the events.

Specific duties   Here you have the opportunity to list the tasks you expect the employee to carry out on a regular basis. In the example, the duties are ranked in order of frequency. Items 1, 2, and 3 are daily and weekly tasks; items 4 through 7 occur on a monthly or semiannual basis. You can extrapolate this section to almost any job in the organization. The wording will be different, but performers, shop staff, ushers, museum guards, curators, and so on all have lists of specific duties.

Requirements for employment   The education, experience, and specific knowledge, skills, and abilities required are listed in this section. The *KSAs*, as they are often called, are important indicators for you in the screening process. Does the person have knowledge of the area of the position you are trying to fill? Does he or she have proven skills in specific tasks you need done? Do the person have the general abilities to succeed in the job as defined? You can further clarify your KSAs by indicating which are required and which are desired. You may require someone to have skills in specific software applications, but desire that he or she speaks a second language. This does not mean that the employee must have these skills. In fact, he or she may bring unanticipated skills to the job that will benefit your organization.

Compensation   There are differing opinions about what to list for salary information. In some cases, unions may require that the salary be stated in the advertisement. In other cases, you may use a range to suggest some latitude in the salary to be offered. For example, "in the mid-

Sample Job Description

The Harper Performing Arts Center invites applications for the position of Ticket Service Manager. This is a full-time, 12-month administrative staff position supervised by and reporting to the Managing Director.

Responsibilities
The incumbent will have general responsibility for the sales and accounting of individual tickets and subscriptions for productions produced by the Performing Arts Center. The Ticket Service Manager will perform the following duties:

1. Provide daily operation of a ticket service in a courteous and efficient manner through telephone sales, exchanges, and reservations. In addition, he or she will process mail order, email and voice mail message sales orders.
2. Using a computerized ticketing system account for daily income and issue timely sales and deposit reports. In cooperation with other staff members maintain a ledger file of revenue from cash sales, credit card charges, money orders, and open accounts.
3. Provide general information in response to inquiries about the Performing Arts Center and various performing arts events.
4. Update information on the Ticket Service web site on a regular basis.
5. Train and supervise a staff of three and volunteer assistants in customer relations, subscription and single ticket sales, and general box office procedures.
6. Assist with marketing projects as needed and specifically with the following: (1) manage the ticket service and supervise the concession operations the night of performances; (2) train and supervise a house manager and ushers.
7. Assist with the maintenance and development of mailing lists for arts events.
8. Provide statistical reports on sales, subscriptions, and attendance at arts events during the year.
9. Perform other related duties as required.

Requirements
Three or more years of experience in box office management and sales required. A proven track record of positive interactions with customers and staff required. Other desired qualifications include a performing arts background, excellent computer skills, and familiarity with office equipment.

Compensation
Salary commensurate with experience, [or you could say the starting salary is in the upper $20s]. Full benefits package available.

Applications
Send cover letter, current resume, and three letters of reference to the Human Resources Dept., Harper Performing Arts Center, and so forth. EEO/AA.

20s" may mean as little as $23,000 to as much as $27,000. Other listings will simply say "compensation commensurate with experience." This could create budget problems for a manager when it comes time to negotiate a salary offer. For example, you would waste time by taking an applicant who is making $40,000 through the entire application process for a $30,000 job. One way to cover this contingency is to be sure that you clearly state the experience level required for the job in the requirements section. If you require a MFA (Master of Fine Arts) or equivalent experience, the applicant may take that to mean at least three years of work. This is based on the fact that most MFA programs require three years to earn the degree. In the long run, you may save yourself and the applicant a great deal of confusion if you are clear about the compensation levels at the beginning.

Benefits   The term *full benefits* usually means the following:

• Health insurance
• Life insurance

- Disability insurance
- Retirement benefits

The benefits package an arts organization can offer is a budget decision in many cases. The costs of benefits can run as much as 30 percent of an employee's salary. In addition, many arts organizations expect employees to pay a portion of the health insurance. The employees share may be as high as 50 percent.

Application method   The final section of the job description explains what is required for the application, when the application is due, and to whom it should be sent. This is the appropriate place to state your concerns about seeking applications from special constituencies. You also will want to include your participation in equal-opportunity employment process.

The Overall Matrix of Jobs

In the initial stages of forming an organization, a great deal of time must be spent determining the minimum number of people required to operate the enterprise. This task is best done by identifying the key functions the organization must do to present its programming. For example, if your organization presents concerts of chamber music, a series of major activities will have be done if you want to sell tickets for performance on a specific night in a specific place. As you begin to get a clearer picture of the overall scope of the jobs required to make the organization function, your job descriptions should reflect how you are going to achieve your objectives. The number of full-time and part-time employees and how they all relate to the performance season or exhibition schedule becomes the foundation of your operating budget. When salary and benefits often account for up to 80 percent of an organization's budget, it is critical that the manager keep the overall picture of the staffing as clear as possible. This overview should make the planning process easier. For example, when it comes time to initiate a new program or project, being able to look at the overall organizational structure can prove helpful. Being able to see where you can make adjustments and predict the possible impact of staffing changes should make the planning process less difficult.

Constraints on Staffing

The costs related to staffing a position play a key part in the constraints placed on managers. For example, if you hire an administrative assistant for $20,000, your first-year costs must include another $8,000 for benefits and taxes. If you consider a $28,000 staff position over a five-year period, assuming an inflation rate of 3 percent, your salary and benefits cost for this position will be in excess of $32,000 by the fifth year. Over five years, you will have paid out more than $153,000 in salary and benefits. This cost does not include any equipment or extra training the employee may require. Assuming that you are able to justify the expense for the staff addition, you must still face the ever-increasing complexity of laws and regulations that control hiring in the United States.

Government regulations   Arts organizations are not exempted from the rules and regulations on hiring. The Equal Employment Opportunity Commission (EEOC) rules generally apply to all private and public organizations that employ 15 or more people. In addition, some state laws supplement various federal laws. In Chapter 4, we discussed the impact of the political and legal environment on arts organizations. Here are examples of some of the major pieces of federal legislation that affect the hiring process:

- The Title VII Civil Rights Act (1964) and the Equal Employment Opportunity Act (1972) prohibit employment discrimination based on race, color, religion, sex, or national origin.
- The Equal Pay Act (1963) prohibits wage discrimination based on sex. The law requires equal pay for equal work regardless of sex.
- The Age Discrimination Act (1967; amended 1973) protects people from 40 to 70 years old against discriminatory hiring.
- The Rehabilitation Act (1973) provides for affirmative action programs for hiring, placing, and advancing people with disabilities.
- The Mandatory Retirement Act; Employment Retirement Income Security Act (1974) was designed to prohibit mandatory retirement before age 70. The law also provides for some pension rights for employees.
- The Privacy Act (1974) gives employees the right to examine letters of reference in their personnel files.
- The Pregnancy Discrimination Act (1978) requires pregnancy and maternity to be treated as a legal disability.
- Immigration Reform and Control Act of 1986 requires employers to check identities and work authorization papers of all employees.
- The Americans with Disabilities Act (1990) requires businesses and public services to open up jobs and facilities to disabled people.
- Older Workers Benefit Protection Act (1990) prohibits age discrimination in employee benefits.
- Civil Rights Act of 1991 strengthens Title VII of the 1964 Civil Rights Act, granting the opportunity for compensatory damages and clarifying obligations of employers and employees in unintentional discrimination cases.
- Family and Medical Leave Act (1993) allows for up to 12 weeks of unpaid leave during a year for the birth or adoption of a child, family health needs, or the employee's own health needs.

Organized labor   An organization required to employ people working under a union contract must adopt rules and policies for employment that fulfill specific legal procedures agreed to by the union and the management. Although union membership has been dropping steadily since 1956,[3] a variety of unions represent various employment groups in the arts and entertainment industries. Unions represent artists and craftspeople, such as actors, singers, musicians, writers, directors, choreographers, and technicians. In addition, specific contracts with unions like the Teamsters (they may control the loading and unloading of trucks at the performance space) might be required in larger metropolitan areas.

The human resource function of an arts organization must take into account the myriad of rules and regulations that typically accompany a union contract. We will discuss this area later in this chapter under the heading "Unions and the Arts."

Recruitment

Depending on the situation, you may face many or few choices in filling a staff position. The range involves the limits placed on the overall contractual relationship between the employees and the employer. If you need an extra electrician for a lighting setup in a union theater, the local sends over whomever it has. If, on the other hand, you need to fill the position of head electrician for the theater complex, you take steps similar to filling a salaried staff opening. The three steps in recruiting for a standard staff position are advertising the opening, screening possible candidates, and critically evaluating possible candidates for a list of finalists.

Internal   As you may know, many jobs are filled before anyone hears about the openings. The internal recruitment process is common in companies that have a promote-from-within policy. For example, if you are hired as the assistant to the marketing director for the museum and you are aware that the promotion policy favors internal candidates, you may have an additional motivation to do your best work. In fact, many organizations lose good employees because there is no room for advancement within the organization.

External   Many arts organizations use a dual policy of internal and external recruitment. As organizations seek to create a more multicultural staff, active external recruitment has become a regular procedure. When doing external recruiting, there are various avenues to pursue, depending on what you seek. Some organizations may arrange auditions just to build files of possible performers for the future. Specialized publications like *ArtSEARCH*[4] can be used to seek out executive and administrative staff members, designers, technicians, and craftspeople. Trade newspapers covering the arts may be found in some of the larger cities. General publication newspapers also may be used. Mailings to universities and colleagues can generate applications. Finally, a professional recruitment service can be hired to find candidates for higher level positions. Although "headhunter" services may be an extra expense, they may also generate the most likely candidates for executive level positions, such as museum director or artistic director. Also, a designated subcommittee of the board may carry out searches for executive-level personnel.

Recruitment philosophy   There are two fairly common philosophies about recruiting.[5] One approach assumes a traditional "selling" of the organization, and the other takes the "realistic," or real-time, approach. In the selling approach, you stress the most positive features of the job and the work environment. Essentially, you try to present an upbeat picture of the organization. The real-time approach tries to depict accurately what day-to-day life is like in the organization. You try to present an objective view of the work situation and are not shy about answering questions about the less positive aspects of working in the organization. Organizations often blend these two approaches in their recruitment campaigns, but the tendency is to sell the organization. After all, who wants to paint a picture that might scare off the applicants? People involved in the recruitment process have been known to use the realistic approach to discourage candidates that they perceive as not being "right" for the company. Obviously care must be taken when selling the organization in the recruitment process. A candidate who frames the wrong picture of the organization could be very unhappy once in the job. This may hasten his or her departure and require yet another employee search.

Recruitment difficulties Arts and other nonprofit organizations have complex personnel needs like any other business. Arts organizations hire people for vastly different jobs in meeting their objectives. Recruiting a soprano for an opera, hiring a marketing director, filling an administrative assistant position, and negotiating a union contract with the musicians or stagehands requires different priorities and strategies. Staff recruiting for salaried positions often is difficult because many arts organizations do not offer competitive pay rates. Artists, on the other hand, often negotiate contracts through their agents that exceed union scale minimums. Employees who work for wages negotiated by union representation may receive pay at rates comparable to those of private industry. This may lead to pay disparities that have a negative impact on recruitment strategies.

Trying to attract quality candidates to staff positions with no advancement possibilities, low salary, minimal—if any—benefits, and an overwhelming workload is a difficult task. It is not surprising that there is a high turnover rate in lower-level staff positions. Ironically, the people in these positions often do the basic work that keeps the organization going, such as payroll taxes, ticket office sales, or shop work. Competent, skilled administrative staff members are needed to ensure that the organization complies with all of the federal, state, and local laws pertaining to collecting and reporting taxes. Your ticket office can help build a positive relationship with the community. Without skilled help in your shops, shows will not be of a high enough quality. Some of the lowest paid positions in an arts organization typically fall into these categories.

Selection Process
Auditions Different selection processes are used for different employee groups. All performers may be selected by audition, depending on how the schedule is organized. For example, most resident theater companies now hold auditions in New York and a few other selected cities at various times during the year. Very few theater companies have actors in residence for a full season. Ballet companies, on the other hand, have yearly auditions for a resident group of dancers. Smaller dance companies try to provide at least 26-week contracts for their dancers. Lead dancers for special performances in the repertory may be contracted as the need arises. The larger regional opera companies, which have lengthy seasons, tend to audition resident choruses, dancers, and musicians and hire the principal singers and conductors on a show-by-show basis. Smaller regional opera companies often work with a minimal staff and contract for all singers, dancers, and musicians on a show-by-show basis. Larger orchestras usually have a blind audition process in which the musician plays behind a screen so the judgment about his or her musicianship is based on sound alone. The competition for places in the major orchestras is very stiff. Regional and smaller orchestras also have some type of audition process. However, the limited performance schedule may mean

In the News 1

American Theatre magazine sponsored a debate entitled "On Cultural Power" in January 1997 at the Town Hall in New York City. Robert Brustein, artistic director for the American Repertory Theatre and playwright August Wilson met to carry on a dialogue about issues of race, casting, funding, multiculturalism and arts and society. The issues raised have implications for arts managers trying to address programming and staffing that reflect the diversity of the audiences and the workforce. As reported by Stephen Nunns, the spirited discussion, which was punctuated by heckling, touched on subjects such as ebonics, colorblind casting, and questions about the validity of Black History Month as a way to effectively serve African-Americans audiences. Discussion raised questions such as "Is the classic American image of the 'melting pot' a thing of the past? Is the country metamorphosing from a democracy to a 'meritocracy'? What does the future hold for (in Brustein's words) the only hyphenated nation on earth"?

Source: "Wilson, Brustein and the Press," *American Theatre* (March 1997), pp. 17–19. *American Theatre* is published by the Theatre Communications Group.

the players hold other full-time jobs as music teachers in schools and universities.

The audition process requires a great deal of data management. Records, which may include photos, lists of special skills, and so on, must be organized so that they can be retrieved easily. An audition space with a piano, tape player, dressing room, and warm-up areas must be secured. If union contracts are in force, restrictions may apply to a variety of actions taken by management. For example, Actor's Equity Association contract with League of Resident Theaters (LORT) contains dozens of stipulations about auditions.[6]

Ultimately, the organization's survival depends on its ability to select the right talent for the positions available. Since the performer is the product that the audience "purchases," it is critical that the artistic management establish criteria that match the company's desired quality level. A poor casting choice or a weak player can bring down the overall quality of the artistic product.

Traditional application process The typical pattern for filling many staff positions in an arts organization follows these six steps: formal application, screening, interviewing, testing, reference check, and hiring.[6] Let's take a brief look at each stage.

Formal application Standard forms are used to take applications for job openings. Arts organizations often invite applications and request a cover letter, a résumé, and three or four references. In some cases, organizations actively seek out specific individuals and ask them to apply for the opening. The advantage of the application form becomes clear when you begin reviewing the candidates for the job. By using a similar format for gathering data, it may be easier to see which candidates have the qualifications you seek. When no formal application form exists, the person responsible for reviewing the files must develop a checklist of qualifications and requirements for the job. This checklist should be easily gathered from the job description you wrote.

Screening The next step requires narrowing the list of applicants by eliminating those who do not match your search criteria. Further fine tuning of the applicant pool usually reveals a short list of qualified candidates for the job. This work may be done by an individual or committee. For example, if the board is trying to hire a new artistic director, a search committee will be established and chaired by a board member. The screening process may become a very difficult stage in the hiring process because of strife within the organization. The search committee may be divided about the kind of person being sought, or the committee may arrive at a set of finalists that the rest of the board finds unacceptable. Needless to say, a significant number of variables can add to the complexity of the screening process.

Interviewing The interview is equivalent to the audition for a staff position. If the search is being conducted by a staff member (not a search committee), the usual procedure is to interview several of the top candidates and schedule second interviews for the best candidates. The committee approach may involve interviews with the top two or three candidates over a day or two by a wide range of people. Because the costs of conducting staff searches can run into the thousands of dollars, it is important to take the time to narrow the list of finalists before beginning the interview process. When pressed, some finalists may withdraw their candidacy, leaving you to fall back on other candidates on the list.

During the scheduled interviews, care must be taken to deal fairly with the candidates. Questions about age, marital status, family, national origin, handicaps, or religion are not legal. The same questions should be asked of each candidate, and they may be structured in such a way that you legally can discover whether the prospective employee can meet your work schedule, can communicate and write effectively, and can perform the specific tasks you require.

Prospective employees should not be permitted to leave the interview process with the impression that you were engaged in discriminatory activities. Your organization may have to answer to a lawsuit if you do not manage your interview process carefully.

Testing, reference check, and hiring   The decision to hire the candidate best suited for the job sometimes rests on intangible emotional responses. After you evaluate and compare the composite skills of the people most likely to fill the staffing needs of the organization, you may still be left with a high degree of uncertainty. Further background checks and additional on-site interviews may help. Ultimately, a degree of chance always is involved in hiring.

Many large corporations use detailed screening tests for applicants in an attempt to narrow down the variables involved in hiring. Psychological, medical, or specific skills tests often are administered in large companies. Because of the very high cost of hiring the wrong employee, corporations are not shy about spending several thousand dollars to hire the right person. On the other hand, the company's needs must be balanced against the individual's right to privacy.

Arts organizations must work with very limited recruitment budgets. High staff turnover creates an even greater burden on the budget because too much time is spent seeking replacements for people who quit. Few arts organizations have the time to conduct an extensive background check on a prospective employee. As a result, the organization may find its self on a hiring treadmill.

Legal issues also enter into the hiring process. If you narrow your candidates down to two or three finalists, the potential for sending misleading signals to the candidates is very high. You will need sufficient documentation to stand up in court about why you did not hire candidate B or C, should your decision be challenged. When you make any hiring decision, you face some risk that the rejected finalists will take legal action. This may sound pessimistic, but more organizations face lawsuits over hiring practices each year.

Orientation and Training
The fourth stage in the process begins once the hiring has been completed. There are countless variations on employee orientation. Some organizations have fixed probationary periods (three or six months) in which very specific activities are planned to acquaint the employee with the organization. In other cases, a new person is hired and told to direct any questions to a specific individual or mentor.

The most important element in the orientation process is the socialization of the new employee into the organization. New employees are often anxious about their new jobs. They want questions to be answered and clarifications made about where they fit into the entire operation.

Hiring Tip

A saying is often heard in the personnel field: "Hire the person who best fits the job, not necessarily the best qualified." This statement implies that you need not force yourself to hire the person with the most qualifications. Remember, the key factor in attaining the maximum productivity from a staff member is finding someone who matches the overall job environment. The person you hire must be compatible with the corporate culture of the organization. In some cases, hiring the most qualified (or overqualified) person can lead to problems.

The informal interactions new employees encounter will help shape their perceptions of the entire organization. To avoid problems later, it is best to schedule a review of the overall policies with new employees near the end of their probationary period. Also important is to note the date that you reviewed all the relevant material with the new employee. You later may incur a problem with an employee who claims to have never been told about a specific policy. It may prove helpful to document when you reviewed a specific problem area with the employee.

Training and development   In corporate America, millions of dollars are spent each year on employee training and development. Many employers need to train their workers in such basic areas as reading, writing, and simple mathematics. Due to their limited resources, arts organizations have no such training programs. Training usually takes place only after costly errors have been made by a new employee. Although employee training is recognized as a real cost to organizations, few take into account the financial impact of not having a training program.

On-the-job training   Most arts organizations use some variation of on-the-job training (OJT). The formal approach includes very specific work abilities that are tested by the supervisor at specific time intervals. The less formal approach usually includes quick demonstration sessions, and then the new employee is expected to get on with the task at hand. More rigorous OJT structures include some combination of job rotation, coaching, apprenticeship, and modeling.

Job rotation and cross-training   In this system, employees move around to different areas to receive training in specific activities. This is helpful when an employee later has to fill in for someone who may be out of the office. Organizations also often engage in cross-training their staff. The idea is always to have two people who can accomplish a set of tasks in the event someone is out of the office or leaves for another job. For example, having only one person who processes subscription orders could prove harmful to an organization dependent on daily sales revenue.

Coaching   As the term implies, a new employee receives very specific help with a skill related to the job. For example, an experienced stagehand may guide a new crew member through the operation of a follow spot. The stagehand watches the employee's performance and offers suggestions on improving his technique as he or she runs the spot.

Apprenticeships   The apprentice system is used extensively in the arts for training. Ideally, the apprentice works alongside a more experienced employee. If the system really is to function effectively, apprentices should be given specific tasks that allow them to assume substantial responsibility.

Modeling   In modeling, a new employee watches the performance of the supervisor or trainer. Personal demonstrations of what is expected help form a consistent presentation of the organization. This is especially important for employees who come into contact with the public. For example, people who sell subscriptions or museum memberships are involved in performance-related skills. They must be able to act out the script they have been provided to make the correct sales presentation. Watching and listening to a more experienced staff member go through the "scene" is a useful way to train a person.

Replacement and firing   You may have a number of reasons to replace an employee. You may have made a selection error that resulted in a poor match between the individual and the organization, or the person you hired may have outgrown the job. You may move someone to a new job and create a vacancy due to reorganization. The person you hired may have violated the rules and procedures of the organization, leaving you no choice but to fire him or her. You may experience a slowdown or budget cut that requires you to lay off someone, or an employee may develop an illness and be unable to work for an extended period. You may need to replace someone due to retirement or death or an employee who quit.

No part of the staffing process is more troubling than firing an employee. Obviously, care must be taken when firing someone because of the legal ramifications. A poorly handled employment termination can cost an organization millions of dollars. *Wrongful-discharge* suits, as they are called, are becoming more common in the not-for-profit sector. Assessing the risks of firing an employee has led to better evaluation and documentation procedures. Verbal and written warnings usually must precede a termination. Although a union contract may stipulate very precise steps that must be taken, it should not be assumed that it is impossible to fire a union employee. Clauses that provide for the rights of management usually address this issue. On the other hand, many people work with no contracts whatsoever. Most arts organizations hire staff under what is called *employment at will*. Simply stated, the employee can be fired at any time with no or limited notice but also may quit with the same limited notice. If you have provided some indication to an employee that his or her job performance is not satisfactory and you are operating in an employment-at-will environment, firing is best done swiftly. Typically, when someone resigns, the notification period is two weeks to 30 days. However, employment at will means that an employee may be fired at 9 A.M. and told to clear the office by noon.

Some upper-level management staff have very detailed contracts developed by their lawyers and the organization's legal advisers. Precise language is used to cover all aspects of compensation, evaluation, retirement, and termination.

Volunteers in the Arts

In addition to the paid staff, volunteers may constitute a significant portion of the workforce in an arts organization. There is a long history of volunteerism in a variety of nonprofit organizations in Americas, and in fact, the IRS provides the opportunity for a tax deduction for volunteers who assist nonprofit organizations.

The management of the volunteers often is a separate functional work area in the organization. The staff volunteer coordinator serves the important role of managing a resource that may save the organization thousands of dollars in staff salaries. However, the time and energy required to recruit, train, supervise, and evaluate volunteers can be considerable. Volunteers also have a different relationship to the organization, and therefore they must evaluated with criteria that are

In the News 2—High Court Extends Job-Bias Scope

WASHINGTON—The U.S. Supreme Court gave new legal protection Tuesday to workers who say their ex-bosses wrote bad references or took other vengeful action against them for filing discrimination claims.

In expanding the scope of federal civil-rights law, the justices handed a unanimous victory to Charles Robinson, a black man who was fired by Shell Oil Co. in 1991 after 11 years as a sales representative.

He filed a racial-bias charge with the U.S. Equal Employment Opportunity Commission. Four months after he was fired, and while his EEOC complaint was still awaiting action, Shell sent an unfavorable recommendation about him to a prospective employer, Metropolitan Life Insurance Co. Robinson did not get the job.

Maureen Mahoney, a Washington lawyer who represents employers, said she now expects employers to refuse to provide references or to require that employees surrender their right to sue in exchange for references.

The decision is expected to also help older people who have been fired, because the Age Discrimination in Employment Acts contains similar retaliation provisions.

SOURCE: "High Court Extends Job-Bias Scope," Knight-Ridder Washington Bureau (February 19, 1997). Copyright © Knight-Ridder/Tribune Information Services, 1997. Used with permission.

relevant. Most active volunteers come to the organization with a commitment that is refreshing. In other cases, the volunteer may possess special skills the organization can use in areas such as advertising, marketing, law, or accounting.

To effectively operate the usually understaffed arts organization, volunteers no doubt will be needed in many areas. They can help realize the mission of the organization and help fulfill the goals and objectives by covering key areas where staff resources are limited. However, for the volunteers to be effective, the same attention must be paid to their job descriptions, recruitment, and training as paid staff.

One obvious consideration in the use of volunteers is the risk factor. Management must assess the risk of using volunteers based on the work to be done. For example, it would probably be unwise to use a volunteer account or bookkeeper to manage the day-to-day financial activity of the organization. On the other hand, volunteers could be effective seeking renewals by calling lapsed subscribers or members. Their personal commitment to the organization may make them ideal salespeople. Assisting with specific group projects such as stuffing envelopes for a big renewal campaign can be a good affiliation-building experience. Many organizations have guilds that sponsor annual fund-raising events. The social element of the volunteer's participation in the organization can be a positive way to strengthen ties to the organization. Ultimately, a well-managed arts organization needs a volunteer staffing system that is an integral part of the overall operating plan.

The volunteer staffing system also has its disadvantages. For example, it is difficult to manage volunteers in the same manner as staff since they are not being paid. The working relationship between volunteers and staff may become strained, as can any working relationship. However, in this case, if your volunteer is also a major donor to the organization, how do you tell the person his or her "job" performance is not adequate? Kotler and Scheff, in *Standing Room Only*, point out organizations often do not anticipate full output from their volunteers:

> One manager of a large volunteer force has developed what he calls his "rule of thirds." One-third work of his volunteer workforce works avidly with very little direction and encouragement. One-third will work only with considerable motivation and are only effective with careful supervision. And one-third will not work at all under any circumstances . . .[7]

Regardless of how productive your volunteers may be, enormous benefit is to be had from a well-managed volunteer system. Since the model of so many arts organizations includes a volunteer board of directors and general volunteers working with a paid staff, the necessity of developing and maintaining a healthy organization requires a staffing plan that allows for and uses volunteers.

Unions and the Arts

Some of the unions involved in the arts are Actor's Equity Association (AEA) for actors and stage managers; American Federation of Musicians (AFM); American Guild of Musical Artists (AGMA); American Guild of Variety Artists (AGVA); American Federation of Television and Radio Artists (AFTRA) for performers; United Scenic Artists (USA) for scenery, costume, and lighting designers; and International Alliance of Theatrical Stage Employees and Motion Picture Machine Operators of the United

Sample Wording from a Contract

The following is from the Actor's Equity Association contract with the League of American Theatres and Producers for the time period of June 29, 1992 to June 30, 1996:

6. Billing
(A) House Boards
1) The names of all Actors employed in the production shall be listed on the house boards in the front of the theatre in letters no less than one-half (1/2) inch in height. Such house board shall be

entitled *"The Company."* Stage Managers, (and) Understudies . . . maybe listed separately.
a) The Producer agrees, in instances where there is no house board outside the theatre, to place one prominently inside the lobby.
b) At least one such house board with names in alphabetical order shall be displayed so as to be clearly visible to the public at all times.

2) Should the Producer fail to comply with this clause prior to the first performance, on the day following the giving of written notice, by the Actor or Equity, the Producer shall pay the Actor whose name is omitted, one-eighth (1/8) of the contractual salary for each performance that the violation continues to exist.

Source: "Agreement and Rules Governing Employment Under the Production Contract," Actor's Equity Association, 1993, pp. 11, 12.

States and Canada (IATSE) representing stagehands. Large organizations like the Metropolitan Opera in New York City must negotiate with multiple unions. The MET management must negotiate contracts with everyone from the musicians to the people who hang the posters in the marquees. Museums located in the larger cities also must work with unions who represent employees from many different groups, such as security guards.

Definition and Purpose

The classic definition of a *trade union* is a "continuous association of wage-earners for the purpose of maintaining or improving the conditions of their working lives."[8] Unions arose to fight the exploitation of employees, which, more often than not, was the norm. Although it might be argued that the unionization of the arts created a division between salaried artists and employees who are paid a wage, the reality is that unions are here to stay.

The union's primary responsibility to the workers is to derive benefits from the working relationship with the employer through a written contract. This contract is carefully negotiated by individuals elected by union members to represent them and designated representatives from management. The life of the contract generally is limited to two or three years. Although there are thousands of variations on the terms in a contract, the six key areas are

1. Compensation and benefits: pay increases and extent of benefits.
2. Job specifications: what exact duties will be proscribed for the employee?
3. Grievance procedures: in the event labor or management has a grievance, how will it be resolved?
4. Work rules: start and stop times, overtime, breaks.
5. Seniority rules: this often affects internal promotions and sets criteria.
6. Working conditions: health and safety, equipment provided, training.

FYI—Actor Salaries

Based on the AEA contract with the League of American Theatres and Producers, the minimum (many performers, stage managers, and designers negotiate salaries above the minimum) salaries for actors and stage managers in many Broadway theaters effective June 28, 1999 are

Actor: $1180 per week, 8 shows per week
Stage Manager:
  (Musical) $1939 per week, 8 shows per week
  (Drama) $1667 per week, 8 shows per week
Assistant Stage Managers:
  (Musical) $1534 per week, 8 shows per week
  (Drama) $1362 per week, 8 shows per week

Source: "Agreement and Rules Governing Employment Under the Production Contract," Actor's Equity Association, 1996, p. 3, of the addendum "Summary of Production Contract Negotiations Results."

In the News 3

Labor disputes usually are a result of a negotiation process that fails to satisfy the union's initial demand. Management typically brings to the bargaining table less than labor is willing to accept. The result can be a work stoppage. For example, on September 22, 1996, the Atlanta Symphony Orchestra went on strike for 10 weeks. The musicians had played for a month without a contract. In December, they signed a four-year agreement that provided an 8 percent increase over the life of the contract, a minimum salary of $62,500, and 95 tenured positions with the orchestra. The orchestra members wanted a greater say in the tenure review, the tour planning, and "revolving seating for string players."[9] Out West, the San Francisco Symphony Orchestra went on strike on December 4, 1996, to force a contract settlement. The negotiations had started in March 1996 and the then-current contract expired November 23, 1996. The musicians were seeking a 5.5 percent increase to bring their minimum salary to $78,520. They also were seeking a reduction in their performance schedule because of the high rate of repetitive stress injuries.[10]

In both cases the work stoppage had a detrimental effect on the orchestra's finances. However, the unions did make some progress in meeting their demand. The issue of repetitive stress injuries and health insurance coverage continues to be a subject in other orchestra contracts around the country.

Disputes

The agency most often involved in labor and management disputes is the National Labor Relations Board (NLRB). This organization investigates unfair labor practices by employers and unions. An NLRB representative listens to both sides of a dispute and renders a decision aimed at resolving the conflict. If either party is unhappy with the ruling, the court system is the next step. The high cost of litigation motivates both sides to try to reach an out-of-court agreement.

Many companies are now making use of mediation services to avoid prolonged NLRB process or the courts. Specialized firms now offer this service on a contract basis, helping companies keep down their legal costs. However, because the results of these mediations are binding, employees do not necessarily do as well as they would if they went to court. In fact, some critics have noted that, since the company hires the mediation firm, it tends to seek out firms that side with management more than labor.

Because the culture of many not-for-profit arts organizations stresses "giving to the cause," nonunion staff members tend to focus on horror stories about union abuses. The most common complaint is featherbedding, or creating jobs that really are not essential to the project. The unions often are blamed for creating a high overhead for professional productions. However, since the union's mandate is to achieve the best wages and working conditions for its membership, equally compelling arguments for the number of employees working an event can be made. From the union's perspective, having the correct number of workers at the event could be an important safety issue. This is especially true if the event has dangerous scenery changes or special effects or complex costume changes. The producer's goal, of course, is to keep the number of staff members as low as safely possible, because over the run of a show one extra person will add thousands of dollars to the cost of a show.

The 1980s saw a major shift in the way in which the business community dealt with unions. Led by President Ronald Reagan's dissolution of the air traffic controller's union, company after company simply let unions call strikes and then hired replacement workers. Management became much bolder in demanding concessions from the unions. Unions continued to fight a losing battle in the 1990s as more companies shifted work overseas. Well-paid union workers were seen by many companies as a liability, not an asset, in a competitive world economy. The cost of labor in the United States was simply too high, so many companies took the work elsewhere. Congress passed legislation requiring advanced notice of plant closings, but this had little effect on the trend.

For companies that stayed in America the strategy became to work in a more cooperative association with labor. Many union contracts began to include differential pay scales for those newly hired, reduced benefits, early retirement buyouts, and a modification of restrictive work rules. Many of these changes trickled down into negotiations between arts organizations, performing arts centers, producers, and the unions. These changes were not met with enthusiasm, and suspicion about the motives of management remained high

Unfortunately, an "us versus them" attitude is still very much a part of the day-to-day relationship of labor and management. The negotiation process often tends to set up a win-lose mentality, and that can lead to internal strife. To a large extent, the corporate culture of the arts organization can play a big part in forming the overall attitude about employees and the perceived value of their contribution to the organization's goals and objectives. If the organization's values express the attitude "We are here to do high-quality work as creatively and efficiently as possible, and we appreciate and reward people who have these work ethics," the odds are that the relations with the union will be fairly positive. However, if management's attitude is "You can't trust them, they always goof off, and they are slow to get work done," a work environment filled with suspicion and mistrust is reinforced. The union members and their leaders will be more likely to respond favorably if the culture of the organization is cooperative, not confrontational. However, if the union members, from the stagehand to the first violinist, feel that management is out to get them the entire artistic product may suffer. Cultivating good labor-management relationships in an arts organization must be a high priority from the board president on down.

Maintaining and Developing the Staff

If an organization is to be successful over the long run, it must have a dedicated and experienced staff. The only way to build such a staff is to monitor the work environment constantly. A good manager should be aware of the staff's changing needs. The degree of intervention exercised by the manager depends on whether problems have arisen that require correction.

The psychological atmosphere of the workplace changes almost every day. One of the most important parts of the manager's job is staying attuned to the mood of the workplace. You can employ several strategies to help you stay in touch with your employees. Organizations must develop ongoing systems to assess regularly employee concerns in the workplace. Annual or ongoing evaluations, scheduled project assessments, production meetings, informal lunch or dinner meetings, and awards for outstanding performance or achievement all form a menu of choices that an organization must have available (see "Performance Appraisal Systems" in Chapter 9).

Career Management

If an organization places a high value on employee retention, a career management system must be established. Employees need to believe that they are learning and growing in their jobs. Some ways to help employees develop a long-term commitment to the organization are to offer support for additional training, provide leaves of absence for outside study, and solicit employee input about job and work expectations. Obviously, there are limits to the amount of career enrichment available for every level within an organization, but the creative application of these ideas can help promote an organizational culture that places a high value on people. For example, it would be a mistake to assume that someone functioning as a receptionist is capable only of answering the phone and directing inquiries. It is true that this job is not a staff position with a great deal of potential for career development. However, by carefully designing the job to provide additional duties, such as assisting with gala event planning or conducting donor research, you may be able to make the job more challenging for an employee.

The "Right Staff"

The importance of staffing the organization cannot be stressed enough. All the neat and tidy organizational charts, beautifully detailed strategic

Personnel Odds and Ends

As this story demonstrates, employee problems can be manifested in various ways.

News of the Weird
Chuck Shepard

In May, Los Angeles Philharmonic bassist Barry Lieberman was suspended without pay for assaulting colleague Jack Cousin as they were leaving the stage after a performance. Lieberman alleged that, because of an ongoing dispute, he was justified in shoving his bass into the back of Cousin's legs to trip him as they were filing off the stage.

Source: Chuck Shepard, "News of the Weird," *Cleveland Plain Dealer* (January 6, 1991). Copyright ©1991 by the Cleveland Plain Dealer.

plans, forceful mission statements, and carefully designed marketing and fund-raising campaigns will be of no use without the people to make it all happen. To function effectively as an organization you must have the personnel with the skills and dedication suited to the mission. As you will see in the next chapter, the success or failure of an organization is related directly to the effectiveness of its leadership. Finding the right people for the jobs you have and building a team of productive staff members is one of the most difficult tasks a manager faces. In situation after situation, the failure to assemble the right combination of people on the workforce leads to the failure of organizations to achieve their aims. A symphony with a brilliant conductor is only as good as the musicians in the orchestra. The finest collection in a museum will fail to live up to its potential without an effective curatorial staff. A dynamic choreographer or director needs equally dynamic dancers, actors, or singers to grab the audience's interest and support.

Summary

The staffing process can be broken down into four major processes: job analysis, job description, recruitment and selection, and orientation and training. The analysis process assumes that you are staffing the organization to realize strategic and operational objectives. Job design helps integrate the staffing plan with specific job responsibilities and duties. Organizations must function within the laws that affect hiring personnel. Union contracts and stipulations are a fact of life in the arts. Arts managers must be well versed in negotiating contracts and structuring their organizations to work effectively with unions. The two major domains for recruitment are internal and external. Recruitment options include auditions and traditional application and screening processes. When interviewing candidates for jobs, managers must follow legal guidelines carefully. The hiring and orientation of new staff members can be aided by formal procedures to ensure that consistent information is presented. Job training and long-term staff development are key components in building an experienced and productive staff. Firing and replacing staff members can be legally risky if handled improperly.

Key Terms and Concepts

Human resources planning
Job description
KSAs
Job matrix
Equal Employment Opportunity Commission
On-the-job training
Wrongful discharge
Employment at will
National Labor Relations Board

Questions

1. Based on your own employment experiences, give an example of how the job requirements differed from the official job description. Relate the problems or benefits of the situation.

2. Discuss the pros and cons of unions in the arts. Make a case for each side of the argument.

3. Write a job description for a position in an arts organization using the style provided in the "Sample Job Description."

4. Have you ever gone through a formal job orientation? Was it an effective tool for bringing you into the work environment?

This 1988 article from the *New York Times* highlights a very important staffing issue facing arts organizations. While many of the participants in this debate have changed jobs or in some cases have passed away (e.g., Joe Papp), the issues remain fresh. The casting of a performance obviously says a great deal about the values and beliefs of the arts organization. Since the artists are the most visible part of the organization, the impression the public forms about the extent of diversity in your organization will be based on what it sees, not on what you say. As you read this article, try to keep in mind the perspective of art forms other than theater.

Case Study

Should Equal Opportunity Apply on the Stage?
Hal Gelb

James Earl Jones as Big Daddy, the patriarch of a powerful white Southern family?

"I'm not interested in seeing it, nor do I think it has any value other than as an actor's exercise," said Douglas Turner Ward, artistic director of the Negro Ensemble Company, when Mr. Jones was being considered for the role in a New York revival of "Cat on a Hot Tin Roof" to be mounted by Fran and Barry Weissler during the next year.

"'Cat on a Hot Tin Roof'," Mr. Ward continued, "came out of a specific historical-context which we are all a part of, a Mississippi in which the existence of a Big Daddy was founded on a racist World, and blacks weren't allowed access to any sort of power. I don't doubt that Jimmy could play the character wonderfully. But what interpretive weight are we giving to this role except to say, 'Oh, we're using this to overcome the social disadvantage of black actors'?"

Yet that is precisely what a current campaign to cast minority-group, female and handicapped actors in parts traditionally played by non-handicapped white males is attempting to do. And in fact, though Mr. Jones will not play Big Daddy in the forthcoming revival, he has already done so—during a symposium sponsored by Actors' Equity and designed to educate producers, directors and others in the merits of nontraditional casting. He has also played white characters in "The Iceman Cometh" and "The Cherry Orchard."

The outspoken opposition of Mr. Ward and other black playwrights to such affirmative-action programs is significant, for the particular concern of Actors' Equity is the under-representation of blacks and other members of racial minorities. The organization has compiled statistics demonstrating that between 1982 and 1987, when such minorities accounted for some 17 percent of the population nationwide, fewer than 12 percent of the acting jobs in regional theaters, where most of the stage work is these days, were filled by actors of color. For Broadway plays, the figure was a mere 6 percent.

To remedy this anomaly, Equity is working closely with the Non-Traditional Casting Project, a nonprofit organization based in New York. The project claims some progress in its two years of existence, but still finds considerable resistance. As noted, some of the strongest resistance comes from black playwrights, who, while supporting the project's general economic goals of increased employment, object to nontraditional casting on historical, esthetic and even social grounds.

Mr. Ward, for one, finds great danger in, in effect, rewriting history. To cast, for example, a black actor as Big Daddy in "Cat on a Hot Tin Roof" is, in his view, to diminish what he sees as the play's depiction of a racist society and a family whose wealth and power are based on the exploitation of blacks.

Lonne Elder, whose "Mummer's Play" was recently produced at the American Place Theater in New York, is concerned more generally that a writer's vision be realized in all its particularity. "A writer has a certain feel about the character, in terms of what his background is, what type of person he is, what he does," says Mr. Elder. "Neil Simon's people are indigenously Neil Simon's people. It would be ludicrous to say, 'Well maybe I'll go with a black in this part.' It might be fine for employment parity, but it would be deadly for the theater."

Moreover, Mr. Elder feels, to assert that white and minority actors are interchangeable is to deny their individual identities, the very subject of art. "Everything that can affect you—pain, joy, etc.—will also affect me, but when you get into this whole area about, 'well, we can just be anybody, just be a human being,' you're saying you don't have any definition, you didn't come from some place. Then you become an invisible person."

August Wilson, author of "Fences," agrees that cultural difference are crucial in art. He, too, rejects the idea of casting blacks in parts normally played by whites, "because it denies them their basic humanity, their right to stand on a stage as who they are: African-Americans." To stage an all black "Death of a Salesman" or "Agnes of God," he contends, would be a mistake. "The important thing is that blacks would not act or talk like white characters in a white play. They have their own culture and their own sensibility, which informs even the way they think. So the whole approach would be different."

For Mr. Wilson, nontraditional casting is simply another instance of blacks being asked to deny their blackness in order to participate in society. "Whenever they say, 'O.K., we'll restrict this color-blind casting thing to plays that are universal,' the 'universal' plays they come up with are always white plays, in which they're going to put a black person on stage and have him deny his humanity in order to participate in the universal. I'm saying the universal exists in black life."

While the Non-Traditional Casting Project would probably not wish to deny it, it finds the situation more complicated. The co-chairman of its board, Clinton Turner Davis, himself a director, complained that while a white actor is perceived as a human being, the third-world actor is seen "as a Hispanic human being, an African American human being." Consciously or unconsciously, he argued, people who make casting decisions—playwrights included—assume minority actors are limited to embodying the thoughts and aspirations of their own races.

Moreover, the project receives strong support from other prominent producers and directors, both minority and white. Joseph Papp, head of the New York Shakespeare Festival, has been producing multiracial theater for three decades. Nontraditional casting, he feels, works particularly well in such productions as A. J. Antoon's version of "A Midsummer Night's Dream" of last January, in which the Festival's casting added new thematic sense to a classic play. With black actors as inhabitants of the forest in a Brazilian locale dominated by white colonial rule, nontraditional casting was "integral to the whole approach of the play, and had a historic basis."

More problematic, according to Mr. Papp, are "color-blind" productions of modern realistic plays, with actors cast regardless of race, simply because they are the best qualified by personality and craft. Given America's race-consciousness, he says, choosing an actor of color to play a white character without incorporating some recognition of the character's race and its effect on relationships will result in "a fairy tale."

Charles Gordone, who takes issue with the Non-Traditional Casting Project, nevertheless believes that minority actors cast in realistic American plays can illuminate both the script and minority experience, but it has to be done without ignoring either the actor's ethnicity or historical context. At the American Stage in Berkeley, Calif., Mr. Gordone cast Hispanic performers as the migrant laborers in "Of Mice and Men," and a Creole as Stanley in "A Streetcar Named Desire."

Lloyd Richards, artistic director of the Yale Repertory Theater and dean of the Yale School of Drama, champions nontraditional casting insofar as it adds a stimulating new dimension to a play. He thinks audiences should be "able to accept and utilize their own imaginations to focus on the essence of what is being presented rather than stumbling over the fact of an actor's size, weight, pigment, whatever."

The greatest impetus for nontraditional casting, however, has come from the ground up—from actors for whom it has become a bread-and-butter issue. There is a crush of minority actors entering the profession, and few roles available to them in Western classics and the modern American realistic genre. According to Charles Fuller, a playwright who generally supports nontraditional casting, actors have to "turn to what is already there and say, 'Let us try this,'" simply to survive.

The playwright Amiri Baraka, who helped create the community-based black arts movement in the mid-60's, takes a more jaundiced view, seeing the current embrace of nontraditional casting by actors as one more example of 80's careerism. He feels that the push for nontraditional casting hides the fact that third-world theaters "have insufficient self-determination and resources" to do the plays and roles they'd like to do, and that there are few minority administrators in regional-theaters, where the repertory remains unchanged. "It's still the great books," he says, "with colored covers."

Other playwrights, too, believe that multiracial casting is often a substitute for productions of plays by minority dramatists. Mr. Ward finds this "a period of intense difficulty" for independent black theaters. Ironically, just when Mr. Wilson's plays emerged—not from a black company, but from the new breeding grounds of the Yale Repertory Theater and regional theaters—Mr. Ward's Negro Ensemble Company had to cancel its season.

Color-blind casting and the production of plays by minority playwrights are not mutually exclusive goals, says Mr. Ward, but "to place the main emphasis on nontraditional casting is out of balance." In his view new plays about the black experience will do more to provide minority employment than racially mixed productions of the classics.

Ultimately, however, the actors can only perform what's out there, and Charles Gordone threw it back on the playwrights, black and white, to create a multiracial theater—by writing for multiracial casts and by dealing with the conflicts that arise within a multiracial society. "Once there are writers who write about an American experience that is all-inclusive, you'll have a vital and vibrant American theater."

SOURCE: Hal Gelb, "Should Equal Opportunity Apply on the Stage?" *New York Times* (August 28, 1988). Copyright © 1988 by the New York Times Company. Reprinted with permission.

Case Study Questions

1. Do you agree with the goals of the Non-Traditional Casting Project? Discuss why.

2. Do you agree with the idea that nontraditional casting is directing energies away from the problems of Third World theaters?

3. How do the issues raised in this article apply to opera singers and ballet and modern dancers? Do casting choices related to ethnicity have the same impact on these art forms? Explain why or why not.

4. What should the role of museums be in providing "equal opportunity"?

References

1. John R. Schermerhorn, Jr., *Management for Productivity*, 2d ed. (New York: John Wiley and Sons, 1986), p. 241.
2. Ibid., p. 243.
3. Howard M. Wachtel, *Labor and the Economy*, 2d ed. (New York: Harcourt Brace Jovanovich, 1988), p. 373.
4. *ArtSEARCH* is published by the Theater Development Fund, New York. Yearly subscriptions are available.
5. Schermerhorn, *Management for Productivity*, p. 249.
6. Actor's Equity Association, *Agreement and Rules Governing Employment in Resident Theatres*, effective February 26, 1996, terminates February 26, 1999.
7. Philip Kotler and Joanne Scheff, *Standing Room Only* (Boston:

Harvard University Press, 1997), p. 427.

8. Sidney Webb and Beatrice Webb, *The History of Trade Unionism* (London: Longmans, Green and Co., 1894), p. 1.

9. Allan Kozinn, "Symphony Strike Is Settled," *New York Times* (December 5, 1996), Section B, p. 1.

10. Allan Kozinn, "San Francisco Symphony Goes on Strike," *New York Times* (December 6, 1996), Section B, p. 8.

Additional Resources

Many textbooks cover the field of personnel management in depth. A quick check of business books in a university bookstore should turn up at least an undergraduate-level book in this area. Three excellent sources for more information about personnel issues may be found in the following books:

Michael Carrell, Frank Kuzmits, and Norbert Elbert. *Personnel: Human Resource Management*, 3d ed. Columbus, OH: Charles E. Merrill, 1989. This text was used in developing this chapter.

Stephen Langley. *Theatre Management and Production in America*. New York: Drama Book Publishers, 1990. Chapter 4 provides much information on personnel for all levels of theater.

Thomas Wolf. *Managing a Nonprofit Organization*. Englewood Cliffs, NJ: Prentice-Hall, 1990. Chapters 3 and 4 provide clear information about putting together a workforce and establishing personnel policies.

A good resource for your own use as an employee in an organization may be found in the Nolo Press book *Your Rights in the Workplace* by Barbara Kate Repa, 1996, ISBN 0-87337-346-4.

8

□ □ □ □ □

Fundamentals of Leadership and Group Dynamics

We now are ready to examine the complex areas of leadership, the management communication process, and group dynamics in arts organizations. This chapter is designed to make you aware of the many theories that exist in the field of management psychology. I strongly urge you to explore the list of books at the end of this chapter.

Up to this point, we have created an organization, given it an overall structural framework, established strategies and plans to realize its mission, and begun staffing the enterprise with the best people we can find. Before we move into the specific operational areas of finance, budgeting, scheduling, marketing, and fund raising, we need to finish building the organization's interpersonal structure. Every day, arts organizations face the changing dynamics of people working together. With sensitive and adaptive leadership, the organization will go far. As you will see in this chapter, developing an organization with effective leadership is a continually challenging process.

Leadership Fundamentals

The subject of leadership is explored in numerous books each year. Stop by your local bookstore, and go over to the section on business books. There, you will find dozens of titles on the topic. The search for the best way to develop leadership skills and use those skills to create an organization that flourishes is a popular topic in today's business literature.

What is the essence of leadership? Simply put, *leadership* is the manager's use of power to influence the behavior of others.[1] *Power*, as we will use the term, is defined as the ability to get someone else to do something you want.

In all of our discussions of leadership, keep in mind that leadership success is a necessary, but not the sole, condition for managerial success. Also important to remember is that, although a good manager should be a good leader, a good leader is not necessarily a good manager. People have ranges of skills, some of which are more developed than others. For example, someone identified as an excellent leader may not be particularly good at planning and organizing. Some managers may be wonderfully organized with detailed plans but lack leadership ability. Let us look at the two basic leadership modes: formal and informal.

Formal and Informal Leadership Modes

Formal leadership is leadership by a manager who has been granted the formal authority or right to command.[2] The director of the play, the conductor of the orchestra, and the chair of the board of directors have been given formal authority by the organization to act in behalf of the organization. *Informal leadership* exists when a person without authority can to influence the behavior of others.[3] Often informal leadership grows out of specific situations where an individual steps in and takes over. For example, suppose that an inexperienced student stage manager is unable to control the cast. A cast member with some stage managing experience steps in and starts giving orders. Because other students have respect for the actor, they listen to this informal leader and ignore the formal leader.

Theory X and Theory Y Approaches to People

Before examining the details of various leadership theories, consider again a topic we touched on in Chapter 3. Douglas McGregor's classic book, *The Human Side of Enterprise*, was noted in the summary of management evolution. His Theory X and Theory Y contrasted the fundamental beliefs that managers have about the people who work for and with them. The Theory X manager assumes that people dislike work, lack ambition, are irresponsible, resist change, and prefer to be led rather than to lead. The Theory Y manager works with people from an opposite perspective. He or she assumes that people like to work, are willing to accept responsibility, are capable of self-direction and self-control, and can be imaginative, ingenious, and creative.[4] McGregor's theory raises the issue of a self-fulfilling prophecy. This psychological term simply translates into a way of viewing how people will perform in their jobs. In other words, if you treat your staff, cast, and crew like idiots, they will tend to fulfill your expectations.

This topic is fundamental to the underlying attitude a manager has about the people he or she works with and supervises. The psychology of the workplace usually is very complex. If you assume a leadership position without having developed an overview about the people you work with, you will probably run into a series of personnel problems that will limit your effectiveness.

Before you can develop your leadership skills, you must seriously evaluate your attitudes about work and people. In many arts organizations, both X and Y attitudes operate. Needless to say, these conflicting approaches usually lead to varying degrees of employee satisfaction. In addition, some arts organizations function with leadership that borders on the tyrannical, while other organizations appear to be without leaders. The leadership sets the tone for the entire organization. The corporate culture of an arts organization is established and reinforced by its leadership.

Power: A Leadership Resource

The word *power* often has negative connotations. Yet, without power, it would be impossible to operate most organizations. As we defined it, power is the ability to get someone to do what you want. However, in most arts organizations (or any organization), you have only as much power as your coworkers are willing to give you.

We begin our investigation of leadership power by posing three questions:

1. What sources of power are available to the manager?
2. What limits are placed on the manager's power?

3. What guidelines exist for acquiring and using power?

Sources of Power

Two sources of power are available to the manager: position power and personal power.[5] The first comes with the job you occupy, and the second is directly attributable to you.

Position power As shown in Chapter 6, the organizational design process should establish the working relationship among employees in the organization. No matter how little vertical or hierarchical structure the organization has, managers are given power by their designated positions. For example, a production manager has more power than a technical director, a technical director has more power than a stage carpenter, and so forth. Management texts identify three types of position power: reward, coercive, and legitimate.

Reward power is the capability to offer something of value as a means of controlling others.[6] For example, a position may carry with it the power to grant raises, promotions, special assignments, or special recognition.

Coercive power is defined as the ability to punish or withhold positive outcomes as a way of controlling others.[7] For example, if you have ever received a verbal reprimand or a demotion or if you have ever been fired from a job, you have been subjected to coercive power. Control over the work schedule may be used as a form of coercive power. (Scheduling also could be used as to gain reward power in some cases.)

Legitimate power is the ability to control others by virtue of the rights of the office.[8] It is asserted in the phrase, "I am the boss, and therefore you must do what I ask."

Personal power Along with the position you hold, you bring your unique attributes and talents to the situation.[9] The two types of personal power are expert power and reference power.

Expert power is simply the ability to control others because of your specialized knowledge.[10] This could include special technical information or experience that others in the organization lack. For example, a stage manager with production experience may have expert power when it comes to planning a scenery shift on stage. This would allow the stage manager to exercise more power in a production meeting when alternative ways of doing a set shift are being discussed.

Reference power is derived from a more personal level of interaction with employees. Reference power is the ability to control others because of their desire to identify personally with the power source.[11] This use of power is often found among strong founder-directors of arts organizations. Their charismatic personality and forceful approach to managing the organization are used as a way of controlling others.

It is fairly easy to apply the five types of power—reward, coercive, legitimate, personal, and reference—to such familiar roles as a conductor, director, production manager, technical director, stage manager, or choreographer. Each of these leadership positions requires the use of some combination of these powers. You have probably realized that some individuals are better than others at using the power they have been given.

Limits to Power

Now that we have looked at the sources of power, let us look at some of the limits to power. In the organizational setting of the arts, the power to control others more often is a potential than an absolute. Although history provides many sad examples of individuals abusing the power they had over others, there are limits to power. In arts organizations, as we have seen, several different groups of employees work to support the organization's stated goals and objectives. Within each employee group, differing degrees of power are exercised. The union stage crew has a different relationship to the power structure of the organization than the senior staff. However, whatever the differences may be within each work group, there are limits to how effectively power can be used to control work output.

Acceptance theory   As noted in Chapter 3, Chester Barnard's 1938 book, *The Functions of the Executive*, articulated what is known as *acceptance theory*. Simply stated, power is realized only when others respond as desired; that is, when they accept the directive.[12] Acceptance theory states that people are most likely to accept orders or requests when one or more of these four conditions are met:

1. They truly understand the directive.
2. They feel capable of carrying out the directive.
3. They believe that the directive is in the best interests of the organization.
4. They believe that the directive is consistent with their personal values.

Zone of indifference   Another part of Barnard's leadership theory focuses on what is called the employee's *zone of indifference*. This theory states that power in organizations is limited to the range of requests and directives that people consider appropriate to their basic employment or the psychological contracts they make with the organization.[13] A directive that falls within the zone of indifference tends to be accepted and followed automatically. For example, a marketing research assistant in a museum asked to check the membership list for zip code distribution in comparison to census data reports would not react negatively. However, if asked to pick up a supervisor's dry cleaning on the way to work, the odds are good that the supervisor has crossed the zone of indifference. The assistant will react by saying, "That is an inappropriate request to make." The assistant still may pick up the dry cleaning, but resentment and negative feelings about the supervisor will no doubt effect the employee's attitude and work behavior.

Both these theories can be easily applied in arts organizational setting. Trying to ignore these theories may make the leadership role very difficult. Put yourself in the position of a cast member, intern, or crew member and think about how the acceptance theory may affect your interaction with your supervisor.

Guidelines for Using Power

Consider using the guidelines that follow when you find yourself exercising formal or informal power. These are very practical applications of Barnard's acceptance theory. They are from an article by John R. Kotter in the *Harvard Business Review*:[14]

1. Don't deny your formal authority. It is acceptable to act like the boss if you keep your perspective and remember that you are dependent on the good will and cooperation of the people who work for you.
2. Don't be afraid to create a sense of obligation. Doing a few favors or clearing the path so that employees can get their jobs done will help establish their obligation to follow your direction.
3. Create a feeling of dependence. Although care must be taken not to create a negative dependence (employees can't make a decision without you), it can be helpful to establish a situation in which people depend on your help to make their job easier. This will make it easier to gain their cooperation later.
4. Build and believe in expertise. A few solid examples of your having accomplished something will help build a belief by others in your expertise. No one likes working for know-nothing bosses who do not seem qualified to hold the positions they do. (A good example of negative employee behavior in this situation may be found in the Dilbert cartoon series.)
5. Allow others the opportunity to identify with you as a person. When you create an environment in which the people you work with know and respect you as a person, they are more likely to follow your direction and supervision.

Approaches to the Study of Leadership

Management researchers have developed several theories that attempt to predict why some people are better leaders than others. The first studies of leadership examined the personal traits and psychological characteristics of people in leadership roles.

Trait Approaches to Leadership

The earliest research was based on the assumption that a person with particular traits has leadership potential. The idea was to establish an inventory of traits and match them to people. This early research focused on physical and psychological attributes. However, little correlation was found between these attributes and leadership. Recent studies have shown that the traits of intelligence, dominance, aggressiveness, and decisiveness do tend to be associated with people identified as leaders.[15] The focus on traits still is secondary to most research on leadership. The actual behavior of leaders is the current focus.

Behavioral Approaches to Leadership

Other researchers have tried to formulate a leadership model by studying recurring patterns of behavior by people in leadership positions. The research focused on the leader's orientation toward tasks and people. Leaders who were highly concerned about the tasks to be done exhibited certain behaviors: planning and defining the work to be done, making clear assignments of task responsibility, setting work standards, and following up on task completion and monitoring. The people-oriented leaders tended to emphasize other behaviors: developing social rapport with employees, respecting the feelings of others, and developing a work environment of mutual trust. These styles of leadership are diagrammed in Figure 8–1. A practical application of this matrix is the relationship

Figure 8-1
Leadership Styles

Four Leadership Styles

More concerned about people than tasks

Examples:
* Director spends long hours working with actors and falls behind on the rehearsal schedule.
* Development director works so closely with donors that he/she does not have time to complete weekly donor research reports.

Concerned about people and tasks

Examples:
* Marketing Director works with staff on large mailing project and leads lively discussions and provides refreshments.
* Technical Director takes time to train crew on difficult scene shifts and explains how crew can remain safe during rehearsals and performance.

Low concern for tasks and people

Examples:
* Conductor gives a half-hearted effort on a concert that they wished they had never agreed to do. Gives little correction to orchestra.
* Long-term shop manager is invested in his new sailing hobby. Supervising construction and crew is of little personal interest.

More concerned about tasks than people

Examples:
* Lighting designer stays late after rehearsal to get cues set. Disregards crew complaints as "whining."
* Choreographer insists section of new work must be redone after long day of classes and rehearsals by dancers.

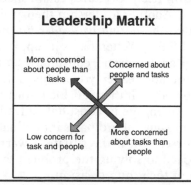

Leadership Matrix

| More concerned about people than tasks | Concerned about people and tasks |
| Low concern for task and people | More concerned about tasks than people |

Different leadership situations require applying task and people concerns in varying intensities.

between a stage director and the cast. Consider your own experience, and try to place an arts leader you have worked with somewhere within this matrix.

Contingency and Situational Approaches to Leadership

Circumstances in the workplace change, and these changes may require different leadership approaches. Researchers questioned the idea that any particular leadership style is effective in all situations. Out of their studies came the theories called *contingency* or *situational leadership theories*. The source for these theories may be found in Fred E. Fielder's 1967 book *A Theory of Leadership Effectiveness*.[16] This study indicated that leaders differ in how oriented they are to tasks and people. Some situations require focus more on tasks and others more toward people. Here are two examples of contingency leadership required in a typical arts setting.

A membership manager for a museum must coordinate a renewal and new members drive each year. Once it is planned, the entire operation is task oriented and specific. The leadership requirements in this situation would be directed toward ensuring that employees were being accurate completing routine tasks. At the same time, because this project requires repetitive work on the part of the staff, the manager's challenge is to keep people motivated and productive. Therefore, the manager might structure the day with frequent breaks or some other form of stress relief for the staff.

After finishing the big renewal campaign, the membership manager has been appointed to chair an ad hoc committee to study and improve management and employee relations. Different leadership skills will be required. The goal is defined, but the specific tasks are not indicated. Other committee members will be volunteers, and the manager will have little direct control over them. This situation requires strong group leadership skills. The manager also must develop clear objectives for all phases of the study. Deadlines will have to be set, objectives defined, and committee procedures established.

Another leadership theory aligned with the situational approach is called the *normative leadership model*. This model from Victor Vroom and Phillip Yetten bases its approach on the idea that a leader acts in either an autocratic, consultative, or group decision making style.[17] As an autocratic leader you either solve the problem or make the decision yourself with the available information or after consulting a subordinate. If you engage in consultative leadership behavior you may gather ideas from your subordinates individually or in group, then make the decision yourself. Or, if the situation warrants, you may decide on a group approach to solving the problem works best, then you accept and implement the group decision.

Yet another model, developed by Paul Hersey and Ken Blanchard, is "based on the premise that leaders need to alter their behaviors depending on one major situational factor—the readiness of followers."[18] *Situational leadership theory* focuses on two leader behaviors: task and relationship. *Task behavior* refers to how much the leader tells people about what, how, when, where, and who is to do something. *Relationship behavior* describes the communication processes used by the leader: listening and facilitating.[19] This model is based on the assumption that, depending on the task and the employee's readiness, the leader may need to use some combination of telling, selling, participating, and delegating to accomplish a task. For example, telling may be used if the employee is "unable or also unwilling or too insecure to take responsibility for a given task."[20] A ticket office manager would be wise to use this approach when training a new employee to process a credit card phone order. Given that errors may be costly, this type leadership is appropriate. On the other hand, this same manager would probably want to use a participating style when establishing the work schedule during a particularly heavy part of the season. Working with employees and gaining their investment in developing a schedule in which the workload is perceived as distributed equally probably will have a positive effect.

Management researchers Robert J. House and Terence R. Mitchell developed the *Path-Goal Theory* as another major approach to the study of situational leadership. This approach focuses on how leaders affect the "way subordinates perceive work goals and possible paths to reach work and personal goals."[21] The situational behaviors of the leader include them being *directive, supportive, participative,* and *achievement-oriented*. The leader needs to assess which combination of the four behaviors will work best depending on the subordinates' current situation and the anticipated result. The challenge in this leadership model is that the leader must understand that what worked in one situation may not work in another. For example, using a directive approach to explain to an intern the process for putting labels on seasonal brochures when, in fact, the intern already has done this task before can lead to the intern thinking "this person must really think I am dumb." In this case, the directive approach places a barrier for the intern whose goal may be to be recognized as someone employable by the organization, not a lowly intern.

Transactional and Transformational Leadership

Leadership expert Bernard M. Bass distinguished between a *transactional leader* (someone who motivates people to perform tasks and achieve stated objectives) and a *transformational leader* (someone who motivates and inspires people to go beyond their normal work behavior).[22] In Bass's model managers are people who "do things right" over and over, while a leader is someone who innovates, inspires, and changes organizations by getting people to the "do the right things."[23] A good leader should be able to perform both leadership behaviors. The leader's analysis of the situation should help clarify how much of each approach to apply. For example, an opera director communicating his or her concept for a production of *The Magic Flute* could outline these ideas for the design team in a more transactional or more directive leadership approach. The director might begin by talking about when the show must be completed, where it is being set in time and place, and how it should look. Or, the director could focus on the larger philosophical issues of the piece and discuss what the music evokes in each of the designer's imagination. In other words, he or she could work from a more transformational style by using a participative process to inspire the group to move beyond a standard vision of a work of art.

Applications to the Arts

Management theory tries to be scientific about creating "experiments" and "controls" in an attempt to "test" the theories. In reading the literature, it becomes apparent that no one theory can explain why some people are dynamic, productive leaders and others are not. There no test you can pass that identifies you as a good leader. As you have seen from the myriad of theories we touched on, a great deal of individual effort must be taken by an arts manager to identify and cultivate leadership skills that are appropriate to the situation and can inspire people to do better.

In an arts organization, keeping the creative spirit alive is a full-time job for a manager. It is extraordinarily easy to be become bogged down in the day-to-day operation of the organization. For example, leadership directed at trying to run an arts organization "just like any other business" could be a formula for disaster. Although an arts organization must function in a businesslike way, arts managers must address the larger issues of the relationship of their organizations to the larger society and culture. For example, authors like Warren Bennis point out that the trend to two- and three-part leadership—distributed leadership—of organizations tends to only dilute the leaders' effectiveness in pursuing their overall goals; instead of leadership, the result is more bureaucracy.[24] Instead of looking to the future, managers spend their time dealing with the routine of supporting the bureaucracy.

Future Leadership?

As more arts organizations move away from a founder-director leadership structure, the trend seems to be toward adopting the multiple-manager leadership model. The older, intuitive leaders with great charismatic appeal seem to be fading from the scene. Corporate structures and distributed leadership may be the only way that arts organizations can gain the required fund-raising credibility in the community, but it seems doubtful that this is a formula for artistic leadership that goes beyond a safe, conventional approach (see the case study in Chapter 6). Many upstart arts organizations of 1970 now are cornerstones in regional arts consortiums. Obviously, artistic leadership need not succumb to conventionality just because it is accepted in the community. However, since so much funding for the operation of arts organizations comes from ticket sales and local fund raising, a point may be reached at which controversial leadership becomes a detriment to the organization.

Arts managers eventually will find themselves solving critical problems and making big decisions through groups. This is the very nature of the contemporary organization. It might be considered a type of "art by committee." The trend toward the committee-style management of arts organizations may prove irreversible. If this is the case, a leader with great skill as a transformational leader and negotiator will be required. Moving boards of directors, staff, and patrons to new frontiers and new challenges takes consummate skill that all too often is rare.

Motivation and the Arts Work Setting

No discussion of leadership would be complete without examining the area of individual and group motivation and the communication process. To lead effectively, you must understand basic concepts about what motivates individuals to make them want to work and create. At the same time, most of the activity that occurs in an arts organization revolves around groups. As we have seen, organizations are divided into work groups that should match the operational and planning objectives the organization has established. Creating, maintaining, and keeping these work groups productive is one of the manager's major leadership responsibilities. To work with individuals and groups, you must communicate your expectations and objectives, and the people you work with must effectively communicate their progress and problems to you.

Let us look at the area of motivation first. The people who make up a large portion of an arts organization usually are highly self-motivated. The discipline and motivation required to become a singer, dancer, actor, designer, or musician are not found universally in society. Ideally, professional performers need not be told to learn their lines, practice the music, or rehearse the movements. However, we do not live in an ideal world. People respond in often unpredictable ways to various challenges they face in work and in life. Therefore, even the most gifted and motivated may benefit from carefully structured communications that help them achieve their goals.

Theories of Motivation

Management texts usually devote large sections to the subject of motivation. Motivation theories and applications arise from research in psychology. These applications are directed toward the workplace and making workers more productive. Researchers have identified four broad theory areas: needs, cognitive, reinforcement, and social learning. *Needs theories* "argue that we behave the way we do because of internal needs we are attempting to fulfill."[25] *Cognitive theories* "attempt to isolate the thinking patterns we use in deciding whether or not to behave in a certain way."[26] *Reinforcement theory* "relies heavily on the *law of effect*, which states that behaviors having pleasant or positive consequences are more likely to be repeated and behaviors having unpleasant or negative consequences are less likely to be repeated."[27] Last, *social learning theory* "argues that learning occurs through the continuous interaction of our behaviors, various personal factors, and environmental forces."[28]

Needs Theories

Abraham H. Maslow's 1954 book *Motivation and Personality*[29] created a foundation on which business psychologists have built. Maslow proposed that human beings have five levels of needs arranged in a hierarchy of importance. These fell into lower-order needs (physiology, safety, and society) and higher-order needs (esteem and self-actualization). The system is based on the assumption that only unmet needs act as motivators. The other key principle is that these needs are arranged in a strict hierarchy. The implication is that an individual can move to the next higher level only after satisfying the needs in the preceding lower level.

Maslow's theory has been embraced by much of the business world, but that does not mean that it can explain all facets of human behavior. Cultural differences, the reality that strict hierarchy does not always describe how people behave in a work environment, and the fact that people's needs change over time were not easily accommodated in Maslow's theory.

Researcher Clayton Alderfer proposed an alternative to Maslow's hierarchy known as *ERG Theory*. His approach took the five need levels and compressed them to three: existence, relatedness, and growth. Existence needs cover things such as food, water, shelter, and work-related desires such as pay, benefits, and the actual working conditions. Relatedness needs encompass things such as relationships with friends and families, work groups, professional associations. Our desires to be accepted by others and to have some control over our lives also fall under this classification. Growth needs cover things such as creativity and innovation. Alderfer argues we could be concerned with more than one level at a time and that, if we are continually frustrated from reaching a level such as growth, we may cease to be concerned about that need. This concept was expressed in what he called the *frustration-regression principle.*[30]

In an arts organization, providing a job in a comfortable work environment (physiological need) that does not endanger health (safety need), has a degree of group stability (social needs), recognizes good performance (esteem need), and provides opportunities for creativity (self-actualization need) should not be an impossible task. However, if employees fear for their lives whenever they go on the stage because the overhead stage rigging system is dangerous, for example, their safety and physiological needs are not being met.

Two-factor theory   Frederick Herzberg and B. Syndermann's 1959 book *The Motivation to Work*[31] became the cornerstone for another need theory of motivation. Their study focused on what they called the *two-factor theory* of motivation. *Hygiene factors* were items that seemed to make individuals dissatisfied with their jobs. For example, people may become less motivated if they think their pay, benefits, company policies, or the working conditions are not as they perceive they should be. *Motivators* were identified as things such as achievement, responsibility, the work itself, recognition, and growth and personal achievement.

The limited scope of the study on which the two-factor theory is based (limited to about 200 engineers and accountants) invalidates the theory to some critics. For example, by studying only professionals, Herzberg and Syndermann do not address the possibility that hygiene and motivational factors might differ for hourly employees. In other words, the staff members in the marketing department of a performing arts center probably will have different perceptions about motivators than the stagehands who unload the trucks at the loading dock.

However, the limited nature of the study does not invalidate the two-factor concept. Managers obviously may adjust the range of hygiene and motivational factors for particular work groups. For example, most employees like recognition. Prominently displayed "employee-of-the-month" plaques with photographs and accompanying praise for some accomplishment can boost morale. Unfortunately, the two-factor theory provides little guidance on how the motivational factors can be translated into measurable increases in productivity.

Acquired-needs theory   The last needs-related motivational theory is a product of psychologist David C. McClelland's research. His studies focused on three needs: achievement, affiliation, and power.[32] The need for achievement, in McClelland's view, was a "desire to accomplish challenging tasks and achieve a standard of excellence in one's work."[33] Affiliation was seen as "the desire to maintain warm, friendly relationships with others";[34] and power was "the desire to influence and control one's enviornment."[35] He further broke down power into *personal power* and *institutional power.*[36] Some individuals enjoy using power over others while others are able to work in organizational settings to express their power needs. McClelland developed a Thematic Apperception Test as a measurement tool to assess the degree to which individuals were motivated by the varying needs. In this theory, one could posit that an individual with a strong need for affiliation probably would not be successful in a high-level leadership position because his or her primary motivation would interfere with the requirements of exercising power and control over people and organizations. A good director, conductor, or choreographer probably will exhibit a strong need to achieve. Success in different institutional settings will depend to some degree on how strong are the needs for power and affiliation. For example, a high-powered and driven guest artist brought in to an academic environment may find he or she lacks the affiliation need required to successfully relate to students and carry on positive work relationships with others.

Cognitive Theories

We now look quickly at two of the cognitive theories of motivation. Essentially, these theories look at how people think about their jobs and their work. The theories attempt to isolate the patterns of thought people use in deciding which behaviors to choose. It is assumed that people find their own sources of motivation and dissatisfaction in the workplace.

Equity theory   The equity theory of motivation is based on the work of J. Stacy Adams in the 1960s.[37] The theory states that *a perceived inequity functions as a motivator*. When employees believe that they are not being treated equitably, they are motivated to try to change the source of the perceived inequity. Employees perceive inequities whenever they feel that they are not rewarded for their work at the same level as someone else who works equally hard. To resolve equity conflicts, Stacy predicts that employees will change how much work they do, try to get their salaries increased, rationalize the inequity, or quit.[38]

Equity issues arise most often with highly separated work groups. For example, an arts organization might have union stage employees with a high school education who receive $20 per hour for their labor and a marketing assistant with a master's degree who receives the equivalent of $8.50 per hour. Based on a 40-hour work week, the stagehand could gross $41,600 a year while the marketing person might earn $17,680. It will not take long for the marketing assistant to pick up on these wage differences, thanks to the informal communication system in most organizations. According to Stacy's equity theory, the marketing assistant will probably create some rationalization to minimize the inequity or quit. If the assistant approaches the head of the marketing area for a pay increase and is told that the budget is too tight, he or she may go back to work but probably will temporarily reduce his or her work output. The inequity will not go away. In fact, the problem may grow as the unhappy employee lets other employees know that they are receiving a lot less money for their hard work than others in the organization. The employees may also say to themselves, "If that's all you think I'm worth, then that's all the work you are going to get from me." The result is dissatisfied employees with low motivation levels and less work output. Of course, our marketing assistant also may have longer-term goals that are based on the assumption that $8.50 an hour job is not a reflection of their true skill and, in the short term, can accommodate the inequity.

This issue of pay equity is a hot topic in the business world. Lobbying groups for the business community are hard at work in Washington, trying to control the growth of the concept of comparable worth. If the marketing assistant is doing work of similar value to the organization as the stagehand, why is she not paid the same rate? Should the organization pay equally for equal work?

Arts managers would do well to read up on equity theory. They must anticipate these issues and formulate strategies to help employees. The employee's perspective is important here. For example, when it is time for contract negotiation with union employees, typically nonunion employees will start talking about wage inequities. Managers might explain that the stagehands often do not work year-round, so they do not make as much as imagined. In fact, they may make less on average per year than salaried employees.

Expectancy theory   Another motivation theory often cited in management textbooks is the expectancy theory. Simply stated, Victor Vroom's *expectancy theory* postulates that people will be motivated to work if they expect that they will be adequately rewarded for their effort.[39] The expectancy theory has three major components: effort, performance, and outcome.

The first component is *effort-performance expectancy*.[40] The employee may ask how probable it is to actually can perform at the required level. If you are given a task such as updating a 20,000-name mailing list in two days or building an entire set of stage platforms in three days with no assistance, your expectancy will be zero. Using these examples, your expectancy probably will be higher if you were given six weeks for the mailing list and three weeks for the construction project.

Next we assess the *performance-outcome expectancy*, or our belief that "our successful performance will lead to certain outcomes."[41] If you are told that you will receive an extra vacation day if you finish the mailing list or the construction project early, you must decide whether the value of the reward is worth the extra effort. In this example, since the value of your performance expectancy is so low ("I can't do all that work in that short a time!"), the outcome expectancy of getting a day off is equally low. Outcome is affected by the type of rewards the employee perceives are available. Vroom identifies *extrinsic rewards* as such things as a day off, a bonus or merit pay, awards, and promotions. *Intrinsic rewards* include things such as feelings of achievement, being challenged, or being given the opportunity to grow.[42]

The last component in Vroom's motivation theory is *valence*, the assessment of the anticipated value of the various outcomes or rewards.[43] The motivational strength of rewards for the work effort is determined by the value we assign these rewards. If, for example, you have not had a day off in weeks, that one day you are promised may be a strong motivator despite the low expectancy that you can complete the task.

This theory suggests the arts manager should be aware of the performance—outcome expectancy—when planning projects and creating tasks to accomplish. For example, suppose you assign four people to the mailing list project and divide the task into four parts, 5000 names each. You give an equal pay bonus to all four employees, even though only two of the four actually did the work on time. Have you not sent a mixed signal about your performance-outcome expectancy to the two employees who actually did the work on time? In this case, the motivational strength of the pay bonus is weakened for the high-achieving employees by the fact the underachievers were paid the same.

Probably the most important element of this theory centers on the intrinsic and extrinsic rewards system you establish in your arts organization. Limited budget resources probably will curtail the use of monetary rewards as a motivator. A good source for ideas for nonmonetary rewards may be found in Bob Nelson's book *1001 Ways to Reward Employees*.[44] He offers a comprehensive list of informal and formal awards as well as awards for specific achievement and activity awards.

Does this theory of motivation offer any help to arts managers? Yes. For example, you can influence expectancy by establishing a general attitude in your work group that the work is important and makes a difference. You also can hire and train people in the work group who are willing to accept the attitude you desire. You can influence preferences by developing an ongoing system of listening to employees' needs and guiding them toward results.[45]

Never underestimate the power of perception and never assume that the people who work for you have the same values and assign the same priority to the work to be done. Your effectiveness in a leadership role is dependent on your ability to motivate the people with whom you work. Understanding what motives them, what they perceive as a reward, and what they value in the workplace are key elements to your success.

Reinforcement Theory

The third area of motivation falls under the broad heading of reinforcement theory. The motivational theories described previously approach behavior from the perspective of how people perceive the value of work, how they satisfy needs, or how they try to resolve inequities. Reinforcement theory focuses on the behavior or the output of the person and does not concern itself with what may be behind the behavior. The use of positive and negative reinforcement is the motivating force that managers use in their leadership roles. As a manager you cannot possibly know the psychological issues all of your employees bring to work with them. Your job is not to be a psychologist but their supervisor or leader. Reinforcement theory requires observing behavior and modifying it to support the mission of the organization. Let us take a quick look at this topic.

Organizational behavior modification (OBM) is an approach that uses the principles of B. F. Skinner's research on human behavior.[46] *Operant conditioning*, a key element in the research, assumes that you can control behavior by manipulating its consequences. By using positive and negative reinforcement, you can increase desired behaviors or eliminate undesired behaviors. Another key concepts in the system include the *law of contingent reinforcement*, which states that for a reward to have maximum impact, it must be delivered only if the desired behavior is exhibited. Equally important is the *law of immediate reinforcement*, which states the quicker the delivery of the reward after the desired behavior, the greater is the reinforcement value. This theory is often summarized as *ABC* or antecedent, behavior, consequence.[47] The antecedent is what proceeds the actual behavior and the consequence is result of the behavior. A policy about lateness to rehearsals establishes an antecedent, showing up on time would be the desired behavior, and the consequence is starting on time. If a performer is late (the behavior) but bears no consequence (a fine?), reinforcement theory predicts this person will continue to engage in this behavior. You may modify the behavior if you enforce a consequence that causes the person to change his or her behavior.

Does behaviorist theory have a place in an arts organization's leadership system? Yes, if carefully applied. Consider a few other examples. Something as subtle as nodding occasionally during a meeting as your assistant makes a presentation about a new marketing plan or revisions to a scene design can have a positive reinforcing effect. As an example of behavior modification through *negative reinforcement*, suppose that you always make a point of saying, "I thought we had a no-smoking rule onstage in this theater" whenever you find the crew head smoking. Then one day you see that the employee is not smoking, and you walk by without saying anything. You stop nagging the employee when he stops the undesired behavior. Negative reinforcement, by the way, is not necessarily the best way to approach behavior modification. Unfortunately, for most of their lives, people hear only about the behaviors that they are not supposed to engage in. In some organizations, negative reinforcement is the main operating mode. It is often summarized by employees who say "The only time I get noticed around here is when I do something wrong."

As an approach to organizational leadership, behavior modification has been criticized because it focuses solely on extrinsic reinforcers. The complex reasons behind a particular behavior pattern are of little interest to the leader who relies on behavior modification. Critics argue that self-motivated artists, who are independent and creative, will laugh at attempts to influence their behavior through simplistic, positive-reinforcement techniques. However, praise is a powerful leadership tool, and as a positive reinforcer, most people do not seem upset when it is used sincerely.

An aware arts manager who carefully and thoughtfully uses some components of operant conditioning usually cannot go wrong. A director, choreographer, or manager of any type will usually get better results with positive reinforcement than negative reinforcement. Berating and belittling people usually instills hostility and resentment among employees or volunteers. Managers who believe that the only way to get top performance from their employees or volunteers is through terror tactics are sadly out of touch with reality.

Social learning theory   The last motivational theory we discuss is based on integrating cognitive and reinforcement theory. Albert Bandura's *social learning theory* posits that "learning occurs through the continuous interaction of our behaviors, various personal factors and environmental forces.[48]

The learning that in turn effects our behavior includes three cognitive processes: symbolic processes, vicarious learning, and self-control.[49] Let us look at each process and how this theory may be applied in motivating employees.

The *symbolic processes* include how we use verbal and imagined symbols to process and store experiences in words and images. We also use *self-efficacy* to imagine and project goals and outcomes we desire.[50] We would be motivated if we imagine the outcome of our completing the labeling or platform construction project will lead to more significant or weighty tasks or a promotion.

"*Vicarious learning*, or observational learning is our ability to learn new behaviors and/or assess their probable consequences by observing others."[51] For example, as a new employee, you observe a particular staff member who seems to be respected and rewarded for the way he or she does a job. You in turn model your behavior along the lines of this person and find reinforcement and rewards for doing so.

Last, we engage in forms of *self-control* in the workplace. We control our behavior and provide for our own self-rewards.[52] You may congratulate yourself for completing a project ahead of schedule by going

Figure 8-2

Leading and Managing

Overview of leadership, motivation and group dynamics

LEADERSHIP THEORIES

Contingency and Situational Approaches

Trait Approach
Acts and looks like a leader
— intelligence
— dominance
— aggressiveness

Fielder: Type of work situation dictates leadership style - Focus on tasks and people

Hersey, Blanchard: Situational Leadership: depending on the task leader either tells, sells, participates, or delegates

House, Mitchell: Path-Goal Theory: Leader is directive, supportive, participative or achievement oriented

Vroom, Yetten: Normative Leadership Model
Leader makes decisions:
— autocratically
— in consultation
— in groups

Behavior Approach
Recurring behavior
— Task oriented
— Sets standards
— Rapport with people

Bass: Transaction and Transformational Leader: Motivates people to perform tasks or inspires people to go beyond circumstances

THEORIES OF MOTIVATION

Need Theory
* Maslow: Hierarchy of 5 needs
* Alderfer: ERG - 3 levels of need
* Herzberg, Synderman: Two-Factor Theory - Motivators or Hygiene (dissatisfiers)
* McClelland: Acquired-needs of achievement, affiliation, and power

Cognitive Theory
* Adams: Equity Theory, Inequity is a motivator
* Vroom: Expectancy Theory, motivation from the belief appropriate rewards will result

Reinforcement Theory
* Skinner: Operant Conditioning, control behavior by manipulating consequences - ABC
* Bandura: Social Learning Theory, continuous interaction of behavior, environments and personal factors

GROUP DYNAMICS

Formal Groups
* Command: manager supervises work groups
* Task: a production team
* Interest: health and safety
* Committee: standing and ad hoc and by functional areas (finance)

Group Development & Behavior
* Stages: forming, storming, norming, performing, adjourning
* Dysfunctions: Groupthink also disruptive behavior by individuals such as aggressiveness, special pleading, withdrawing, etc.

Effective Group Management
* Task Activities: initiating, information transfer, summarizing, elaborating
* Maintenance Activities: gatekeeping, following along, harmonizing, reducing tensions

A good leader will draw on all these approaches to effectively manage organizations and people

out to dinner or simply given yourself a break. In other words, social learning theory recognizes self-reinforcement as part of behavioral response that motivates people.

In an arts organization, social learning theory can be applied as a motivational tool by establishing clear and visible rewards for learning and developing new skills. Encouraging and rewarding employees who acquire new skills or who provide models for interns should have a positive outcome. Establishing and supporting a corporate culture of learning makes a great deal of sense in a workplace that tend to attract highly educated people in the first place.

Theory Integration

Figure 8–2 summarizes the various theories about leadership, motivation, and group dynamics discussed in this chapter. The manager's objective is to be as effective as possible in getting people in the organization to achieve the results that support the organization's goals and objective. An organization does not reach or exceed its goals. The motivational theories are tools to be used by the manager by chance or through the efforts of one person. Within an arts organization, some employee groups are motivated by extrinsic rewards, others by how they perceive their role and status, and still others by the need to achieve some degree of self-actualization. It will take time and experimentation to find the best mix of motivators in any work situation. The investment of time by the leaders of an arts organization in establishing a coherent and effective motivational system will help maintain a positive work environment. The fact that so many organizations, arts and business, operate with motivationally and psychologically dysfunctional cultures speaks directly to the lack of training in working with people by the leaders and managers. It is safe to say that employees, no matter how highly educated or self-motivated, are not maintenance-free entities.

Group Dynamics

A fact of organizational life is that leaders must work effectively with many different groups. Whether the group is formal or informal, when you put together several people, a collective behavior pattern emerges that usually is different than an individual acting singly. Therefore, a leader should understand that group dynamics is the actual behavioral output exhibited when the various standing groups interact on a daily basis within an organization. Arts organizations are made up of several groups: a cast, corps de ballet, ensemble, crew, board of directors, committees, subcommittees, task forces, and so on. The effective leadership of all these various groups can result in a dynamic, creative organization that has a positive impact on the community. By the same token, ineffective group leadership can result in low-quality events and productions, poor use of resources, high turnover of staff and board members, labor problems, and marginal community support. Let us look at some of the basic terms and concepts of group management and leadership.

Group Management Activities and Forms

A *group* is a collection of people who regularly interact with one another in the pursuit of one or more common objectives.[53] A *formal group* is created by the formal authority structure within an organization to transform inputs into product or service outputs.[54] For example, a theater company sets up a formal group (e.g., a cast) by deciding to do a play and present it to the public. A board of directors creates a formal group when it selects a personnel search committee to find a new museum director. Organizations may establish permanent work groups to carry on specific operational activities. For example, the production staff in an opera company or the curatorial staff in a museum may meet regularly as a group to make plans, assign work, and evaluate progress. Temporary groups, such as a personnel search committee, may be established to accomplish a particular task. The group is disbanded after it completes the job.

An *informal group* is "one that emerges in an organization without any designated purpose."[55] These informal groups can satisfy employee needs for socialization, security, and identification.[56] Informal groups also can help people get their jobs done by establishing a network within an organization. For example, a production manager in an arts organization may establish a formal working relationship with the crew heads through regular staff meetings. However, within the crews, various informal groups will form that can help or hinder the overall operation. An informal group may form within the crew (usually with an informal leader), centering on the belief that the production manager is incompetent. This informal group may try to influence others in the formal work group about the manager's incompetence. Soon, the production manager finds that things are not getting done or are being done in the way that the informal group decides is best. Direct intervention by the formal leader of the group may be the only way to disrupt the influence of the informal group.

Types of groups   Various types of groups are formed in organizations, including command, task, interest, and committee groups.[57]

Command groups are established in the organizational chart in the working relationship between supervisors and subordinates. Figure 6–2 depicts the command group relationship between the managing director and the directors of marketing, finance, and fund raising.

Task groups are groups of employees who work together to complete a project or job. A major portion of the activity in arts organizations is accomplished by task groups. Show A in Figure 6–4 is a task group.

Interest groups form when employees unite around a particular issue. The members of this group could be from different work groups who are brought together to resolve a short-term problem. For example, when a symphony orchestra announces that, due to a shortfall in fund raising, all medical benefits for the regular staff will cease, an interest group forms to deal specifically with this issue.

Finally, the *committee* is a group that has been humorously defined as "the only life form with twelve stomachs and no brain."[58] The seasoned manager in an organization might see the operations of a committee falling under Old and Kahn's law: "The efficiency of a committee meeting is inversely proportional to the number of participants and the time spent on deliberations."[59] A more formal definition of a "*committee* is a group of two or more people created to perform a specific task."[60] Organizations establish standing committees to fulfill ongoing needs (e.g., a finance committee) or ad hoc committees to fulfill specific needs (e.g., a search committee). Numerous books offer suggestions for making committees function effectively in organizations. Such issues as committee composition, size, clarity of purpose, and ability to bring resources to bear on a problem are covered in a variety of texts and business books. The disadvantages of compromised decisions, long deliberation periods, and the expense often are cited in the literature. However, committees tend to proliferate in organizations. Care must be taken to avoid using the committee approach to avoid taking individual responsibility for decisions.

Stages of group development   The study of groups shows that when a new group is formed, it typically undergoes five stages: forming, storming, norming, performing, and adjourning.[61]

In the *forming stage*, the group tries to establish its purpose, define its operational rules, establish the identity of members of the group and what they have to offer, and define how people will interact with each other.

The *storming stage* may be very emotional or relatively calm, depending on the personalities of the group members. For example, an ad hoc committee to examine employee benefits that is made up of staff and hourly workers could experience substantial personal style differences that take some time to work out. It could take several heated discussions to move everyone to a common agenda.

The *norming stage* is characterized by building group cohesiveness, developing consensus, and clarifying roles. Typically, the group leader will emerge at this stage. Constructive ways of handling disagreement will be found, and group discussions will allow differences to be expressed. Group members will feel more confident about their specific responsibilities and help keep the group focused on the problems that must be solved.

As a group reaches the *performing stage*, it begins to actively address its purpose. If the group leader is able to effectively engage everyone, the entire group should be contributing to the committee's work. Unfortunately many groups do not reach this stage. More often than not, a few members of the committee will actually work and a few others are marginal. The group still performs, just not as effectively as it could if everyone were contributing.

In the final stage, *adjourning*, the committee wraps up its work and disbands. The search committee completes it job and no longer needs to meet.

A group such as a cast of a play will go through some variation of this process as it moves from auditions to rehearsals. Other ensemble efforts share similar patterns of development. When a committee is formed by a board of directors, patterns similar to those noted take place. An arts manager must watch vigilantly for committees that become dysfunctional. For example, some committees never achieve norming and performing. The committee output may be slow in coming or marked by minority reports by differing subgroups that form within the larger committee.

Group norms and cohesiveness   *Group norms* is a familiar phrase related to leading and managing groups. Norms are the rules that guide group behavior.[62] The leader of a group must establish behavior norms ("One person talking at a time, please") as well as performance norms ("We must finish deliberations and report to the board by March 1").

At the same time, a leader must develop cohesiveness among the group if it is to be effective. *Cohesiveness*, in this case, refers to the degree of motivation of members to stay in the group. For example, a running crew for a production is a task-specific group that often requires a high degree of cohesiveness. You can use specific circumstances such as having to do a complex scene change in a limited time, as a way of building cohesiveness among a group. For example, if the performance norm is to complete the scene change in one minute, the group may be challenged to beat that norm and do the shift in 45 seconds. When this new norm is established, the group usually feels some sense of collective accomplishment, which is a way of building cohesiveness.

Successfully managing groups in an arts organization requires careful thought about establishing norms, performance expectations, and building cohesiveness. In arts organizations, group performance extends from the board through the construction shops. We now look at some of the problems that can arise with groups.

Groupthink, a dysfunctional group activity   A well-noted problem with groups that are too cohesive has been termed *groupthink*. In a 1971 article, Irving Janis defined the groupthink phenomena as "a tendency for highly cohesive groups to lose their critical evaluative abilities."[63] Unless a member of the committee or work group is designated as the devil's advocate, there is the danger that groupthink will establish itself in an organization. The peer pressure to appear to agree is enormous. A group leader should make it a point to have conflicting points of view aired before the group.

Some symptoms of groupthink are rationalizing data that contradict the expectation, self-censorship by group members, and creating an illusion of unanimity by stopping the discussion of a topic prematurely. As an example of groupthink, imagine a design-development discussion that includes a director, the designers, and key technical staff. The production manager, who is running the meeting, knows that the proposed set design is too big and expensive to produce, but the designer and director do not want to hear that. In fact, the director has said on several occasions, "Don't tell me what you can't do, tell me what you can do." The technical director has tried to tell everyone that this design is more than the shop can handle. Every time the technical director tries to bring up the subject of time, money, and personnel constraints, the production manager cuts off the conversation. The schedule dictates that construction start immediately. The group "decision" is really nothing more than a groupthink trap. The technical director knows it cannot be done but goes along with the group decision anyway. The shop proceeds to construct the set as designed. Later, when the show is over-budget and behind schedule, the technical director may be asked, "Why didn't you say something before we started building the set?"

Strategies for Making Groups More Effective

Many predictable, common problems occur when people get together to function as a group. An aware leader must act immediately to stop these dysfunctional behaviors from disrupting the group. Here are some behaviors you may find disrupting a meeting:[64]

- *Aggressiveness.* One or more members of the group uses an aggressive tone of voice to dominate discussion. "Well that's a stupid idea, I think with should do this."
- *Blocking.* Committee members who go off on tangents or bring unrelated personal experiences in to the meeting can side track discussion. For example, a season selection committee is trying to pick programming and one member chimes in

with, "I remember several years ago when we performed a piece by Philip Glass, people walked out of the concert."

- *Self-confessing.* Sometimes committee members interject their personal, nongroup feeling into meeting. In a budget planning discussion, a committee member chimes in with, "I am uncomfortable with this investment plan and it just seems to me we should be rethinking this whole approach."
- *Competing.* Some committee members think they must have the final idea on how something should be done. After a lengthy discussion about a change in the season schedule and as the group starts to approach consensus a committee member offers, "Yes, well that's all well and good, but I think my idea is best and in fact, this current idea lacks merit."
- *Seeking sympathy.* Some committee members feel compelled to share their ideas for purposes that do not advance the agenda. For example, a ticket office manager uses the meeting as a chance to whine about how out of date the computers are. "If the budget committee would only pay attention to my pleas, this equipment is so slow and I just can't do my job with this junk."
- *Special pleading.* The ticket office manager not only seeks sympathy but is providing an example of someone trying to get his or her special need or pet project addressed by the committee.
- *Horsing around.* Some members of the committee may find that clowning, joking, or mimicking someone is enjoyable. While a little humor is useful to move a group along, these types of behaviors usually are disruptive.
- *Seeking recognition.* On occasion you may have a committee member who feels it necessary to propose extreme ideas or try to dominate discussion. "I think we should do away with the concerts in the park. It is too hot outside and I don't like sitting on the ground."
- *Withdrawing.* A committee member who becomes passive, does not engage in discussions, daydreams, doodles, or starts whispering to others is disrupting the meeting by withdrawing or acting preoccupied.

To counter act some of these behavioral problems in meetings it would be wise to build in some simple behavior patterns as norms at the very beginning. The first set of behavior patterns fall under the heading of *task activities.* The second group of patterns are called *maintenance activities*, and they support a set of healthy group interactions.

Edgar H. Schein, in *Organizational Psychology*, lists these *task activities* as

1. Initiating: Setting agendas, giving ideas, defining problems, and suggesting solutions.
2. Giving and seeking information: Offering information directly related to the problem, asking others for ideas, and seeking facts.
3. Summarizing: Restating the highlights of the discussion can help keep everyone on track.
4. Elaborating: Clarifying ideas by citing relevant examples can help keep the group working effectively.[65]

The *maintenance activities* include the following.

1. Gatekeeping: Allowing various members of the group to talk. Sometimes one person will try to dominate the discussion and direct the group to his or her opinion by monopolizing the discussion.
2. Following: Going along with the group and agreeing to try out an idea.
3. Harmonizing: When appropriate, reconciling differences and promoting compromise can help keep the group going.
4. Reducing tensions: Using humor as an antidote when the situation becomes emotional. This can help shift the energy of the group long enough to put the conflict in perspective.[66]

Distributed Leadership

For any organization to function effectively as a group, there must be a healthy interchange among its members. Arts organizations, especially performing arts organizations, spend a lot of time engaged in group activities. The management of these various group efforts calls for the recognition of the concept of *distributed leadership*. Simply put, it means that the group members share the leadership responsibility. As a member of a committee, a work group, or a cast, you share the responsibility to keep the group from becoming dysfunctional. Leaders who point out effective strategies and dangerous behaviors have the best chance of bringing distributed leadership to life for the group. As noted earlier, distributed leadership can create another layer of management and add more bureaucracy in an arts organization. However, if all members of the group adopt the attitude that being a leader means making decisions, the organization need not become mired in inaction.

Communication Basics and Effective Leadership

Underlying the entire area of leadership is the assumption that good communication and listening skills are used daily. Success as a leader directly relates to the ability to send, receive, interpret, monitor, and disseminate information. However, because the process of communication is so simple and, at the same time, so complex and subtle, we often overlook the obvious when we hunt for the source of a problem. The consequences of miscommunication—ranging from the simple "go" on a cue by the stage manager to a complex report by the director of finance to the board—can be devastating. A missed special effects cue may be life threatening to a performer, and a misunderstood financial report may lead to bankruptcy for the enterprise. Almost all organizations say, "We have a communication problem around here." Whether this is true or not is irrelevant. If the phrase is repeated often enough, the perception that a communication problem exists will be created.

We next look at the communications process and explore some strategies to minimize its problems.

The Communications Process

We use the following definitions as a starting point.

Communication is the creation of meaning through the use of signals and symbols. Furthermore, meaning is defined as the perception that takes place when we formulate the relationship between two statements or images. Lastly, signals and symbols are key components in a message. Signals mean the messages which a communicator feels are beaming from a source, and they suggest very limited but concise meaning. Symbols suggest broader and more complex meanings assigned to the verbal and nonverbal language of the communicators.[67]

Suppose that a museum director, on Monday morning, scowls at everyone, goes into the office, and slams the door. This nonverbal behavior communicates a wealth of information to the office staff. People in the office speak more quietly, become anxious, "What's wrong?" Or imagine that the director of a play watches a scene and says to the cast in a monotone, "Very good." The message is mixed. The verbal tone communicating a half-hearted endorsement contradicts the meaning of the words." *Very good* might mean, "You did fine, but I really was not impressed."

As you can see from these examples, the communication process carries many nuances that have different meanings to people. Figure 8–3 depicts a simplified overview of the communication process. Let us briefly review what takes place in a typical interchange between two people.

The communication process includes a sender, who encodes and delivers a message through a communication channel, and a receiver, who decodes the message and perceives a meaning. The sender receives some feedback or an acknowledgment that the message has been received. At the same time, the communication channel is directly affected by noise that interferes with the message. *Noise*, in this case, means anything that disrupts the message or the feedback.

Perception

For the communication process to be effective, both the sender and the receiver should be aware of four key elements that modify the perception of the communication by each party: stereotypes, the halo effect, selective perception, and projection.[68]

Stereotypes   When you speak of "dumb dancers," "techie types," or "musicians!" you are communicating in stereotypes. When you refer to the board of directors as the "board" you are implying they all are the same with one mind. You are stereotyping the individual members as if they all acted and thought the same way. If you are to become a credible leader, you must drop the stereotypical thinking patterns.

Halo effect   The halo effect is the perception of an individual based on one strong attribute. For example, a person who shows up late for a rehearsal or a meeting more than once will suddenly be known throughout the organization for "always being late." The halo effect can be used positively as well. For example, a recent report on the long-term funding prospects for the organization may make a staff member a star just in time for the annual board meeting when, in fact, this individual has been coasting all year and does not deserve the praise.

Selective perception   *Selective perception* refers to noticing only those incidents or behaviors that reinforce what you already strongly believe about a situation or a person. You may choose not to see problems that

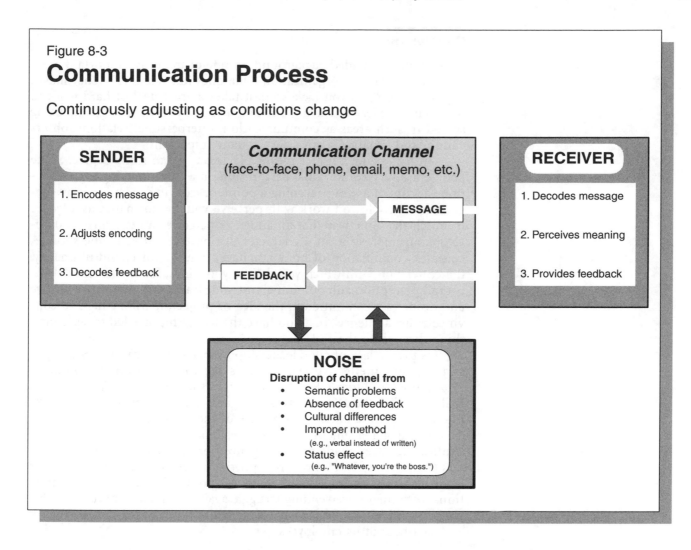

Figure 8-3
Communication Process

Continuously adjusting as conditions change

SENDER

1. Encodes message

2. Adjusts encoding

3. Decodes feedback

Communication Channel
(face-to-face, phone, email, memo, etc.)

MESSAGE

FEEDBACK

RECEIVER

1. Decodes message

2. Perceives meaning

3. Provides feedback

NOISE
Disruption of channel from
- Semantic problems
- Absence of feedback
- Cultural differences
- Improper method
  (e.g., verbal instead of written)
- Status effect
  (e.g., "Whatever, you're the boss.")

particular employees are having because it is inconsistent with your perception of them.

Projection   When you project, you assign your personal attributes to someone else. The classic example of projection is when you assume that everyone who works for you shares your attitudes and beliefs about the job and the organization.

Formal and Informal Communication
Within an arts organization, formal and informal networks exist to communicate with and among employees. Managers must give constant attention to how well both systems are serving the organization's communication needs. Memos, e-mails, small group meetings, forums, newsletters, and annual meetings make up a part of the organization's formal communication system. The informal communication system exists at every level in the organization. Phone conversations, waiting in line to use the copy machine, coffee breaks, and rehearsal breaks all may be touch points for informal communication. The informal system may seem impossible to manage, but by simply recognizing its existence and monitoring the information (or misinformation) being communicated, a manager can creatively intervene when required.

Conclusion

This chapter provided background on one of the most important areas in operating an arts organization. One question remains, "What makes a good leader?" As you have seen, it takes a great deal of hard work to be an effective leader. Having a vision of where you want to go and being skilled in such areas as communication, interpersonal relations, observation, and situation analysis are equally important.

In fact, being a leader means playing a role to some degree. Some people are very comfortable performing on a stage, making a presentation in front of a group, arguing a point, or carrying on an intensive negotiation. People you work with perceive your performance as a leader in much the same way that an audience perceives a performer and develops an impression of a character during the course of the show. A complex combination of body language, tone of voice, and ultimately, the conviction with which you deliver your lines, form your coworkers' overall perception and opinion about your leadership. If you are unsure and do not act committed to the idea or project, it will be hard to convince your "audience" that you have the leadership needed to see something through to the end.

Is there a lack of good leadership in many organizations? Sadly, yes. Coping with ineffective leadership is the topic of Muriel Solomon's *Working with Difficult People.*[69] Chapters such as "When Your Boss Is Belligerent," "When Your Boss Is Arrogant," and "When Your Boss Is Exploitative" paint a fairly grim picture of the workplace.

Good management and good leadership do exist. Although few studies have been made of arts organization, some people like Tom Peters (*In Search of Excellence*) are reporting on companies that meet their goals and keep their people happy and productive. For arts organizations, with their never-ending struggle against limited resources, it is especially critical for the leaders to recognize and reward the hard work and sacrifices of its employees.

Summary

Leadership is the use of power to influence the behavior of others. Power means getting others to do what you want. Formal leadership is granted to a manager by the organization. Informal leadership arises from special situations. A manager can draw on position power and personal power. Power is limited by acceptance theory and the zone of indifference.

Leadership theories have developed from trait studies that tried to identify leadership qualities by evaluating personal attributes. Behavioral theories are based on the study of the leader's attitudes about tasks and people. Contingency or situational theory works from the concept that leadership approaches must be adjusted based on the particular situation. Transactional leaders work to motivate people to perform tasks and achieve objectives; transformational leaders work to inspire people to exceed their capabilities.

An effective leader must understand the four main motivation theories and how they apply in the workplace. Need theories argue we behave the way we do because of internal needs we are trying to fulfill. Maslow, Alderfer, the two-factor theory, and McClelland's acquired-needs theory all offer variations on the concept that we seek to met needs such as recognition, self-esteem, responsibility, growth, and self-actualization. Various factors such as working conditions, pay benefits, and organizational polices may reduce motivation. Cognitive theories are based on isolating and studying the thought processes used to select work behavior. The idea is that people find their own sources of motivation in the workplace. Adams equity theory argues that people use perceived inequities to motivate them to action. Vroom's expectancy theory states that we work most effectively if we believe the effort we put in will produce a desire outcome. If the probability of success is believed to be low, we will be less motivated to attempt a task or project. Reinforcement theory assumes that through operant conditioning and controlling rewards people will be motivated to repeat behaviors that are productive to them and the organization. Last, social learning theory ingrates cognitive and reinforcement theories to create a model in which the continuous interaction of the behaviors of processing words and images, vicarious learning, and self-control motivates a person to action. Real-life situations require that managers recognize that different work groups are motivated by different things. Theory integration is a possible model.

Managers must lead and effectively work with groups. Both formal and informal groups are a part of every organization. Group dynamics include understanding what happens when people are brought together to achieve certain objectives. Norms of behavior and cohesiveness are key elements of group development. Like people, groups can become dysfunctional over time. Groupthink is one symptom of ineffective group management.

An effective leader understands and uses the communications process between people and among groups. Elements of the process include the sender, the receiver, the channel, and the effects of noise on communication.

Key Terms and Concepts

Leadership
Power
Formal leadership
Informal leadership
Theory X
Theory Y
Position power: reward power, coercive power, legitimate power
Personal power: expert power, reference power
Acceptance theory
Zone of indifference
Approaches to leadership: trait, behavioral, contingency or situational, transactional and transformational
Theories of motivation
Needs theories: hierarchy of needs by Maslow, ERG theory by Alderfer, two-factor theory by Herzberg and Syndermann, acquired-needs theory by McClelland
Cognitive theories: equity theory by Adams, expectancy theory by Vroom
Reinforcement theory: organizational behavior modification, ABC
Social learning theory
Group dynamics: formal and informal groups; command, task, interest, and committee groups; group development stages; group norms and cohesiveness; groupthink

Distributed leadership
Communications process: stereotypes, halo effect, selective perception, projection

Questions

1. The use of power is a key component in leadership. Discuss examples from your work experience in which power was used effectively or ineffectively.

2. What are some additional examples of acceptance theory and the zone of indifference in the psychological contract people have with an organization?

3. Can trait theory be effectively applied in evaluating arts leadership? Explain how.

4. A directive or autocratic leadership style often is exhibited in an arts setting. Is it possible to have a strong artistic vision for a project and a participative leadership style? Explain how.

5. Cite examples in which situational leadership worked or failed.

6. Analyze a recent motivation problem you encountered in your work or school. What steps would you have taken to motivate the individual or group involved?

7. Can you cite a recent example of a dysfunctional group? How would you have solved the problem knowing what you now do about group behavior?

Case Study

As you will see in this article, if there is a gap between the direction a leader in which wishes to go and the board's perception of the organization, it can lead a dismissal.

Hartford Ballet Dismisses a Director
Jennifer Dunning

The Hartford Ballet has dismissed Kirk Peterson, a former member of the American Ballet Theater and the artistic director of the Connecticut troupe since 1993.

Peggy Kyman and Endi Kynn have been named to succeed Mr. Peterson. Ms. Lynn directs the School of Hartford Ballet. Ms. Lyman, a former Martha Graham dancer, directs the bachelor of arts program offered jointly by the school and the Hartt School at the University of Hartford.

The ballet troupe also did not renew the contracts of Raymond Lukens, the company's rehearsal assistant, and Maria Youskevitch, a prominent teacher at the ballet school. Mr. Peterson's contract would have expired in 1999.

Branko Terzic, chairman of the ballet, said that budget problems had led to the dismissal but declined to comment further, saying the company was in discussions about severance pay with Mr. Peterson.

Mr. Peterson did not significantly enlarge the company or increase the number of engagements each year. But one of his aims, he said on Thursday, had been to upgrade the troupe from a regional company to a nationally known group, developing a more international and glamorous repertory and creating an American Indian version of "The Nutcracker."

"I didn't want to put on the Bolshoi Ballet," he said. "I wanted Hartford Ballet to be a powerful artistic entity. I wanted to make the company a company that could stand side by side with any other company in the country."

An opinion piece written by Trevor Cushman, executive director of the ballet, and published in *The Hartford Courant* on Wednesday suggested that the company's administrators intended to focus on local audiences, with the dancers devoting 50 to 75 percent of their time to programs aimed at young people. "We have an internationally known dance company," Mr. Cushman wrote, "but how well is it known on Wethersfield Avenue or in the North End or at the Fox school with a fifth grader there named Joshua?" Hartford will never be "a dance connoisseur's town, "he continued, "but there is no reason why it cannot be a great place for kids to discover ballet."

SOURCE: Jennifer Dunning, "Hartford Ballet Dismisses a Director," *The New York Times*. Copyright © Tuesday, May 26, 1998, The New York Times. Used with permission.

Case Study Questions

1. Summarize the primary difference in the ballet artistic director's vision of the organization and vision of the administration.

2. Based on this article what would be your overall strategy as a leader to help make the ballet recognized nationally and locally? What specific leadership steps could you take to serve the two differing approaches?

3. It appears the executive director has a point of view about the company and its place in the city of Hartford. If you were artistic director of the ballet what leadership choices would you make to effectively work with the executive director?

References

1. John R. Schermerhorn, Jr., *Management for Productivity*, 2d ed. (New York: John Wiley and Sons, 1986), p. 275.
2. Ibid., p. 276.
3. Ibid.
4. Ibid., p. 46.
5. Ibid., p. 279.
6. Ibid.
7. Ibid.
8. Ibid.
9. Ibid., p. 280.
10. Ibid.
11. Ibid.
12. Chester Barnard, *The Functions of the Executive* (Cambridge, MA: Harvard University Press, 1938), pp. 165–66.
13. Schermerhorn, *Management for Productivity*, pp. 280–81.
14. John R. Kotter, "Acquiring and Using Power," Harvard Business Review, 55 (July-August 1977), pp. 130–32. Adapted from Schermerhorn, *Management for Productivity*, pp. 282–83.

15. Kathryn M. Bartol and David C. Martin, *Management,* 3d ed. (Boston: Irwin McGraw-Hill, 1998), p. 417.
16. Fred E. Fielder, *A Theory of Leadership Effectiveness* (New York, McGraw-Hill, 1967).
17. Victor H. Vroom and Phillip W. Yetten, *Leadership and Decision Making,* (Pittsburgh: University of Pittsburgh Press, 1973). The source material for this discussion is the table from the book entitled *Normative Leadership Model Decision Styles.*
18. Bartol and Martin, p. 429.
19. Ibid.
20. Ibid., p. 430.
21. Ibid., p. 431.
22. Ibid., p. 434.
23. Ibid.
24. Warren Bennis, *Why Leaders Can't Lead* (San Francisco: Jossey Bass, 1989).
25. Bartol and Martin, p. 385.
26. Ibid., p. 392.
27. Ibid., p. 400.
28. Ibid., p. 405.
29. Abraham H. Maslow, *Motivation and Personality* (New York: Harper and Row, 1954).
30. Bartol and Martin, p. 388.
31. Frederick Herzberg and B. Syndermann, *The Motivation to Work* (New York: John Wiley and Sons, 1959).
32. Bartol and Martin, p. 389.
33. Ibid., p. 390.
34. Ibid.
35. Ibid., p. 391.
36. Ibid.
37. J. Adams Stacy, "Toward an Understanding of Inequity," *Journal of Abnormal Psychology* 67 (1963), pp. 422–36.
38. Schermerhorn, *Management for Productivity,* pp. 338–40.
39. Victor Vroom, *Work and Motivation* (New York: John Wiley and Sons, 1964).
40. Bartol and Martin, p. 392.
41. Ibid., p. 393.
42. Ibid.
43. Ibid., p. 394.
44. Bob Nelson, *1001 Ways to Reward Employees* (New York: Workman Publishing, 1994).
45. James H. Donnelly, Jr., James L. Gibson, and John M. Ivancevich, *Fundamentals of Management* (Homewood, IL: BPI-Irwin, 1990), pp. 313–16.
46. B. F. Skinner, *Science and Human Behavior* (New York: Macmillan, 1953); *Contingencies of Reinforcement* (New York: Appleton-Century-Crofts, 1969).
47. John N. Marr and Richard T. Roessler, *Supervision and Management* (Fayetteville: University of Arkansas Press, 1994), pp. 9–12.
48. Bartol and Martin, *Management,* p. 405.
49. Ibid., p. 405.
50. Ibid.
51. Ibid., p. 405.
52. Ibid., p. 406.
53. Schermerhorn, *Management for Productivity,* p. 359.

54. Ibid.
55. Ibid., p. 361.
56. Ibid.
57. Donnelly, Gibson, and Ivancevich, *Fundamentals of Management*, pp. 346–47.
58. Arthur Bloch, *The Complete Murphy's Law* (Los Angeles: Price Stern Sloan, 1990), p. 48.
59. Ibid., p. 71.
60. Arthur G. Bedeian, *Management* (New York: Dryden Press, 1986), p. 508.
61. Bartol and Martin, *Management*, p. 490.
62. Schermerhorn, *Management for Productivity*, pp. 370–71.
63. Ibid., p. 374.
64. J. William Pfeiffer and John E. Jones, eds., *Annual Handbook fir Group Facilitators* (San Diego, CA: Pfeiffer and Co., 1976).
65. Edgar H. Schein, *Organizational Psychology* (Englewood Cliffs, NJ: Prentice-Hall, 1970), p. 81.
66. Ibid, p. 82.
67. John J. Makay and Ronald C. Fetzer, *Business Communication Skills: Principles and Practice*, 2d ed. (Englewood Cliffs, NJ: Prentice-Hall, 1984), pp. 5–6.
68. Schermerhorn, *Management for Productivity*, pp. 310–15.
69. Muriel Solomon, *Working with Difficult People* (Englewood Cliffs, NJ: Prentice-Hall, 1990).

Additional Resources

Judith M. Bardwick. *Danger in the Comfort Zone.* New York: American Management Association, 1991.

Phillip L. Hunsaker and Anthony J. Alessandra. *The Art of Managing People.* New York: Touchstone Books, Simon and Schuster, 1986.

Marilyn Loden. *Feminine Leadership.* New York: Times Books, 1985.

Henry Mintzberg. "The Manager's Job: Folklore and Fact." *Harvard Business Review* (July–August 1975).

Noel M. Tichy and Mary Anne Devanna. *The Transformational Leader.* New York: John Wiley and Sons, 1986.

Abraham Zaleznik. *The Managerial Mystique: Restoring Leadership in Business.* New York: Harper and Row, 1989.

9

Control: Management Information Systems and Budgeting

Before we move on to the topics of finance, marketing, and fund raising, we need to examine one more area in our look at the overall management process: control. We saw how planning helps us set the organization's direction and allocate its resources. We studied the organizing process to see how best to bring together people and resources. The leadership part of the process focused on directing people in the utilization of resources. We now look at control, the part of the management process that ensures that the right things happen, in the right way, and at the right time.[1]

In an arts organization, the word *control* carries connotations that often make people uncomfortable. People generally do not like to think of themselves as being controlled by others. At the same time, however, they are not comfortable in situations that could be described as being "out of control." If an arts manager is to lead an organization successfully, systems of control must be in place and function effectively. Far too often we hear of the results of a lack of a control process in an arts organization. When you read an article about a dance company that ran up an unanticipated deficit of $200,000 in one season, you have to ask yourself how this could happen. The assumption is that the budgetary and financial control systems must have broken down. After all, $200,000 does not just appear in a budget report one day.

Control as a Management Function

Here, we use the term *control* to mean "a process of monitoring performance and taking action when needed to ensure the desired results are achieved."[2] The elements that enter into this process and affect how well the system works are uncertainty, complexity, human limitations, and the degree of centralization in the organization.

Uncertainty exists in all planning. Without the ability to see into the future, every organization must plan for uncertainty, and the control system must take this element into account. One useful way of accommodating uncertainty is to evaluate regularly the progress being made in meeting the defined objectives. This becomes a control point at which you may make adjustments in the activities being performed.

Issues related to complexity sometimes are more elusive. Over time, organizations grow and become more diverse. The controls required to monitor activity in an organization often lag behind growth. For example, if you shift from processing all your ticket and subscription revenue through your own box office to a new performing arts center, your old control for tracking revenue probably will be inadequate for the new system. At the same time, you still need accurate, up-to-date reports. New processes and procedure will be put in place and the level of complexity will increase.

All control systems must take into account human limitations. Errors will be made. An incorrect amount will be entered in the computer, an order form will be misplaced, a costume or set piece will be constructed incorrectly, or a purchase order or invoice will be lost. The control system must recognize that these things will happen and must have in place adequate monitoring capabilities. For example, the accuracy of the cash accounting could be enhanced if two different people counted ticket sales before depositing funds in the bank.

The basic design of your organization may require different control processes because of the degree of centralization or decentralization. If you operate a decentralized organization, authority normally will be delegated to more people in middle- and lower-level management positions. Control systems that ensure accountability will be required. For example, if the scenery construction shop is five miles from the administrative offices, you do not want to make a staff member drive to the office every time a purchase order is needed. Instead, you probably will delegate the authority to approve purchases to a staff member at the shop, who will submit the purchase orders and invoices for the week to a member of the accounting staff for review. The control points now include the staff member who authorizes the purchase and the staff member who reviews the purchase before entering it into the accounting records.

Elements of the Control Process

The control process comprises four elements: *establishing performance objectives, measuring results, comparing the actual outcome with the objectives,* and *implementing corrective procedures*[3] Figure 9–1 diagrams this process with an example of a missed sales target.

The first area to examine in the control system is the *performance objectives.* What were the expectations about how much, how good, how expensive, or how timely the work being performed was? How many membership or subscription orders do you want to process in a day, in a week, in a month, in a year?

The second step in the control process is to measure and compare what was achieved. How much did sales increase? How long did it take to build the scenery or costumes? In order for the measurement system to work you must have the mechanisms in place to track the data.

The third step requires an assessment of what caused the difference between your objective and the actual results. Was there a lack of resources, poorly trained staff, high turnover, or weak management?

The fourth step culminates in action taken by the manager to correct the problem. Assuming your control system is providing feedback in a timely manner you may increase staff, institute new training programs, or replace the manager leading the work group.

The control system extends into areas that may not be quantified as easily. For example, what is the appropriate output standard for the rehearsal process of a play, opera, dance, or concert? Assuming that all of these events have a deadline for opening night, the leader (director, choreographer, and so on) must make it clear through the rehearsal

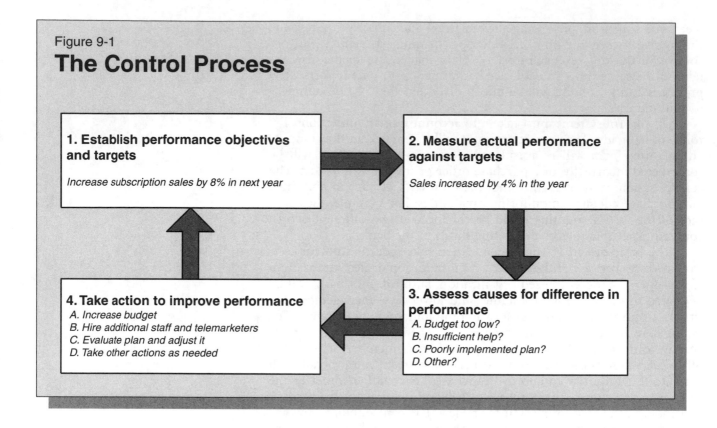

Figure 9-1

The Control Process

1. Establish performance objectives and targets

Increase subscription sales by 8% in next year

2. Measure actual performance against targets

Sales increased by 4% in the year

4. Take action to improve performance
A. Increase budget
B. Hire additional staff and telemarketers
C. Evaluate plan and adjust it
D. Take other actions as needed

3. Assess causes for difference in performance
A. Budget too low?
B. Insufficient help?
C. Poorly implemented plan?
D. Other?

schedule what will be expected during preparation for the event. However, if no one monitors the process, the control system breaks down. For example, if the artistic director is directing the play and spends the first five weeks of a six-week rehearsal period on the first act, who is left to take corrective action? The stage manager may point out that the play is behind schedule, but if the person in charge of the whole operation does not stick to the schedule as written, little can be done.

For many arts organizations, there may be no solution to a dysfunctional control system. The artistic director may hold others to the established output standard while personally ignoring it. The result is an organization in a constant state of panic about getting the production ready for the opening.

This is a circumstance where strong board leadership could influence the control systems. For example, the board president and the personnel committee could mandate that a different working relationship between an artistic director and a managing director be established. The board would have to grant the managing director has some real authority to monitor the schedule and take corrective action when required. Under this scheme, the managing director would point out at the appropriate times that the published rehearsal schedule is not being followed. He or she would request adjustments in the schedule be made and, it is hoped, get the show back on schedule.

In the real world, of course, it is much harder to get people to accept intervention in their projects. Often, in arts organizations, people occupy multiple positions of control. The artistic director may be very effective at setting the output standards for a guest director and others in the organization while reacting violently to being criticized for falling behind schedule. Ultimately, the ability of the organization to effectively realize its mission depends to some degree on how well the control systems function.

Another component of the control process is to set *input standards*. The process involves evaluating the effort that goes into a task. One way to evaluate the work is to look at how well the person used the available resources. For example, a staff member might ask for two extra helpers to complete the subscription orders within the six weeks allotted for the task. If the orders actually take nine weeks to complete and, halfway through the schedule, two more people had to be hired, the supervisor might wonder about the staff member's ability to estimate the resources needed to complete a project.

Once you establish objectives for output, you face the issue of *measuring performance*. In some cases, a manager can define clearly the quantitative measures and communicate them to the employees. For example, a manager expects at least 45 subscription orders to be processed each day. The actual number of orders filled in one day gives the manager a specific piece of information. A lower output would lead to an investigation of the work process, and it may be found that, by changing the order in which the work is completed, the average number of orders filled daily exceeds 45.

Since many areas in an arts organization deal with specialized craft and custom construction techniques, it is much harder to make accurate projections about the performance level of a staff member. Suppose that eight chairs must be built for a dining room scene in a play or opera. The shop supervisor asks the properties master how long it will take to build the chairs, and they agree on five days as the output standard. At the end of that period, only three chairs have been completed. The shop supervisor notes that the expected output level was not met, intercedes, and changes the input standard. Two extra people are assigned to assist the properties master complete the remaining chairs.

The previous examples demonstrate how a manager will compare the actual performance with the standards and make adjustments to correct any problems. The success of any of the projects cited in these examples depends on active and involved management of the control process.

In an arts setting, the critical work of all the creative artists must undergo a similarly active interaction with management. For performers, the roles they act or sing and the music they play represent a complex mix of talent, ego, and ensemble interaction. How do you set standards, evaluate performance, and take corrective action when a performer does not measure up to the expectations? You can call on your communication skills to tactfully present the problem, suggest alternatives, and ultimately, if the work does not meet the expected standards, replace the performer. Circumstances may prevent taking such direct action, however. For example, a union contract may prevent or hinder abrupt changes in casting.

In some situations, you may have no recourse. For example, suppose that the scene designer you hired to do the sets for your opening production misses the deadline for submitting the plans. Your shop staff cannot start building the set, and the entire construction process begins behind schedule. Your only recourse would be to refuse to hire that designer for your next show. By the time you confront the problem of failing to meet an output standard, it is too late to take much corrective action.

Management by Exception

One way of creating a control system is to establish a *management by exception* (MBE) process within the organization.[4] Essentially, the MBE process (shown in Figure 9–2) works as a part of the comparative element outlined in the control system. Once you establish clear performance standards and communicate them throughout the organization, you focus your energies on the exceptions to the norm. In this approach, you spend time on the less-than-standard performance. However, you can boost morale and productivity if your management team recognizes and rewards people who exceed the standards.

For management by exception to work, internal control must be at a high level in the organization. High standards for performance must be central to the culture and value system of the organization. From this strong culture should come attitudes among your staff that support them in setting high goals for their own work output. An arts manager who approaches the staff from the perspective of McGregor's Theory Y, as you may remember from Chapter 8, will assume that staff members want to do a good job. Of course, if clear standards are not communicated to employees, you cannot expect even the most highly self-motivated people to meet your expectations.

Another element in the MBE process is a system of external controls. Every organization needs some ongoing policies and procedures to guide work behavior and state expected standards clearly. When the organization sets these standards (smoking policy, break periods, vacations, sick days, and so forth), it frees the manager from expending energy on routine expectations. The manager need be concerned with only the exceptions to the external controls.

Management by Objectives

In the late 1960s, the concept of *management by objectives* (MBO) began to be applied widely in the business world. Simply put, MBO is an integrated planning and control system that involves a formal agreement between a supervisor and subordinate concerning[5]

1. the employee's performance objectives for a specific period of time;
2. the plan(s) to be used to accomplish the objectives;
3. agreed upon standards for measuring the work accomplished;
4. and, procedures for reviewing results.

When properly applied, management by objectives is integrated into the overall strategic plan for the organization. For example, if one of an organization's goals is to increase the level of donations from corporations, and the objective is to increase corporate giving by 10 percent this year, then the development staff can specifically develop quantitative objectives for the year. Specific methods would be developed to meet the objectives (phone, mail, and direct contact campaigns), and standards of achievement would be set for each employee (each staff member is given a specific dollar amount as the goal for a specific time period). During regular meetings, the employee and the supervisor would evaluate the employee's progress in meeting the objective.

As you can see, the MBO process can be very time consuming. When you begin to account for all the time spent drawing up objectives, meeting regularly to review and revise objectives, and documenting the MBO of each employee, you can begin to see some of the problems. You also may encounter problems if the objectives you set

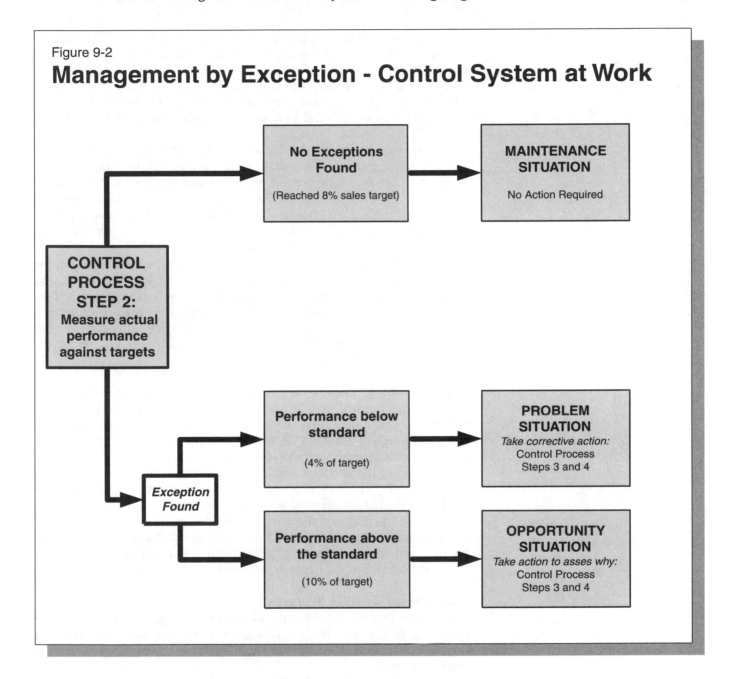

Figure 9-2

Management by Exception - Control System at Work

are reached too easily. In a sense, you begin to establish lowered performance expectations.

In an arts organization, different employee groups have different time frames in their work. As a system, MBO does not make much sense for performers. Elements of MBO may make sense in administrative and production areas in the organization, provided that the time and commitment to support the extensive demands of MBO really exist.

Performance Appraisal Systems

When an arts organization grows big enough to keep a staff employed year-round, a *performance appraisal system* will have to be established. Performance appraisal simply means formally evaluating work performance and providing feedback so that performance adjustments can be made.[6] Performance appraisal is part of the overall control system for the organization. If the system is working well, it should provide employees with constructive feedback about their strengths and weaknesses and concrete suggestions for improving and developing their careers. The objective of the appraisal system should be to benefit the employee and the supervisors and to help the organization reach its goals.

Appraisal methods   The business of evaluating people should be tailored to the organization's overall design and structure. Arts organizations probably would be put off by the various numerical rating scales devised by business specialists. For example, there is dubious value in giving an employee a rating of 7 on a scale of 1 to 10. However, a rating of "unsatisfactory" on a behavioral scale in a specific job area ("relates well to others") might draw more attention.

Arts organizations find the *critical incident appraisal* technique more acceptable. The supervisor keeps a running log of positive and negative incidents of work performance over a given time period and reviews it with the employee at specific intervals. Arts organizations also could use a *free-form narrative* to evaluate employees. This essay format usually notes overall job performance, specific accomplishments, strengths, and weaknesses.

Timely feedback   The annual evaluation is a key part of an organization's overall control system but does not provide feedback on work performance on a day-to-day basis. An effective control system must give employees regular feedback about their work output. Some organizations tend not to comment about the good work someone is doing until the annual evaluation. As a result, the employee spends a year working in a vacuum. Even worse, a serious problem in an employee's work habits will be left unattended for a year.

A good manager realizes that each employee has a different need for feedback. Some people need constant monitoring, and others are happy when left alone. An appraisal system must be flexible enough to accommodate a range of employee needs.

Summary of Control Systems
The control process extends into all areas of an organization. The planning, organizing, and leading functions of management interact with the control systems in a way that should provide an effectively managed organization.

At the beginning of this chapter, we noted that the word *control* is a source of discomfort to many people. How can you have a dynamic, creative arts organization and still have effective control systems? The two elements need not cancel each other out.

An arts organization, ideally, will contain an element of creative chaos. The creation of an evening of theater, dance, opera, or music or the installation of an exhibit will develop a life of its own. It may be messy. It may he filled with conflict and passion. My experience is that no two events will ever come together in exactly the same way. Being an adaptable manager is a requirement for survival and for effective monitoring.

What, then, is an effective way to establish a control system in this environment? One simple approach is to recognize that producing art is not the same as producing large quantities of a product or service. The unique event being presented needs a set of mutually agreed-on rules, regulations, and guidelines specific to that project. Recognizing that the event must interact with an ongoing organizational structure, the challenge to the arts manager is to find a way to create bridges between the two approaches.

For example, the financial and accounting aspects of the organization require a great deal of control. Rules, regulations, and laws must be obeyed. You can increase compliance with the rules by making them clear and simple to follow. If, to purchase three yards of fabric for a costume, a staff member must fill out six forms in triplicate and have them signed by two different people, the odds are good that people will do whatever they can to avoid using the "correct" procedures. In this example, the organization would benefit from a different control system for its purchasing procedures.

Management Information Systems

Let us now look at a key supporting system that makes the organizational control work effectively: the management information system. A *management information system* (MIS) is formally defined as "a mechanism designed to collect, combine, compare, analyze, and disseminate data in the form of information."[7] For an arts organization, a well-designed MIS should serve as an almost invisible element. The design, implementation, and maintenance of the MIS may not be particularly exciting to people working in the arts. In fact, many organizations never establish a formal MIS; one evolves. The evolution of the MIS often comes from the crisis management style exercised by many organizations.

For example, it is the middle of summer before you find out that subscription sales revenue is down 15 percent and your cash flow has all been spent to meet creditors' bills and last month's payroll. This has never been as big a problem before. What happened? In this case, maybe the MIS, as it existed, simply did not get financial information about sales and accounts to you quickly enough.

The MIS currently in place may be too informal. Suppose that you are planning a major tour in which your ballet company will perform in five large cities. Two days before the tour starts, you are informed by the management in the first city that only 35 percent of the house has been sold. Whenever you asked about how sales were going, you were told, "Orders are coming in at a steady pace." Because you were led to believe that the sponsor would easily be able to sell 60 percent of capacity, based on previous dance company performances, you signed a contract based on a percentage of the house, not a flat fee. This example of a lack of a hard data delivered in a timely manner very well could mean bankruptcy for the dance company.

Both examples demonstrate the importance of a good MIS. A key function of the MIS is to help managers make decisions. To make a decision implies you have a choice. To exercise choice means that you select from alternative plans of action. The choices you have may become increasingly limited as time passes. In the case of a subscription campaign, you have to make the sale before the season opens. If you learn early enough that sales are down, you can implement planned courses of action to increase sales. If you learn too late about the shortfall in revenue, all you can do is plan for an operating deficit.

Let us look at how to establish an effective MIS so that many of these problems can be avoided.

Data and Information

When we defined an MIS, we used the terms *data* and *information*. Each term implies a great deal about the MIS. With the advent of the personal computer, the term *data* has found its way into our daily vocabulary. Data comes to us in the form of facts and figures, which we process to form a meaningful conclusion. We disseminate this conclusion to others in a regular pattern of information within the organization. The actual number of subscriptions sold and the revenue collected each day at the box office represent raw data that we process and disseminate to those who need the information.

Data and information are not neutral terms. Because people process data, certain biases may affect this part of the process. For example, 25 subscriptions sold in one day may seem like a basic piece of data. You might ask how this number compares to the number sold at this time last year or how the number compares to projections of expected sales to date. If, on the other hand, the box office manager took in revenue from only 18 sales and the other 7 sales were phone calls from people who said they would be renewing, the data collected implies something quite different. The box office manager may have been telling you what he or she thought you wanted to hear to present as optimistic a sales picture as possible. The point is that the MIS you have in place is meaningless if individuals manipulate the data to present misleading information.

Management Information Systems in the Arts

Figure 9–3 shows a partial MIS for an arts organization. Ideally, the system would be set up so data and information can be shared. A small arts organization does not require a supercomputer to function as its central data bank. Although computerization certainly would assist the management decision process, simply walking from department to department to gather information is far less costly. For example, daily reports from the stage manager and technical director to the production manager support the design and production information system. Reports made in weekly staff meetings by the production manager to the managing director complete the cycle of data gathering and distribution.

Most arts organizations start with a small staff of two or three people. The MIS exists as an informal communication among people who are often part of a well-established social unit. The group may have morning meetings to review the day's activities, and this meeting becomes the core of the MIS. One person may deal with accounting, finances, and logistics, while someone else covers marketing and fund raising. A personnel system is not even needed. As the organization grows, more staff members are added, and specialization and departmentalization occur.

Organizational design has a direct impact on the MIS. For example, the MIS of a regional theater company with three theaters in different locations in the city must take into account the potential problems of decentralization. How will these remote locations operate in relation to the accounting department? How will accounting know about purchases unless the MIS includes the accounting department in the ordering stage? If the information system is required to keep track of and control funds expended, it cannot record purchases based on invoices that may come 15 to 30 days after an item has been purchased.

Figure 9-3

Management Information Systems (MIS)

Partial schematic of equipment and information flow in an organization

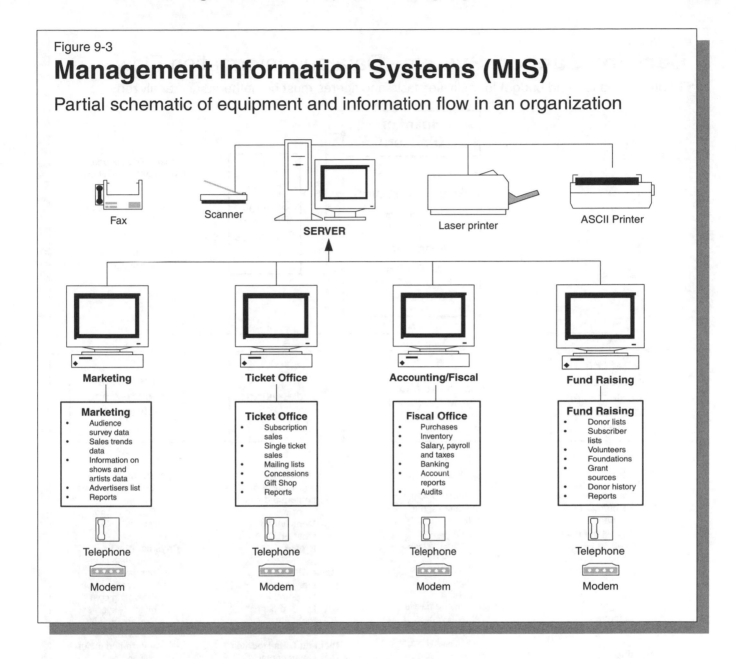

Computers and the Management Information System

Computers and management information systems seem to have been made for each other. The computer's ability to store large amounts of data and distribute it through networks within an organization has had a major impact on the business world. The ability to gather, store, and manipulate data now is very cost effective. The smallest arts organization usually has at least one computer to do the bookkeeping or manage a mailing list. Large businesses spend more on a computerized MIS than 10 regional theater companies spend for all their needs. Whatever the scale of operation, careful planning is required if the maximum benefit of computerization is to be realized.

Figure 9–4 shows a simple flow of information from areas such as the box office, marketing, fund raising, and facilities departments. Information is needed to make decisions and this system fulfills that need. Word processing, e-mail, file transfers and facsimile capabilities enhance

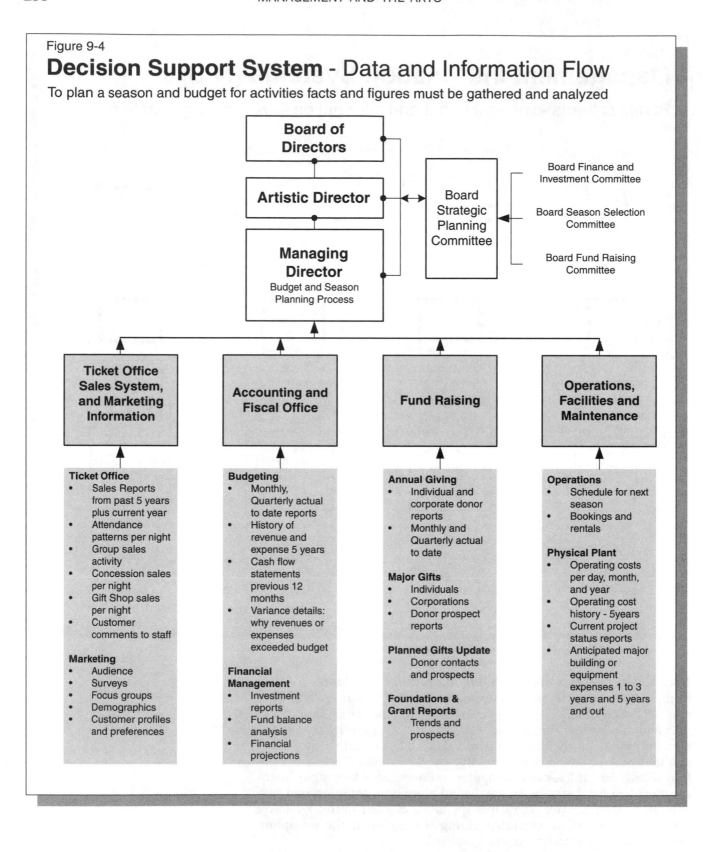

Figure 9-4

Decision Support System - Data and Information Flow

To plan a season and budget for activities facts and figures must be gathered and analyzed

the effectiveness of the overall system. Typically, such a system provides daily reports of ticket and subscription income, as well as year-to-date and previous-year comparisons. Regardless of the scale of the system, a good flow of information needs to exist in the first place. Adding computers does not mean a poorly designed MIS will work.

An Effective Management Information System

The purpose of any MIS is to facilitate the accomplishment of the organization's objectives through improved problem solving and decision making. In shaping and revising a MIS, three factors must be taken into account: the uncontrollable, partially controllable, and fully controllable factors that determine how effective the MIS will be.[8] Let us look at each type.

Uncontrollable factors   Some factors, such as organizational structure and the organization's relationship to its external environments, are beyond the control of the MIS. For example, in a highly decentralized organization in which subgroups have a great deal of autonomy, it may prove difficult to implement an MIS effectively. A regional theater, opera, or dance company may have administrative offices in one location, rehearse in two or three different spaces, build sets and props in yet another locale, and perform in two different venues during the year. This structure would make it more challenging to set up a MIS linked by computers. The flow of information would be possible by using various data transmission formats, such as fax machines and modems hooked up to remote computers that report back to the administrative offices. A computer that functions as a server in the central office may be installed to help manage the data flow. However, the resources needed to pay for all of this may limit the overall system.

An unstable internal or external business environment also has an effect on the MIS. For example, suppose that you are trying to track audience response by collecting data from your mailings. Between the first and second mailing, a fiscal crisis forces the organization to drop two shows from the season. How will you collect meaningful data about the effectiveness of a second mailing if the season package keeps changing?

Many small arts organizations simply lack the resources to install computer networks. The uncontrollable factor in this case may be that the five personal computers in the organization all use different software and are isolated from each other. The fund-raising staff uses one type of software to track the donors, and the box office uses different software to collect sales and subscription information. Data are not shared and information transfer is limited.

Partially controllable factors   It is possible to gain some short-range control over a poorly structured MIS by bringing available resources to bear on the problem. In the previous example, for instance, a managing director might be able to intercede and make sure that the different computer systems use common software. Data files then could be copied from one machine to another, and information could be shared over what is called a *shoe leather network*. For this to succeed, people in the organization must understand the importance of creating a data gathering and information dissemination system.

Fully controllable factors   An MIS that has fully controllable factors is supported and encouraged by the organization and its management. In this ideal world, a staff member would be designated to oversee the data and information system. This person would hold a senior-staff position with support staff to assist with system maintenance. The MIS would be fully integrated into the overall organizational operation.

Integrated computer systems and ongoing operating procedures would support regular data gathering and storage. For example, an effective MIS would allow a marketing staff member to track subscription sales by type of purchaser over the previous five years by accessing a database of subscriber files. When a staff member in the press office needs information about a singer who was in an opera produced by the company three years ago, that information would be available in a database of artist biographies.

Common Mistakes

Care must be taken to avoid some common mistakes in establishing a MIS. As noted earlier, many arts organizations evolve and grow without paying much attention to any MIS. Often, much time is wasted hunting down information that should be readily available. However, trying to force an MIS on an organization that is not yet ready for it can damage the credibility of the system. Even when the MIS is accepted, there are still pitfalls to avoid. Here are four problems with bringing a management information system into operation.

More information is not always better. The issue here is quality, not quantity. Data that are translated into too much information may turn out to be more of a hindrance than a help. It does not take a great deal of effort to overwhelm people with too much information.

Do not assume that people need all the information they want. When designing a MIS for an organization, it is important to review with the various staff members exactly what information they need to be more productive. People tend to request more information than they will have time to process and synthesize.

Despite receiving more information, decision making might not improve. Information does not translate into more effective management. In some cases, too much information may result in decision paralysis for some managers.

Do not assume that computers can solve all of your information management problems. Arts organizations, which are often resource poor, have benefited greatly from the continuing decrease in cost and increase in power of computer systems. The greatest benefits come when a well-designed software system is carefully integrated with a clear vision of the organization's information management needs. However, organizations tend to forget that time is needed to train people to use a computer-based MIS effectively. A poorly designed and managed MIS will probably be abandoned by the users, and everyone will return to the old procedures.

Management Information System Summary

If you ask a staff member in an arts organization how well the management information system is working, you might get a puzzled look. If, on the other hand, you ask the person whether the monthly account statements that detail the expenses of the department are informative, he or she probably will say yes. In this case, the MIS appears to be working.

The effectiveness of an MIS in an arts organization often boils down to integrating the existing systems that produce data and information. The accounting reports of expenses, bills, and payroll; the box office re-

Computers in the Arts—Putting Technology to Work

An example of a heavy use of computers in helping to manage an arts organization may be found in the United State Institute for Theatre Technology (USITT). USITT is a 3,500-member international organization of designers, technicians, stage managers, craftspeople, manufacturers, and companies primarily associated with the performing arts and entertainment industry. Since the late 1980s, USITT has been working with its sister organization, the Canadian Institute for Theatre Technology (CITT), to establish a "virtual organization." Through a server in Calgary, Canada, which functions as the home base for CultureNet, USITT conducts business on a daily basis. The board of directors has an electronic forum where it may vote on action items that come up between board meetings. The executive, finance, planning, publications, and conference committees all "meet" and communicate on a regular basis. Through the use of portable document format (PDF) files, full-color graphics and detailed schedules, budget reports, and other documents are up and downloaded on a regular basis. Using free software such as Adobe Reader™ allows people who lack the source software to view and print documents. Electronic Forums are places where meetings and discussions are held. Votes are taken and the organization keeps it's members informed via its WWW site.

On the whole the system allows board and staff members to meet and keep in touch from around the world. Of course, the effectiveness of all this technology is only as good as the computers and training of the people at the other end. A few holdouts still are sent hard copy of documents and phoned or faxed when a critical vote is being taken. While certainly more effective as a management tool than five years ago, limitations in the computer skill of some of its members compromises the system.

---

ports of sales; and the fund raising reports of donor amounts may simply need to be pulled together in an overview for the staff and board. Probably the most effective way to quickly pull together a MIS is to ask some very basic questions about what information the organization and the staff need on a daily, weekly, monthly, quarterly, and annual basis. A chart that lists the data, reports, and so on needed in each time frame can become the foundation for a very simple and effective MIS.

The Future

Arts organizations as well as many other businesses have only begun to tap into the potential of computers as an organizational support and a MIS tool. The current application of computers in arts organizations has focused on automating manual procedures. This has resulted in productivity gains in isolated parts of the organization. It now may take minutes to gather the information that used to require days.

As computer networks become more common and computer processing speed increases, the arts manager of the future will need to be creative in extending the effectiveness of the automated MIS beyond record keeping and data management. The new technology is leading systems that will allow the multimedia use of computers. For example, designers, directors, and data managers will be able to update designs, visualize a staging, or manipulate data many times faster than ever imagined.

Budgets and the Control System

In this final section on control systems, we look at the area of budgeting. Budget control very quickly can become the major focus of an arts manager's job. Being able to project revenue accurately and to monitor and control expenses for a small organization with a limited budget is an extremely valuable set of skills to possess. The very survival of an arts organization often depends on being able to keep current with income and expenses. As a control center, budgeting is a key element in the overall MIS of the organization.

What exactly is a budget? One common definition of a *budget* is "a quantitative and financial expression of a plan."[9] A budget represents an allocation of resources to activities. If the control process is to be effective, the person supervising the use of the funds must be held responsible for the budget. Depending on the organization's culture, the budget development and implementation process may range from highly structured and formal to informal. Formal budgeting implies a proposal and review process before budget changes are approved. Depending on the structure of the organization, proposing and making changes in the budget could involve very precise procedures. See Figure 9–5 for an overview of the process.

Budgetary Centers

Before an arts organization begins the process of trying to fulfill mission it has set for itself, a budget must be prepared. Even the smallest organization will need to look at two key centers: revenue and expenses. The *revenue centers* include income from the sale of tickets or memberships, donations, grants, concessions, program advertising, rentals, and merchandise. *Expense centers* generally follow the organizational structure that has been established. These two components form the overall operating budget of the organization.

Budgets as Preliminary Controls

A budget is a preliminary control because it establishes the resources allocated to achieve the objectives outlined in the operational plans for the organization. An opera company that allocates one-third of its production budget to one show in a five-show season is making a statement of artistic priority. The monthly budget reports should give the production manager a clear sense of whether the resources allocated for each show are being used as projected. A budget functions as a preliminary control when the production manager tells the designers that they have a specific amount for sets, costumes, and so forth.

Types of Budgets

The types of budgets that an organization could use include fixed, flexible, zero-based, operating, short-term, and long-term budgets.[10]

In a *fixed budget*, allocations are based on the estimated costs from a fixed base of resources. For example, the salary budget is set for the year, and resources are allocated to cover that expense. Typically, the fixed budget becomes the base budget for the work area and is increased or decreased on an incremental basis according to activities and plans proposed each year.

A *flexible budget* assumes that activity levels will influence resource use. For example, a museum's payroll budget may respond to increased traffic flows due to programming. If the museum has a big exhibit that brings in a larger than average number of paid admissions (increased revenue), it also may have to hire additional part-time guards to control the crowds (increased expense).

A *zero-based budget* is a planning and objective-setting tool used by some arts organizations. At the end of a fiscal cycle, all budget lines are

Figure 9-5

The Budgeting Process

A budget is a financial expression of the plans of the organization

Factors That Affect Budget Development

A. Board & Management Plans

1. Overall organizational strategic & operational plans are formulated or reviewed each year
2. Management and Board make decisions that establish objectives for the year based on overall strategic plan
3. Staff estimates costs to fulfill objectives and costs of any new initiatives
4. Assess overall impact on continuing budget

B. Existing Operations

Based on current operations & new tasks budgets are prepared for each area

Revenue:
   Ticket sales
   Memberships
   Donations
   Investments

Expenses:
   Personnel
   Benefits
   Marketing
   Fund raising
   Operations & facilities
   Productions
   Miscellaneous

Evaluation, Revisions & Approval Process

C. Budget Formulation

Staff presents budget to finance or budget committee of the board
   1. Draft 1- Typically more expense than revenue
   2. Revision process to balance income and expense
   3. Committee approves and brings final budget to full board for action
   4 Board approves
   5. Staff implements
   6. Control systems monitor revenue and expense activity
   7. Start over again for next season at steps A and B

Implement, Monitor & Adjust

D. Yearly Operating Budget Implementation

1. Monthly reports to management and finance committee
2. Summary reports to board members
3. Budget reviewed & adjusted as conditions warrant
4. Issue accounting and audit reports as required by law

zeroed out. Revenues and expenses must be projected and justified in relation to the plans and objectives for the whole organization for the coming year. Compared to the fixed budget with its yearly incremental increases, the zero-based budget can be an effective tool to help keep an organization from creating budgets filled with underutilized line items.

An *operating budget*, as already noted, normally is a yearly budget created to carry out the organization's operational plans.

A *short-term budget* describes expense and revenue activity during a period of one year or less. An individual project or production may have a short-term budget that covers its activities, and this is situated within the overall operating budget of the organization. A *long-term budget* is used for projects or programs of more than one year, such as a five-year fund raising campaign. The objective of a long-term budget is to allocate resources that are not subject to year-to-year budget cutting.

The Budgetary Process

As noted in Figure 9–5, the budgeting process usually begins with a projection of the organization's various sources of revenue. In arts organizations, revenue comes from a variety of sources. The organization's MIS should be able to provide detailed reports of all revenue from the previous year or years. Evaluation of the previous revenue distributions and comparison with the budget projections for the coming year are the next step. Care must be taken when projecting revenue. A few too many optimistic revenue projections could lead to a midseason budget crisis.

The same type of activity takes place in the organization's various expense centers. Comparing the recent year's expense patterns and evaluating the project and programming plans for the next year must be done in the context of the overall revenue for the organization.

The next stage in the process compares and adjusts budgets based on expected revenue. If, after subtracting revenue, expenses still exceed the available resources, a series of revision's are made in the expense budgets.

Arts organizations sometimes find themselves adjusting revenue projections to match expenses. This dangerous game usually leads to chronic financial trouble for the organization. For example, unrealistic projections of fund raising or subscription sales revenue may result in a balanced budget to present to the finance committee of the board, but such budget practices are nothing short of fraud.

Budget Reality

A manager in an organization soon discovers that the control process in budgeting extends into anticipating behavior patterns by staff members. Staff members become very territorial about budgets, for example. Some people overestimate needs, while others try to make the budget allocation process a competition for resources within the organization. (One tool for controlling this problem is to work with zero-based budgets.) Very few staff members will loudly proclaim, "I don't need this much. Here, take back some of my budget."

Budget Controls

Trying to control a budget can be a full-time activity. Theoretically, the organizational MIS will provide the manager with the required information about revenue and expenses. For budget control to be effective, the manager must have this information as quickly as possible each month. Without computers, this work becomes more time consuming, but it is not impossible. Simple year-to-date percentage expectations for revenue and expenses can give a manager some element of control over a budget. For example, at the end of a specific period of time, a specific percentage of the budget should have been expended. The manager's efforts then can be focused on variances from the expected distributions.

Another key element in the budget control process involves the authorization procedures for expending funds. A system of review and approval must exist if the organization is to control its budget effectively.

Finally, the manager must recognize and develop strategies for dealing with the political nature of budgets. Organizational politics play a role in the budget control process. Staff members try to obtain as many resources as possible for their work areas. The information a manager receives may have been filtered by department heads to distort the true budgetary condition of a subunit within the organization.

Chapter 11 examines in detail the actual workings of a budget. Sample budgets are shown within an overall financial management information system.

Summary

Control is the process of monitoring performance and making adjustments as required to meet planned objectives. Uncertainty affects all planning. The degree of complexity, human limitations, and the degree of centralization also influence how effective an organization's control system will be.

Output and input standards must be clearly established. Measurement standards must be in place so that a manager can compare what was done with what was expected. A control system requires that mechanisms be in place for correcting work that fails to meet the standard. Management by exception (MBE) allows a manager to focus attention on variances to expected performance. Management by objectives (MBO) encourages the integration of planning objectives and work objectives.

Performance appraisal systems are formal methods for providing feedback to employees on a regular basis. Numerical rating scales, behavioral rating scales, critical incident method, and free-form narratives are techniques used to appraise work output.

Effective control systems depend on data and information gathered from the organization's management information system (MIS). The MIS extends into all areas of the organization, influenced by factors related to the controllability of the information flow through the organization. The organizational design might promote or hinder the effectiveness of the MIS. Some of the possible shortcomings in a MIS include providing too much data, providing irrelevant data, or assuming that computerizing operations will improve the MIS.

Budget control systems are a critical component of an organization. Controlling the distribution of resources and monitoring how effectively the resources are used is a full-time job. Organizations must identify revenue and expense centers and project monetary activity accordingly. A budget can function as a preliminary control on a project by defining the limits on the available resources. Budgets can be fixed, flexible, or zero-based and cover the short or long term. Budget controls concentrate on the timely monitoring of revenue and expenses for all areas of an organization.

Key Terms and Concepts

Organizational control system
Output and input standards
Internal and external controls
Management by exception
Management by objectives
Performance appraisal system
Management information system
Budget
Fixed and flexible budgets
Zero-based budget
Short- and long-term budgets
Budgetary process
Budget controls

Questions

1. What is the relationship of control to the manager's other functions?

2. What are the four steps in the control process? Give a specific example of the control process in an arts setting.

3. Describe the typical steps involved in applying the management by exception process. As a system, how does MBE effect an organization's planning process?

4. From your personal experience, describe a situation in which the control system for an organization did or did not work well. Offer suggestions for appropriate improvements, if applicable.

5. What are the four main appraisal methods used in a control system? Briefly evaluate some of the things you have accomplished in the last year.

6. Define the term *management information system*.

7. What will be some of the future applications of MIS computers in the arts?

8. How is a budget part of the control system?

9. What are the five types of budgets? Which type or types would be most effective in supporting an arts organization?

10. Outline the budget process.

Case Study

The following article points out problems with an organization's control system. You should be able to find numerous flaws in the system used to keep staff activities in check.

Radio Station Officials Got Free Cruises

Officials with a college's public radio and television station have received tens of thousands of dollars worth of free ocean cruises through fund-raising promotions of questionable value to the stations.

Last year, the station manager and his wife were sent on an all-expenses-paid cruise to China, Korea, and Japan by a travel agency that had a promotional contract with the stations—a contract that the station manager signed. The travel agency also paid

$2,700 toward a cruise package for one of the radio station's program directors, records show.

A glossy, full-color promotional brochure sent to 33,000 of the station's donors described the 18-day excursion as a once-in-a-lifetime opportunity and boasted of the ship's excellent chefs and fine dining. Ports of call included Shanghai, Hong Kong, Pusan, and Nagasaki, with three nights in Peking.

Although the cruise was heavily promoted as a fund raiser to benefit the area's only public broadcast outlets—with $200 from every cruise package sold being donated to the stations—the chief benefit appears to have been to station officials.

The cruise packages given to the station manager, his wife, and the program director were worth a total of $11,000 to $15,000. The cruise line sold more than $125,000 worth of cruise tickets through the station and received thousands of dollars worth of free advertising.

Meanwhile, the station received a $4,800 "contribution" from the cruise line and an additional $7,250 from auctioning off two cruise packages donated by the cruise line for the station's annual membership drive. The 24 people who bought the cruises received a $200 tax write-off per person.

The station manager said that he and his wife were asked by the travel agency to host the trip because the agency thought that having the couple host the trip would sell more cruises.

But the station manager, his wife, and the program director, who has been on most of the cruises that the station has sponsored, were listed in the station's promotional brochures as the hosts of the cruise.

A special assistant to the president of the college and legal counsel to the college said that he approved the idea of the station manager taking his wife along and said that the manager asked his permission before doing so.

As manager of a college-owned station, the station manager is a public employee, the legal counsel said. State law prohibits public employees from using their official position "to secure anything of value" for themselves that they would not ordinarily receive in the performance of their official duties.

The station manager said that the official duties that required him to go on the cruise were "being the head of the station and having the expertise in the East."

The station's marketing director said that the station had done only one cost-benefit analysis of the cruise promotions since they began in the early 1990s, and those records showed that the promotion cost more than it raised.

According to documents provided by the station, the previous year cruise promotion brought in a $6,800 "contribution" from the cruise line and $9,500 from a donated cruise that was auctioned off.

But to get that money, it cost the station $20,941 for such things as providing 71 free 30-second ads on the FM radio station, numerous television spots for the cruise, additional-air fare for the auction winners, staff salaries, and full-page ads in the station magazine.

The travel agent, who began arranging the cruises for the station in the three years, said that the station manager complained during the negotiations for last year's China trip that the station was not getting enough out of these promotions.

During the negotiations, records show, the cruise line initially offered to pay most of the costs of the cruise for the station manager's wife, which was described in a letter the travel agent wrote to the station as "a favor" from the cruise line but that created "an additional expense (for the station) that is difficult to explain."

In the end, the station paid for part of the cruise expenses for the program director and all the expenses for the station manager's wife.

The travel agent said it was routine for cruise lines to provide free trips in an effort to entice groups to sell cruise packages. "It's the carrot they hold out. Everyone wants a free cruise," she said.

The marketing director said that the station no longer is receiving free cruises for station personnel because the college's alumni association now is cosponsoring the promotion. She said that the cruise line now handling the arrangements simply donates one cruise for the annual fund-raising auction.

According to the marketing director, the station decided last year that the cruise promotions were taking up too much of station personnel's time and not producing enough revenue.

SOURCE: The information in this case study was developed from an article by Gary Webb and published in the *Cleveland Plain Dealer* in 1988.

Case Study Questions

1. Was there a conflict of interest when the station manager signed a contract that gave him free cruises?
2. The case study alleges that the station manager and his wife used station funds to cover their personal expenses. If you were on the board of directors for the station, how would you handle this issue?
3. The legal counsel said that the station manager sought permission before accepting the cruise, and the station manager claimed that his travel was part of his job responsibilities. Was there a violation of the control mechanism implied in the regulations prohibiting state employees from accepting gifts?
4. If the cost-benefit analysis indicated that the station was taking a loss on the cruise promotions, why do you think it continued to offer them for four years?
5. What kind of controls should have been in place to prevent the station from entering into such a costly promotional campaign?

References

1. John R. Schermerhorn, Jr., *Management for Productivity*, 2d ed. (New York: John Wiley and Sons, 1986), p. 397.
2. Ibid.

3. Ibid., pp. 398–99.
4. Ibid., p. 400.
5. Ibid., pp. 414–16.
6. Ibid., pp. 404–05.
7. Arthur G. Bedeian, *Management* (New York: Dryden Press, 1986), p. 588.
8. Schermerhorn, *Management for Productivity*, pp. 447-450.
9. Ibid., p. 428.
10. Ibid., pp. 429–30.

10 □□□□ Economics and the Arts

Arts organizations, as we saw in Chapter 4, function in multiple environments. Economic, political, cultural, demographic, technological, and educational environments shape and change an arts organization over time. The economic environment is the focus of this chapter. The objective here is to gain an understanding of many of the economic forces with which an arts organization interacts and the impact of the economy on the organization. This chapter and the next one on financial management are not intended as a substitute for courses in economics and finance. If you currently are an undergraduate interested in a career in arts management, take courses in these areas before you graduate.

The economy has a direct effect on artists and arts organizations every day in the United States. Staying aware of the economic environment allows an arts manager the opportunity to prepare plans of action designed to ensure the survival of the organization. An arts manager might consider the following questions related to the economy:

1. Will there be a downturn or an upturn in the economy?
2. Will people have more or less disposable income?
3. How will inflation affect operating costs?
4. How will changes in interest rates affect the budget and the organization's other investments?

Ultimately, the answers to these and many similar questions remain uncertain. The economic information that a manager needs to make decisions often is out of date or contradictory. One report says that the economy is headed for recession, and another says that the growth economy will continue for another year. An abundance of common sense and skepticism are essential. Rather than plotting out abstract data on charts and graphs, an arts manager's time is better spent analyzing the threats and opportunities in the economic environment. The objective is to translate the potential impact of these conditions into practical courses of action to help the organization survive.

Introduction to Economics

This section will highlight some of the economic principles that have an impact on arts organizations. It is assumed that the reader has not yet taken any courses in economics. If you have a background in this subject, you may want to skip ahead to "Microeconomics."

We begin by defining some basic terms. An *economy* is "a system of organization for the production, distribution, and consumption of all things people use to achieve a certain standard of living."[1] *Economics*, on the other hand, is "the study of how people and society choose to employ resources to produce goods and services and distribute them among various persons and groups in society."[2] The study of economics can be broken down further into macroeconomics and microeconomics. *Macroeconomics* is concerned with the entire economy or large sectors of it. *Microeconomics* focuses on the individual units (a household, business, or arts organization) that make up the entire economy.[3] Microeconomics also studies how individual markets (a place where buyers and sellers come together) are organized, grow, develop, and change over time.[4]

Inherent in the discussion of the economy is the assumption that *goods* (tangible things such as a car or groceries) and *services* (intangible things such as a live concert) are scarce. That is, there is not enough of either to satisfy everyone's needs. Prices for goods or services are based on two factors: (1) the demand for them and (2) their supply (how scarce or plentiful they are). At the most basic level, a dance concert performance scheduled for one night is a scarce entertainment service. The "product," in this case, is the dancers' performance. The price that audience members will have to pay to see the performance depends in part on the overall market for one-night dance concerts in that area. On the other hand, the level of demand for dance events in the area might be so low that the tickets must be inexpensive to attract an audience.

People desire goods and services because these things provide a form of satisfaction to the purchaser. The complex interaction of individual tastes and preferences, advertising, the socialization process, and the educational system influences what people perceive as desirable. Billions of dollars are spent each year on advertising designed to convince people that they will find satisfaction if they consume this product or that service. Producers of goods and services attempt to increase the demand through advertising and ultimately make a profit. Nonprofit arts organizations seldom, if ever, have the money budgeted to advertise their product with the same frequency as many consumer goods. These limited resources result in a fairly low level of awareness among the general public about the fine arts and the live performing arts in U.S. society.

The Economic Problem

Economists argue that the underlying *economic problem* is "the combination of scarce resources and unlimited wants."[5] Scarcity forces us to choose which goods and services we are willing to pay for with the resources we have available. These choices lead to what is referred to as an *opportunity cost*, or "the cost that equals the amount of the good that must be given up in order to have more of another."[6] For example, if we have a limited natural resource that can be processed to manufacture both weapons and hospital instruments, we would say that the opportunity cost of making more weapons will be that we will have fewer hospital instruments. Such trade-offs take place at all levels in an economy.

For an arts organization or artist, the concept of opportunity cost could be applied along similar lines. For example, if you decide to become a concert violinist, you will have to forgo other opportunities because you will only have a limited amount of time to train, rehearse, travel, and perform. The opportunity cost of becoming a soloist therefore might be a social life or a position in an orchestra.

Organizations can have the same problem. For example, arts groups often believe that they can do more than they can with the resources available. There is an opportunity cost if the organization decides to undertake a tour to all of the schools in a 200-mile radius. The organization will be unable to do other things if it expends the required human, financial, and time resources on this new project. Unfortunately, many arts organizations start up new programs without evaluating the opportunity costs. As a result, staff time and budget resources are overextended.

Three Problems for an Economy

When we talk about an entire economic system, we need to remember three basic questions:[7]

1. What and how much should be produced?
2. How should the means of production be organized?
3. For whom should the goods and services be produced?

In the U.S. economy, the question of what and how much to produce is determined by a complex mixture of the market system, government control, and politics. Recent trends to deregulate or remove some elements of government control from segments of the economy (agriculture, airlines, banking) have met with varying degrees of success. On the other hand, thousands of laws and policies at the federal and state levels affect what and how much should be produced in the economic system. For example, a system of tax exemptions and grants fosters a system of government support for arts organizations that could not depend solely on the marketplace to provide enough income to operate. By freeing some organizations from paying income tax, the government in effect subsidizes services of benefit to the whole society.

Organizing the means of production has proven to be very difficult. There is little agreement in the United States about the best way to organize the economy. In an ideal world, some economists see the market system as the key to solving the issues related to distributing all resources to maximize productivity of the workforce and produce the optimum mixture of goods and services to further everyone's standard of living. Until recently, the planned or command economy, such as the centrally controlled systems of what was formerly the USSR, was seen as the major alternative to the market system. In fact, this system had limited success. Much of the turmoil in the former USSR and Eastern Europe continues to revolve around the changes brought about by shifting to a more market-driven economy. Combinations of market and command systems are in place in most contemporary economies in Europe.

The third question, for whom to produce the goods and services, is no easier to answer. The distribution of the total output of the economic system is uneven. Should only those who contribute to the system get something back? The U.S. economic system answers that question by providing social support for those members of society who do not directly contribute to the total output of goods and services. However, the political issues related to supporting all members of society have yet to be settled.

Government funding, for example, is used for everything from AIDS research to grants for new composers. The continuing battle over NEA funding further reflects a fundamental political conflict about who should get a share of the limited resources. Looking at the world around us, it is easy to see that neither the free-market economies nor the centrally planned systems are providing for all of their people.

Arts organizations have been affected directly by the shifting political attitudes about all three of these questions. Since the early 1980s, much time and energy have been spent in reducing the government's role in the day-to-day operation of the economy. For example, the competition for funds has increased as policies have shifted from government support to private support.

Macroeconomics

An arts manager operates an organization in a macroeconomic system that is always undergoing change. The macro level in any economy is concerned with such issues as the overall price level or the unemployment rate not the cost of an arts subscription or a new car. Because an arts organization is a part of the entire system, economic conditions will have an impact on such areas as the organization's strategic planning or financial management.

The Role of Government

In the U.S. economy, the government provides the following:

- The legal and institutional structure in which the markets operate,
- Intervention into the allocation of resources in areas of the economy in which public policy deems it beneficial to intervene,
- Redistribution of income through taxes and payments of entitlements (e.g., Social Security),
- Stability in prices, economic growth, and economic conditions in general.

In the world of macroeconomics, the scale of operation and the amount of financial activity defy comprehension. When you read that the gross domestic product (GDP, the market value of all final goods and services produced by the economy in a year) has increased by 1.2 percent, it may not mean much to you. When the numbers being tossed around are in the trillions of dollars, it is difficult to relate to them at the micro level of an organization. When you read that the Federal Reserve Bank has dropped the prime interest rate by a half a point or has increased the money supply, you may wonder if this has any relationship to your impoverished arts organization. The answer is that it does. For example, an increase in the GDP may translate into a healthier economy in which people have more money to spend or give. If the cost of borrowing money declines as a result of actions taken by the Federal Reserve Bank, an organization will not spend as much on loans, which in turn will free up resources that can be used for other purposes.

Although an arts organization may not immediately feel the impact of changes in the macroeconomic environment, adjustments in strategy and operational objectives eventually will become necessary. For example, if the GDP is falling and the entire economy appears to be headed into a downturn, an organization should activate a series of operational adjustments to cope with these external changes.

Microeconomics

An arts organization is a small business. It functions in the world of microeconomics and, as such, is subject to a constantly changing market. The term *market* refers to all the sale and purchase activity that affects a product or service. In the case of an arts organization, the market activity occurs in the larger market of the entertainment industry. This industry includes film, television, theme parks, personal recreation, and spectator sports. Let us take a brief look at some economic principles from the perspective of the arts.

Law of Demand

Trying to identify the demand for a particular show or exhibition requires that a manager weigh numerous factors that influence the behavior of consumers. The well-known factors of supply and demand are directly translated into activities at the core of an arts group's financial planning. We begin by looking at the area of demand.

The *law of demand* explains the relationship between the amount of a good or service a buyer both desires and can purchase and the price charged for the good or service. In other words, the lower the price charged for a good or service (the vertical axis, or *y*-axis, of the graph), the larger will be the quantity demanded (the horizontal axis, or *x*-axis). Conversely, the higher the price, the lower will be the quantity demanded. Figure 10–1 shows this relationship. The quantity demanded (QD-1) for concert tickets priced from $10 to $42 is plotted. In this example, the estimated demand for $22 tickets is 600. The downward sloping line is called a *demand curve*.

This graph, a fixed demand curve, is based on important assumptions: *Only the price change affects the quantity demanded*, and *the change in quantity occurs only along the demand curve*. Other factors that influence the ticket buyer, such as the prices of other goods and services, income levels, and individual tastes, do not change.

Demand Determinants

Figure 10–1 also shows what happens to the demand curve when other factors are taken into account. Each factor may cause the entire demand curve to shift to the left or right.

Price of other goods   *Substitute goods* or services may cause a shift in the demand if their prices change. In Figure 10–1, the line (QD-3) to the left of QD-1 shows a drop in demand when another similar service was available to the consumer. In this case, only 700 people are willing to pay $10 for tickets instead of 900. QD-2, the line to the right of QD-1, shows an increase in demand. Now 1,100 people are willing to pay $10 for tickets. To understand how these factors work, suppose that another group is presenting a classical music concert featuring the same Mozart symphony on the same night. Because the other group is charging $5 less per ticket, the demand line for your concert might shift to the left (QD-3), meaning that the overall demand will go down. Likewise, if the other group is charging $5 more than your group, the demand may increase, as shown in the shift to the right (QD-2). In summary, when the price of a substitute good or service goes down, the demand curve shifts to the left. When the price of the substitute good or service goes up, the curve shifts to the right.

The demand curve also will shift if a *complementary good* is introduced into the interaction. A complementary good, which is defined as a good or service used jointly with the original good, can cause the demand curve to shift to the left or right, depending on a rise or fall in the price of the complementary good. Such a relationship is illustrated by compact discs (CDs) and compact disc players. If the price of CDs declines, the demand curve for CD players should show an in-

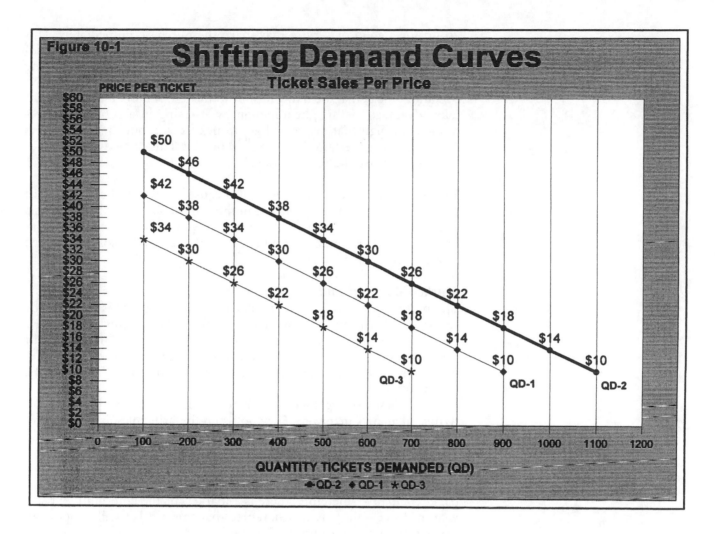

Figure 10-1
Shifting Demand Curves
Ticket Sales Per Price

crease (represented by a shift to the right). If the price of CDs goes up, there should be a decrease in the number of CD players sold (a shift to the left).

An arts organization may feel the effect of this shifting demand curve in many ways. For example, if parking fees rise sharply, some consumers may be discouraged from purchasing tickets.

Income Another factor that could affect the demand curve is individual income. If income increases, the demand for normal goods and services will increase as well. Conversely, if income levels decrease, the demand for normal goods and services will decrease. *Normal goods and services* are those things that people want as their income increases. *Inferior goods or services* are those things people will choose when their income decreases. For example, if there is a significant drop in income levels, people might choose less expensive forms of entertainment. Instead of buying a $300 season subscription to the symphony, people may shift their spending to a less expensive community orchestra series. The community orchestra may not perceive itself as an "inferior" good or service, but in economic theory, it fits the definition.

Expectations Demand is affected by individual expectations about the overall economic situation. A consumer who thinks that the price may go up for a good or service may make the purchase immediately. This expectation would shift the demand curve to the right, increasing demand. On the other hand, a consumer who thought the price was going to drop may delay making the purchase. If enough people share this expectation, the demand curve will shift to the left. An arts manager might take advantage of this phenomenon by stressing in a subscription renewal campaign that prices will go up next season but that subscribers who renew by a certain date can save money. This tactic would probably help increase the renewal rate.

Tastes   Personal consumer tastes also cause the demand curve to shift to the left or right. If a significant number of people shift their interests away from classical music and toward bluegrass, the curve will shift to the left. An increase in demand might result if a popular soloist is added to a concert performance.

Market Demand and the Arts
The market demand for a particular product or service is obtained by summing all the individual demand curves. When this is done, we must consider the overall size of the market as a factor that will shift the demand curve to the left or right. Overestimating the market demand for any product can lead to a series of financial problems for the organization.

Do these concepts have any place in the day-to-day planning activities of an arts manager? They do when the principles are applied realistically. For example, a dance group with the mission of bringing postmodern dance to the masses would be wise to start with the expectation that there will be limited demand for the product. Although the community may regularly support dance performances by the regional ballet company—therefore, there is a market for the entertainment service of dance—there is no guarantee that this market will support an experimental dance troupe.

Advertising is one way to affect the demand for a particular product within an overall market. However, reaching individual consumers with the message about a particular dance organization and being able to make a sale are two different matters.

To understand the entire relationship of the arts organization to the economic environment, we must look at the supply of the product or service.

Law of Supply
We have seen that there is a relationship between price and quantity demanded for a product or service. Now let us look at the supply side of the theory. The application of these concepts to the operation of an arts organization requires some explanation.

The relationship between the amount of a product and its price is at the center of the *law of supply*, which states that "suppliers will supply larger quantities of a good at higher prices than at lower prices."[8] Figure 10–2 shows the supply curve for concert tickets. The normal revenue curve based on the venue would allow the supplier to sell 900 tickets at $50 each (QS-1). The supply curve shows how few tickets would be provided at the lowest price of $18. The supplier has an incentive to provide the $50 ticket because the costs of producing the event remain constant within the single performance. In fact, the supplier may want

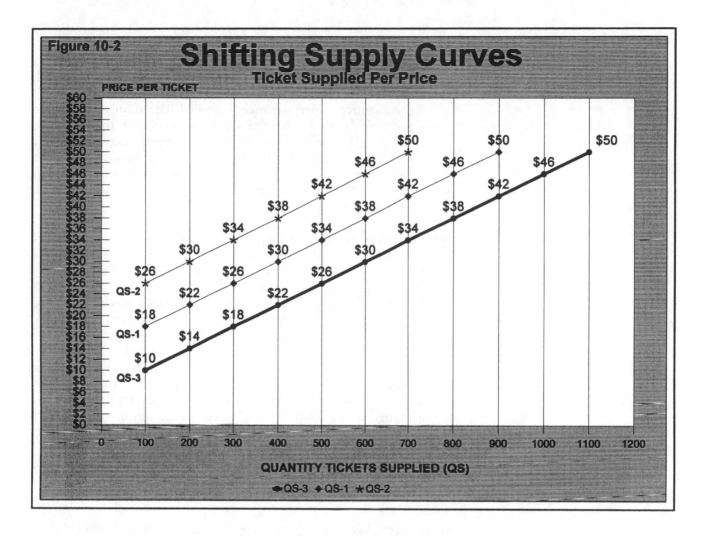

Figure 10-2

Shifting Supply Curves
Ticket Supplied Per Price

to provide multiple performances of the concert to bring in as much revenue as possible. For example, if you are the supplier of a symphony orchestra performance and all your players are under contract, it is to your benefit to offer this service as many times as possible.

The fixed *supply curve* (QS-1) shown in Figure 10–2 shows a change in quantity supplied based on a change in one variable: price. Change in the quantity supplied therefore occurs only along this supply curve. Other variables will have an effect on the shift of the entire supply curve to the left or right. These variables are called *supply determinants*.

Supply Determinants

Price of resources If the price of resources used in creating the good or service rises or falls, the supply curve will shift to the left or right, respectively. Figure 10–2 shows examples of what a shift in the supply curve would look like. In economics, the term *factors of production* is used to describe the "inputs of labor services, raw materials and other resources" used to create the final product or service.[9] For suppliers, a drop in the factors of production translates into greater profits. Therefore, suppliers have the incentive to supply more (QS-3) because they can make more profit. Conversely, if the factors of production go up, suppliers have an incentive to supply less (QS-2) because their profit margin goes down. Hence, suppliers reduce output to bring production costs into line with the quantity supplied.

In the case of arts organizations, we seldom see the behavior exhibited by the theoretical supplier of concert tickets. The law of supply, as applied to this example, does not translate into the ticket supplier reducing the quantity of performances supplied. The supplier is not motivated to provide as much of a good or service if the factors of production rise. If costs increase, the typical concert ticket seller would simply pass the cost along to the consumer in the form of a price increase. The other alternative is to go further into debt by not charging enough to cover the costs of production. Ironically, this is what many nonprofit arts organizations do.

Prices of other goods   The fixed supply curve (QS-1) assumes that the prices of other goods remain constant. If the prices of other goods rise, the supply curve will shift to the right or left. In other words, a change in the price of one good produced by an industry may be expected to shift the supply curves of all other goods produced by that industry.[10] If, for example, the supply curve for the particular type of paper used for newspapers increases, or shifts to the right, the costs of paper for programs and brochures will increase as well. Why does this occur? If paper producers increase the quantity of paper supplied for newspapers and cut back on the paper supplied for brochures and programs, the supply of the latter is decreased; and its price will rise. Such a change is demonstrated in Figure 10–2 when the supply curve shifts from QS-1 to QS-2. Printers will have to pay more for paper, and that price increase will be passed along to the organization. This in turn will affect the organization's overall operating budget. More funds will have to be allocated to printing or a lower quality of paper will have to be selected.

Technology   Advances in technology reduce the costs of production for suppliers and increase the productivity of the industry. This translates into lower costs for suppliers, and it is an incentive to supply more. The concert ticket seller may sell the performance rights to a television station with a new pay-per-view system. In addition to selling 1,000 tickets for the live performance, the concert supplier may now find a whole new distribution system for the product; and this may become an incentive to schedule more performances.

Number of suppliers   When the number of suppliers in a product area increases, the supply curve shifts to the right; and conversely, when the number of suppliers decreases, the supply curve shifts to the left. The entertainment industry, taken as a whole, generally has a great many suppliers at various prices. The supplier of classical music concerts might be able to increase prices if a great number of alternative forms of entertainment disappeared. On the other hand, if you have the only performance available of a specific work with a special performer, you may be able to raise the price despite the number of suppliers in the entertainment industry.

Suppliers' expectations   When establishing the quantity to produce, suppliers consider many different factors. For example, the concert supplier expects that this will be the final performance before the famous soloist retires and thus increases the number of concerts.

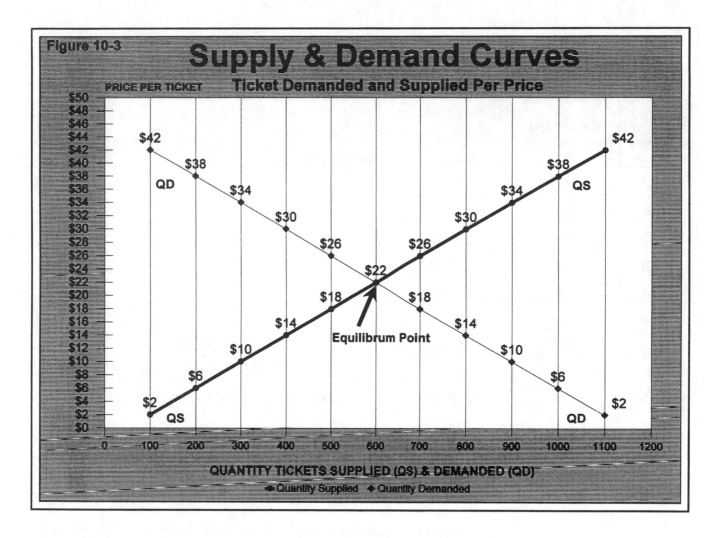

Figure 10-3
Supply & Demand Curves
Ticket Demanded and Supplied Per Price

Market Equilibrium: Supply and Demand Curves

Now let us see what happens when we bring together supply and demand.

Figure 10–3 shows the supply and demand curves brought together for the concert. The point at which the two curves intersect is called the *market equilibrium*, the "price where the quantity of the good or service buyers demand and purchase is equal to the quantity suppliers supply and sell."[11] The area directly below the equilibrium point reflects a shortage of tickets, and the area directly above the equilibrium point represents a surplus of tickets. In other words, if all of the tickets were priced at $42, some would be left over. If, on the other hand, they were all priced at $2, there would be a shortage of tickets.

Revenue maximization Figures 10–4 and 10–5 show one application of how revenue maximization relates to demand. In this case, the theoretical demand (QD-2) generates the most revenue from tickets priced $18, $22, and $26 per ticket. As we lower or raise the ticket price beyond that range, the estimated revenue changes. Assuming that the demand moves along the curve estimated, we will make less money selling $14 or $30 tickets than selling $26 or $18 tickets.

If we distribute the seat prices by location and charge more for seats in the better viewing areas (scale the house), we can generate even

Figure 10-4

Price and Revenue Matrix

Ticket Price	Estimated Demand (QD-2)	Revenue	Comments
$50	200	$10,000	
$46	225	$10,350	
$42	250	$10,500	
$38	300	$11,400	
$34	350	$11,900	
$30	400	$12,000	
$26	500	$13,000	**Range where ticket prices and demand generate maximum revenue.**
$22	600	$13,200	
$18	700	$12,600	
$14	800	$11,200	
$10	900	$9,000	

greater revenue. For example, Figure 10–5 illustrates an example of differential pricing using a 900-seat venue. If you were producing an event that was relatively inexpensive, you may be able to charge $14 and $22. Based on our estimated demand (Figure 10–1, QD-2), you might be able to generate $13,400 in gross sales. On the other hand, this same 900-seat venue could produce almost three times more revenue by pricing your tickets with four levels. The assumption is that a number of people will want to see the event and are willing to pay $50 to sit in a good location to do so. Also an assumed is that a larger number of people are willing to pay only $34 to see the same artists. Depending on your project goals, either pricing approach may be appropriate.

The price reduction scaling of the house becomes a demand-increasing tactic that may have long-term benefits to an organization trying to build an audience. Economists refer to this as the *income effect*. A price reduction gives people more money to spend. When faced with a choice of paying a minimum ticket price of $34 or $ 50 for the same event, most people would rather make their dollar go further.

This is a simplification of the entire ticket pricing process, but it is also a reminder that fundamental concepts in economics are a part of the arts manager's job. Most arts and membership organizations base their prices on a complex mix of financial need and educated guesses about what the market will bear. Seldom, if ever, do arts organizations respond to demand issues. For example, if you price tickets at $20 for an event and sell out in the first day, you underpriced the tickets. Ob-

Figure 10-5
Scaling Ticket Prices
Revenue maximization using principles of supply and demand
Assumes 900 seat capacity

Ticket Prices	Quantity to Sell	Revenue	Comment
Based on QD2 - see Figure 10-1			
$50	100	$5,000	Pricing based on $4 increments and
$42	150	$6,300	placing a premium on location.
$38	300	$11,400	Assumes a demand for more & less
$34	350	$11,900	expensive seats for the event.
TOTAL	900	$34,600	

OR

$46	200	$9,200	Pricing based on $4 difference in top
$38	300	$11,400	prices and $8 difference with the lowest
$30	400	$12,000	priced ticket.
TOTAL	900	$32,600	

OR

$22	600	$13,200	Pricing based on $16 difference
$38	300	$11,400	between low and high price.
TOTAL	900	$24,600	

OR

$14	800	$11,200	Pricing based on customers looking
$22	100	$2,200	for a bargain. Assumes event costs
TOTAL	900	$13,400	are low.

viously, demand for tickets at that price was very high. If you priced the tickets at $50 each and only sold 100 of the 900 available you overpriced the event. Either pricing decision creates problems for the organization.

General Applications of Economic Theories

Throughout this chapter, examples are cited to show how economic theories can be applied to the arts environment. A few other general theories have a direct impact on the arts.

Economic Impact

A key area on which the arts have focused in the last few years is the economic impact of the organization on the community. Arts organizations expend funds; pay salaries, wages, taxes, and benefits; and use goods and services in the community. They also help stimulate the local economy through the *multiplier effect* of money. "Cashing in on Gotham's Culture-Hungry Guests" and "Spoleto Means Profits to

Cashing in on Gotham's Culture Hungry Guests

Dinitia Smith

. . . Spring is the season of cultural tourism [in New York]. About 25 million people visit the city each year from out of town, according to the most recent estimates by the New York Convention and Visitors Bureau. Of those, about 2.6 million say they come just to see something cultural, an increase of almost 20 percent from 10 years ago. And millions more business and leisure travelers visit a museum or see a show while they're here.

According to the most recent comprehensive study of tourism and the arts by the Port Authority of New York and New Jersey, tourists make up about 30 percent of the attendance at major cultural institutions in New York. "Arts-motivated visitors," as the survey calls them, spend about $1.3 billion on hotels, restaurants and other "ancillary expenses."

Charleston Vendors" provide evidence of the economic impact of the arts on a community.

The impact of the basic operation of the arts organization extends beyond the community. The salaries paid to staff members are used to pay rent, make car payments, or buy groceries. The money is used again by the property owner, bank, or store to purchase things or to make loans. In effect, the money that the arts organization puts into the local economy ripples throughout the region. In addition, when consumers buy tickets and make the journey to the performance, they may pay for a baby sitter, gas for the car, a meal at a restaurant, parking, and a purchase at the arts center's gift shop. The $42 paid for the ticket may generate four or five times that amount in other goods and services.

Organizational Impact

Several basic economic principles relate to how an organization operates in the total economic environment. For example, calculating the impact of such things as total fixed costs, total variable costs, average fixed and variable costs, and marginal costs helps the organization with financial and operational planning. The ideas related to the law of diminishing returns, long-term operational costs, and economies of scale also have some application to the arts. Let us take a brief look at some of these theories and laws.

Fixed, variable, and marginal costs   All organizations must identify the fixed costs of operation to form the base operating budget. Expenses for such things as renting or leasing space, buying equipment, and repaying loans, must be carefully calculated as part of the *total fixed costs* (TFC) of operating. These costs will not change whether you do 2 or 200 performances; they often are called *overhead*. Salaries for a minimum or core staff and the various benefits paid to them also might be part of the fixed overhead of an arts organization.

When performers, designers, and technicians are hired for a given production (assuming a season of several shows), these expenses are added to the *total variable costs* (TVC). Materials purchased for the scenery and costumes, phone calls, blueprints, paint, and labor to produce the show are all part of the TVC. The *total cost* (TC) represents the total of the fixed and variable costs (TC = TFC + TVC). You could divide the TFC and TVC by the number of shows in the season to derive the *average fixed costs* (AFC) and *average variable costs* (AVC) per show. Added together, the AFC and AVC equal the *average total costs* (ATC).

Another key indicator of costs is the *marginal cost* (MC), which is the cost of producing an additional quantity of the product. In the performing arts, the most obvious output increase would be the number of performances scheduled. For example, when you plan for an evening concert performance, you can estimate the total variable and fixed costs associated with that concert. The marginal cost of doing another performance that afternoon would probably be less than the marginal cost of scheduling another performance for the next day. One reason why the MC might be lower is that the rental of the performance space is based on a daily rate of eight hours. If you use the space for only four hours in the evening, you still pay for time you do not use the space. The matinee performance would not add to the variable costs of the hall.

Diminishing returns   On the other hand, your payroll and production costs would rise with the extra performance. These variable costs would

Spoleto Means Profits to Charleston Vendors

Joe Drape

The following article is an example of the multiplier effect in action.

CHARLESTON, S.C.—They come to this port city in search of avant-garde dance, startling opera stagings and the bonhomie shared by like-minded lovers of arias and teasing denouements. But Spoletogoers also dig hot dogs, die for lemonade, scarf up souvenir T-shirts and gulp brews with the same gusto as a baseball crowd.

In short, the French, Italians, Georgians and others who converged here beginning yesterday for the annual international arts festival are tourists.

And local hoteliers and hucksters look to the festival's 17 days of high-minded art as an economic opportunity akin to fishing in an aquarium.

"It's 17 days of extra cash and extra hard work," Meeting Street vendor Brenda Williams explained, squirting mustard on some hot dogs for an Italian couple outfitted in sailor caps with "Charleston" emblazoned on the front.

"All you got to do is be out on the street when the doors open and you've got it made."

Nearly 100,000 people are expected to attend the festival. . . . They will spend almost $2 million on tickets to attend more than 120 performances. The spin-off economic impact of the festival, according to Spoleto and city officials, exceeds $50 million.

"It's a really big time for everyone," said Patty Downs, a desk clerk for the Planters Inn.

Innkeepers and restaurateurs are the biggest beneficiaries of the arts dollars. As with most inns and hotels in The Battery, all 41 rooms at the Planters Inn are booked throughout the festival, and have been for 5 months.

She-crab soup and other native seafood will be spooned out at more than double the rate at 82 Queen, a favorite downtown eatery. Nearly 150 lunches and 450 dinners per day will be served in the antique indoor dining rooms and balmy patios of the 19th-century estate.

Because this is a pedestrian-oriented city fraught with the opulence and charm of a Confederate yesteryear, retailers also experience dramatic profit increases.

---

offset the gains from the decreased hall rental and would allow the organization to gain firsthand experience with the *law of diminishing returns.* The law states that "as more and more of a variable factor of production, or input (e.g., labor) is used together with a fixed factor of production, beyond some point the additional, or marginal, output attributable to the variable factor begins to fall."[12] To put it simply, at some point the costs rise enough to reduce the marginal gain from creating the additional output.

Profit-making ventures must constantly watch all costs related to making, selling, distributing, and advertising the product as well as the marginal costs. Otherwise, no money will be left to call a profit. Not-for-profit organizations may not try to generate revenue above costs for owners or investors, but they still must carefully control fixed, variable, and marginal costs. In fact, a not-for-profit organization may generate a surplus of revenue, as we will see in the next chapter. To generate a surplus or break even, the arts manager must draw on a great deal of skill in controlling costs, setting prices, and estimating demand. Chapter 11 examines various fixed and variable costs in the process of designing budgets and managing cash flow.

Economies of scale   Another issue related to overall cost is how economies of scale operate in an organization. The technical definition of *economies of scale* is "a decrease in the long-run average total costs

(ATC) of production that occur when larger facilities are available for manufacturing a product."[13] These economies are achieved because the business is able to specialize production techniques, its labor force becomes more expert, volume discounts are available for materials used to produce the product, or the by-products of manufacturing reach a large enough quantity to become salable.

Applications of economies of scale are limited in aspects of the production process. For example, instead of setting up and equipping its own scenery and costume production shop, an organization could develop a central production center to be used by all of the major arts organizations in the region. This production center could achieve costs savings from scale through construction techniques and bulk purchases. For example, by grouping various construction projects and buying in quantity, the organization may be able to achieve a large enough scale of operation to reduce overall costs.

Another example of economies of scale is a performing arts center with multiple spaces. The assumption that it is less costly to run three theaters under one roof than three theaters under three roofs helped motivate the construction of these types of facilities. However, *diseconomies of scale* also can affect such centralized operations if management is not careful to control growth as the organization matures. A diseconomy of scale might be achieved by having to hire extra people and buy extra tools to take on the increased scale of production. This would increase the average total costs to produce the sets in the central shop. The savings realized by the scale of the operation would be quickly negated.

Economic Problems Facing the Arts

Up to this point, we examined many of the basic economic principles as they relate to the arts. A limited number of studies have been done and a few books have been written about the arts and economics. One that is required reading for all arts managers is William J. Baumol and William G. Bowen's landmark study, *Performing Arts: The Economic Dilemma*,[14] published in 1966. The book was the first detailed analysis of the economic conditions of the arts. In addition, the 1993 publication of *The Economics of Art and Culture*, by James Heilburn and Charles M. Gray,[15] provided a comprehensive and updated view on the microeconomics of the arts and public policy in America. This book also addressed the arts audience with new information and provides an excellent analysis of trends in the arts. Other writers also explored the relationship of the arts and economics. Their works are listed at the end of the chapter.

The Cultural Boom

During the mid-1960s there was much talk of a "cultural boom" in America. Attendance at arts events was up, the number of performing arts groups was increasing yearly, and regional performing arts centers were being built everywhere. Baumol and Bowen found that, despite a lot of activity, the actual growth of the *arts in relation to all other factors of the economy* was very modest. By adjusting and correcting the data for inflation, population increases, and income growth, they found very little change since 1929. Figure 10–6 shows a sampling of data from the Department of Commerce's *National Income and Product Accounts of the United States* report related to disposable income and

Figure 10-6

Disposable Income Spending on Admissions

Years	1929	1939	1947	1970	1975	1980	1985
Total of all spending	**5.301**	**4.953**	**5.479**	**5.966**	**6.161**	**6.022**	**6.384**
Total Spectator Entertainment	1.118	1.178	1.187	0.457	0.375	0.341	0.314
Performing Arts	**0.155**	**0.092**	**0.111**	**0.074**	**0.068**	**0.092**	**0.089**
Motion pictures	0.881	0.945	0.944	0.226	0.191	0.132	0.112
Spectator Sports	0.081	0.141	0.132	0.157	0.116	0.117	0.113

NOTE: Spending total in billions of dollars and adjusted for inflation

SOURCE: Department of Commerce, *National Income and Product Accounts of the Untited States,* various years.

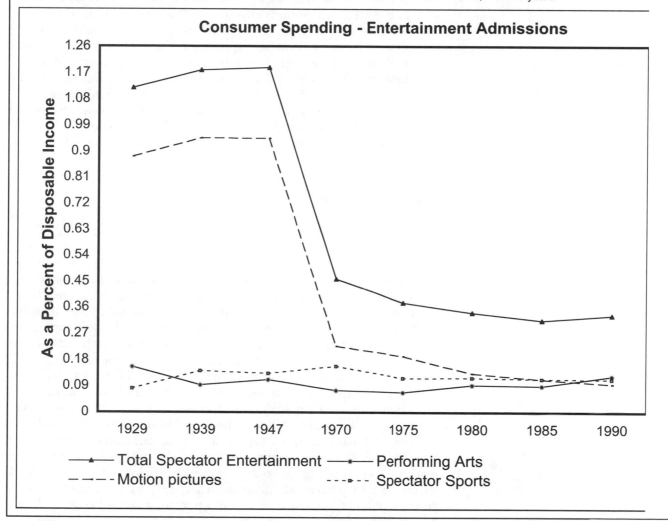

spending on entertainment. For example, the line designated "performing arts" has not varied a great deal since 1929. In 1929 the percentage of disposable income expended on attending arts events was 0.155, and it fell during the Depression to 0.92. As a percentage the low point was 1975, and it has increase through 1990. In other words, as a percentage of disposable income, people are spending about what they have been spending on the performing arts for the last 50 years. Of course, the population has increased and so all the signs point to increased activity, but relative to all the other growth that has occurred since the 1930s, arts spending is fairly flat. The large drop in motion pictures as a percent of disposable income spent on entertainment is linked to the arrival of television after World War II.

Despite these numbers the widespread perception was the arts were booming. More dance companies, regional orchestras, theater companies, and arts centers were opening every year. Heilburn and Gray note that,

> ... it is not unreasonable to suggest that the high growth of performing arts activity in the 1970s and 1980s may have resulted not so much from rising consumer demand as from increased supply. The availability of government subsidies and of additional private contributions encouraged the formation of new performing arts companies in places that previously had few or none. The same financial support greatly increased the number and range of performance tours into previously untapped markets. In this process, a latent demand for the arts was satisfied by a sudden burst of new activity, and consumer spending on the arts increased much faster than income. If that is what happened in the 1970s and 1980s, it is a pattern that will be difficult to duplicate in future decades, when the number of unserved markets will have diminished in relative importance.[16]

The Arts Audience

Before Baumol and Bowen's study, very little statistical data was available about who attended the various theater, dance, opera, and concert performances in the United States. The authors used detailed audience surveys to gather data on income levels, education, age, gender, and preferences. They found that the "common man" was fairly uncommon among those who attended live professional performances. They found a predominance of people with white-collar occupations and high levels of education and income. Forty-five percent of the audience members were between 35 and 60 years of age. Their research led them to estimate that in 1966 about 4 percent of the U.S. population over 18 years of age attended some professional arts event. Taken at today's population levels, that would translate to around 10 million people.

Heilbrun and Gray's book updates Baumol and Bowen's work with the assistance of various NEA studies done in the 1980s (the NEA Web site contains many statistical reports about current attendance patterns). For example, one survey comparison pointed out 93 percent of the population 18 years of age and older watched television; 63 percent attended movies; 19 percent attended musicals; 13 percent, symphonies; 12 percent, plays; 4 percent, ballet; and 3 percent attended opera.[17] In addition, they found similar results when profiling the participation rates at music, theater, and arts museums. Of those attendees with incomes over $50,000, a total of 70 percent held college or advanced degrees, 30 percent were professionals, and 19.3 percent were managers.[18]

In the 30 years since Baumol and Bowen's study, not a great deal has changed when it comes to audience composition. The audience for "high culture" events such as opera, theater, dance, and museum exhibits continues to be a relatively small segment of the population. However, some sources claim there was a higher attendance at arts events than at sporting events in 1990, indicating that, on the surface at least, the arts are doing much better than at the time of Baumol and Bowen's study.

However, when the millions who watch sports on television are taken into account, it probably would be reasonable to assume that more people, representing a greater cross section of the population, would consider themselves to be sports, not arts, fans. In fact, the economic values of our society are expressed clearly in such things as the salaries now paid to some athletes. In many cases, one athlete's salary is often more that the budget for a whole season of a regional orchestra, ballet, or theater company.

The apparent growth experienced by arts organizations in the 1980s was very much a product of the baby boom population increase driving up arts attendance and participation. The diversity of interests of the people educated in the 1960s and 1970s is reflected now in the many small arts organizations that specialize in more nontraditional work. However, the actual audience demographic profile has not changed significantly.

The Productivity Issue

Baumol and Bowen's detailed economic study uncovered data that support the conclusion that the financial difficulties arts groups were experiencing would only worsen over time. The basis for this finding is directly related to how the entire economic system has seen slow but steady growth in productivity. In theory, new technologies and processes of production increase the quantity of work output for each employee; that is, they increase productivity. This, in turn, should reduce the cost per unit for production and increase profits. If profits can be increased, then suppliers have an incentive to produce more, and the entire supply curve and all of the goods and services produced should shift to the right. At the same time, if businesses are able to achieve higher levels of productivity and profit, then the overall income level of the workforce should rise. The result, in theory, is economic growth as the demand curve moves to the right with the supply curve.

To stay ahead of *inflation*, which is a constant increase in the price levels of everything, a business must find ways to more productively use the labor force and any other inputs needed to produce the product or output. Without productivity gains, the producer would have to raise the unit price higher and higher to cover the increasing input costs. If other companies that make a similar product are able to increase productivity, the prices they charge could be kept lower. This would cause consumers to buy the less costly product and eventually would put the less productive company out of business.

Baumol and Bowen applied this theory to arts organizations and found the basis for the gap between the organizations' income and their expenses. The authors argued that the technology of presenting an arts event was subject to limited increases in productivity

The time it takes to rehearse and perform a play, opera, dance, or symphony is not subject to increases in productivity. In addition, the supply of the product is limited. A live performance can be repeated only a certain number of times in a day. From that conclusion and from the income-expense gap data they collected over a 15-year period, Baumol and Bowen predicted that arts productivity actually would decline over time as other segments of the economy became more productive. The long-term effect of this is the ever-increasing income gap. They predicted that, without regularly increasing donations, the income gap would continue to increase despite increasing ticket prices.

The application of technology to almost all phases of American business has helped increase productivity. In fact, technology in the offices or production areas of arts organizations have helped make people more productive. However, no amount of technology will have a significant impact on shortening the time spent on rehearsing a scene or repeating a musical passage until it is perfect. The final product will take about the same amount of time to present. The result is that whatever gains in productivity are realized by computerizing the office will be offset by increasing costs to present the basic product.

Cost increases caused by inflation coupled with limited productivity and supply gains in operations further increased the income gap for the arts. In most cases, salaries, benefits, utilities, supplies, and so forth are increasing each year. Unless ticket prices increase, more performances are scheduled, or more funds are raised, arts organizations will be doomed to an ever-increasing income gap.

This gap, sometimes called *Baumol and Bowen's disease*, is a fact of life for arts and service organizations. Any arts group that attempts to ignore the implications of the income gap in its strategic planning, marketing, or fund-raising efforts eventually will find itself going broke. In the long run, the only way the arts will continue to survive is if the overall economic system places enough value on this activity to subsidize it.

Other Findings

Baumol and Bowen's study had many other key findings. Here are just a few:

1. Costs per performance were rising faster than the consumer price index (CPI).
2. Increases in ticket prices often exceeded the CPI, but because these increases were below the increases in the costs per performance, there was no real gain in additional revenue.
3. Cost pressures and the demand to provide artists with a living wage placed many arts organizations in a state of almost constant budget crisis.

The problems Baumol and Bowen saw 30 years ago are still with us. In Chapter 4, a quote from McDaniels and Thorn's *Quiet Crisis in the Arts* noted that the financial problems facing arts groups today are worsening. The number of organizations facing economic difficulty seems to multiply daily.

Conclusion

What do Baumol and Bowen's and Heilbrun and Gray's studies and this chapter on economics lead us to conclude? An optimist might conclude that the economic system has worked well enough to get us to the point where more arts organizations are operating in a wider geographical distribution than ever before. On the other hand, a pessimist could conclude that arts organizations have expanded too much in relation to the real market demand for their products. As a result of this overexpansion, too many arts groups are chasing too few dollars.

Somewhere between these two viewpoints resides the realist, who believes that market forces, government subsidies, and private sources will provide enough support to keep a limited number of arts organizations alive. The realist would argue that a culture is expressed in part through its artistic creations and activity. Society will continue to invest its resources in the arts because enough people want and need what the arts provide. The satisfaction gained from creating and consuming the arts ensure their place in the overall economic system. However, if the system is to work for the benefit of everyone, artists and arts organizations must play an active role in shaping public policy about the place of the arts in society.

The basic economic principles and theories discussed in this chapter have application to the arts. The relationship of the organization to the macroeconomic environment and the conditions in the microeconomic environment in which the organization operates should affect planning. Understanding the supply and demand issues facing the organization is critical. Being able to predict and control fixed and variable costs accurately and being able to predict marginal costs and gains can help keep the organization from falling into financial trouble. Finally, it is important for nonprofit organizations to accept that the income gap is a fact of life. Strict cost-control strategies and plans can be adopted to minimize the negative consequences of this underlying problem.

Summary

Arts organizations function in macro- and microeconomic environments that affect the long-term financial health of the organization.

The economy is the organization of the production, distribution, and consumption of all things people use to achieve a certain standard of living. Economists study how societies employ scarce resources to produce goods and services and distribute them among people. Goods are tangible things, and services are intangibles. The price for a good or service is based on how plentiful or scarce it is and how much it is demanded by people in the economic system. Opportunity costs are the costs of giving up one thing in exchange for another.

Macroeconomics considers to the overall relationship between business, government, and households. Microeconomics deals with the sales and purchases that affect a good or service.

The law of demand states that there is a relationship between the costs of a good and what people are willing to pay. In most cases, the higher the price, the lower is the quantity demanded; and the lower the price, the higher is the quantity demanded. The entire demand curve may be increased (indicated by a shift to the right) or decreased (shifted to the left) by changes in the prices of other goods or consumer income levels. In addition, consumer expectations and tastes also may cause a change in the demand curve.

The law of supply states that suppliers will provide larger quantities of goods and services at higher prices. Supply curves are affected by the price of production resources, the price of other goods, technological advances, the number of suppliers, and suppliers' expectations. Market equilibrium is said to exist when the quantity demanded matches the quantity supplied.

Organizations face fixed, variable, and marginal costs in all phases of operation. Calculating these costs helps determine the organization's baseline operating budget and the costs of doing additional activities. Some aspects of the arts organization may benefit from economies of scale, which are savings derived by decreasing the average total costs of operation.

Baumol and Bowen found that the cultural boom in the United States was driven by the baby boom, and when measured against real growth, per capita expenditures on the arts had declined a little. Their study also found that a small segment of the population—mostly white-collar, highly educated, and economically advantaged people—were regular consumers of the arts. The key finding of the study was that increased costs of production coupled with limited productivity gains created a growing income gap in the long run. They predicted that, unless arts organizations regularly increased donated revenue, the gap would far outdistance their ability to raise revenue through ticket prices.

Key Terms and Concepts

Economics
Macroeconomics
Microeconomics
Goods and services
Economic problem
Opportunity costs
Gross domestic product
Market
Law of demand
Demand determinants
Substitute goods
Complementary goods
Law of supply
Supply determinants
Market equilibrium
Fixed, variable, and marginal costs
Economies of scale
Productivity
Inflation
Baumol and Bowen's disease

Questions

1. What is an economic system?
2. Define macroeconomics and microeconomics.
3. What are some opportunity costs that arts organization might have to face?
4. Give three examples of the laws of demand and supply at work in the arts.
5. To what degree do public taste and expectations affect the demand and supply curves for arts events? Give examples.
6. Give two examples of economies of scale that could be applied to an arts organization's daily operation.
7. Summarize the key findings in the Baumol and Bowen study of the economics of the arts.

Ticket Pricing Exercise

Use graph paper to create a demand curve based on what you think would be the quantity demanded for tickets for a symphony orchestra concert in your area if the prices ranged from $10 to $45 in $5 increments. Assume the performance hall contains 2,000 seats.

1. Based on this demand curve, what would you estimate to be the equilibrium point in demand and supply?

2. How much revenue do you think this event would generate if you had four different prices for the tickets (e.g., $15, $25, $35, and $45)?

3. Discuss some other variables you think that affect ticket pricing.

References

1. Roger N. Waud, *Economics*, 3d ed. (New York: Harper and Row, 1986), p. 4.
2. Ibid.
3. Ibid., p. 12.
4. Ibid., p. 13.
5. Ibid., p. 24.
6. Ibid., p. 25.
7. Ibid., p. 33.
8. Ibid., p. 70.
9. Ibid., p. 72.
10. William J. Baumol and Alan S. Blinder, *Economics-Principles and Policy*, 4th ed. (New York: Harcourt Brace Jovanovich, 1988), p. 63.
11. Waud, *Economics*, p. 77.
12. Ibid., p. 503.
13. Ibid., p. 514.
14. William J. Baumol and William G. Bowen, *Performing Arts: The Economic Dilemma* (Cambridge, MA: MIT Press, 1966). This section of the chapter summarizes Baumol and Bowen's key points.
15. James Heilbrun and Charles M. Gray, *The Economics of Art and Culture* (Cambridge, England: Cambridge University Press, 1993).
16. Ibid., p. 22.
17. Ibid., p. 38.
18. Ibid., p. 43.

Additional Resources

The following articles and books relate to the topic of economics and the arts.

M. Blaug, ed. *The Economics of the Arts*. Boulder, CO: Westview Press, 1976.

H. Hanasman. "Nonprofit Enterprise in the Performing Arts." *Bell Journal of Economics* 12 (Autumn 1981).

Peter Passell. "Broadway and the Bottom Line." *New York Times* (December 10, 1989).

The Rockerfeller Panel. *The Performing Arts: Problems and Prospects*. New York: McGraw-Hill, 1965.

Harold L. Vogel. *Entertainment Industry Economics: A Guide for Financial Analysis*. Cambridge, England: Cambridge University Press, 1986.

In addition, the NEA WWW site contains information about arts economics statistics at:
http://arts.endow.gov/Guide/NewLook/Other.html#Research.

11 □□□□□ Financial Management

In the last chapter, we examined the basic theories and principles of economics and studied some of the ways in which the economic environment affects an arts organization. The topics of supply and demand, utility, and variable, fixed, and total costs were studied to build a foundation for understanding the financial management of an arts organization. In *Managing a Nonprofit Organization*, Thomas Wolf notes that "financial management is, for many, one of the most forbidding aspects of the administration of nonprofit organizations."[1] This in part is due to phobias that people have about anything having to do with quantitative thinking. When faced with a budget or a balance sheet, board members may develop a glazed look and suddenly lose the ability to reason. Even worse, they approve budgets and accept financial statements without understanding the numbers. Unfortunately, comprehension usually comes to the board of directors when it is too late to correct a financial problem that has been staring them in the face for months.

This brings us to the goal for this chapter: to unravel some of the mystery about financial management and provide a clear picture of the relationship of planning, organizing, leading, and controlling to the financial health of the organization. We look at an overview of financial management in for-profit and not-for-profit organizations and then move on to the financial management information system. We look next at budgeting, cash flow, and record-keeping systems. Finally, we integrate the whole system into the balance sheet and statement of account activity.

Overview of Financial Management

In many arts organizations, the responsibility for financial records, budgets, payroll, and money management falls to a business manager who works under the supervision of a general manager or managing director. In a smaller organization, an accountant or bookkeeper may do the processing and record keeping. This person reports to the artistic director and the chair of the board of directors. As we saw in Chapter 9, many arts organizations do not start up with a management information system. Instead, a system evolves as the organization grows. The same often is true for the financial management of the organization. If it is to be effective, *a financial management information system* (FMIS) must be a comprehensive investment, reporting, control, and processing system that helps managers realize the financial objectives of the organization. The financial management of the organization is one of the manager's most important responsibilities. The long-term health of the enterprise depends on the arts manager's vigilance in monitoring the revenue, expenses, and investments of the organization.

Let us look at the responsibilities and evolution of financial management.

For-Profit Organizations

In the for-profit sector, a vice-president of finance usually supervises the controller and treasurer of the organization. The controller usually supervises the accounting system and the tax operations of the organization. The treasurer manages the firm's investments and cash and oversees the management of the capital resources (the plant and equipment) and planning.[2]

The financial manager's biggest responsibility in a for-profit business is to plan for the acquisition and use of funds to maximize the overall value of the business. Therefore, the financial manager makes decisions focused primarily around three areas: forecasting, investing, and control.

The financial manager's forecasting and planning role involves interacting with other executives who are charting the strategic course for the organization. Growth or change usually requires funding. The financial manager must be involved in advising and directing how the organization will pay for its plan.

The financial manager also actively works to raise money to finance the growth of the organization or pay for equipment or the acquisition of other businesses. The financial manager must be able to tap into the stock and bond markets, and the banking community to pay for the future of the organization.

Finally, the financial manager must be able to help the company operate as efficiently as possible with the resources it currently possesses. It is safe to say that all business decisions have financial implications. For example, if marketing decides to expand into a new product line, finding the money needed to pay for the new product line will be the responsibility of the financial manager.

Profit in the arts   Commercial theater, popular music presentations, films, television, and the entertainment industry are very concerned with maximizing revenue and creating a profit. For example, Stephen Langley's *Theatre Management and Production in America*[3] contains very clear examples on how to calculate the costs, profit, and break-even points for Broadway and Off Broadway productions. Techniques for budgeting, cost control, and cash flow analysis, which are discussed later in this chapter, can be applied to for-profit or not-for-profit organizations. The process for incorporation, acquiring a property (the work to be produced), and forming a for-profit arts company will be touched on in this chapter. However, the definitive text on the subject of producing commercial theater is *Producing Theatre* by Donald C. Farber.[4]

Not-for-Profit Financial Management

Because the primary objective of most not-for-profit arts organizations is not focused on increasing the wealth of the owners or stockholders, the financial manager's job is somewhat different than in the for-profit sector. A not-for-profit organization is still a business, though, and it must collect as much or more revenue than it expends or it will go out of business. The financial manager's job in a nonprofit organization is critical to planning and using the limited resources available. For example, if the artistic director wants to add another show to the season, do a world premiere, or take a production on tour, how will the organization pay for this activity? Understanding the cash flow, current debt load, fund balances, and so on is the first step in analyzing what can and cannot be done.

A good financial manager maximizes the use of the available resources. For example, funds raised through ticket sales or donations should be invested to generate further revenue. If an organization collects $200,000 from subscription sales for next season's shows, that money should be invested in interest-earning accounts before it is needed for the new season's operating budget. A financial manager also actively seeks out ways to minimize costs for insurance (health and life) and to reduce other operating costs.

Financial Management Information System

In Chapter 9, we learned that the management information system is responsible for gathering data, formulating information, and distributing it throughout the organization. The financial management information system is a key part of the overall MIS. Figure 11–1 is a schematic drawing of a FMIS.

The FMIS ultimately must provide the board of directors and upper management with accurate, timely, relevant information based on the data the system gathered. Without this information, the planning process will not work. The questions usually are very simple: How are we doing? Did we spend more than we budgeted? Why? Did we raise less than we budgeted? Why? Did we increase or decrease our debt? Will we have sufficient resources to continue operating?

If the system is working properly, the answers to these questions pose no problem for management. For the system to work properly, the operating system noted in Figure 11–1 must accurately gather the data needed to process the records. These data become the information used in reports and the analysis of the current financial health of the organization. At the same time, the organization has specific legal responsibilities to report on its financial activities to various state and federal agencies. The FMIS must be capable of gathering and reporting this information if the organization is to retain its nonprofit legal status.

Before delving into the details of the FMIS and the accounting system, it is important to clarify the legal status of the organization. The FMIS serves two important purposes. It provides information about the fiscal health of the organization to people inside the organization, and it reports to external agencies, such as the IRS, and to granting agencies, such as the NEA and state and local arts councils.

Legal Status and Financial Statements

When a business or arts organization starts up, it may be owned and operated by one individual. However, once the operation grows to the point that a staff and office space are required, it may be time to incorporate the enterprise. Individual artists also may incorporate themselves to gain some specific tax advantages. In many areas of the country, the Volunteer Lawyers for the Arts help individuals and organizations with the incorporation process.

Incorporation
The major reason why an individual or organization decides to legally incorporate is to provide protection for the people who operate the

Figure 11-1

Financial Management Information System (FMIS)

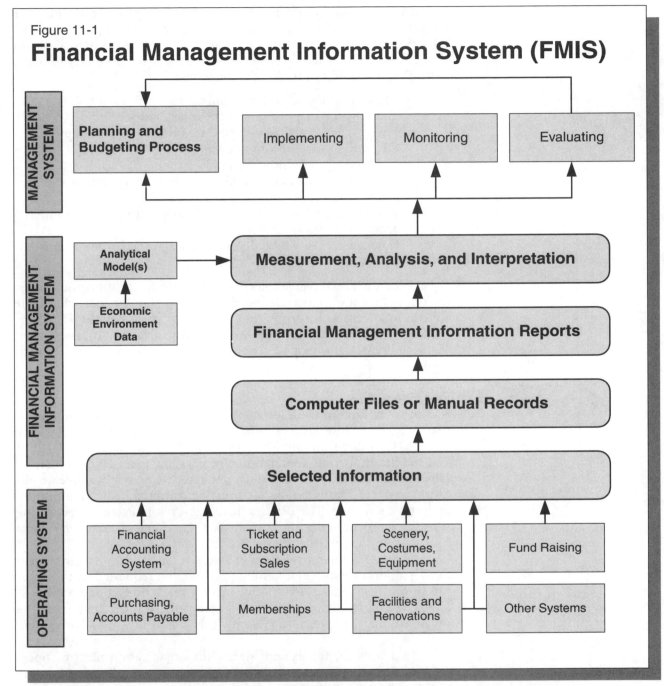

business. Without the protection of incorporation, the owner is legally responsible for all debts incurred and may be sued personally. A legal settlement against an individual might mean that all personal assets could be sold to pay the organization's debts.

In the case of most arts organizations, filing for incorporation as a not-for-profit business (or a for-profit one, for that matter) is fairly straightforward. Provided that the proper papers are filed, the state bestows on the organization the legal right to operate. Filing for exemption from state and local taxes requires additional paperwork. Filing for incorporation usually is covered under the operational procedures established by the Secretary of State. Forms and detailed instructions on filing are usually available on the WWW site for the Secretary of State. Typically, you need to provide the following:

- The official name of the organization;
- The purpose or purposes of the organization;
- The scope of activities—if you are filing for tax exemption, this limits what you can and cannot do;
- Membership provisions (if any);
- The name of the person registering the incorporation and the place of business;
- The names and addresses of the incorporators and the initial board of directors (if any);
- How any assets will be distributed when the corporation is dissolved.

Additional legal regulations may affect not-for-profit corporations, including business or occupation licenses and state or local charitable solicitation licenses. Incorporation and not-for-profit status, if accompanied by tax exemption, empowers the organization to raise funds. Vending licenses also may be required if you plan to sell items through a gift shop.

Tax Exemption

As noted, exemption from local, state, and federal taxes does not automatically come with not-for-profit incorporation. The Internal Revenue Service (IRS) Code, section 501(c)(3), exempts charitable organizations and public and private foundations from paying taxes on net earnings. However, an organization still must pay some taxes. For example, in addition to payroll taxes, a sales tax must be collected if the organization operates a gift shop. The IRS has many tax-exempt categories, covering social welfare organizations, such as the League of Women Voters (501,c,4), and even cemeteries (501,c,19).

When applying for tax-exempt status, financial data for the current fiscal year and the three preceding years will be requested. If the organization is just getting started, the current year's budget and a proposal for the next two years will be accepted. A form that fixes the organization's fiscal year—for example, July 1 to June 30—is required, too.

To qualify for tax-exempt status, the organization must be operated for a charitable purpose. The exemption status is bestowed on organizations that fulfill some of the following purposes: religious, charitable, scientific (research in the public interest), literary, educational, or testing for public safety. In addition, some restrictions pertain to making a profit from enterprises not directly related to the exempted purposes of the organization. These activities will be subject to the *unrelated business income tax* (UBIT). For example, if an arts organization starts acting as a travel agent and sells bookings for cultural cruises, the IRS might rule that this is unrelated to the organization's stated mission, and any surplus revenue from this activity would be subject to income taxes. Certain lobbying and propaganda activities also are prohibited.

A 501(c)(3) organization is not restricted from making a profit. As long as the profit making relates to the stated purpose of the organization, net earnings (profit after deducting expenses) may be accrued and retained. However, these earnings may not be distributed to members of the organization. Net earnings usually are placed in endowment funds or a restricted account and then put to a use that helps fulfill the mission of the organization.

As should be expected, the rules and regulations contain a lot of fine print. Hiring a lawyer, using legal services donated by a board member, or contacting the Volunteer Lawyers for the Arts is a prerequisite to filing the incorporation papers. Once an organization has attained the legal status to operate, it is obligated to provide reports and documentation to local, state, and federal agencies. The organization also will be required to file forms related to Social Security taxes and withholding taxes. The organization must file tax forms with the IRS that list revenues, expenses, and changes in net assets (the not-for-profit organization's equivalency of worth, often called a *fund balance*). The details of the organization's liabilities, assets, programmatic activities, revenues, donations, and expenses for the previous four years must be filed every year.

A financial management information system and a person designated to oversee this important area become vital once the organization reaches the level of legal incorporation. The preparation of required reports—such as a balance sheet, a statement of account activity, and a financial statement of the worth of the organization—will be required. In addition, the organization's finances must be in order to the degree that an outside auditor could come in and analyze the financial operation. A complete audit, which could be very costly, often is required.

(The Nolo Press, on the Web at http://www.nolo.com, is a good source for books about the legal aspects of incorporation. Anthony Mancuso's *How to Form a Nonprofit Corporation*, fourth edition, and Fred S. Steingold's *Legal Guide for Starting and Running a Small Business*, third edition, were the sources for much of the information in this chapter.)

Budgeting and Financial Planning

To attain a clear understanding of the entire financial management system, we return to Figure 11–1. The top left box represents planning and budgeting as a key component in the FMIS. The budget is the framework around which the entire operation is organized. Decisions about how the organization will establish its budget and manage its income, expenses, and investments in a fixed time period are critical if artistic goals and objectives are to be met.

The Budget

As noted in Chapter 9, a budget is a quantitative representation of the organization's plans for a given period of time. Budgets usually cover what is called a *fiscal year* (FY), which can be any designated 12-month period of expense and revenue activity. Most financial planners suggest that organizations set their fiscal year around the programmatic profile of the organization. The IRS tax year, for example, is January 1 to December 31. However, a performing arts group with an eight-month season of October to May would probably find that a fiscal year of July 1 to June 30 better fits their programming and expense patterns.

The summary budget usually works well for smaller operations with a limited number of account lines. Figure 11–2 shows part of a

Figure 11-2

Summary Budget - Theater Company

INCOME	Current Year Budget	Proposed Budget Next Fiscal Year	$ Change	% Change
Subscription Ticket Sales	817,000	970,000	153,000	18.7%
Single Ticket Sales	602,000	600,000	(2,000)	-0.3%
Group Sales	56,000	60,000	4,000	7.1%
SUBTOTAL Sales	1,475,000	1,630,000	155,000	10.5%
Advertising	77,000	85,000	8,000	10.4%
Concessions	56,000	65,000	9,000	16.1%
Gift Shop Income	15,000	14,000	(1,000)	-6.7%
Interest	16,000	23,000	7,000	43.8%
Costume & Scenery Rentals	3,500	2,500	(1,000)	-28.6%
Space/Equipment Rentals	7,000	5,000	(2,000)	-28.6%
Education	5,200	8,000	2,800	53.8%
Miscellaneous	6,500	5,000	(1,500)	-23.1%
Surcharges on Ticket Sales	17,000	18,000	1,000	5.9%
SUBTOTAL Other Income	203,200	225,500	22,300	11.0%
TOTAL EARNED INCOME	1,678,200	1,855,500	177,300	10.6%
DONATED INCOME	Current Budget	Proposed	$ Change	% Change
Individuals	250,000	300,000	50,000	20.0%
Corporations	100,000	125,000	25,000	25.0%
Foundations	100,000	125,000	25,000	25.0%
Co-producers	75,000	100,000	25,000	33.3%
Special Events	205,000	250,000	45,000	22.0%
Matching Contributions	250,000	300,000	50,000	20.0%
TOTAL DONATED INCOME	980,000	1,200,000	220,000	22.4%
GOVERNMENT FUNDING	Current Budget	Proposed	$ Change	% Change
State Grants	48,000	45,000	(3,000)	-6.3%
City/County Grants	94,000	100,000	6,000	6.4%
Federal Grants	0	0	0	
TOTAL GOVT FUNDING	142,000	145,000	3,000	2.1%
TOTAL INCOME	2,800,200	3,200,500	400,300	14.3%
EXPENSES	Current Budget	Proposed	$ Change	% Change
Artistic Salaries/Fees/Expenses	872,045	1,060,000	187,955	21.6%
Technical Salaries/Fees/Expenses	615,907	665,000	49,093	8.0%
Production Cost	139,669	150,000	10,331	7.4%
Administrative Salaries/Fees/Expenses	152,409	160,000	7,591	5.0%
Marketing Salaries and Expenses	542,522	652,500	109,978	20.3%
Development Salaries and Expenses	162,942	192,500	29,558	18.1%
Special Events & Receptions	128,000	88,000	(40,000)	-31.3%
Concessions	35,858	40,000	4,142	11.6%
Gift Shop Expenses	6,435	6,500	65	1.0%
Occupancy (Utilities, phones, etc.)	70,352	75,000	4,648	6.6%
Contingency	33,561	36,000	2,439	7.3%
TOTAL EXPENSES	2,759,700	3,125,500	365,800	13.3%
VARIANCE - Surplus OR (Deficit)	40,500	75,000	34,500	

proposed budget for a small theater group. This budget is simplified for presentation here. In addition, the budget does not show benefits costs (health insurance, retirement, and so forth). What is shown is a sample list of the income and expenses for the organization. In a typical fiscal year, the income and expense lines form the most active part of the budget. The budget does not reveal whether the organization is financially healthy. It simply tells what is expected in revenue and what is planned in expenses. In this example the theater company has a current year budget that is designed to produce a $40,500 surplus of income over expenses. The budget planning for next year anticipates an even larger surplus, $75,000. As you read this budget you will see certain

Figure 11-3

Detailed Budgets - Theater Company

SAMPLE INCOME ACCOUNT LINES   Assumes 11 months into FY

Acct Num	Account Title	Budget	To Date	Balance	Percent
300	Subscription Sales	817,000	775,000	(42,000)	94.9%
321	Single Tickets - Show 1	85,000	84,000	(1,000)	98.8%
322	Single Tickets - Show 2	85,000	82,500	(2,500)	97.1%
323	Single Tickets - Show 3	148,000	152,000	4,000	102.7%
324	Single Tickets - Show 4	85,000	79,000	(6,000)	92.9%
325	Single Tickets - Show 5	85,000	87,000	2,000	102.4%
326	Single Tickets - Show 6	114,000	116,000	2,000	101.8%
	SUBTOTAL Single Tickets	602,000	600,500	(1,500)	99.8%
421	Group Sales - Show 1	8,000	7,700	(300)	96.3%
422	Group Sales - Show 2	7,200	6,800	(400)	94.4%
423	Group Sales - Show 3	22,000	24,000	2,000	109.1%
424	Group Sales - Show 4	5,800	6,000	200	103.4%
425	Group Sales - Show 5	5,000	7,200	2,200	144.0%
426	Group Sales - Show 6	8,000	8,500	500	106.3%
	SUBTOTAL Group Sales	56,000	60,200	4,200	107.5%
	TOTAL TICKET SALES	1,475,000	1,435,700	(39,300)	97.3%

SAMPLE EXPENSE ACCOUNT LINES

Acct Num	Account Title	Budget	To Date	Balance	Percent
3000	**MARKETING**				
3001	Salaries	221,000	202,000	(19,000)	91.4%
3002	Payroll Taxes	20,322	18,600	(1,722)	91.5%
3003	General Advertising	7,000	7,400	400	105.7%
3004	Newspaper Advertising	50,000	47,000	(3,000)	94.0%
3005	Broadcast Advertising	32,000	30,000	(2,000)	93.8%
3006	General Printing	30,000	32,000	2,000	106.7%
3007	Season Program Printing	53,700	52,223	(1,477)	97.2%
3008	Telemarketing Expenses	6,325	6,500	175	102.8%
3009	Telemarketing Commissions	50,025	48,000	(2,025)	96.0%
3010	Displays and Signage	6,000	6,200	200	103.3%
3011	Photography	13,000	15,000	2,000	115.4%
3012	Postage & Distribution	12,000	11,950	(50)	99.6%
3013	Distribution of Brochures	1,800	1,500	(300)	83.3%
3014	Program Ad Sales Commission	15,000	14,000	(1,000)	93.3%
3015	Group Sales	15,000	14,000	(1,000)	93.3%
3016	Hotel Commissions	3,000	2,800	(200)	93.3%
3017	Dues/Subscriptions/Clippings	2,000	1,850	(150)	92.5%
3018	Materials and Supplies	3,500	2,900	(600)	82.9%
3019	Miscellaneous	850	250	(600)	29.4%
	SUBTOTAL MARKETING	542,522	514,173	(28,349)	94.8%

planning expectations are funded. For example, the company plans to increase its marketing expenses by 18.1 percent, slightly less than the 18.7 percent expected rise in subscription sales. This would indicate some major effort will be undertaken to increase the subscriber base.

The detailed budget, shown in Figure 11–3, goes into more depth. Account numbers are assigned to the individual line items in the budget. The account numbering system helps identify the type of transaction that took place, and the system can be broken down further into account subcodes to provide as much detail as possible. For example, under the marketing budget (3000) are line items for a season program (3009) and telemarketing (3010 and 3011). Figure 11–3 also shows, in each line, expenses incurred to date and the percentage of the budget expended. This information is very important to the person responsible for issuing budget reports in the FMIS. For example, the marketing area has used 94.8 percent of its budget to date. The information in the revenue lines shows that the theater company has completed 11 months of the season and is at 97.3 percent of its revenue budget. Thus, the marketing department has kept on its budget track in relationship to the season. However, a closer look shows certain expense lines exceeded the budget. For example, general advertising (3005), printing (3008), and photography all have gone over budget. The marketing manager would need to assess why and determine whether adjustments in next year's budget are called for in those lines.

Another way to organize a budget is along project or department lines. A project budget distributes revenue and expense centers across the organization. Figure 11–4 shows one way the theater company could express its budget by using this approach. In this example, the account titles are distributed across five major operational areas: regular season, touring, educational outreach, building fund, and special events. This new distribution gives much more information about how the organization distributes its income and expenses. For example, we see that the educational outreach activities are generating more expenses than revenue. The variance section of the report at the bottom of the page shows a deficit of $120,700 in the outreach program. In effect, other activities of the organization are subsidizing this activity. Of course, this may be a management decision and the deficit may have been anticipated.

The project budget is an excellent way to help with the fund-raising needs of the organization. For example, the educational outreach area could make a case for an additional $120,700 to achieve its objectives. If the $120,700 could be raised from outside sources, funds could be shifted to help pay for other high-priority projects that the organization has established in its planning process.

Another useful element of the project budget is its ability to show the proposed distribution of resources across the entire organization. The salary lines for the regular artistic, technical, and administrative staff present a clear picture of how much of the budget has been allocated to support the educational outreach program. The FMIS becomes a tool for helping the manager evaluate whether the budget is best serving the organization. For example, in looking at this budget, the manager might wonder why so little of the organization's resources are required to put on the shows. Based on the information in Figure 11–2, the company does six shows a season and the $139,699 production budget seems rather meager. That averages to $23,283 per show for materials for sets, costumes, and props. Since the revenue budget (Figure 11–3) indicates at least two of the six shows generate substantial single ticket revenue ($148,000 and $115,000), one could surmise these are large-scale productions. Therefore, it is likely one or more of these six shows costs more to build and costume than $23,000.

The project budget also may be broken down in various graphic representations to help make the FMIS more effective. This is especially important when a manager must work with a board of directors or a finance committee that is not close to the daily operational activities of the organization. The pie graphs (shown in Figure 11–5) illustrate how the revenue, expenses, and salaries are distributed by amount and percentage. These graphs help a board member see that nearly 60 percent of the budget is committed to staff salaries and that ticket sales account for 53 percent of the operating revenue.

Figure 11-4

Budget Distribution - Project Basis   Current Year

INCOME	Regular Season	Touring	Educational Outreach	Building Fund	Special Events	TOTAL
Subscription Ticket Sales	653,500	163,500	0	0	0	817,000
Single Ticket Sales	481,600	120,400	0	0	0	602,000
Group Sales	36,400	11,200	8,400	0	0	56,000
Advertising	61,600	15,400	0	0	0	77,000
Concessions	47,600	8,400	0	0	0	56,000
Gift Shop Income	12,000	3,000	0	0	0	15,000
Interest	12,800	3,200	0	0	0	16,000
Costume & Scenery Rentals	3,500	0	0	0	0	3,500
Space/Equipment Rentals	7,000	0	0	0	0	7,000
Education	0	0	5,200	0	0	5,200
Miscellaneous	6,500	0	0	0	0	6,500
Surcharges on Ticket Sales	12,000	0	0	0	5,000	17,000
SUBTOTAL	**1,334,500**	**325,100**	**13,600**	**0**	**5,000**	**1,678,200**
DONATIONS & GOVT FUNDING						
Individuals	100,000	0	0	50,000	100,000	250,000
Corporations	45,000	25,000	25,000	5,000	0	100,000
Foundations	40,000	10,000	40,000	10,000	0	100,000
Co-producers	45,000	15,000	15,000	0	0	75,000
Special Events	0	0	0	0	205,000	205,000
Matching Contributions	200,000	50,000		0	0	250,000
State Grants	0	25,000	23,000	0	0	48,000
City/County Grants	29,000	30,000	35,000	0	0	94,000
Federal Grants	0	0	0	0	0	-
SUBTOTAL	**459,000**	**155,000**	**138,000**	**65,000**	**305,000**	**1,122,000**
TOTAL	**1,793,500**	**480,100**	**151,600**	**65,000**	**310,000**	**2,800,200**

EXPENSE	Regular Season	Touring	Educational Outreach	Building Fund	Special Events	TOTAL
Artistic Salaries/Fees/Expenses	557,745	175,000	130,800	0	8,500	872,045
Technical Salaries/Fees/Expenses	389,407	125,000	95,000	0	6,500	615,907
Production Cost	96,669	28,000	15,000	0	0	139,669
Administrative Salaries/Fees/Expenses	84,059	30,500	15,000	7,600	15,250	152,409
Marketing Salaries and Expenses	425,000	102,000	10,000	0	5,522	542,522
Development Salaries and Expenses	72,942	10,000	5,000	10,000	65,000	162,942
Special Events & Receptions	9,000	0	0	12,000	107,000	128,000
Concessions	35,858	0	0	0	0	35,858
Gift Shop Expenses	3,735	1,200	0	0	1,500	6,435
Occupancy (Utilities, phones, etc.)	70,352	0	0	0	0	70,352
Contingency	25,061	3,500	1,500	0	3,500	33,561
TOTAL EXPENSES	**1,769,828**	**475,200**	**272,300**	**29,600**	**212,772**	**2,759,700**
VARIANCE - Surplus or (Deficit)	**23,672**	**4,900**	**(120,700)**	**35,400**	**97,228**	**40,500**

From the Budget to Cash Flow
The budget shows the manager the planned revenues and expenses for the fiscal year. The budgeting process that took us to the point of preparing a detailed budget still does not tell us if we have enough resources to operate the organization during the year. To make the budget work, a cash flow chart must be developed. It will provide a detailed look at the budget before the organization begins to spend money.

Cash flow statement   It is possible to anticipate periods during the fiscal year when the organization may not have enough cash to pay its bills. Figure 11–6 shows the theater company's budget distributed over the current fiscal year that begins in July and ends in June. The

Figure 11-5

Revenue and Expense Distribution

INCOME

Ticket Sales	$1,475,000	52.7%
Other Income	$203,000	7.3%
Donations	$980,000	35.0%
Grants	$142,000	5.1%
TOTAL	**$2,800,000**	**100.0%**

EXPENSE

Staff Salaries	$1,640,361	59%
Productions	$139,669	5%
Marketing	$542,522	19%
Development	$162,942	6%
Special Events	$128,000	5%
Other Expenses*	$186,706	7%
TOTAL	**$2,800,200**	**100%**

* Includes $40,500 surplus

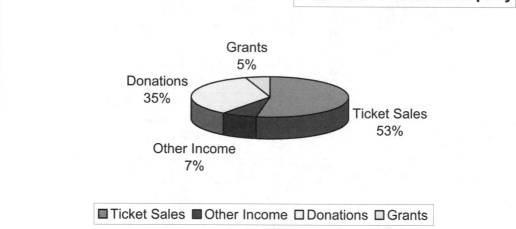

Revenue - Theater Company

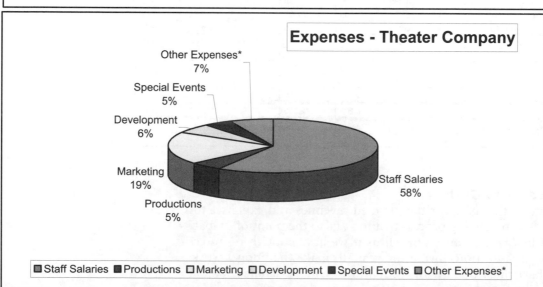

Expenses - Theater Company

Figure 11-6

Cash Flow Projections - Theater Company

INCOME	July	Aug	Sept	Oct	Nov	Dec	Jan	Feb	Mar	Apr	May	June	TOTAL
Subs Ticket	100,000	175,000	150,000	25,000	0	0	0	0	42,000	75,000	125,000	125,000	817,000
Single Ticket	0	0	7,000	50,000	125,000	150,000	75,000	65,000	60,000	70,000	0	0	602,000
Group Sales	0	10,000	15,000	6,500	7,500	5,000	5,000	2,500	2,000	2,500	0	0	56,000
Advertising	25,000	22,000	22,000	0	0	0	0	0	0	0	1,000	7,000	77,000
Concessions	0	0	0	7,500	8,000	11,000	9,000	8,000	7,500	5,000	0	0	56,000
Gift Shop	0	0	0	1,500	2,500	3,500	2,000	2,000	1,500	2,000	0	0	15,000
Interest	1,300	1,500	1,700	1,200	1,200	1,450	1,400	1,200	1,200	1,300	1,350	1,200	16,000
Set/Cost Rental	0	0	0	0	0	0	3,500	0	0	0	0	0	3,500
Space Rentals	3,500	0	0	0	0	0	0	0	0	0	0	3,500	7,000
Education	0	0	0	0	0	2,500	0	0	0	0	2,700	0	5,200
Miscellaneous	0	0	0	0	0	0	0	0	0	0	3,500	3,000	6,500
Surcharg Tkts	0	0	0	2,100	2,500	2,600	2,500	2,500	2,500	2,300	0	0	17,000
Individuals	8,500	9,500	10,000	10,000	25,000	35,000	30,000	30,000	35,000	30,000	15,000	12,000	250,000
Corporations	6,500	7,000	7,500	9,000	15,000	20,000	15,000	8,000	6,500	3,500	1,000	1,000	100,000
Foundations	0	0	25,000	0	0	25,000	0	0	25,000	0	0	25,000	100,000
Co-producers	10,000	10,000	20,000	0	0	30,000	0	0	5,000	0	0	0	75,000
Special Events	0	0	0	0	0	0	45,000	55,000	100,000	5,000	0	0	205,000
Matching	0	0	0	100,000	0	10,000	100,000	40,000	0	0	0	0	250,000
State Grants	0	0	0	24,000	0	0	0	0	24,000	0	0	0	48,000
Grants	0	0	31,000	0	0	31,000	0	0	0	32,000	0	0	94,000
Federal Grants	0	0	0	0	0	0	0	0	0	0	0	0	-
INCOME	154,800	235,000	289,200	236,800	186,700	327,050	288,400	214,200	312,200	228,600	149,550	177,700	2,800,200

EXPENSES	July	Aug	Sept	Oct	Nov	Dec	Jan	Feb	Mar	Apr	May	June	TOTAL
Artistic Staff	0	0	87,045	110,000	110,000	125,000	110,000	110,000	110,000	110,000	0	0	872,045
Technical Staff	0	61,591	61,591	61,591	61,591	61,591	61,591	61,591	61,591	61,591	61,591	0	615,907
Production	0	38,000	25,000	15,000	10,000	10,000	10,000	10,000	10,000	10,000	1,699	0	139,699
Administrative	12,701	12,701	12,701	12,701	12,701	12,701	12,701	12,701	12,701	12,701	12,701	12,701	152,409
Marketing	18,022	24,500	35,000	100,000	60,000	50,000	5,000	50,000	50,000	50,000	75,000	25,000	542,522
Devel Sal & Exp	13,500	20,000	13,500	13,500	20,000	13,500	13,500	13,500	13,500	13,500	8,000	6,942	162,942
Special Events	0	0	0	0	1,500	1,500	25,000	97,000	1,500	1,500	0	0	128,000
Concessions	0	0	0	4,800	5,000	6,200	5,358	5,500	4,500	4,500	0	0	35,858
Gift Shop	0	3,500	0	0	0	2,935	0	0	0	0	0	0	6,435
Occupancy	5,863	5,863	5,863	5,863	5,863	5,863	5,863	5,863	5,863	5,863	5,863	5,863	70,352
Contingency	0	0	0	15,000	15,000	3,561	0	0	0	0	0	0	33,561
TOTAL EXP	50,085	166,154	240,699	338,454	301,654	292,850	249,012	366,154	269,654	269,654	164,853	50,505	2,759,730
VARIANCE	104,715	68,846	48,501	(101,654)	(114,954)	34,200	39,388	(151,954)	42,546	(41,054)	(15,303)	127,195	40,470

CASH FLOW PROJECTIONS													
RESERVES	0	104,715	173,560	222,061	120,407	5,453	39,653	79,041	(72,913)	(30,367)	(71,421)	(86,725)	$ 40,470
BALANCE	104,715	173,560	222,061	120,407	5,453	39,653	79,041	(72,913)	(30,367)	(71,421)	(86,725)	40,470	$ 80,940
	July	Aug	Sept	Oct	Nov	Dec	Jan	Feb	Mar	Apr	May	June	TOTAL

Comment: The company is projected to have a $80,940 cash balance at the end of the season.

performances will take place October through April. The touring activity is scheduled for December and April.

In this example, the variance line of the cash flow statement shows that the company will spend more than it makes in sales and donations for five months out of the year. The actual cash flow projections at the bottom of the page show that, four months of the year, the company will have a cash flow deficit. However, by carefully planning the use of cash reserves, the company should be able to make it through the year.

In this example, if the company starts the year with no cash reserves (see the Cash Projections section of Figure 11–6), it will have enough funds to get through the season. The bank account would be in the negative in February ($72,913) and would stay that way through May. By the end of the season, the company would have a positive cash flow of $80,940. How did this come about? The decrease began in February when revenue was $214,200 and expenses totaled $366,154.

It is easy to see from this simple example how an arts organization can get into financial difficulty. Even though the company is projecting ending the season with a $40,470 surplus (see the Variance line under the Total column), the cash flow though this account ends $23,775 less than in July ($104,715 − $80,940 = $23,775). The financial manager for the theater company of course would take action to create a reserve to begin with so the account would not be depleted.

Often an arts organization will lack sufficient reserves to cope with the difference between when you receive money and when you spend it. Once an arts organization begins to find itself in a cycle of borrowing to make up cash flow and paying very high short-term interest rates, the erosion of the fiscal foundation begins. It may take two or three years, but overestimating revenue in combination with overspending and poor cash flow management eventually will lead to a deficit that could bankrupt the organization.

Fixed and variable costs   The previous chapter introduced the concept of fixed and variable costs. The total operating costs of the organization were derived from the combination of these two figures. The theater company's operating budget is an expression of these figures in the designated account lines. However, an arts organization is a type of service business. Therefore, the distribution of fixed and variable costs will differ from that of a manufacturing enterprise. Identifying fixed costs becomes the starting point in the financial manager's quest to establish how much it will cost to run the arts organization.

In economics, a fixed cost is "the cost of the inputs needed to produce any output and it is a cost that does not change when the outputs are changed."[5] For example, the theater company will have a fixed annual occupancy cost for leasing office space. Regardless of how many productions the company mounts, it still will have to pay the rent. The same applies to the shop space it rents to build the scenery and costumes. A case also can be made for budgeting a core staff, payroll taxes, insurance, minimal office supplies, telephone lines, and specific equipment charges as part of the fixed costs of the organization. Without these core elements, it would be impossible to operate the organization. Obviously it is in the organization's best interest to control these core costs or baseline budget carefully.

After the organization has designated the fixed costs, the variable costs are any other costs required to run the company. The variable costs relate directly to the myriad of decisions that the theater company made about works performed in the season, the scale of production, the marketing campaign, and so forth as part of the planning process. If the company decides to produce six shows, all of the variable costs related to supporting that effort should be reflected in the budget.

Until an organization has a clear picture of all of its fixed and variable costs and understands how to adjust those figures to budget realistically, the financial management system will experience recurring problems. In the long run, the chances are good that the company will find itself growing into a larger deficit each year. Once an organization reaches its debt threshold, it becomes very difficult to pay back the borrowed money and continue to meet its stated objectives.

Developing a Financial Management Information System

The financial management information system illustrated in Figure 11–1 requires that data from the operating system be transmitted to the records system. These data are assembled in various reports used by the different departments in the operation. To report accurately on the fiscal activity of the organization, an accounting and record-keeping system must be in place. Figure 11–7 shows one version of an accounting system. In this case, the flow is from the top of the page to the bottom.

The personal computer and inexpensive accounting software has had a tremendous positive impact on arts organizations. Inexpensive systems are available to help organizations quickly enter data and print reports. However, due to the nature of not-for-profit businesses, different reporting formats are required when discussing how much the "business" is worth and how it is using its assets.

Accounting

Accounting usually is defined as identifying, collecting, analyzing, recording, and summarizing business transactions and their effects on a business. A *transaction*, which is a key element in this definition, is an exchange of property or services. *Bookkeeping* involves the clerical work of recording the transaction. In a sense, the accountant begins where the bookkeeper leaves off by summarizing and interpreting the records or books. In many cases, the bookkeeping and accounting are done by the same person.

The Financial Accounting Standards Board (FASB) oversees the practices of the profession and regularly updates what is referred to a the *generally accepted accounting principles* (GAAP).

Accounting has evolved its own specialized language to describe transaction activity. Let us look at a few key concepts.

Cash-based accounting A personal checking account is one example of a cash-based accounting system. You make a deposit, write checks, and at the end of the month, have a positive or negative balance. The major problem with the cash-based system is that it gives you no information about how much you are worth, how much you owe, or how much is owed by others. However, it is simple to keep this account and many small organizations keep cash accounts to record their business activities.

Accrual-based accounting The accrual system recognizes expenses when they are incurred and income when it is committed. The primary advantage of this system is that it shows future commitments and

Figure 11-7
Accounting System Overview

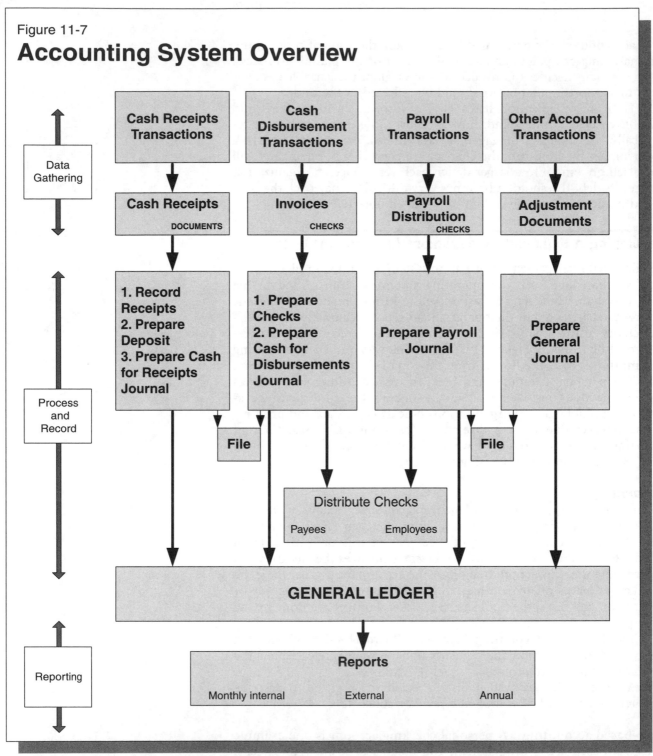

how much money you owe. When you charge something to a credit card, you are using an accrual system. You will have to make a future payment to an ongoing account in your name.

An organization typically opens accounts with several different vendors. Office supplies, lumber, and paint are purchased with the understanding that the organization will pay for the materials when they are billed. For example, when $250 worth of office supplies are purchased from a local supplier, the $250 becomes a *payable*, and when the bill is paid, it becomes an *expense* item in the budget. A foundation grant for $5,000 awarded to the organization is called a *receivable*. When the check arrives and is deposited, it becomes *revenue*. The accounting system deducts the payables, adds the receivables, and arrives at the balance with which the organization will operate.

Fund-based accounting   Because not-for-profit organizations receive money in such forms of income as grants and gifts, the FASB has a special set of standards for not-for-profit organizations to use to report the overall account activity. Fund accounting is a system of classifying resources into activities or projects so that each area can accurately report account activity during a fiscal year.

Frederick J. Turk and Robert P. Gallo note that "the fundamental principle in fund accounting is stewardship," and the "funds are accounted separately according to restrictions established by donors" or the board.[6] In Figure 11–4, for example, the activities related to the regular season, touring, education, and the building fund all could be established as fund accounts. Each account becomes a separate entity and may be designated as either a restricted or an unrestricted fund. A *restricted fund* is designed to control how the funds are used from a specific account. For example, if an organization has an endowment fund, the money received or expenses incurred will need special approval. In the project budget shown in Figure 11–4, the building fund could be a restricted account because gifts and expenses would be intended for a specific purpose. In this example, the theater company has decided to designate funds as temporally restricted. This allows the flexibility to use "restricted" funds to support other activities in the event of an financial emergency. The regular season fund, on the other hand, would be *unrestricted*, meaning that resources could be expended for a wide variety of organizational activities, as approved by the board. The revised financial accounting terminology used by the FASB now allows organizations to classify various fund accounts as restricted or unrestricted net assets. The term *net assets* often is used in place of *fund balances* in many financial statements.

The accounting system   To extract the information required for an effective FMIS, the accounting input must be as detailed as possible. Figure 11–7 shows how a typical system takes the input of cash receipts, invoices, payroll, and other documentation and processes the data to produce monthly external and annual reports.

When an organization establishes its accounting system, specific account numbers and designated subcodes are used to identify *liabilities* (money owed or funds committed) and *assets* (property or resources owned by the organization). When expenses are incurred, they are recorded as liabilities that reduce the organization's overall worth. When money is received in the form of revenues or gifts, it is classified as an asset that adds to the organization's overall worth.

The accounting system shown in Figure 11–7 identifies a data-gathering area where cash is received, checks are written (disbursement transactions), payroll is processed, and all other account activity takes place. A general ledger processes the four other journals (receipts, disbursements, payroll, and general journal) and allows reports to be assembled that provide the feedback required by the management and the board. Computers and software automate the bookkeeping to the point that the journal and ledgers are modules within the software. However, all accounting systems still generate a tremendous amount of paperwork. Check stubs, invoices, receipts, purchase orders, requisitions, credit card slips, and so forth quickly can overwhelm an organization. Organizations are required to keep all of this documentation—sometimes called a *paper trail*—to successfully complete a full audit or simple review by an outside accounting firm. Since all not-for-profit organizations must file a 990 tax return with the IRS, it is a good idea to review the categories of assets and liabilities used by the IRS when establishing your account system reports. If nothing else, it will make it easier to transfer data when filing taxes each year.

Accounting formula   The record-keeping system used in accounting is based on the simple formula that assets must equal the liabilities plus the net assets ($A = L + NE$), and the net assets must equal the assets minus the liabilities ($NE = A - L$). For example, an arts organization starts with $5,000 in cash. The accounting formula expresses this relationship as $5000 (A) = $0 (L) + $5,000 (NE). The assets total $5,000, and because no debts have been incurred, there is $0 in liabilities and $5,000 in net assets. (In the profit sector, the net asset would be called *equity*, and the formula would read $A = L + E$.)

The organization buys a computer system for $2,000 on credit. The business takes on a liability it must pay. The cash assets are reduced by $2,000 and the liabilities are increased by $2,000. To recalculate the net assets of the business, we apply the formula. In this case, we find a net asset balance of $3,000 by subtracting liabilities from assets ($NE = A - L$).

Financial Statements

So far, we have been looking at accounting documentation from the FMIS that was designed for internal use by the staff and board. These various budget reports do not tell us about the overall fiscal health of the organization. Does the theater company have any money in the bank? How much does it owe in short- or long-term debt? To locate this information, we need to review two reporting formats in the accounting system: the balance sheet and the statement of activity. The example used in Figures 11–8 and 11–9 depicts a theater company that is not in serious financial trouble. As you will see, it has an excess of revenue over income and funds to see it through some tough times.

Balance sheet   The balance sheet shown in Figure 11–8 is an example of the $A = L + NE$ formula. The top half of the balance sheet details the current and previous years' total assets as of June 30. The bottom half of the sheet shows the organization's liabilities and fund balances. On this day, June 30 of the current fiscal year, the organization had $326,812 in cash, $37,426 in accounts receivable, and so forth. In comparison, in the previous year the organization had $144,000 in cash and $12,000 in accounts receivable. The total assets for the current year were $427,670 and $231,000 in the previous year. Therefore, the organization increased

Figure 11-8

Theater Company Balance Sheet

Balance Sheet as of June 30   *ASSETS = LIABILITIES + NET ASSETS*

Assets	Unrestricted Funds		Temporally Restricted Funds			
	Operating Fund	Gala Fund	Building Fund	21st Century Fund	Current Year TOTAL	Last Year TOTAL
Cash	$70,812	$106,000	$100,000	$50,000	**$326,812**	$144,000
Accounts receivable	2,800	19,626	15,000	-	**37,426**	12,000
Shop Equipment	25,000	0	0	0	**25,000**	22,000
less depreciation	(9,000)	0	0	0	**(9,000)**	(3,000)
Office equipment	25,000	0	0	0	**25,000**	20,000
less depreciation	(12,568)	0	0	0	**(12,568)**	(4,000)
Scenery & Costume inventory	35,000	0	0	0	**35,000**	40,000
TOTAL ASSETS	**$137,044**	**$125,626**	**$115,000**	**$50,000**	**$427,670**	**$231,000**
Liabilities						
Accounts payable	$47,299	$2,500	$0	$0	**$49,799**	$18,000
Accrued payroll and taxes	18,933	0	0	0	**18,933**	6,000
Bank notes payable	25,000	0	0	0	**25,000**	24,000
TOTAL LIABILITIES	**$91,232**	**$2,500**	**$0**	**$0**	**$93,732**	**$48,000**
Net Assets (Fund Balances)						
Unrestricted fund balances	$45,812	$123,126	$0	$0	**$168,938**	33,000
Temporally restricted fund balances	$0	$0	$115,000	$50,000	**$165,000**	150,000
TOTAL NET ASSETS	**45,812**	**123,126**	**115,000**	**50,000**	**$333,938**	**$183,000**
Total Liabilities & Net Assets	**$137,044**	**$125,626**	**$115,000**	**$50,000**	**$427,670**	**$231,000**

its assets in the current year. The liabilities the organization incurred also increased. The company has much higher liability for the accounts its owes (accounts payable) and it owes $25,000 for a bank note (a loan) it took out during the year. The company has good news in its various fund balances accounts. Except for the operating fund, all the other funds (Gala, Building, and 21st Century) were positive at the end of the current year. Overall, the net assets increased from $183,000 to $333,938.

Statement of activity The second of the financial reports is the statement of activity and changes in net assets. The example shown in Figure 11–9 makes clear the source of the operating fund deficit and what changes took place in the net assets or fund balances.

The revenue section tells us how much money came into the organization from various sources. In comparison to last year, the overall revenue rose by $155,216 (to a total of $2,800,200), and expenses increased by $151,819 (to a total of $2,759,700). On closer examination, we see the operating fund ended the year with a $135,128 deficit. The other funds ended with a positive balance (expenses minus revenues or "changes in net assets"). The operating fund ended the year in a positive balance due to the transfer of $100,000 from the Gala Fund to operating. This was done to offset the overexpenditure in the operating

Figure 11-9

Statement of Activity and Changes in Net Assets
Theater Company

As of June 30

Revenue	Unrestricted Funds		Temporally Restricted Funds		Current Year TOTAL	Last Year TOTAL
	Operating Fund	Gala Fund	Building Fund	21st Century Fund		
Ticket Sales	1,475,000	0	0	0	$1,475,000	$1,425,826
Other Income	198,200	5,000	0	0	$203,200	$198,522
Donations	567,000	305,000	65,000	43,000	$980,000	$895,636
Grants	142,000	0	0	0	$142,000	$125,000
Total Revenue	$ 2,382,200	$ 310,000	$ 65,000	$ 43,000	$2,800,200	$2,644,984
Expenses						
Staff Salaries	1,602,511	30,250	7,600	0	$1,640,361	$1,510,963
Productions	139,669	0	0	0	$139,669	$142,895
Marketing	537,000	5,522	0	0	$542,522	$535,892
Development	87,942	65,000	10,000	0	$162,942	$154,258
Special Events	9,000	107,000	12,000	0	$128,000	$135,259
Concessions	35,858	0	0	0	$35,858	$27,891
Gift Shop	4,935	1,500	0	0	$6,435	$7,259
Occupancy	70,352	0	0	0	$70,352	$64,895
Contingency	30,061	3,500	0	0	$33,561	$28,569
Total Expense	$ 2,517,328	$ 212,772	$ 29,600	0	$2,759,700	$2,607,881
Changes in Net Assets (Fund Balances)						
	-$135,128	$97,228	$35,400	$43,000	$40,500	$37,103
Net Assets - Beginning of Year						
	$80,940	$125,898	$79,600	$7,000	$293,438	$145,897
Board Designated Fund Transfers						
	100,000	(100,000)	0	0	$0	$0
Net Assets - End of Year						
	$45,812	$123,126	$115,000	$50,000	$333,938	$183,000

fund (–$135,128). The overall good news for the theater company is that it ended the year with net assets of $333,938, up from $183,000 the previous year. While the company has no endowment account, it has a building fund and what has been designated a 21st Century Fund. Although both of the funds are modest (they total $165,000), they represent a little insurance for the organization. However, if a serious financial situation arose (a significant drop in single ticket and subscriptions sales), these fund balances represent a small percentage of the overall operating budget.

Ratio analysis Ratio analysis is a quick way of examining the organization's balance sheet and statement of activity. These ratios, and dozens of others, are detailed in Chapter 8 of Turk and Gallo's book.

Figure 11–10 compares two key indicators of the theater company's fiscal health. In this example, the *ratio of expendable assets to total liabilities* has declined in the current season. Turk and Gallo recommend that organizations have at least a 1:1 ratio of assets to liabilities. The balance sheet for the theater company shows that assets exceed liabilities, and the

---

Figure 11-10

Ratio Analysis - Theater Company

1. Ratio of Expendable Assets to Total Liabilities

Expendable Assets
 Total Liabilities

Current Year

Cash	326,812
Accts Receivable	37,426
Assets $	364,238 = 3.89
Liabilities $	93,732

Last Year

Cash	144,000
Accts Receivable	12,000
Assets $	156,000 = 3.25
Liabilities $	48,000

Comment: In the current year the organization had fewer liabilities in relation to its assets. The ratio of expendable assets to total liabilities is lower therefore.

2. Ratio of Expendable Net Assets to Total Expenses

Expendable Net Assets
 Total Expenses

Current Year

Net Assets	333,938 = 0.121
Expenses	2,759,700

Last Year

Net Assets	183,000 = 0.070
Expenses	2,607,881

Comment: In the current year the organization increased its net assests in a higher ratio to expenses than in the previous year.

---

ratio formula reveals an increase in financial health. In this case the increase in the ratio from 3.25 the previous year to 3.89 tells a manager and board member that they are doing a good job despite the fact liabilities increased from $48,000 the previous year to $93,732 this year.

The *ratio of expendable net assets* (fund balances) *to total expenses* for the current year is 0.121, up from 0.070 the year before. This ratio is a measure of how well organization is building its financial base. Gallo and Turk suggest this ratio should be closer to 0.3:1. For the theater company in this example to achieve that ratio, it would have to increase its net assets to over $800,000 in relation to its expenses in the current year.

Problem areas If, as a member of the board of directors of the theater company, you read the cash flow projections, balance sheet, and statement of activity, what would be your reaction? In this case, the financial management information system reveals that the organization has some cash flow problems (Figure 11–6) and increasing account payables (Figure 11–8). The reports also show that operating expenses exceed revenue (Figure 11–9) and a substantial interfund transfer of $100,000, was required to offset overexpenditures (Figure 11–9). The total net assets of

In the News

In the business world, diversification can bring new revenues to an enterprise. This article points up how the financial planning for arts organizations could be affected by operating additional businesses.

Beyond the Box Office: Arts Groups Find New Ways to Generate Income
Vince Stehle

In recent years, leaders of non-profit arts groups have heard a constant refrain from their supporters in the business and foundation worlds: Become more self-reliant by becoming more entrepreneurial.

For some groups that have answered the call, the experience has been profitable. But others have found that running a business is easier said than done. For them, the lure of big profits has led to wasted efforts, lost money, and disillusionment.

Some of the most successful ventures by arts groups have involved little more than an expansion of long-standing mercantile enterprises, such as museum stores, or branching out into areas that they know best—like the Portland Opera, which has been applying the ex-

pertise it gained in presenting classical opera to become the largest presenter of touring Broadway shows in Oregon. Last year, the opera earned more than $100,000 through such shows.

But several arts groups have created, bought, or even been given for-profit businesses that fall farther afield from their main pursuits.

In most cases, the arts groups hope that the money they earn from those business ventures will help them further their artistic missions. But many of the ventures have a second bottom line that is more difficult to measure: building audiences.

Even so, some in the non-profit world worry that the distraction of running a business is too much for many non-profit groups, and will cause traditional marketing and fund-raising activities to suffer.

"The most important thing is to make sure you are operating at capacity," says Cynthia Massarsky, president of CWM Marketing Group in Tenafly, N.J. For instance, before a theater group contemplates opening up a high-technology consulting firm, she says, it should make sure it is

doing everything it can to sell all of its tickets.

[Some of the examples of these venture include]

- In San Francisco, the profits of a cutting-edge information-technology company called the Content Group are used to underwrite experimental theater.

- In Seattle, a classical-music radio station is owned by an arts consortium. And Opera America, a Washington, D.C., association of opera organizations, recently bought a catalogue company that sells opera recordings and other merchandise, even though the group had never run a private business before.

- In New York, the non-profit group Art Matters devoted a large amount of its human and financial resources to building a successful and critically acclaimed art catalogue—only to see its investment go down the drain after the group was unable to attract adequate funds to keep the enterprise going.

the organization increased by $150,938 (Figure 11–8), but the net assets still are a smaller ratio of expenses than is desirable.

The immediate problems facing the theater company include balancing the operating fund and better controlling its cash flow. Continued overexpenditures in the operating fund will only erode the financial health of the organization. It will be very difficult to build an endowment if funds constantly have to be transferred to the operating fund to offset deficits. As a board member or manager for this organization, it is important to solve these problems because, in the long run, the ability of the organization to attempt new programs or enhance existing operations will be hampered by these financial problems.

Investment

One of the most important responsibilities of a financial manager in a nonprofit arts organization is to work with the board of directors to develop investment strategies that will help ensure the survival of the enterprise. Earlier in this chapter, we discussed the responsibility of the stewardship of the funds for an organization. This fiduciary responsibility, or trusteeship of the organization's resources, is the fundamental role of the board of directors. To exercise this fiduciary responsibility, the board must have accurate information about the assets and liabilities of the organization. At the same time, a finance committee should work with the financial manager to seek out ways to maximize the assets available. The management of the various fund balances of the organization must be monitored closely by the board.

In *Financial Management Strategies for Arts Organizations*, Turk and Gallo detail the best way to approach the asset management of the organization.[7] Their suggestions include developing a system for managing the cash available to the organization. Cash control can be realized through limiting access to cash accounts, timing the payment of bills, and closely monitoring the organization's accounts receivable. They recommend that the organization invest in a mix of short-term interest-earning instruments, such as certificates of deposits (CDs), Treasury bills (T bills), and money market funds. The objective of short-term investment is to maximize the interest-rate return while maintaining quick access to the funds should an emergency arise.

The board of directors also needs a long-term investment policy. One strategy is to take a conservative approach and invest in a variety of well-known stocks and bonds. Higher-risk investments usually provide greater returns, but board guidance is necessary to ensure that the financial manager invests the organization's assets safely.

Finally, Turk and Gallo urge managers to monitor the fixed assets of the organization, including inventories and expensive capital equipment and property. Maintaining sufficient insurance for equipment, inventories, and buildings helps minimize the financial risk to the organization if a disaster strikes.

Another approach an organization might adopt would be to establish another business to supplement its cash flow. The In the News article "Beyond the Box Office" describes several ventures undertaken by arts groups.

Conclusion

It is important to remember that the FMIS is a tool designed to help the organization fulfill its mission. Maximizing revenue, building the endowment, controlling cash flow, and conducting ratio analyses are important, but these activities should not be the organization's controlling force. The primary objective of the FMIS is to support the organization in achieving its mission and artistic goals. If the FMIS is working effectively, it should help, not hinder, goal achievement. Also remember that the system is only as good as the people who use it. Inexperienced or poor management, not the FMIS, usually leads an organization into a financial crisis.

For example, if the artistic director insists that the only way to attain a high level of production quality is to build the costumes and sets in the company's own shops, it is the financial manager's responsibility to explain how much this will cost. If it can be done with the resources available in the short and long run and the board approves the idea, then it should be done. If the organization cannot afford to build its own costumes and sets, the financial manager has an obligation to say so. Unfortunately, this scenario is not always followed. Instead, either the manager cannot stand up to the artistic director or the cost analysis is done without a real understanding of the organization's fixed and variable costs. When poor management is combined with a lack of understanding about the fiscal health of the organization, even the most sophisticated FMIS will not help.

Managing Finances and the Economic Dilemma

Without cash coming in, there is little chance that the show will go on or that the exhibit will open. The noble artists and staff can come to the rescue by working for free or for half pay once in a while, but in the long run, trying to operate an arts organization by using a crisis financial management technique will spell doom. Limited productivity and ever-increasing labor costs means that all arts organizations must adapt a flexible plan to keep up with the income gap. For example, if we take the hypothetical theater company's budget for $2,800,200 and project the budget for five years with a 3 percent per year increase to allow for inflation, the budget will grow to $3,246,200. Finding the additional $446,000 in revenue to offset expenses will be daunting, especially if ticket prices are not raised each year. In reality, the cost increases that the company will face probably will exceed 3 percent per year. Salaries, artist fees, construction materials, rents, and so on will increase at rates that are very difficult to project accurately.

Without careful planning, the organization will be susceptible to this familiar cycle: A growing deficit leads to a budget crisis, followed by a high visibility fund raising campaign and a last-minute rescue by a group of donors.

These realities make it all the more important for arts organizations to have at least a five-year plan that establishes expense and revenue projections. Longer-range plans make sense for organizations with very high fixed costs, such as museums. The changing economic conditions will require that arts managers and board members revise the financial plans at least every year. In times of recession or when inflation rates begin to exceed 6 percent per year, organizations may need to revise the long-term plans every quarter.

Reserve funds   The question of how much should be set aside for reserves is not easy to answer. As we have seen, most arts organizations operate with a very thin margin between the cash coming in and the expenses going out. As you will see in Chapter 13, "Fund Raising," donors prefer giving to financially healthy organizations. A donor does not want to see his or her money being used to support an organization that does not know how to manage its resources. However, since most arts organizations start out undercapitalized (i.e., insufficient startup funds) a cycle of cash flow shortages plagues many arts groups. Controlling costs and not being overly optimistic still remain the best strategies for cash-poor organizations. However, also setting a goal to have "rainy day" funds that would allow the organization to remain solvent despite a 25 percent drop in revenue in two consecutive years would be prudent. For example, the sample theater company used in this chapter should have about $1.4 million in net assets (unrestricted fund balances) to see it through two seasons of poor sales and weak fund raising.

Looking Ahead

In the next two chapters, we study various approaches to maximizing the financial resources needed to realize the organization's goals and objectives. We look at how the key areas of marketing and fund raising relate to the FMIS of the organization.

Summary

In most arts organizations, financial management is supervised by a business manager under the supervision of a general manager or managing director. The financial management information system is a comprehensive investment, reporting, control, and processing system designed to realize the organization's objectives.

In the profit sector, the financial manager is responsible for forecasting, investing, and control. He or she is concerned primarily with increasing owner and shareholder wealth.

Not-for-profit financial management implies a fiduciary responsibility for the net assets (fund balances) of the organization. *Net asset*, or *fund balance*, is the not-for-profit sector's term for the equity, or the financial worth, of the organization. Both for-profit and not-for-profit organizations share the same challenge: More money must flow in to the organization than it spends.

A not-for-profit organization must incorporate to be legally recognized in a state. Tax exemption will be granted only if the organization can meet the legal conditions set down by the federal and state governments. Even tax-exempt organizations must pay payroll and social security taxes. Any revenue earned from business operations that are not directly related to the main mission of the organization is taxable as well.

The key to a successful FMIS is financial planning through a realistic budget. Budgets for small organizations simply list revenues, expenses, and the balance or deficit that remains after operations. Larger organizations usually distribute the budget across revenue and expense centers. Each area is budgeted as if it were an independent fund balance.

After a budget is created, the organization estimates the cash flow required to meet the budget during the fiscal year. The organization must establish its baseline budget of fixed costs and then analyze the variable costs of operation.

The FMIS depends on accurate data processing of all revenue and expense transactions. Arts organizations are expected to follow accepted accounting practices so that they may be audited by outside accounting firms.

Most arts organizations use a combination of accrual and cash-based accounting to keep track of their transactions. The accrual system records receivables and payables, which later are recognized as revenues and expenses. The system allows financial statements about the organization to be developed. The accounting system is composed of three main components: assets, liabilities, and net assets. The system is based on a simple formula: The assets of an organization equal the liabilities plus the net assets.

The accounting system allows data to be collected for internal and external reports. The balance sheet shows what assets, liabilities, and fund balances the organization has. The statement of activity shows in more detail how the revenue, expenses, and fund balances were used during the fiscal year. A ratio analysis helps pinpoint problems in such areas as the relationship of assets to liabilities and of fund balance to expenses.

Organizations should develop short- and long-term investment plans to manage their assets. Certificates of deposit, treasury bills, and, money market funds are typical short-term investment tools. Stocks and bonds can be used for long-term investments.

Key Terms and Concepts

Financial management information system
Incorporation
Tax exemption
Section 501(c)(3) of the IRS Code
Unrelated business income tax
Account number
Account line items
Cash flow statement
Fixed and variable costs
Baseline budget
Cash-based accounting
Accrual-based accounting
Payables
Receivables
Fund-based accounting
Net assets
Restricted and unrestricted funds
Liabilities
Assets
Accounting formula
Financial statements
Balance sheet
Statement of activity
Ratio analysis
Fiduciary responsibility
Asset management
Short- and long-term investments

Questions

1. What are the key components of an FMIS?

2. What are the three major responsibilities of a financial manager in a for-profit business?

3. What are two advantages of incorporating?

4. What is the importance of Section 501(c)(3)?

5. Define the term *budget.*

6. What is the major advantage of the project or department budget?

7. What is the main purpose of a cash flow statement?

8. Why is it important to establish a baseline budget?

9. Define the term *accounting.*

10. Are there situations in which both cash-based and accrual-based accounting systems might be used in an organization?

11. Why is it better for organizations to have unrestricted, rather than restricted, net assets?

12. What is the accounting formula, and what does it reveal about an organization's fiscal health?

13. Solve for the ratio of expendable assets to total liabilities and expendable fund balances to total expense and explain whether this organization has a financial problem or not. The organization has $250,000 in expendable assets, $125,000 in total liabilities, $1.25 million in expendable net assets, and $225,000 in total expenses at the end of a fiscal year.

Creating a Financial Report for a Dance Company

The Wing and a Prayer Dance Company just finished its third season of operation. The company performs four weekends distributed as one weekend in October, December, February, and April. It performs Thursday through Saturday in a 1,000-seat theater. The single ticket prices are $10 and $16, and the series subscription prices to the four weekends are $32 and $52. During this last season, 60 percent of the subscriptions were sold at $52. The single ticket revenue was distributed through sales of 55 percent for the $16 tickets and 45 percent for the $10 tickets.

This year, the company was able to generate $99,950 in revenue. It sold $30,000 in single tickets and $39,855 in subscriptions. It received a grant from the state arts council for $10,000 and donations of $13,545. It raised $6,550 from a benefit dinner.

The expenses for the year totaled $96,450. The total was distributed in the following manner: $25,500 for salaries and benefits, $30,000 for guest artist fees, $2,400 for the office, $6,450 for travel, $7,800 for marketing, $15,000 for productions, $1,800 for utilities, $6,500 in mortgage payments, and $1,000 for miscellaneous expenses. They had net assets of $11,500 in their operating fund, $1500 in a restricted endowment fund, and $24,400 in assets represented by their building.

The dance company started with net unrestricted assets of $11,500 for the year. According to the bookkeeper for the company, the year ended with $79,400 in restricted and unrestricted assets. The unrestricted assets were made up of the following: $13,800 in cash, $1,200 in accounts receivable, $2,500 in prepaid expenses (deposits it made), a $13,000 inventory of scenery and costumes, $1,500 in a restricted endowment fund, and $47,400 in a restricted account for land and a building. The unrestricted liabilities were listed as $500 in accounts payable, $15,000 in a loan due to the bank, and the $23,000 in restricted liabilities from the balance due on the mortgage. The total liability was $38,500.

Problem Questions

1. Prepare an annual financial report for the dance company, showing the preceding information in the standard form of a balance sheet and a statement of activity (Figures 11–8 and 11–9).

2. Based on the balance sheet you created, what is the change in the dance company's net assets? Did net assets increase or decrease this year?

3. Assuming that cash, accounts receivable, and prepaid expenses are totaled to make expendable assets, what is the ratio of assets to total liabilities? What does this figure tell you about the company's financial condition (Figure 11–10).

4. Based on a total of 12,000 seats (a 1,000-seat theater times four weekends times three performances per weekend), what was the average number of tickets sold per performance by the dance company?

5. What is the percentage of total income earned through sales versus the total amount from donations, grants, and other sources?

Case Study

The following article gives you a good overview on how leadership of an arts organization can put you in and get you out of trouble.

Dance Center Lands back on Its Feet
Jacob's Pillow rises from deep debt through good management, creative grant making—and luck
Vince Stehle

Sali Ann Kriegsman was a battle-weary warrior in early 1995 when she agreed to take charge of the Jacob's Pillow Dance Festival, which was so deep in debt that it was on the brink of closing.

After a decade as head of the dance program at the National Endowment for the Arts—which had been under siege by conservative lawmakers seeking to dismantle the agency—Ms. Kriegsman worried that she did not have the energy to lead Jacob's Pillow back to solvency. "I was not interested in another very demanding position after being at the endowment during the hardest years of the culture wars," she says.

But she could not bear the idea of letting Jacob's Pillow, one of the largest and most influential dance festivals in the country, go under. During its 65-year history, the festival had become internationally renowned for presenting and educating some of the finest dancers in the world, especially among the avant-garde.

So she agreed to take up the challenge.

Less than three years later, she has announced that she will leave the festival next month, after having brought about a dramatic transformation in the financial health of the arts institution.

When she took charge, the festival faced an accumulated deficit of more than $650,000, including $250,000 in short-term bank debt and over $400,000 in overdue interest on an ill-advised $4.8-million bond issue that was used to finance capital improvements. In addition, donors were reluctant to give to an institution on the verge of disappearing, and the group's most important multiple-year foundation grants were about to expire.

Seeking $10.4-Million by 2004
Now, the festival is out of debt and has even established a cash reserve. What's more, it has taken in more than $7.5-million toward a fund-raising goal of $10.4-million by 2004, and it has renewed commitments for foundation grants of nearly $1-million over the next few years.

The story of the festival's turnaround involves more than just good management, however. It includes creative grant making, forgiving lenders, and a little serendipity. For other non-profit organizations, the lesson to be learned is not that deficits can easily be erased, Jacob's Pillow officials say. The lesson is: don't get into such a position in the first place.

Victim of Its Own Success
In a way, Jacob's Pillow was a victim of its own success. From 1981 to 1990, its budget grew from $300,000 to more than $2-million. Much of that increase came from government grants and private contributions, which together amounted to $860,000 in 1990.

As Jacob's Pillow expanded, its physical plant, nestled here in the Berkshires, began to deteriorate. By the end of the decade, water and sewage systems were outmoded. Kitchen and dining facilities had to be modernized. Housing for dancers and students was limited, and rehearsal and performance spaces were inadequate.

To top it off, the foundation under the main performance venue—the Ted Shawn Theatre, named after the modern dance pioneer who founded the festival—was crumbling.

Although construction and renovation work desperately needed to be done, the festival did not have the needed money in hand. The organization's contributions were steadily increasing, but many of the donors restricted their gifts to particular projects, rather than giving unrestricted money that could be used as the festival's leaders saw fit.

While many other organizations might have decided to start a capital campaign to raise money specifically for building projects, the festival instead decided in 1990 to obtain a $2.9-million bond, which it then expanded to cover $4.8-million of capital repairs in 1992.

"It Was Irresponsible"
The details of bond financing can be complicated. But the basic concept is as simple as a mortgage. A bond is a type of loan, which must be paid off over time according to a schedule.

Tax exempt bond financing relies on the participation of a government financing authority—known as the issuer—and an underwriter. When the issuer determines that a charity is performing a function that benefits society, it may issue a bond. But the issuer accepts no liability for the bond. The money comes from the underwriter, typically an investment banker who purchases the bond then resells it to private customers.

The festival's current treasurer, Caroline Williams, a New York financial adviser who joined the board to help straighten out the group's tangled accounts, says the organization got in trouble by not following the standard practice of figuring how it would meet its payment obligations before the bond was issued.

"My automatic reaction was that it was irresponsible," says Ms. Williams, a former partner with the investment-banking company Donaldson Lufkin & Jenrette. Although the festival's leaders may have felt a compelling need to borrow the money, she says, "Nobody thought through the potential consequences."

Managers and board members at Jacob's Pillow "were thinking soft," says Robert Crane, president of the Joyce Mertz-Gilmore Foundation in New York, who was instrumental in getting the festival back on its feet. "They loved the dance, but they were not people who understood the financial implications of what they were doing," he says.

The former management team at Jacob's Pillow acknowledges that their business acumen was flawed and that they were naive to believe that if they fell short on their payments, the issuer of the bonds would be tolerant. But the pressures to make capital improvements were too great to ignore, says Samuel A. Miller, who resigned as the festival's executive director in 1994 to become the executive director of the New England Foundation for the Arts.

Skepticism About Bonds

Many non-profit board members and managers view bonds skeptically, arguing that they should be used sparingly by charities. Most people familiar with non-profit capital financing believe that traditional fund drives make more sense.

At Tanglewood, the summer home of the Boston Symphony Orchestra in nearby Lenox, the institution built the $10-million Seiji Ozawa Hall at about the same time that Jacob's Pillow undertook its construction projects. But the orchestra ran a capital campaign before it broke ground, says Daniel Gustin, director of Tanglewood. "We were facing the same situation, and my board would not let me build it until we raised most of the money," says Mr. Gustin.

"I never would have voted to borrow the money," says Irene Hunter, who recently rejoined the Jacob's Pillow board after several years' absence. "I have been involved in enough not-for-profit groups to know that first you raise the money, then you do the improvements," says Ms. Hunter.

Nobody on the Jacob's Pillow board felt strongly enough to argue that a capital campaign would be better than a bond. The Massachusetts bond agency agreed to issue tax exempt bonds for Jacob's Pillow, and the Fidelity Massachusetts Tax-Free Fund, run by the Boston-based mutual-fund giant, agreed to sell the bonds.

But it soon became clear that the festival could not come up with the $420,000 annual payments on top of its more than $2-million in regular operating expenses. In 1994, the bond went into default and the festival's future was in jeopardy.

New Leadership

Jacob's Pillow's Board of Directors called upon Neil Chrisman, a board member who had recently retired from a career in investment banking, to take over as chairman. Not only had Mr. Chrisman worked the other side of the table, scowling at forlorn debtors as a managing director of Morgan Guaranty Trust Company, he had also been chairman of the Board of Directors at the Brooklyn Academy of Music. A decade earlier, Mr. Chrisman helped the academy eliminate a nagging, if less severe, accumulated deficit.

Ms. Kriegsman was chosen to lead the dance festival, in part because of her deep knowledge of the art form and the artists. But her main asset was her network of colleagues among foundation and corporate grant makers, says Mr. Chrisman. As head of the dance program at the arts endowment, she was an influential peer, and the festival expected her to use her contacts to attract financial support to the organization.

But first, the issue of the defaulted loan needed to be resolved. In May 1995, Ms. Kriegsman and Mr. Chrisman entered into negotiations with Fidelity. After commissioning a full review by Coopers and Lybrand, in which no hidden assets were discovered, Fidelity offered to forgive Jacob's Pillow's outstanding interest payments and agreed to accept $1.25-million to pay off the $4.8-

million bond on the condition that the group make the payment in 60 days.

Visibility an Asset

Jacob's Pillow was in such a bad financial position that Fidelity would have gotten very little had the company decided to fore-close on the festival, says Mr. Chrisman. Besides, he adds, "The Pillow was so visible that no financial institution would want to have its hands bloodied by putting it under."

To raise the $1.25-million, Ms. Kriegsman made the rounds to the usual suspects, calling upon large foundations and past supporters for financial help. None of the grant makers were willing to put money into an organization that was on such shaky ground, she says, particularly on such short notice. The biggest funds—those that make grants large enough to clear the organization's debt—could not respond quickly enough to help out, because it usually takes many months to propose, approve, and pay out big grants, she says.

Frustrated by her lack of success, Ms. Kriegsman went to Mr. Crane, then vice-president for programs at the Joyce Mertz-Gilmore Foundation, to seek his advice. His foundation had clear guidelines that limited support for the arts to organizations operating in New York City. Even so, Mr. Crane had achieved a reputation among his peers and among arts groups as a creative grant maker. And Ms. Kriegsman hoped that he could guide her to other foundations whom she had not already solicited.

Mr. Crane and Ms. Kriegsman quickly determined that no secret angel was going to materialize, that it was highly unlikely that anyone would come forward to bail the organization out, and that the festival was very likely to go bankrupt.

"The weight and severity of the situation began to roll over me," Mr. Crane recalls. Then it suddenly occurred to Mr. Crane that his own foundation was in a better position than many larger funds to take an extraordinary step to save the institution.

The dance festival's needs, however, far outstripped the foundation's normal grant-making budget. And there was little time to develop a new grant proposal anyway, with just two weeks to go before a meeting of the fund's Board of Directors.

$1.25-Million Loan

Instead, in a dramatic departure from past practice, Mr. Crane suggested that the fund could offer the festival a five-year loan for $1.25-million out of the fund's $70-million endowment.

The foundation's board approved the loan, which enabled the dance group to pay off Fidelity on time. With the bond debt paid off, the festival was once again in a position to seek support from its past backers, many of whom pitched in.

Key festival supporters thought it would be easier to keep donor enthusiasm high—and improve morale of staff members who suffered through the debt crisis—if the loan were paid off ahead of schedule, instead of sticking to the five-year schedule. To demonstrate his strong feeling that such an action was necessary, one supporter offered the festival $400,00—on the condition that the group's leaders ask Mr. Crane to forgive the balance of his foundation's $1.25-million loan.

"Beyond Our Capacity"

Mr. Crane refused. "The purpose was not to make a grant, and it was beyond our capacity to do it, anyway," he recalls.

Using his ties to another of the Mertz families' philanthropies, the Lu Esther Mertz Charitable Trust, which had a long history of association with dance groups, Mr. Crane arranged a grant which stipulated that Jacob's Pillow would get $250,000 if it was able to raise the balance of the Joyce Mertz-Gilmore loan. Combined with $400,000 from the anonymous donor, that meant the festival had to seek an additional $600,000 to pay off the loan.

Once the loan was paid off, the trust provided an additional $250,000 that Jacob's Pillow was required to use for efforts to make its fund raising more sophisticated. When the festival raises at least $1-million in new contributions, the trust will kick in an additional $500,000.

"It is a set of incentives that kept their feet to the fire," says Mr. Crane. "We pushed them to the limits of their capacity and then we rewarded them for doing it."

The festival was delighted to adhere to those terms, and by the time this year's festival began, Ms. Kriegsman and Mr. Chrisman had put the festival on a firm financial footing. With the incentives in place—and with all but $50,000 of the donations needed to create a $500,000 cash reserve—Jacob's Pillow appears to be on the way to fiscal health.

But Mr. Chrisman says that non-profit arts organizations can never feel completely at ease financially, no matter how successful their fund-raising efforts are.

Sitting on the shaded lawn near the Ted Shawn Theatre, Mr. Chrisman glances around and says, "You're never out of the woods up here."

Case Study Questions

1. Summarize the key actions that took place to put the festival in financial difficulty.
2. Although the article never mentions why bonds were selected over a capital campaign as the way to finance improvements, what arguments, if any, can you make for the choice the board made at the time?
3. Summarize the steps taken to solve the financial problems and put the dance festival back on its feet.

References

1. Thomas Wolf, *Managing a Nonprofit Organization* (Englewood Cliffs, NJ: Prentice-Hall, 1990), p. 139.
2. J. Fred Weston and Eugene F. Brigham, *Essentials of Managerial Finance*, 8th ed. (New York: Dryden Press, 1987), pp. 3–24.

3. Stephen Langley, *Theatre Management and Production in America* (New York: Drama Book Publishers, 1990), pp. 317–26.
4. Donald C. Farber, *Producing Theatre* (New York: Limelight Editions, 1987).
5. William J. Baumol and Alan S. Blinder, *Economics—Principles and Policy*, 4th ed. (New York: Harcourt Brace Jovanovich, 1988), p. 506.
6. Frederick J. Turk and Robert P. Gallo, *Financial Management Strategies for Arts Organizations* (New York: American Council for the Arts, 1984), p. 102.
7. Ibid., pp. 141–54.

Additional Resources

Thomas Ittelson. *Financial Statements*. Franklin Lakes, NJ: Career Press, 1998.
Franklin J. Plewa, Jr., and George T. Friedlob. *Understanding Cash Flow*. New York: John Wiley and Sons, 1995.

12 ☐☐☐☐ Marketing and the Arts

An arts manager must plan, organize, implement, and evaluate various marketing and fund-raising strategies in an effort to maximize revenue to meet the organization's established objectives. An enormous satisfaction can be derived from seeing a full house, a packed museum, or the groundbreaking for the new building made possible by the efforts of a well-designed marketing or fund-raising campaign. However, no amount of managerial brilliance or sophisticated marketing efforts will amount to much if the basic product does not meet the needs of the consumers for whom it is intended. It is important to remember that, like a management information system or a computer, marketing and fund raising are nothing more than tools. Marketing and fund raising cannot make a bad script good or a weak performance strong. At best, marketing and fund raising can help support a long-lasting relationship between the individual consumer and the organization. If properly managed, this relationship can evolve: The consumer can grow from a single ticket buyer to a subscriber or member and finally to an annual supporter. Unfortunately, this operational objective is much easier said than done.

In the United States today, it is almost impossible to avoid the efforts of someone trying to sell you something every day. We are bombarded with thousands of messages every week in the form of television commercials, newspaper and magazine advertisements, flyers and letters in the mail, or phone calls from total strangers. Thousands of new consumer products are released in the market every year. Billions of dollars and millions of hours of labor are expended on product research, design, and distribution.

Promotional activities related to the profit sector of the entertainment industry relentlessly let us know that a new film is opening, a new book is coming out, the ice show is in town, or a new ride is starting at the theme park. The escalating mixture of media blitz, promotional hype, and advertising competitiveness used to get the consumer's attention leaves little room for local arts organizations to make an impact. For example, it is not unusual for a movie studio to spend more money advertising one new film than a major regional arts organization has in its operating budget for an entire year.

As we have seen, the economic environment in which arts organizations must function requires constant effort to find the resources to survive from year to year. The need to retain and increase the number of subscribers, ticket buyers, members, or donors also places an enormous amount of pressure on the arts manager. Arts managers with the expertise and a successful record of managing marketing and fund-raising campaigns are very much in demand. However, because organizations depend so heavily on revenues generated from sales, when there is a decline in income, once-successful managers may find themselves suddenly unemployed.

An Event in Search of an Audience

No matter how lofty the aesthetic aims of an organization, without the regular support of an audience, patrons, or members, not enough money will come in to keep the enterprise alive. In other words, demand for the product must be sufficient or the enterprise will be out of business.

Before the advent of "marketing," arts organizations had a fairly standard set of activities that they undertook in an effort to create enough demand for a show or an exhibit. A press release announcing the upcoming event was sent to the local papers (a photo or two may have accompanied the release) and posters were put up wherever they were allowed. Flyers sometimes were distributed, a few very small advertisements were placed in the paper, and a low-cost brochure was mailed out to names on the mailing list. If the organization was lucky, a preview article might appear in the arts section of the local paper. Organizations with larger budgets placed bigger ads in the paper, and they sometimes ran a few radio or television commercials.

Many managers and board members wondered why after marketing came into vogue, arts organizations continued to do the same things but spent twice as much money to get the same audience. What happened was that organizations were really not engaged in marketing. They were still trying to sell events in a scattershot method to an ill-defined public. As a result, they wasted a great deal of money trying to convince people to buy their product without really knowing to whom they were selling. Spending more on advertising, in this case, was wasted effort.

As we will see in this chapter, real marketing requires that the organization adapt and change its fundamental perceptions about its relationship to consumers. Marketing requires the adoption of a customer-oriented perspective that often unfortunately is perceived as being incompatible with the fundamental mission of high-culture arts organizations. Selling, on the other hand, which is what most organizations still do, means that the organization tries to get the consumer to buy the product because it believes the product is inherently good and would be beneficial to the consumer.

A Means to an End

Whatever term is applied to the energy and resources used to find, develop, and keep an audience or membership base, all of this activity still is only a means to an end. Philip Kotler and Joanne Scheff noted in their definitive text, *Standing Room Only*, that we must view marketing as "a *means* for achieving the organization's goals, and using marketing and being customer-centered should never be thought of as the goal in itself."[1]

Let us look more closely at marketing and many of the key concepts inherent in this vital area of study.

Marketing Principles and Concepts

A key part of any arts organization's strategic plan is how to market itself. The marketing plan normally forms a major section in the foundation of an organization's strategic approach to its long-term growth. We will see how the term *marketing* often is used incorrectly to describe various promotional activities that organizations undertake.

The American Marketing Association's definition of marketing, is "the process of planning and executing the conception, pricing, promotion and distribution of ideas, goods, and services to create exchanges that satisfy individual and organizational objectives."[2]

Needs and Wants

The marketer strives to achieve a match between human wants and needs and the products and services that can satisfy them. Theoretically, the better the match, the greater is the satisfaction. Marketers define a *need* as "something lacking that is necessary for a person's physical, psychological, or social well-being."[3] Charles D. Schewe's textbook notes that food, shelter, and clothing are universal needs. Psychological needs (such as knowledge, achievement, and stability) and social needs (such as esteem, status, or power) are shaped by the overall value system of the culture.

A *want* is defined as "something that is lacking that is desirable or useful."[4] Wants are intrinsic to an individual's personality, experience, and culture. You may have a need for knowledge, but you want to pursue an idea from a specific book. You need to eat, but you want a particular brand of pizza.

When you have needs and wants to satisfy, two other marketing principles come into play: functional satisfaction and psychological satisfaction. When we purchase an item like a refrigerator, we achieve a *functional satisfaction* because of the tangible features of the product. When we purchase a car, we may satisfy a functional need, but a particular make and model may provide an intangible *psychological satisfaction* for recognition or esteem.

Obviously, *functional satisfaction* and *psychological satisfaction* are not neutral terms. Americans have attitudes about products that have been shaped by the advertisements on television and radio and in print. Accordingly, the "goal of [the] marketers [is] to gain a competitive edge by providing greater satisfaction."[5] Unfortunately for many consumers, the idea that a fine arts event could provide a degree of satisfaction is foreign. In many cases, arts organizations would probably not see their mission as providing satisfaction to customers. After all, in the minds of those inside an arts organization, a symphony concert is not a mass consumer product like soft drinks or toothpaste. However, the reality is that arts organizations function in a highly competitive entertainment market. Ultimately, if the symphony concert does not provide some degree of satisfaction to audience members, they will not continue to purchase the product.

Exchange Process and Utilities

Wants and needs are satisfied through the process of *exchange*, which occurs when "two or more individuals, groups, or organizations give to each other something of value in order to receive something of value. Each party to the exchange must want to exchange; must believe that what is received is more valuable than what is given up; and must be able to communicate with the other parties."[6]

For example, suppose that you want to hear a piano recital and the pianist wants to perform. You believe that the time you are spending to listen and the money you give up for the ticket are worth the exchange. The pianist believes that the fee and the satisfaction derived from playing will be personally rewarding. The performance and the recognition of applause form the communication to complete the exchange process.

Performers sometimes forget just how important this final communication really is for the audience. The level of satisfaction felt is greatly diminished when the performer walks off the stage without acknowledging the audience.

The exchange process depends on four utilities that marketers have identified as form, time, place, and possession. The utilities interact as part of the exchange process in ways that promote or hinder the final exchange or transaction.

The *form utility* simply means the "satisfaction a buyer receives from the physical characteristics of the product."[7] Attributes such as style, color, shape, and function affect the exchange. Arts organizations that have gift shops must be very sensitive to this utility because the customers usually have fairly sophisticated tastes, and filling the shop with cheap products will do more harm than good for the organization. Unique, high-quality items may provide the organization with a chance to build a strong bond with the discriminating buyer.

Except for the printed program, a performance offers no form utility. The live performance, as we all know, is an intangible event. However, the psychological satisfaction gained from the event can form a powerful bond between the audience and the organization. The memories that trigger emotional and intellectual responses in relation to a particular performance or exhibit can help build a lifelong relationship between the arts organization and the consumer.

The *time* and *place utilities*, which involve "being able to make the products or services available when and where the consumer wants them,"[8] have a direct impact on arts organizations. Arts organizations usually have little flexibility when it comes to time and place. The customer has the choice of either coming to the performance at a specific time and a specific place or not seeing it at all. Experimenting with different performance schedules or locations or different exhibit hours may offer arts organizations occasional opportunities to increase consumer access to their products. However, the live performing arts, by their very nature, always will be limited in their manipulation of the time and place utilities. The advent of television and home videotaping offers a way of partially overcoming the inherent limitations of the live performance. *Live from the Met*, for example, has provided a way for opera to reach audiences that would never be able to attend the production in New York City. Art museums have experimented with different programming and exhibit schedules. (See the "In the News 1" article, "Art Museum Thrives with Marketing.")

The *possession utility*, which refers to "the satisfaction derived from using or owning the product,"[9] has some application in the live performing arts. The tangible items offered by the organization can create a degree of consumer satisfaction in much the same way as the form utility. For example, long-time subscribers often view the seats they regularly sit in as their possessions. For two or three hours on a given night, they indeed possess those seats. Allowing subscribers to keep their seats each year can be a powerful tool for maximizing on the possession utility. It also is possible to reinforce the experience of having attended through the secondary means of selling souvenir programs or other related material.

As we have seen, the exchange process for consumers of arts products and services fits within the theoretical framework of basic marketing principles. As part of an arts organization's core strategic planning, it makes sense for the staff and the board to ask very fundamental questions about exactly what they are offering to the public. For example, how does the organization's corporate structure and philosophy affect its relationship with its audience? Do its programs and activities satisfy the wants and needs of the audience? What mechanisms are in place to get feedback from the audiences about the organization's programming?

If an organization is to survive, it must be able to adapt to and plan for changing conditions in the marketplace. "*Strategic market planning is a managerial process of developing and implementing a match between market opportunities (i.e., unsatisfied wants and needs) and the resources of the firm.*"[10] This process is not exclusive to the profit sector. One need only look at the changes that nonprofit hospitals have had to make in the mix of services they offered in the 1990s to see how essential organizational adaptability is.

Evolution of Modern Marketing

Marketing has moved through three eras in its evolution. It is important to note that although these phases represent a progression, many organizations still hold to attitudes and beliefs about their product or service that have not changed much in 75 years. As a result, there are no clean break lines in this evolutionary development.

The first era is tied to the production and manufacturing techniques that began with the industrial revolution in the eighteenth century.[11] The main emphasis up through the beginning of the twentieth century was on fulfilling the basic needs of consumers. Mass production techniques dictated an approach of deciding what the consumer wanted and then manufacturing the product in the most cost-effective way. The assumption was that consumers would buy whatever was manufactured.

During the second era, more attention was focused on sale of the mass-produced products. The rise of the salesperson as a dominant figure in a system of getting goods to consumers is a part of the American myth. The period after the Civil War was marked by economic growth and expansion. Masses of immigrants came to the United States, which also fueled rapid growth. Thousands of salespeople spread out over the country, trying to sell products to people whether they wanted them or not.

The marketing era, the third era, is an outgrowth of the diversification of consumer wants and needs that resulted from the demands of unprecedented growth in the economy after World War II. More companies began to pay attention to what consumers were saying about the available products. The idea of a consumer-driven economy meant that companies needed to consider their basic relationship with the consumer. The research and testing of products and the application of psychological theories about purchase behavior led to a greater emphasis on developing a long-term relationship with the consumer.

Modern Marketing

By the 1990s, the concepts of marketing had been applied in just about every segment of for-profit and not-for-profit business in the United States, including as a tool for electing candidates to office. The use of computers to store massive amounts of information about consumer preferences and provide almost instant feedback to companies about what is selling has revolutionized the marketing industry. The ability to track sales via *point-of-purchase systems* offers marketers immediate access to information about what people are buying. The ubiquitous bar code now gives the store and the suppliers up-to-the-minute sales information about what people are buying.

The proliferation of products designed to satisfy consumer needs and wants has led to an explosion of specialty goods and services. A journey to the supermarket provides evidence of products designed to meet special health and nutritional concerns. In fact, the reality of global marketing has led companies to use satellite communications to monitor worldwide sales and make adjustments in production much more rapidly.

Marketing and Entertainment

The news article "Off the Street and into the Audience: Tourists Help Pick Fall TV Schedule"[12] provides an accurate description of the degree to which the commercial entertainment industry is committed to consumer feedback. People were asked to watch pilots of television shows and rate them with a handheld counter that registered whether they liked what they were seeing. Writers, directors, and producers are not always happy with the prospect of their shows being subjected to this simplistic evaluation system.

The commercial film industry uses test screenings and similar audience feedback methods to find out what people like or dislike. Endings may be edited or even reshot if there are negative reactions to a film at a test screening. Theme parks do extensive surveying to get feedback about rides, exhibits, and services. The economic pressure to have a hit in the entertainment industry no doubt will lead to the application of more intensive prescreening and testing. (See the case study at the end of this chapter for an opinion about surveying audiences.)

It is easy to see why there is so much suspicion about the place of marketing in the high-culture industry. As we will see, there are limits to the practicality of consumer feedback and how consumer oriented an organization can be. For most arts organizations, being totally consumer driven in the choice of programs and presentations remains a totally alien concept.

Marketing Approaches

A company attempting to make a profit usually has different values and goals than a local not-for-profit health care center or symphony, but both rely on establishing a positive relationship with individual consumers and the general public. Both private and public sector companies make plans and state their missions based on satisfying the public's wants and needs. The mission statement is the source of the organization's goals and strategic plans. The planning process includes defining the function of marketing in the organization. First, we look at two approaches to marketing used by a great many arts organizations; then, we focus on customer-oriented marketing.

Product Orientation

Kotler and Scheff characterize the *product orientation* as one in which the organization believes that "consumers will favor those products that offer the most quality, performance, and features."[13] They cite as examples "a chamber music association that calls itself a 'society,' performs only traditional music, advertises in only a suburban weekly and doesn't understand why it doesn't attract a younger audience."[14] Another example might be colleges and universities that continue to offer courses evaluated as being below standard or for which there is very low enrollment and museums that feature specific works of art from the collection even when there is little public interest in the exhibit. Product-orientated organizations "have a love affair with their products."[15]

Sales Orientation

The organization with a *sales orientation* thinks that "consumers show buying inertia or resistance and have to be coaxed into buying more . . ."[16] Most arts organizations engage in sales activities that they misidentify as marketing. Rather than make any changes in the product or how it is presented, they increase the resources allocated to advertising, direct mail, or telephone solicitations. These efforts usually result in short-term gains in audience. However, because it does not really adopt the consumer's perspective, the sales-oriented organization constantly has to replenish a large number of nonrenewing subscribers or members.

Customer Orientation

All the marketing texts seem to agree that organizations that have evolved or start with a customer orientation have the best chance of competing in the world market today. An organization with a *customer orientation* must "systematically study customers' needs and wants, perceptions and attitudes, preferences and satisfactions."[17] To further clarify this definition as it applies to the arts, Kotler and Scheff go on to say,

> *This does not mean that artistic directors must compromise their artistic integrity.* Nor does it mean that an organization must cater to every consumer whim and fancy, as many manager fear. Those who warn of such consequences if the devil (marketing) is let in the door simply misunderstand what a customer orientation truly means. To restate: marketing planning must *start* with the customer perceptions, needs, and wants. Even if an organization ought not, will not, or cannot change the selection of the works it performs or presents, the highest volume of exchange will always be generated if the way the organization's offering is described, priced, packaged, enhanced, and delivered is fully responsive to the customer's needs, preferences, and interests. Furthermore, who the customer will be is largely up to the performing arts organization. Marketing will help maximize exchanges with targeted audiences.[18]

As this quote should make clear, an organization that takes a customer's perspective, for example, would use text to describe an upcoming performance in terms that an audience can respond to rather than in the jargon of the profession. If a potential ticket buyer believes that arts events are only for the wealthy and well educated and everything the organization does with its promotional activity (ads, brochures, and so on) only reinforces this image, the arts promoter should not be surprised if the consumer feels reluctant to enter into the exchange process. On the other hand, arts organizations usually believe that they should not have to describe a play like *Hamlet* as a "gut-wrenching tale of a family caught up in an whirlwind of lust and murder" to sell tickets. However, to discover the language that makes the most sense to its potential au-

In the News 1—A Customer Orientation

Art Museum Thrives with Marketing
David I. Bednarek

Through aggressive marketing, the Milwaukee Art Museum is attracting more visitors and members at a time when attendance at art museums nationwide is declining.

Since 1984, attendance at art museums in the US has gone down almost 5%, according to a Lou Harris poll, and is putting some museums on shaky footing because the higher cost of art and insurance demand greater attendance.

In the face of that national trend, attendance at the Milwaukee Art Museum has risen dramatically—from 129,000 in 1984 to 197,000 in 1989, an increase of 53%. Membership went up 56%, from 6,500 to about 10,000.

The museum's success with marketing stands out as a model for other arts groups and similar organizations as leisure time becomes more scarce.

Rebecca Turner, director of marketing for the museum, attributed the increases to a decision in the early 1980s to get into marketing instead of simply relying on public relations to keep the museum going.

In addition to the increases in attendance and membership, Turner said the number of people taking classes at the museum went up from 771 to 2,000, the number attending special events increased from 9,000 to 49,000, and the number taking museum tours rose from 25,759 to 53,000.

Since 1984, the museum also has attracted more docents, the volunteers who work as guides.

In deciding what to do to sell the museum, the marketers first found out why people did not go and then set up programs to counter those reasons.

To the response, "I have no time for arts," for example, the museum set up mini-lectures on gallery nights, First Friday events with live jazz, "Bagels and Bach" on Sunday mornings and lunch time lectures.

To those who say, "I don't know enough," the museum set up audio tours of exhibitions, using tapes to tell about the arts on display, the "Bluffer's Guide to Art," and Master of the Month gallery talks.

And to the complaint, "I won't fit in," the museum organized or helped organize Senior Days, Grandparents' Day, Free Days, Lakefront Festival of the Arts and Music in the Museum.

---

dience, the organization must engage in some basic consumer research. Research may show that a more dramatic description would make sense in their market.

The key to successfully adopting a customer orientation resides in the organization's having done research on its community. What are people's attitudes and perceptions about the value of the music, opera, theater, dance, and art programs offered in your community? Based on that research, the customer-oriented arts organization would have several different approaches to communicating with the different audiences in the community. In some cases, the promotional campaign might be targeted to educating people about a new work or new author. In other cases, the organization may focus on the strong emotions that a story or a piece of music conveys. *Hamlet* may spark the interest of some potential audiences if described in more lurid terms. The arts marketer, of course, must be careful about crossing a line that distorts or debases the product. On the other hand, the risk of offending the sensibilities of a small number of the old guard patrons may prove worthwhile if it brings in new customers. However, unless the organization has a method for tracking the impact of different advertising tactics, these efforts will be wasted.

In the News 2—Price as a Marketing Tool

This article demonstrates the marketing principle of price manipulation as a method for attracting and increasing attendance.

This Theater Tells Patrons: Pay What You Can Afford
Associated Press

PROVIDENCE, RI—At a time when the price of theater tickets is soaring beyond the reach of many, Trinity Repertory Theater will try a one-night experiment Tuesday of letting patrons pay what they will.

"The objective is to give everyone an opportunity to come to the theater," said E. Timothy Langan, managing director of the theater company.

The normal ticket price for the preview performance of Maxim Gorky's "Summerfolk"— a story Langan described as one about the Russian Empire's version of yuppies before the 1917 revolution—is $24. Based on similar experiments in Baltimore and San Diego, Langan said he expected people would be willing to pay $3 to $4.

"But that's OK," he said. "The whole purpose of this is for someone to be comfortable in coming to the theater."

Trinity has set aside $5,000 from a grant to cover projected losses.

The problem that most customer- or audience-oriented arts organizations face when it comes time to communicate effectively about the product is a lack of money. The cost of multiple target promotional campaigns usually is well beyond the reach of most groups. However, a marketer would argue that this is money well spent because the objective is to build up long-term audience support and consumer identification with the product. Unfortunately, many arts organizations take a middle ground and ultimately communicate a bland image by trying to straddle too many marketing perspectives in their brochures and publications.

Marketing Management

The Four Ps

Using these principles of marketing now allows us to move into the process of marketing management. To market its products or services effectively, an organization must carefully design its marketing mix. *Marketing mix* is defined as "the combination of activities involving product, price, place, and promotion that a firm undertakes in order to provide satisfaction to consumers in a given market."[19] Each of these elements will have an effect on the exchange process.

The *four Ps*, as they are often called, can be manipulated as part of the organization's overall strategy. For example, if you have a product with a brand name, such as the Metropolitan Opera, you may be able to manipulate the price based on the customer's perception of quality while stressing the place with its crystal chandeliers and red carpet in your promotional material.

The promotional aspect of the marketing mix is the most visible element, and it usually is divided into a further mix of types of advertising: newspaper, magazine, radio, television, direct mail, raffles, and other public relations activities (e.g., getting a soprano on a local television talk show or radio program).

The overall marketing strategy for the organization may have several different marketing mixes. Depending on the target audience, you may stress price or product. For example, a group sales flyer sent to a retirement center may be accompanied by a letter that stresses price first and then product. The same group flyer may be accompanied by a different letter that stresses product first and then price when sent to a college or university drama department.

Market Segments

A marketing manager is expected to have a good grasp of the overall marketplace. As discussed in Chapter 10, there are many markets in the system of supply and demand, and within the large markets, there are smaller markets for goods and services. Marketers use the term *market segment* to identify "a group of buyers who have similar wants and needs."[20] Once a market segment has been identified, the marketer begins the process of *target marketing* by "developing a mix of the four p's aimed at that market."[21]

In planning the marketing mix, information is the key ingredient in designing a successfully targeted campaign. For example, if you buy a mailing list from the state arts council with the names of 10,000 people interested in the arts in the state, you have identified a broad market segment. If this list of names is to be useful to you, it will need further analysis. How many of these people attend particular types of performing arts events? Narrowing the list further, how many of these people are geographically close to your performance or exhibition space? After you finish narrowing down the list to people within a three-hour driving distance, are there enough names left to make it worthwhile trying to target this group?

Mailing lists, which are purchased all the time in profit-sector marketing, may be far too costly for many arts organizations. For these groups, the existing audience is the best and most cost-effective resource of additional customers. The marketer's assumption is that if you consume the arts product, your friends or colleagues may share similar values.

Market Research

To engage effectively in target marketing, much detailed information about the potential arts consumer must be known. Having a demographic profile (age, income, education, gender, race) and an informed psychographic profile (consumer beliefs, values, attitudes) of the potential consumer is crucial to designing the marketing mix for the target market.

Marketing researchers in the profit sector have been developing various behavioral and psychological models in an attempt to make target marketing as cost effective as possible. The thrust of this work is to divide consumers into lifestyle segments based on such things as activities, interests, and opinions. An example of the psychographic approach (based on a behavioral profile) to understanding consumer behavior can be found in Arnold Mitchell's *The Nine American Lifestyles.*[22] His research resulted in a more elaborate version of Maslow's hierarchy of needs. Mitchell developed a hierarchy chart representing segments of the population as a way to identify consumer behavior. Mitchell called his chart a values and lifestyles segment, or VALS, distribution.

The Association of Performing Arts Presenters (APAP) hired Mitchell in 1984 to conduct a study of arts audiences. In his report, *The Professional Performing Arts: Attendance Patterns, Preferences and Motives,*[23] he found that four groups, which at that time made up about 66 million people, were the primary market for arts organizations. He called these groups the achievers, the experientials, the societally conscious, and the integrateds. Of these four groups, the societally conscious (12 percent of the population) were the best market per capita. Mitchell also found that among these four lifestyle groups, the most common reason cited for attending an arts event was to see a specific show, performer, or group. He also found that, even among these targeted groups, large percentages admitted that they never attended arts events. For example, an average of 28 percent never attended music concerts, 40 percent never attended theater productions, and 68 percent never attended dance events. His research found that lack of leisure time (30 percent), preferences for other leisure activities (34 percent), and not wanting to commit to season or series purchases (33 percent) were the primary reasons given for not attending.

Another approach to target marketing—one designed to help businesses connect with the consumer—is detailed in *The Clustering of America* by Michael J. Weiss. Weiss examines the work of a market research company. Claritas Corporation developed a system that uses a vast mix of census data to produce information that marketers buy to locate the people who might be disposed to buy their product. The Potential Rating Index for Zip Markets (PRIZM) system uses a zip code

Research Update

A recent article in *American Demographics* magazine raised questions about market research techniques and the validity of certain assumptions about customers. The excerpts that follow will give you some ideas to ponder.

What Your Customers Can't Say
David B. Wolfe

Conventional marketing research depends on the assumption that people can accurately report their values, needs and motivations. But many scientists no longer believe this. "We have reason to doubt that full awareness of our motives, drives, and other mental activities may be possible," says neurologist Richard Restak. "Our inability to accurately report intentions and expectations may simply reflect the fact that they are not qualitatively conscious," adds Bernard J. Baars, author of *In the Theater of Consciousness*.

Consumer research's problems originate in psychology, a field that has long struggled to define human behavior with the same precision physicists use to describe the movement of bodies of atoms to stars. But human behavior is too unpre-

dictable to describe with such precision. An increasingly desperate search for cause-and-effect explanations leads many psychologists to "retreat to abstract ideas that ignore contexts completely," writes Harvard psychologist Jerome Kagan. Consumer research reflects similar tendencies.

Models of consumer behavior tend to extract their subjects from the complex, often unpredictable, but completely natural contexts in which people live and make purchasing decisions.

Research Is Too Rational

For years marketers have complained that consumers often indicate one thing in research, yet behave differently in the marketplace. But consumers are not pathological liars. They have split personalities, according to University of Iowa neurologist Antonio Damasio. To be more specific, their decisions are split by the function of reason and emotion.

Damasio's research shows that different brain sites and different mental processes are involved with different kinds of decision-making. We use one set of mental tools when we consider hypothetical matters,

and another when we make personal decisions.

Emotions have a powerful effect on our consumer choices, because they push us toward decisions we think are best for us. We often bypass reason when making decisions because experience endows us with what Damasio calls "somatic markers." Somatic markers are like computer short-cuts that incorporate many keystrokes into one or two.

Many research questions fail to deeply stimulate consumers' somatic markers (or hot buttons). Instead, they invite respondents to develop a reason-based explanation that often distorts reality. Instead of the real reasons for buying or not buying something, researches get a rationalization based on the respondent's idealized self-image. If they do not account for this bias, researches are left with a model based on how people think they ought to be motivated, instead of a model based on their actual motivations.

Source: Excerpts from David B. Wolfe, "What Your Customers Can't Say," *American Demographics* (February 1998). Copyright © 1998 by American Demographics. Used with permission.

analysis of various neighborhood types. For example, Claritas's research has identified the top five clusters for classical music and named them Urban Gold Coast, Blue Blood Estates, Young Influentials, Bohemian Mix, and Money and Brains.[24]

The objective for an arts marketer using the Claritas system is to develop a database of the zip code distribution of its list of current subscribers and, at the same time, to gather information about the zip code distribution of the single ticket buyers, then to compare the data with the neighborhood types. At this point, the marketer could determine which areas the organization has not reached. Buying a list of labels from the local utility company would allow the organization to send targeted mailings to households in the zip code neighborhoods that the organization has identified as potential customers.

Ultimately, a system such as the one Claritas has developed, should allow an arts marketer to target potential audiences by very narrow segments. After all, why should an arts organization waste its limited resources doing mass mailings when carefully targeted mailings to "the right people" will yield much more cost-effective results?

Demographic studies by Baumol and Bowen on the 1960s and recent studies by the NEA have contributed to this profile of the average arts consumer. The arts audience is equally split in gender distribution, has a median age of 35, and a median income of more than $20,000 (in 1980). The average consumer works as a professional, manager, or teacher or is part of a clerical or sales staff and is highly educated.[25]

In 1996 NEA published a comprehensive report, *Age and Arts Participation*.[26] The data were gathered as part of a Survey of Public Participation in the Arts (SPPA). The report identified seven age groups, or cohorts, and analyzed the attendance patterns at classical music, opera, ballet, musicals, jazz, plays, and art museums. The highlights of their research included this:

- The generation born 1936 to 1945 had very high attendance percentages at classical music, opera, musicals, and plays.
- Younger cohorts (people born after 1946) had higher attendance percentages at jazz concerts and museums.
- Concerns were raised in the report because the generations born after World War II, despite better education levels, were not attending arts events to the same degree as the older generation.
- The report indicated that younger cohorts (after 1946) substituted television, cable, and radio broadcasts or videotapes and compact discs for live performing arts events.

Other arts research The PRIZM and VALS approaches to market research can be very expensive. Although Mitchell's study for the APAP goes into great detail about such things as reactions to different types of advertising, audiences will react unpredictably to various marketing plans. Other sources to consider for marketing information include the research division of the National Endowment for the Arts regularly publishes useful data, and the *Journal of Arts Management and Law*. Articles in a special issue of the journal ("Consumer Behavior and the Arts"[27]) cover the general topic of marketing and provide detailed information on price theory. For example, one article applies psychologist Clare Graves's theories of personality to audiences. Another closely examines the variable of price on "discretionary income purchases."

Arts organizations regularly should survey people in their community for feedback on new programs and problems with existing operations. A properly designed survey can give an organization the opportunity to adjust and change its marketing mix. In fact, the use of the Internet and WWW sites can be a low-cost way for arts organization to gain continuing feedback from audiences. On-line surveys or e-mail feedback about the shows can be a useful way of keeping in touch with customers. The use of small *focus groups* is another low-cost alternative for arts organizations. Focus groups of up to 10 or 12 may provide useful insights about the attitudes and perceptions of your audiences to your image and your advertising. Suggested resources for surveys are noted at the end of this chapter (see Additional Resources).

Marketer Profile: Danny Newman—The Godfather of Subscription Ticket Sales

Danny Newman's book *Subscribe Now!* is the source for many arts managers on a quest on how to sell subscriptions.[29] Mr. Newman has been a working for the Chicago Lyric Opera since 1954 and has helped lead their successful subscription sales efforts. In 1997, he was nominated for a National Medal of Arts for his efforts as a marketer and consultant. Despite the shift away from enlisting subscribers in favor of more flexible purchasing options, Mr. Newman remains firm in his belief that the best way to build a long-term relationship with audiences is through subscription plans. Many performing arts centers, college and university arts departments, theaters, opera, dance companies, and music groups copy Mr. Newman's approach to building audiences with much success. Gregory Mosher, a well-known theater director, noted in a 1997 article in the *New York Times* on Mr. Newman that, "He's like Henry Ford . . . I must have read his book 100 times." Mr. Moser went on to note that the subscription series was the cornerstone of the regional theater boom in the United States. The model was based on "a board of directors, a staff lead by an artistic director and a managing director, and a six-play subscription series."

Marketing Ethics

Whatever approach is used in marketing research, the goal is to find out what the consumer thinks about the product or service. Marketers believe that with the right information they could better predict which combination of product, price, place, and promotion is needed to complete the exchange process on a regular basis with consumers. To bridge the information gap, marketers look to even more sophisticated applications of computers in their work. As a result, the line between market research and invading people's privacy has grown very thin today. The selling of vast amounts of information about consumers is a fact of life today. Michael Weiss points out that "the top five credit-rating companies have records on more than 150 million Americans. And Federal data bases contain some 288 million records on 114 million people, with 15 agencies mixing and matching data."[28] As computers have increased their data storage capabilities and programmers have become even more sophisticated in programming the software, the ability to profile consumers will only continue to intensify.

Arts organizations, which depend on the sales of tickets and subscriptions for 60 percent or more of their operating budget, face a dilemma. How intrusive should they be when trying to reach potential arts consumers? Arts organizations want to identify and target the people most likely to be long-term consumers of their product. Techniques such as telephone marketing, if handled properly, can lead to direct contact with consumers. On the other hand, people resent phone calls and "sales pitches" that intrude into their private lives. Marketers for arts organizations also must face the ethical issue of selling information about their customers to commercial firms. The arts consumer is a prime target for the marketer of upscale goods and services. Research has shown that arts consumers have more than the average amount of discretionary income and therefore are good targets for a wide variety of marketing assaults.

Strategic Marketing Plans

Now that the basic principles of marketing have been outlined, we examine in greater detail the critical planning process. As noted earlier in this chapter, if a marketing plan is to be effective, the entire organization must consider carefully how all phases of the operation relate to the dynamics of the marketplace. The simple fact facing all organizations is that new opportunities and new threats arise every day in the marketplace. An organization that can adjust to these changing conditions has the best chance of surviving in the long run.

Some board members may wonder why an organization such as a museum or some other well-established performing arts institution would need to worry about the changing dynamics of the marketplace. After all, won't people always go to the museum or to the symphony? Why should an organization spend time planning, reviewing its mission, devising strategies, and developing objectives when what it does is so obvious? Citing the examples of dance companies that have failed; museums that have had to reduce their hours and staff; and orchestras, theaters, and opera companies that have filed for bankruptcy should be enough to counter any argument that strategic marketing plans are a waste of time.

Planning Process

The organization's overall strategic plan (discussed in Chapter 5) incorporates the marketing plan (see Figure 12–1). The organization's objectives drive the mission, goals, and objectives of its marketing plan. In addition, an analysis of opportunities and threats from the external environments, noted in Chapter 4 (economic, demographic, political and legal, social and cultural, technological, and educational) are weighed against the organization's strengths and weaknesses. Once the basic mission and objectives of the marketing plan have been defined, the core marketing strategy can be developed. The target markets and the proposed marketing mix can be articulated. The process now moves to the final stage by providing the system for carrying out the marketing plan, including what performance criteria will be used to monitor progress. In addition, specific tactics can be created. Implementation plans and an evaluation system complete the process. The evaluation process feeds back to the core marketing strategy for long-term adjustments and directly back to specific tactics for short-term changes. For example, a short-term change might be to revise an advertisement in the paper when there is poor response to a particular offering. A long-term adjustment might be to evaluate all of the print media.

Marketing Audit

One method an organization might use to assess its ability to carry out a marketing plan in this chapter is to do a marketing audit. Essentially, an audit consists of asking and answering a series of questions that explore the organization's markets, customers, objectives, organizational structure, marketing information system, and marketing mix. The Sample Marketing Plan gives you a starting place for preparing an audit. The audit section gives the staff and the board a common ground on which to build a marketing plan that fits the organization's mission and function.

Consultants

Usually, the perspective of an outside consultant is helpful when formulating any strategic or marketing plan. Someone with expertise in planning can save an organization a great deal of valuable time struggling through the planning process. As noted in Chapter 5, planning is hard work, and because of the pressing daily needs of keeping the organization afloat, this essential process often is given a low priority by managers. A consultant, if used effectively, can go into an organization, shake up the status quo, and act as a catalyst to put planning at the top of the priority list. A word of caution though, consultants are not infallible, and they have been known to make mistakes. They can give bad advice and make recommendations that make conditions worse, not better. A background check of former clients is a requirement for organizations that want to protect themselves.

Strategies

The profit sector uses terminology borrowed from warfare when developing marketing strategies. Marketers use such terms as *frontal, encirclement, flanking,* and *bypass* attacks to describe marketing plans. Words such as *preemptive, counteroffensive,* and *contraction* are used to describe strategies.[30] Other options for organizations to explore include generic, market leader, market follower, and market niche strategies. We next look briefly at the competitive environment facing many arts organizations and discuss strategy options.

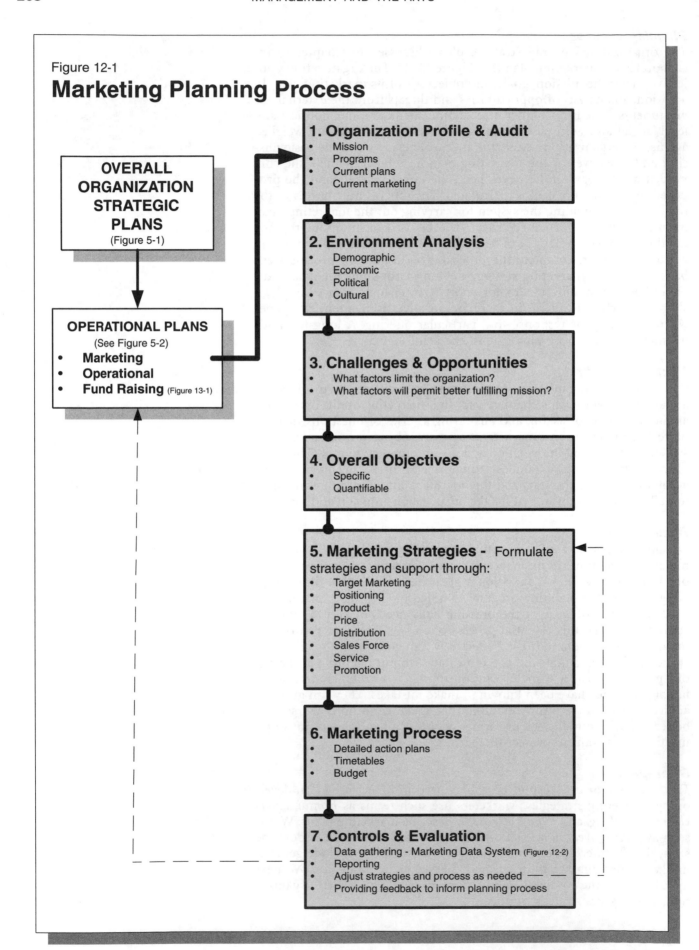

Figure 12-1

Marketing Planning Process

OVERALL ORGANIZATION STRATEGIC PLANS
(Figure 5-1)

OPERATIONAL PLANS
(See Figure 5-2)
- **Marketing**
- **Operational**
- **Fund Raising** (Figure 13-1)

1. Organization Profile & Audit
- Mission
- Programs
- Current plans
- Current marketing

2. Environment Analysis
- Demographic
- Economic
- Political
- Cultural

3. Challenges & Opportunities
- What factors limit the organization?
- What factors will permit better fulfilling mission?

4. Overall Objectives
- Specific
- Quantifiable

5. Marketing Strategies - Formulate strategies and support through:
- Target Marketing
- Positioning
- Product
- Price
- Distribution
- Sales Force
- Service
- Promotion

6. Marketing Process
- Detailed action plans
- Timetables
- Budget

7. Controls & Evaluation
- Data gathering - Marketing Data System (Figure 12-2)
- Reporting
- Adjust strategies and process as needed
- Providing feedback to inform planning process

The Competitive Marketplace and Core Strategies

When a community reaches the point in its growth where it has at least one professional arts organization from each of the major disciplines, the struggle for resources among these organizations probably will intensify. Arts people may carry on a cordial and friendly dialogue in public, but the simple fact of the matter is that the competition is tough and there are only so many dollars that people will spend on subscriptions, tickets, memberships, and donations. As we have seen, arts organizations also face competition for the entertainment dollar from videotape rentals, films, television, and amusement parks. Therefore, in formulating a plan of attack, an arts organization might consider a *niche strategy*. Such a strategy focuses on the qualities that make a live performing arts event or a trip to the museum a unique activity. The niche strategy can be combined with a *differentiation strategy* in an effort to feature those things that are unique about the product. This strategy combination allows the organization to concentrate on what is special about its product while appealing to a targeted market.

If the organization's planning process leads to a decision to expand its audience base beyond the typical demographic blend, a strategy to increase market share would be appropriate. In this *growth strategy*, the organization takes an aggressive advertising approach to reach new audiences. For example, if a theater company wanted to develop its market among African-Americans in the community, an advertising campaign using specific media publications and radio stations with a high ratio of such consumers would make sense. Also, targeting group sales by using the local network of African-American religious groups might prove successful. However, if the arts organization does not regularly offer a product that has some market appeal to members of various minority groups, there is little chance that this strategy will succeed.

Whatever overall marketing strategy an arts organization selects, it is important to remember that it must fit with the mission of the organization. Care must be taken to avoid shifting the organization away from its mission to meet a market strategy. For example, museums are not in the gift shop business, but because these operations can become very healthy sources of cash, it is tempting to overstress their importance in marketing the organization.

Project Planning and Implementation

The details of preparing, budgeting, and implementing the marketing plan require careful attention. Decisions about where to put the usually very limited marketing resources available to the organization can make or break a plan. The research done on the community and a detailed cost analysis of various media campaigns will pay off in the project planning stage. Organization and project management skills are required to prepare the overall schedule and budget distribution for the marketing campaign.

Evaluation

After establishing the marketing mission, the core strategy, and specific tactics and implementing the plan, the organization must carefully evaluate and monitor how well its objectives are being realized. For example, if the costs of implementing the strategy exceed the budget and the number of new subscribers or members is below the levels established for success, the organization must be able to adjust its tactics or revise the entire strategy before it is too late. As noted in Chapter 5, the failure to abandon a plan that is not working can lead to numerous problems.

In the News 3— Marketing Strategies

This newspaper article shows how an arts organization can expand consumer awareness for a very modest investment.

Toasting Cabbies to Tout Visitors
Associated Press

CHICAGO—The Art Institute of Chicago hopes a free breakfast will go a long way toward steering visitors in its direction.

The museum treated about 100 taxi drivers to Danish pastry, juice, coffee and a tour last week in the hope that the steering-wheel philosophers will talk up the place to their fares.

"Chicago taxi drivers really are roving ambassadors," museum spokeswoman Eileen Harakal said. "Not only do they answer passengers' questions on Chicago's attractions, but they help steer people to them."

"It's a great idea," said cabdriver Bill Hogan as he contemplated Henri Matisse's 'Still Life With a Blue Table Cloth.' "When people ask what there is to see in Chicago I usually say the Sears Tower, the Museum of Science and Industry and the Shedd Aquarium. Now I'll mention the Art Institute."

Source: Associated Press, "Toasting Cabbies to Tout Visitors" (October 3, 1990). Copyright © 1990 by the Associated Press (AP). Used with permission.

Sample Marketing Plan

The first step in developing your marketing plan requires you assess the current status of the organization. Depending on your organization, you may need to pose additional questions. Therefore, the items that follow should be viewed as a guide and not the only questions you could raise.

1. Organization Profile and Audit

- Name, type of arts organization, location, brief history, and years in existence.
- Programs and projects currently listed by organization or special performance or exhibition activities.
- Are the mission, goals, or objectives statements published? Is the mission clear? Are the goals connected to the mission and do they seem achievable? Are the objectives clear about who, what, when, and at what priority?
- Is the organization operating under a current strategic organizational or marketing plan? If yes, what is the background of the planning and implementation process. Review brochures, flyers, and the like used by the organization in its current marketing activities. Are these pieces effective?
- Is the organization operating within its budget? Is it a healthy organization? Does it have a budget surplus or deficit? Is the board and the leadership functioning effectively?

2. Environmental Analysis

- Demographic
  What major demographic developments and trends pose opportunities or threats for this organization?

What actions, if any, has the organization taken in response to those developments?

- Economic
  What major developments and trends in income, prices, savings, and interest rates are affecting the organization?
  What major changes are taking place in the sources and amounts of contributed income (from individuals, corporations, private and public foundations, and government agencies)?
  What actions has the organization taken in response to these developments and trends?

- Political
  What recent legislation has affected this organization?
  What federal, state, or local agencies should be monitored for future actions relating to the organization?
  What actions has the organization taken in response to these developments?

- Cultural
  What changes are occurring in consumer lifestyles, values, and educational opportunities that might affect this organization?
  What actions has the organization taken in response to these developments?

3. Challenges and Opportunities

- Challenges. Depending on how you answered the preceding questions, you may have a series of specific challenges facing the organization such as, but not limited to
  Declining subscriber base,
  Increased competition from other arts organizations,

Lack of single ticket buyers or members,
A need to diversify audiences,
Poorly focus target marketing,
Lack of commitment to customer orientation by organization.

- Opportunities. State the opportunities you see that will help meet the challenges facing the organization. State these opportunities as facts, not strategies or objectives. For example, suppose you found a challenge facing the organization was a declining subscriber base. The opportunity is "potential exists to increase subscriber base." Even if your organization is "perfect" you still may have opportunities to venture into new areas such as merchandise or adding an experimental performance series.

4. Objectives. Formulate objectives for the marketing plan based on your factual statements. For example, if you stated opportunity exists to increase the subscriber base, you could state objectives for each of the areas that follow. For example,

- Marketing. The objective will be to increase the subscriber base by a net of 5 percent in the next fiscal year.
- Financial. The objective will be to increase earned income from subscriptions by 5 percent above the previous fiscal year.

5. Marketing Strategy. In this section, you outline your *game plan* for achieving all the objectives you set for yourself in

- Target Markets. Who will targeted?

Marketing Data System

Within the organization's overall management information system and financial management information system, you should find a marketing data system (MDS). The purpose of an MDS is parallel to that of the MIS. The MDS should be designed to gather and analyze data regularly and to issue reports on the success of current campaigns. Figure 12–2 shows a typical MDS for an arts organization. The four major sources of data are the sales system (box office), audience, staff, and various external environments. If the system is working properly, the feedback provided the marketing staff will arrive in time to make corrections and adjustments in the marketing plan. With some sources of information, such as surveys, the data gathered can be translated into information that is useful in planning future seasons or programs.

Computers can play a central role in gathering and processing data for the MDS. As we saw in Chapters 9 and 11, the MIS and the FMIS must be linked with the marketing data system if the organization is to monitor its operations effectively (see Figures 9–3, 9–4, and 11–1). It is essential that the organization have a network of computers that share data among the marketing staff and other members of the management team to enable the marketing plans to be successfully evaluated. The complexity of such a system may require hiring outside consultants to coordinate and advise the marketing manager. Without the ability to track all sales data quickly and accurately, the marketing manager's effectiveness will ultimately be seriously undermined.

Conclusion

Marketing can be an effective tool for keeping an organization growing and evolving. However, marketing also is a long-term investment. A well-organized marketing campaign should be integrated with operational and long-term organization plans. It makes no sense to attempt a marketing plan without first having clearly defined the mission and goals of the organization. Like any tool, marketing can be misused. Thousands of dollars can be wasted on advertising campaigns or printed brochures that have little or no impact on sales.

Ultimately, it is important to recognize how complex the purchase and attendance decision process is for the potential audience members. First, they must achieve awareness of the event, then they have to decide if what you are offering is of interest to them. Next, they must check their schedules to see if the dates and times you are performing fit in their schedule. Assuming all those decision points are unproblematic, then they must make contact your ticket office and engage in the whole actual purchase process. Last but not least, they probably need to get dressed up, travel to your venue, find a place to park, find their way to their seat, and participate as an active audience member by enjoying your show. Then, they have to negotiate the traffic and get back home before they can actually complete the experience. In other words, your average frequent attendee must be well motivated to go through this process. While we in the performing arts stress the "live performance" experience, it is apparent that it is much easier to rent a video or select a cable channel if one needs to satisfy a need for entertainment.

Unfortunately, there are no guarantees that your best plans to attract audiences will work. For organizations with limited resources, experimenting with different approaches to marketing is out of the question. However, finding the most cost-effective way to reach audience

Sample Marketing Plan (cont.)

- Positioning. What will be your positioning statement to sell to these target markets? "We are the only orchestra group performing the work of composer X in the tricities area."
- Product. Describe the product in customer terms your research says these target markets find appealing.
- Price. How will you use price as part of achieving your objectives?
- Distribution. Will you expand the access to tickets by selling through TicketMaster™ ?
- Sales Force. Changes needed to achieve objectives? Hire more staff?
- Service. Any changes in how services are delivered? Extra hours? 800 number?
- Promotion. All forms of promotion? What specifically do you plan to do? Will you use direct mail or telemarketing, radio ads, PSAs, or what? In other words, what will be your media plan?

6. Marketing Process
- Detailed Action Plans
  What will be done?
  Who will do it?
  What will be the benefit?
- Timetable. When will the action plan items be done? (Detail each action plan in list, calendar. or GANTT chart format.)
- Budget. How much will it cost? (Detail all the costs of the plan—graphics, printing, advertising, etc.)

7. Controls and Evaluation. How will you monitor your progress? If reports, what kind and how frequent? Create forms and reports of how you will measure your success in achieving the objectives you set for yourself and the organization.

Figure 12-2
Marketing Data System

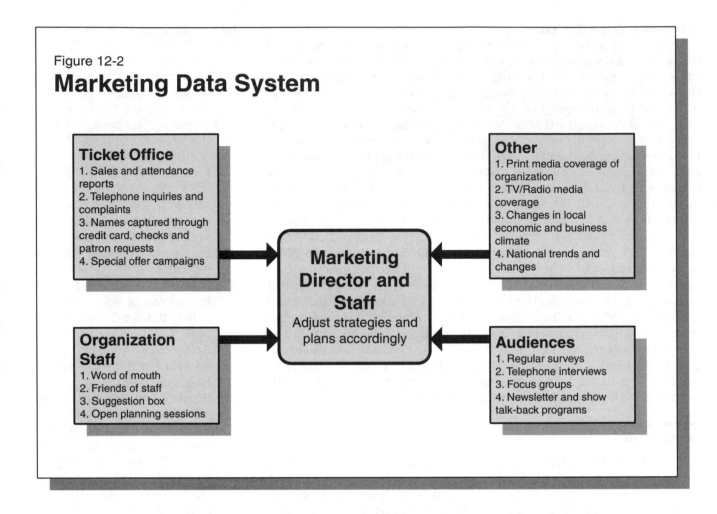

Ticket Office
1. Sales and attendance reports
2. Telephone inquiries and complaints
3. Names captured through credit card, checks and patron requests
4. Special offer campaigns

Other
1. Print media coverage of organization
2. TV/Radio media coverage
3. Changes in local economic and business climate
4. National trends and changes

Marketing Director and Staff
Adjust strategies and plans accordingly

Organization Staff
1. Word of mouth
2. Friends of staff
3. Suggestion box
4. Open planning sessions

Audiences
1. Regular surveys
2. Telephone interviews
3. Focus groups
4. Newsletter and show talk-back programs

members when there are no funds for research also places impossible constraints on the marketing staff. It is not surprising to find 100 percent yearly turnover in an arts organization's marketing staff. Impossible goals, limited resources, and poorly conceived plans take their toll on even the most ambitious people. Upper management involvement and commitment to planning and implementation can go a long way toward remedying the problems that arts marketers face.

The most daunting task facing any arts marketer is the development of future audiences. The simple reality of a very limited audience base coupled with the ever-increasing competition from other entertainment options makes for a difficult mix of circumstances. As most arts marketers know, unless you can establish a pattern of arts consumption at an early age, it is both difficult and costly to change people's leisure behavior later in life. The arts marketing effort no doubt will continue, and wherever appropriate, the arts marketer will borrow from the commercial marketing world those techniques that work.

For students interested in a challenging field of work, arts or not-for-profit marketing has a great deal of potential. The use of language and images to express an idea or to convey an organization's mission demands skill and creativity. Because this chapter is just a glimpse into the world of marketing, students are urged to explore the additional readings from the references cited in this chapter. A college undergraduate course in marketing also will be helpful to the future arts marketer.

Summary

The arts manager must plan, organize, implement, and evaluate marketing strategies to maximize revenue and meet the organization's objectives. Because of the bombardment of marketing efforts by a multitude of businesses and causes, the arts manager must dedicate significant resources to marketing if the organization is to be visible in the highly competitive entertainment marketplace. Marketing is a means to an end, and it therefore should be thought of as one more tool available to the arts manager to use in realizing the overall goals of the organization.

Contemporary marketing attempts to match the wants and needs of consumers with products and services. Needs are physiological and psychological things that are necessary but lacking for people's well-being. Wants are desirable or useful things that people lack. People can gain functional and psychological satisfaction from tangible and intangible features of products or services.

Marketing activity is designed to facilitate the exchange process. This process involves a transfer of something of value between two or more parties or organizations. The exchange process is successful to the degree that the utilities of form, time, place, and possession can be satisfied through the exchange. The arts exchange usually involves satisfying a psychological want through the intangible features of an experience, which is modified by the inherent constraints placed on the four utilities by the delivery system (the performance).

Marketing has evolved over the last 300 years. The production era, which grew out of the Industrial Revolution, concentrated on satisfying basic needs. It was assumed that people would buy whatever was manufactured. The sales era, which concentrated on increasing demand, began sometime after the Civil War. More emphasis was put on customers' wants, but the manufacturers still dictated what would be available to purchase. The marketing era, which came to the fore after World War II, reversed the relationship between the consumer and the manufacturer. The consumer-driven market relationship starts with what the consumer wants, not the product.

Marketing today is classified along the same historical line of evolution. A company may have a product, sales, or customer orientation. The product-oriented company assumes that its product is inherently good and needs no changes. The sales-oriented company concentrates on trying to increase demand for existing products and services. The customer-oriented company determines the perceptions, needs, and wants of the market and creates a product to fit those needs. Arts organizations use all three orientations. The market-oriented arts organization thrives if it understands the market's perception of its product and describes, prices, packages, and delivers its product to reflect those perceptions. It does not mean that the organization must change the product to attract customers.

Marketing management is based on the organization's manipulation of the four Ps—product, price, place, and promotion—or the market mix. The market mix can be adjusted to suit the target market. Market research has shown that people with various demographic and psychographic profiles react differently to various marketing mixes.

The entire marketing process is directly related to the organization's strategic plans. The main objectives of the strategic plan are incorporated into the marketing plan. An analysis of external environments and the strengths and weaknesses of the organization also are included. A detailed audit process may be used to assess the organization's capacity to undertake an effective marketing campaign. From the marketing plan, specific strategies and detailed tactics can be designed to meet the defined objectives. The success of the marketing campaign depends on accurate and timely information gathered by the marketing data system.

Key Terms and Concepts

Marketing
Needs
Wants
Functional satisfaction
Psychological satisfaction
Exchange
Form, time, place, and possession utilities
Production, sales, and marketing eras
Product orientation
Sales orientation
Customer orientation
The four Ps: product, price, place, and promotion
Marketing mix
Market segments
Target marketing
Demographic profile
Psychographic profile
Focus groups
Marketing audit
Strategic marketing plans
Niche strategy
Differentiation strategy
Growth strategy
Marketing data system

Questions

1. Define the term *marketing*.

2. What are some wants and needs satisfied by the following: a brand-name soft drink, a meal at a French restaurant, a visit to an art museum?

3. Does marketing make you buy things that you do not need? Explain why or why not.

4. Give an example of an exchange process in which you recently participated that was not satisfying. What went wrong in the exchange? What would you change to make the exchange satisfying?

5. What suggestions would you offer about form, time, place, and possession utilities to a museum and a children's theater company that are planning new outreach programs?

6. When you are considering the purchase of an arts product, which of the four Ps is most important to you? Explain why. Do you react differently to various marketing mixes? How?

7. What are some of the different market segments you would identify for theater, dance, opera, symphony, and museum organizations? How much attendance crossover do you think exists among

the different segments? For example, do opera audiences go to the theater?

    8. Do demographic and psychographic profiles of audiences match your perception of arts consumers? How do you think the profile of the audience will change over the next 20 years? How will changes in demographics affect arts organizations?

    9. If you were managing a small modern dance company in a community with a well-established ballet company, what marketing strategy would you adopt to gain a market share?

    10. According to "Art Museum Thrives with Marketing," what was the basic marketing strategy attempted by the Milwaukee Art Museum? Why was it so successful?

Portrait of the Artist as a Focus Group

Case Study

Too often these days, the creative types have only the courage of their audience's convictions.

    Michiko Kakutani

If you took a pool what would America's best-loved painting look like? In their playful new book, *Painting by Numbers*, two Russian émigré conceptual artists decided to find out. With a little help from some polling experts, Vitaly Komar and Alexander Melamid queried 1,001 Americans about their tastes in color, form and style, and concluded that the most wanted painting in the country is a bluish landscape painting, populated by George Washington, a family of tourists and a pair of frolicking deer. The canvas is the size of a dishwasher and looks like something that might adorn the walls of a third-rate motel. It is the apotheosis of art created by consensus.

    Komar and Melamid's exercise, of course, is a sly comment on the democratization of creativity and America's mania for polls. What is more disturbing is that their satiric project unwittingly underscores another trend at work in American culture: our eagerness to substitute public opinion for personal belief, market demands for authentic artistic and political vision.

    From the world of advertising, consumer research has already spread to Washington, where President Clinton has rarely made a move without checking with his pollsters, and to Hollywood, where test audiences can affect the content, pacing and tone of big-budget pictures and determine which TV pilots get scheduled. From Hollywood, it is now spreading into music theater, novels and journalism. The result is a brand of carefully positioned art and a culture-wide embrace of that old advertising slogan "The customer is always right"—even if that customer has no expertise, no knowledge and no taste.

    MTV's new show "12 Angry Viewers" gives audience members a chance to add a video to the station's playlist, and focus groups similarly determine what songs many radio stations will or will not play. In his insightful new book, *Dreaming Out Loud*, Bruce Feiler points out that a growing number of country-music stations now employ market-research companies to tell them exactly what their audiences want. The process, he suggests, systematically excludes tracks that provoke the strongest reaction, positive as well as negative—and the resulting picks tend to be predictable, homogenized and cheerfully upbeat.

The sales imperative—be popular, be accessible, be liked—is also threatening to turn writing into another capitalist tool. In an effort to raise circulation, newspapers like *The Miami Herald* and *The Boca Raton News* have used reader-preference surveys to determine their "coverage priorities," and some novelists are adopting the literary equivalent of the applause-o-meter as well. The best-selling author Andrew Greeley has used focus groups to shape his marketing campaigns, and the novelist James Patterson has conscripted groups of test readers to analyze his books before publication. Patterson recently changed the ending of his new thriller, *Cat and Mouse*, in response to reader feedback; the novel reached No. 2 on the *Times* best-seller list.

This shameless second-guessing is not simply a money-grubbing attempt to give audiences what they think they want. It also represents the abdication by creative types of their artistic freedom and judgment. Just as today's politicians have elected to become mirrors of the national Zeitgeist rather than leaders, so have poll driven "artists" elected to become assembly-line manufacturers, in thrall to the opinions of mall rats deemed demographically correct.

No one has tried harder to turn the messy process of artistic creation into a systematic, risk-free proposition than Garth Drabinsky, the producer of the Broadway musical "Ragtime." A 20-year veteran of the movie business, Drabinsky is methodically transferring Hollywood practices to the stage. He insists that a show's prospective book writer submit an initial treatment to insure that the writer is not "going off on a tangent and doing something that is incongruous to the philosophy or ideas of the producer." For "Ragtime," he hired a polling firm to help calibrate audience reactions. The show's book eventually went through some 20 drafts.

"We want to hear what audiences have to say about what they're seeing," Drabinsky says, "and most importantly; we want to find out if the work is coherent—if it's making sense emotionally and dramatically." The "Ragtime" focus groups, he argues, helped his creative team "learn about the response of audiences to what characters we've chosen to put in the show," as well as "whether they feel the show is too long."

So what if critics complained that "Ragtime" lacked a distinctive voice? So what if they thought it had the feel of a corporate committee? "Ragtime" has already racked up a $17.5 million advance, and other producers and theater owners are being encouraged to use surveys and exit polls as a means of boosting business. In an article in the theatrical magazine *Back Stage*, George A. Wachtel, president of a firm called Audience Research & Analysis, writes: "Response cards distributed during previews can produce objective feedback from which the creative team can learn what is working and what isn't." In five years, Wachtel says, "when you open the Playbill for a show and it says, advertising by . . ., publicity by . . ., it will also say market research by . . ., because it's going to become part of what happens on Broadway. In five years, I predict that most shows will be doing audience surveys and will be better understanding their audience from the get-go, and that the majority of new shows will have some kind of preview research."

Such predictions eerily limn a future in which Pop Art gives way to Poll Art—a future in which reproductions of Komar and Melamid's cloying painting will hang on every museum's walls.

Source: Michiko Kakutani, "Portrait of the Artist as a Focus Group," *The New York Times Magazine* (March 1, 1998). Copyright © 1998 by The New York Times. Used with permission.

Case Study Questions

Compare and contrast the point of view of this article with the quote from Kotler and Scheff beginning "This does not mean that artistic directors must compromise . . ."

1. Discuss the differences in the positive and negative effects of marketing research and polling.
2. What is your conclusion about the prediction that marketing research firms will be credited in programs in Broadway theaters in the future? Is this a good or bad thing? Why?
3. The "Artist as a Focus Group" article assumes marketing is geared toward "shamelessly second-guessing" and is an "attempt to give audiences what they think they want." Kotler and Scheff argue this approach is unnecessary to market your event and that understanding your audience only will help you communicate better what you are offering. Is it possible to not give audiences what they want and still expect them to attend your arts event? Discuss.

References

1. Philip Kotler and Joanne Scheff, *Standing Room Only* (Boston: Harvard Business School Press, 1997), p. 44.
2. "AMA Board Approves New Marketing Definition," *Marketing News* (March 1, 1985), p. 1.
3. Charles D. Schewe, *Marketing Principles and Strategies* (New York: Random House, 1987), p. 5.
4. Ibid.
5. Ibid., p. 7.
6. Ibid.
7. Ibid.
8. Ibid., p. 8.
9. Ibid., p. 10.
10. Ibid., p. 19.
11. Ibid., pp. 14–16.
12. Joy Horowitz, "Off the Street and into the Audience: Tourists Help Pick Fall TV Schedule," *New York Times* (July 7, 1991).
13. Kotler and Scheff, *Standing Room Only*, p. 33.
14. Ibid.
15. Ibid.
16. Ibid.

17. Ibid., p. 34.

18. Ibid., pp. 34–35.

19. Schewe, *Marketing Principles and Strategies*, p. 33.

20. Ibid., p. 36.

21. Ibid.

22. Arnold Mitchell, *The Nine American Lifestyles* (New York: Warner Books, 1983), pp. 13–24.

23. Arnold Mitchell, *The Professional Performing Arts: Attendance Patterns, Preferences and Motives* (Washington, DC: Association of Performing Arts Presenters, 1984), pp. ES-1–ES-4 and 21–24.

24. Michael J. Weiss, *The Clustering of America* (New York: Harper and Row, 1988), p. 130.

25. Lynne Fitzhugh, "An Analysis of Audience Studies for the Performing Arts in America," Part I, *Journal of Arts Management and Law*, no. 13 (Summer 1983), pp. 51–60.

26. Richard A. Peterson, Darren E. Sherkat, Judith Huggins Balfe and Rolf Meyrson, *Age and Arts Participation*, ed. Erin V. Lehman, NEA Research Division Report #34 (Santa Ana, CA: Seven Locks Press, 1996), pp. 1–5.

27. *Journal of Arts Management and Law* 15, no. 1 (Spring 1985).

28. Weiss, *Clustering of America*, p. 25.

29. Danny Newman, *Subscribe Now!* (New York: Theatre Communications Group, 1977).

30. Schewe, *Marketing Principles and Strategies*, p. 55.

Additional Resources

There is no shortage of books on marketing. A quick trip to a bookstore should turn up numerous titles on marketing and marketing research. Listed here are some additional resources that will prove helpful in your arts marketing efforts.

David H. Bangs, Jr. *The Marketing Planning Guide*, 4th ed. Chicago: Upstart Publishing Company, 1995.

Michael Blimes and Ron Sproat. *More Dialing, More Dollars: 12 Steps to Successful Telemarketing*. New York: American Council for the Arts, 1984.

Fred E. Hahn and Kenneth G. Mangun. *Do It Yourself Advertising and Promotion*, 2d ed. New York: John Wiley & Sons, 1997.

Roman G. Hiebing, Jr., and Scott W. Cooper. *The Successful Marketing Plan*, 2d ed. Lincolnwood, IL: NTC Business Books, 1997.

Jay Levinson and Seth Godin. *The Guerrilla Marketing Handbook*, New York: Houghton Mifflin Company, 1994.

Joseph V. Melillo, editor and compiler, *Market the Arts*, revised and reprinted by Arts Actions Issues, Patricia Lavender, editor, New York: Arts Action Issues, 1995.

Bradley G. Morison and Julie Gordon Dalgleish. *Waiting in the Wings*. New York: American Council for the Arts, 1987.

Surveying Your Arts Audience, Research Division manual. Washington, DC: National Endowment for the Arts, 1985.

David Parmerlee. *Preparing the Marketing Plan*, Lincolnwood, IL: NTC Business Books, 1995.

Priscilla Salant and Don A. Dillman. *How to Conduct Your Own Survey*, New York: John Wiley & Sons, 1994.

Fund Raising

13

*Apart from the ballot box, philanthropy presents the one op-
portunity the individual has to express a meaningful choice over
the direction in which our society will progress.*
—George G. Kirstein

The act of giving to good causes is well established in U.S. culture. The
charitable system developed by various religious organizations to provide social services in the United States still depends on individual donations of funds, goods, and services. The intervention of direct
government support in this system is a fairly recent phenomenon. In
fact, government subsidies became widely institutionalized only after
1933 in the United States. Today, the United States has a unique mixture
of public and private support for health, education, social services, and
culture. Government support of giving also is reflected in the tax benefits available when a person files a tax form and itemizes expenses.

Organized fund raising by entities other than churches dates back
to the nineteenth century. For instance, the International Red Cross operated the first disaster relief fund drives as early as 1859.[1] One source
cites Lyman L. Pierce and Charles S. Ward as the fathers of modern fund
raising, based on their work for the YMCA in the 1890s. The techniques
they developed were used in 1905 to raise money for a new building in
Washington, D.C., and these techniques made them pioneers of the
major capital campaign. In fact, they may have been the first fund-raising consultants, judging by the work they did assisting the U.S. government sell war bonds to help finance World War I.[2]

From these humble beginnings has risen a multibillion dollar industry. In 1997, for example, more than $143.5 billion was given to not-
for-profit and charity organizations by individuals corporations and
foundations. Of that total, more than $10.62 billion was distributed to
U.S. arts and culture organizations.[3] According to *Giving USA* the total
was up 7.5 percent in that year, but arts donations were down 4.93 percent when adjusted for inflation. Arts donations constituted 6.7 percent
of the total given that year, with 47 percent targeted to religious organizations. Education was the next largest sector at 13.5 percent.

Why Do People Give?

The act of giving is a particular behavior motivated by a complex set of
reasons and emotions. While the giving process mirrors the exchange
concept discussed in Chapter 12, another layer behavior is encapsulated
in this behavior. The personal satisfaction people derive from giving is difficult to quantify, but fund raisers must carefully consider this factor in
how they formulate their approach to seeking support in the community.

People give to particular causes or organizations because the believe in what is being done is helping society in some way. Joseph R. Mixer's *Principles of Professional Fundraising* cites numerous survey's and theories about giving behavior. Mixer focuses on the "Social Exchange Model for Giving"[4] to detail the individual giving process. He goes on to say,

> The charitable organization or agency presents client needs and services to a prospect along with a request for funds. If the request is favorably received, the prospect responds with a donation of funds and possibly time. To continue the relationship, the recipient provides some form of satisfaction to the donor.
>
> The essence of what is returned to the donor is not a commodity or service that can be used profitably by the giver, but an intangible, psychic satisfaction that relates to the donor's personal motivations. An enhanced degree of self-esteem, a feeling of achievement, a new status, and a sense of belonging are among the most powerful rewards donors can receive. Giving satisfies donors' fundamental human needs and desires.[5]

Fund Raising and the Arts

Perhaps no area of managing an arts organization comes under closer scrutiny or is subject to more pressure than fund raising. For many organizations, 40 percent or more of the yearly operating budget may come from gifts or grants by individuals, foundations, arts councils, and corporations. If there is a decline in gifts from any of these sources, arts organizations with little or no cash reserves often find themselves in serious financial difficulty.

As discussed, the changing external environments (economic, political and legal, cultural and social, demographic, technological, and educational) create opportunities and pose threats for arts organizations. Each environment may have an impact on the organization's fundraising efforts. A recession probably will signal a slowdown in giving because people feel the need to retain more of their discretionary income. In an election year, major donors may give more to candidates and less to cultural organizations. Changes in the tax laws also could affect giving. If people who make a donation to an arts organization lower their overall tax liability, they will become donors. However, the cause-and-effect relationship between these environments and donations is unpredictable. Therefore, the arts manager must keep a watchful eye on the donation flow.

Direct government support of the arts in the United States still represents a minimal commitment of resources, even 30 years after the establishment of the National Endowment for the Arts. Direct government subsidy of the arts in many parts of the world are hundreds of times greater per capita than in the United States. The unique partnership of individual and private support for the arts defines the conditions under which all fund raisers must work.

Fund-Raising Plans

Because fund raising is linked so closely to the overall fiscal health of the organization, management of fund-raising activities must be thoroughly integrated into the strategic planning process. In fact, many arts organizations place marketing and fund raising under the control of a development director. This person hires specialists in each area of development to realize the objectives formulated in the short- and long-term organizational plans.

In organizations with inadequate staffing (which describes many arts organizations), one person may try to manage and implement annual giving, major gifts, a capital campaign (for a new building, for example), foundation contacts, and local, state, and federal fund raising. It becomes very difficult to meet these diverse fund raising objectives effectively given this type of work setting. As we have seen in the chapters on planning, organization, and control, a manager needs adequate resources to carry out the organization's overall objectives. Because each of these fund-raising areas requires a working knowledge of a vast amount of detail, it is unrealistic to expect one person to keep any sense of perspective with this impossible workload.

As we will see, much of the work involved in fund raising is research and writing. Much preparation is involved in carefully cultivating a match between the organization and the donor. On the other hand, a great deal of fund raising also involves socializing with potential donors. Without the time and help to research and cultivate donors, the fund raiser's success will be very limited. The rewards usually are not immediate. Years may go by before an individual finally makes a donation to the organization. People who seek instant gratification will find development a very frustrating area in which to work.

On the whole, fund raising seems to be a growth industry. There is a constant high demand for people who can organize and effectively manage the fund-raising activities of a not-for-profit corporation. The downside of this high demand is the often unrealistic expectations about how much money actually can be raised. The tendency to overestimate eventually leads an organization into a deficit operating mode. The net result is a high level of turnover in the development area in the not-for-profit sector.

In this chapter, we explore the requirements an organization must meet before it tries to raise money. We also discuss strategies to use in approaching different target donors and organizations that specialize in giving to the arts.

Preparing Fund-Raising Plans

James Gregory Lord, a recognized expert in the field of fund raising, notes that "people give to people." He goes on to say, "People don't give to an institution. They give to the person who asks them. Often, a contribution is made because of how one person feels about another. The institution may be almost incidental. People also give for people—not for endowments or swimming pools."[6]

If fund-raising managers keep this fundamental fact in the forefront of all planning and solicitation efforts, they probably will be successful in establishing a lifelong pattern of giving in donors. No matter what strategy an organization plans to adopt in its fund-raising efforts, the bottom line depends on regular donations. Without the regular support by individuals, corporations, foundations, and government (even if it is only a tax break), most organizations would not be able to survive. Let us examine in more detail how to establish a pattern of regular giving.

Strategic Planning

Most fund-raising activity begins with a great deal of background work. Unless the organization happens to have a wealthy benefactor who hands out money with no questions asked, countless hours must be

Figure 13-1
Fund-Raising Planning and Process

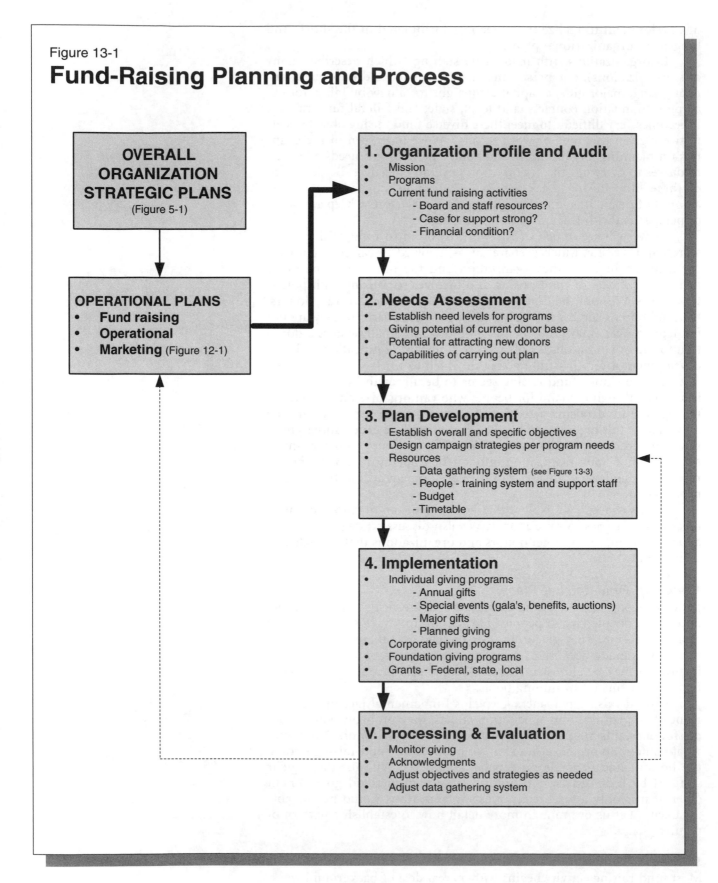

OVERALL ORGANIZATION STRATEGIC PLANS
(Figure 5-1)

OPERATIONAL PLANS
- **Fund raising**
- **Operational**
- **Marketing** (Figure 12-1)

1. Organization Profile and Audit
- Mission
- Programs
- Current fund raising activities
  - Board and staff resources?
  - Case for support strong?
  - Financial condition?

2. Needs Assessment
- Establish need levels for programs
- Giving potential of current donor base
- Potential for attracting new donors
- Capabilities of carrying out plan

3. Plan Development
- Establish overall and specific objectives
- Design campaign strategies per program needs
- Resources
  - Data gathering system (see Figure 13-3)
  - People - training system and support staff
  - Budget
  - Timetable

4. Implementation
- Individual giving programs
  - Annual gifts
  - Special events (gala's, benefits, auctions)
  - Major gifts
  - Planned giving
- Corporate giving programs
- Foundation giving programs
- Grants - Federal, state, local

V. Processing & Evaluation
- Monitor giving
- Acknowledgments
- Adjust objectives and strategies as needed
- Adjust data gathering system

spent preparing to ask people for their support. The flowchart in Figure 13–1 depicts a typical system for organizing the fund raising for an organization.

An organization's strategic plan normally contains a specific operational plan for the proposed fund-raising efforts. In Chapter 5, the concepts of the overall organizational strategy and the operational strategies for special areas were discussed. In Chapter 12, we saw how the marketing plan would be integrated with the strategic plan. Now we consider how the fund-raising needs would be integrated into the overall strategic plans.

The overall strategy the organization adopts will affect the development of the organization's profile and audit. Take the example of an organization that adopts a growth strategy. It is safe to assume that the fund-raising management staff would need to address the issue of finding more new sources of funds for the organization. This in turn requires that much time be spent on donor research. On the other hand, if the organization adopts a stability strategy, the fund raisers might concentrate their efforts on the current donor base. As with any planning process, multiple strategies can be incorporated into the overall master plan. However, the staff and budget resources required to support this approach can become burdensome.

Profile and Audit

The fund-raising process shown is broken down in to five major activity areas (see Figure 13–1). Of course, the starting and ending points in any process are not always clear and distinct, assessment must be taken before action.

The organization's mission and programs are the source for all fund-raising activities. These elements will be the core from which you will build your fund-raising goals. If your mission is to bring opera to schoolchildren in your community, then it will be clear to donors why you need funding for a truck or a van. In addition, you more than likely engage in fund raising now. Ask how well the current process is working. Do you have a clear, strong case for support? And is the financial condition of the organization healthy? Focus groups from the community may be helpful in gathering outside input about your organization. As noted in Chapter 12, marketing and fund raising usually are less successful when presented in a product- or sales-oriented manner. A general appeal that says, "Give to us because we make great music and we are world class," will not promote the exchange process. A letter mailed to a parent that says, "Your gift will help a child experience the wonder and joy of music," might prove more successful.

The next step, determining the amount needed, is based on a careful analysis of the budget and the fiscal health of the organization. For example, if the strategic plan calls for establishing an operating endowment fund to provide an annual income of $50,000, the fund-raising goal could be as high as $1.25 million. This figure assumes that the $1.25 million would earn a conservative interest rate of 8 percent, yielding $100,000 per year. After deducting $50,000 for the operating fund, the remaining $50,000 would be reinvested in the endowment to overcome the annual effects of inflation, which is assumed to be 4 percent in this example.

The actual campaign planning and development involves formulating written material, creating the graphics and brochures to communicate the project or program, planning special fund-raising events (such

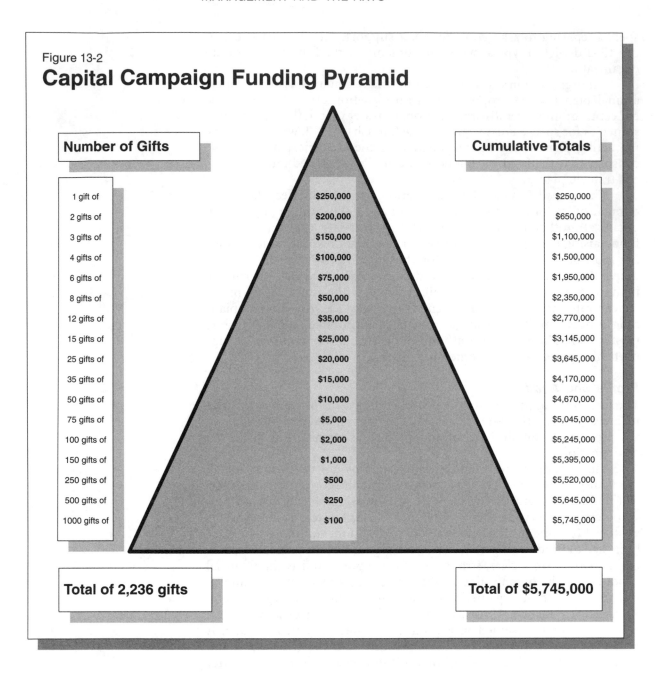

Figure 13-2

Capital Campaign Funding Pyramid

Number of Gifts		Cumulative Totals
1 gift of	$250,000	$250,000
2 gifts of	$200,000	$650,000
3 gifts of	$150,000	$1,100,000
4 gifts of	$100,000	$1,500,000
6 gifts of	$75,000	$1,950,000
8 gifts of	$50,000	$2,350,000
12 gifts of	$35,000	$2,770,000
15 gifts of	$25,000	$3,145,000
25 gifts of	$20,000	$3,645,000
35 gifts of	$15,000	$4,170,000
50 gifts of	$10,000	$4,670,000
75 gifts of	$5,000	$5,045,000
100 gifts of	$2,000	$5,245,000
150 gifts of	$1,000	$5,395,000
250 gifts of	$500	$5,520,000
500 gifts of	$250	$5,645,000
1000 gifts of	$100	$5,745,000

Total of 2,236 gifts   **Total of $5,745,000**

as auctions, dinners, and costume balls), and tactics such as telephoning donors to ask for support. Training staff and volunteers, establishing a detailed timetable, and performing donor research all must be done before launching a campaign.

The implementation stage typically occurs on several fronts. Gifts from all categories of donors are solicited with the intent building the long-term relationships necessary for future campaigns. The cycle of preparing, asking, evaluating, and starting to plan all over again is inherent in the fund-raising function of an arts organization.

Funding Pyramid

The capital campaign funding pyramid shown in Figure 13–2 is one approach used to establish how many gifts at which amounts will be needed to meet a specific goal. A major campaign with a goal of $5 million usually concentrates its initial efforts on raising at least half of the money before publicly announcing the campaign effort. A lead gift of $250,000 and gifts of at least $25,000 are secured before the campaign is announced to build momentum. With at least half of the money raised, fund raisers can tell people, "Here's a project that others are willing to support."

To succeed in building the pyramid from the top down, the fund raisers must do their homework. Identifying possible funding sources, evaluating their giving potential, ranking them within the pyramid, and finding the right contact person could take a year or more. All this work can amount to nothing if the wrong person asks for the gift. As James Lord says, "People give to people. " It is critical that the fund-raising staff educate board members and other volunteers about how and when to ask for support. As we will see later in this chapter, the entire fund-raising effort is a marketing effort. The fund raiser tries to match the wants and needs of the donor with the goods and services of the organization.

Assuming success, the process is completed by legally accounting for the gift and acknowledging the support. As with the marketing campaign, evaluation and adjustment go on constantly in an effort to fine-tune and maximize the gift-giving program.

Marketing and Fund Raising

An effective fund-raising campaign requires the implementation of a well-organized marketing system. As in the marketing campaign, the goal is to achieve a close match between the donor and the funding need. In this case, the exchange process should make donors feel that the money, goods, or services they are donating will help solve a specific problem. For example, the money they donate to the operating endowment, if marketed properly, becomes a gift that supports any number of aspects of the organization. Finding the proper "hot button" for each donor—for example, the young artists' program or the museum arts classes for children—is a way to maximize the satisfaction of giving. The fact is, if the fund-raising campaign is not donor driven in the way it is packaged and presented, it probably will not be as effective or successful.

Fund-Raising Management

Fund raising involves what by now should be the familiar aspects of project management: budgets, schedules, timetables, problem solving, and group leadership techniques. An individual with excellent group and project management skills is required for a successful campaign. Excellent communication skills are a must for development personnel.

Thousands of details must be coordinated into a unified whole if the organization is to reach its fund-raising goals. We begin by examining the background work required for getting ready to ask for support. Then, we review the techniques and tools used to maximize the possibility of support from various funding entities.

Background Work

What Does the Organization Do?

After completing the fund-raising audit and assessment, the process should shift to formulating what the organization can do to address a range of needs in the community. How does the symphony orchestra,

Study Philanthropy?

An article in the *New York Times* noted that over 75 graduate schools were offering masters programs in philanthropy in America. Schools such as Yale, Indiana University–Purdue University, and numerous centers for not-for-profit business study have proliferated over the last 20 years. The article also points out salaries for professionals are one-third lower in general in the not-for-profit sector.

SOURCE: Dirk Johnson, "A Master's Degree in Philanthropy Teaches the Business of Doing Good," *New York Times* (December 24, 1997), p. C-19.

Study to Give away Money?

Another newspaper article focused teaching the rich how to give money away. The Rockefeller Foundation offers a course in Practical Philanthropy. Tuition is $10,000 for a weeklong series of courses on reading financial statements to sharing information with guest speakers about the need and impact of giving. Weekend training sessions by consulting firms in Boston also were noted.

SOURCE: Alex Kuczynski, "The Very Rich Pay to Learn How to Give Money Away," *New York Times* (May 3, 1998), p. A-1.

museum, or dance, theater, or opera company satisfy the current needs of the community? What needs are not being met? Can the arts organization fulfill any of these needs? In *Managing a Nonprofit Organization*, Thomas Wolf identifies three important steps in this process, which he calls the *case for support*:[7]

1. Identify the important problems or needs that the organization intends to address with the help of the contributions.
2. Demonstrate the organization's ability to address these needs.
3. Match the proposed areas of organizational activity with the funder's own philanthropic interests.

The obvious starting point for an organization attempting to identify problems or needs is to address the current programs and projects. For example, the fictitious theater company examined in Chapter 11 had established a home season, touring operation, education program, and a building fund (capital campaign) to meet the various needs of the community. To make its case for support, the theater company would offer proof of how it is uniquely qualified to meet the community's needs through its regular season, which enriches the cultural life of the community by presenting quality productions. The theater could argue that the touring operation provides a service to a wide geographical area and a diverse audience and that the education program offers a school or apprentice program to teach acting skills to young people. The building fund is targeted to provide a permanent home for the theater company so it may increase its effectiveness in presenting its season and its projects in the community.

After the theater company outlines what it is doing and how it is effectively addressing the community's needs, the important process of matching activities to funders takes place.

Accurate research about potential donors is critical to making the optimal match. For example, a foundation may focus on education, a corporation may support high-visibility activities such as touring, and individual donors may want to be associated with a new facility. A significant amount of time can be wasted if the wrong donor is approached. Even worse, a potential donor may be turned off to your organization because of an inappropriate approach. A closer examination of this matching process is presented later in this chapter when the various funding sources are discussed

Staff and Board Participation

One expectation of any fund-raising campaign is that staff and board members will actively participate to help reach the goal. Potential donors may ask how much support staff and board members provide the organization. Answers about the average contribution per staff or board member must be at hand. After all, why should donors give to an organization that does not have the support of its own people?

Many not-for-profit organizations expect their board members to contribute a particular amount each year. This could range from a few hundred to many thousands of dollars. For some organizations, especially organizations made up of board members selected for their expertise and not for their wealth, there are expectations about contributing specific amounts of time to projects each year. In addition, not-for-profit organizations now are asking staff members to make an annual donation. The amount usually is significantly smaller on average than the board member's gift, but the demonstration of strong internal support for the organization is important when talking to outside donors.

Data Management

A well-designed management information system to gather data about potential donors is critical if the organization is to organize its fund-raising campaigns. Chapters 9, 11, and 12 provide examples of management information systems designed for the overall operation, the financial system, and marketing. In arts organizations, which usually have very limited staff resources, the data gathered about donors should be integrated with the sales and marketing systems. This integration can be achieved if the computer software is designed to capture and store information about sales and giving. Several companies specialize in fund-raising software for not-for-profit organizations. Any issue of the *Chronicle of Philanthropy* will contain advertisements for such systems. A careful analysis of the software's capabilities is required, and the support available from the company after the system is purchased should be explored to ensure that the organization's data management needs will be met in the long term. For example, the fund-raising financial record-keeping system must be able to track revenue through the entire accounting system. As we saw in Chapter 11, the balance sheet and account statements must reflect changes in the fund balances based on these donations. The donor tracking system therefore must be integrated with the accounting software used by the organization.

Data system needs   Members of the development staff should be able to sit down at a computer terminal; enter the name of a subscriber, single ticket buyer, or member; and pull up a complete list of all transactions or donations made by that person. Staff members also might want to identify everyone who donated more than $50 and less than $250 in the last year. Donor tracking systems usually contain data fields about the estimated salary and giving potential for each subscriber or member. Staff members might want to know who gave from a particular range of zip codes. The ability to cross-reference donors with sales of subscriptions or memberships is important, too. For example, if some patrons purchased only single tickets to the musicals that the theater company performed, this information could be effectively incorporated in a fund-raising letter. The letter would mention the individual's fondness for musicals and suggest a donation to support the production fund so more great shows could be produced for his or her enjoyment.

The donor data management system is critical in developing confidential financial information. For example, if the business section of the local newspaper announces that one of your patrons just received a promotion, this information should find its way into the data file. A promotion probably means a larger paycheck. This information is noted so that the next time a solicitation is made, a higher gift amount is requested.

A word of caution is in order about confidential information. The tendency to put large amounts of irrelevant personal data in a computer is directly proportional to the ease with which the data can be entered. A clear policy about what information may be kept in the donor file and who may have access to such data is important if the organization is to have any credibility in the community. Policies about the confidentiality of the data gathered by the development staff must be enforced. Passwords or security codes to access the donor data will be meaningless if

In the News 1

The *Chronicle of Philanthropy* pointed out that fund raisers in resource-strapped organizations are using the Internet as a tool to assist in fund-raising research. The ability to download foundation reports, application forms, and other relevant information represents a major shift in the whole information gathering process. The ability to secure frequent updates from funding entities, to participate in electronic discussion groups, and to locate new sources of funding help make the Internet a useful tool for an arts manager. The major challenge in using the Internet is that too much data are available. It is easy to become overwhelmed with data or waste time looking for yet one more Web site. The article lists several Web sites for organizations such as the Foundation Center and the Grantsmanship Center, as well as various grants discussion groups.

SOURCE: Marilyn Dickey, "Fund Raisers Turn to the Internet," *Chronicle of Philanthropy* (May 1, 1997), p. 23.

staff members sit around the lounge discussing how much someone gave to the operation. Any breach in security should be dealt with quickly and visibly.

Fund-Raising Costs and Control

The annual campaign and the various capital fund drives contain a mix of activities designed to reach as many potential donors as the budget will permit. Development managers always seek ways to keep the costs of raising money as low as possible. The impact of these costs cannot be ignored. Potential donors want to know whether the organization is capable of using their gifts efficiently. Although fund-raising costs may vary with different types of campaigns, if they reach 20 percent of the total raised, it is time for the organization to reassess its methods. Organizations that can keep fund-raising costs under 10 percent are viewed favorably by donors.

An effective budget control system must be in place before an organization undertakes any fund raising activity. In addition, legal requirements must be met when reporting income raised through donations on federal and state tax forms. Some states require special licenses before any fund raising may begin.

Direct and indirect costs Arts organizations usually have direct fund-raising costs for salaries, wages, and benefits. These costs should be distributed across the budget if several fund raising activities are supervised by one staff. Developing a project budget such as the one shown in Figure 11–4 makes it easier to track costs. Consultant fees also would be listed as a direct cost to the project. Other costs include supplies and services (paper, copying, printing, telephones), equipment (computers), and travel. Indirect fund-raising costs reflect such items as a portion of the rent, lease, or mortgage, utilities, and the maintenance of general office equipment used for fund-raising activities. The financial manager must calculate the various costs of each area's use of the common resources and formulate a distribution that can be used to prepare fund-raising budgets.

When applying for government grants, the organization can be reimbursed for indirect costs if these costs are reflected in the budget. For example, if a museum gets a grant for $1 million to run an educational program, 30–50 percent of the budget could be allocated for indirect costs. The organization therefore could expect that an additional $300,000–500,000 would be provided above the $1 million to support the costs of supporting the project. Grant applications to foundations and corporations normally show indirect costs as part of the overall project budget. Foundations and corporations may place restrictions on or refuse to support indirect costs. The application guidelines for these granting agencies normally outline the costs they consider to be legitimate.

Fund-Raising Techniques and Tools

A successful fund-raising campaign never ends. Most organizations must seek donations continually if they are to survive financially. As soon as the annual campaign has been completed for one fiscal year, it is time to get started on next year's fund drive. The overall goal remains the same each year: to establish a regular pattern of giving to the organization. We next examine some of the specific details of the various ongoing campaigns that an organization must maintain. In addition to the occasional large capital campaign (usually conducted every three to five years), annual campaigns targeted to individuals, corporations, foundations, and government agencies require constant attention and fine-tuning.

Individual Donors

All organizations want a substantial number of individual donors who make regular unrestricted gifts to the organization. An unrestricted gift carries no stipulation as to how the funds may be spent. Unrestricted gifts give the organization the flexibility to shift funds to fill the greatest need. Restricted gifts, on the other hand, are given on the assumption that the funds will be used for a specific project or program. The organization has a legal obligation to use restricted funds in the manner designated by the donor. An unrestricted gift might be added to the operating fund balance or be used to cover the expenses of a specific production or project. A restricted gift might be designated only for the building fund endowment. Because solicitations to corporations, foundations, and the government often carry distribution restrictions, the more unrestricted gifts the organization can regularly gather, the better.

The actual percentage of your audience that may donate to your organization will vary with how effective you are in making your case. For example, if you have 1,500 regular season subscribers, between 10 and 30 percent might regularly donate to your annual fund. Obviously, the find-raisers' goal is to achieve the highest percentage donors from the subscriber base as possible. As you will see from "FYI— Giving," the mainstay of support comes from individuals.

Because regular giving is the lifeblood of many organizations, it is fairly common for organizations to maintain a standing committee of board and staff members to coordinate the fund-raising activity. Yearly funding goals and objectives are set, a detailed timetable is created, specific details—such as who makes the calls, who signs the letters—are worked out, and assignments are distributed to the board and the staff. This is an example of all the management theories coming together. The fund-raising committee must plan, organize, and lead effectively if the organization is to remain strong.

The techniques for building a large base of individual donors include donor research, offering numerous funding options, personal contact, telephone solicitation, direct mail, and special events.

Donor research   Many of the techniques used to develop an audience are used in donor research. The current subscribers, members, and single ticket buyers form the core of the active donor base. This core group should be subjected to the most intense research, and as complete a donor file as possible should be compiled on each person (see Figure 13–3).

The next level of research focuses on less active supporters and prospects. Vast amounts of data about prospective donors must be gathered and rated in terms of potential for further use. As Thomas Wolf says, "Only prospectors find gold."[8] The organization must commit personnel to go through lists of former subscribers, patrons of other arts organizations, country club members, and members of social or business organizations. They also must explore school phone directories (including college or university phone books), references given by current

FYI—Giving

While corporations and foundations get all the attention and headlines, individual giving in 1997, according to *Giving USA*, accounted for 76.2 percent of all giving for philanthropy in the United States, with corporate support at 5.7 percent and foundation support at 9.3 percent. The remaining 8.3 percent came from bequests.

Source: "Donations to Charity Rise 7.5%," *Chronicle of Philanthropy* (June 4, 1998), p. 29.

Figure 13-3

Donor Cultivation and Solicitation

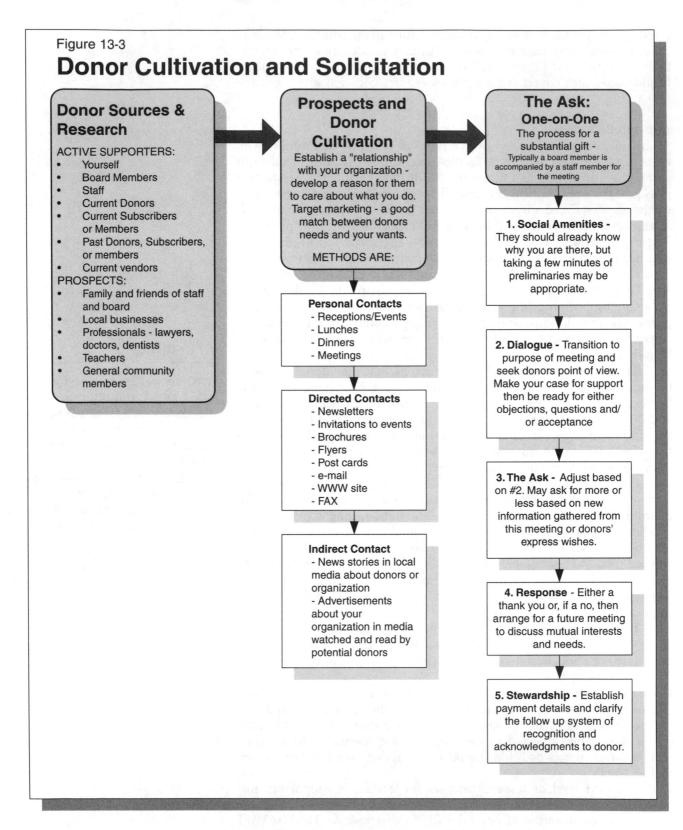

Donor Sources & Research

ACTIVE SUPPORTERS:
- Yourself
- Board Members
- Staff
- Current Donors
- Current Subscribers or Members
- Past Donors, Subscribers, or members
- Current vendors

PROSPECTS:
- Family and friends of staff and board
- Local businesses
- Professionals - lawyers, doctors, dentists
- Teachers
- General community members

Prospects and Donor Cultivation

Establish a "relationship" with your organization - develop a reason for them to care about what you do. Target marketing - a good match between donors needs and your wants.

METHODS ARE:

Personal Contacts
- Receptions/Events
- Lunches
- Dinners
- Meetings

Directed Contacts
- Newsletters
- Invitations to events
- Brochures
- Flyers
- Post cards
- e-mail
- WWW site
- FAX

Indirect Contact
- News stories in local media about donors or organization
- Advertisements about your organization in media watched and read by potential donors

The Ask: One-on-One

The process for a substantial gift -
Typically a board member is accompanied by a staff member for the meeting

1. Social Amenities - They should already know why you are there, but taking a few minutes of preliminaries may be appropriate.

2. Dialogue - Transition to purpose of meeting and seek donors point of view. Make your case for support then be ready for either objections, questions and/ or acceptance

3. The Ask - Adjust based on #2. May ask for more or less based on new information gathered from this meeting or donors' express wishes.

4. Response - Either a thank you or, if a no, then arrange for a future meeting to discuss mutual interests and needs.

5. Stewardship - Establish payment details and clarify the follow up system of recognition and acknowledgments to donor.

donors, and published social registers. Sources such as *Who's Who in America*, which publishes regional directories, may also be of use.

Funding options Fund raisers like to speak of gift giving as an "opportunity" or a chance to make an "investment in the future." Well-organized development managers design several choices for donors using a concept not unlike a menu. For example, gifts can be targeted for the current operating fund for those people who want their gifts to be put to use immediately. Others may want their gift to go to an endowment fund, which is invested and only a portion of the interest is used to fund operations or special programs. A scholarship fund is a good choice for donors who want their gifts to have maximum longevity. Others may want to offer their funds in the form of a deferred gift; that is, a promise to provide funds, property, stocks, bonds, life insurance, property, or jewelry at some future date. Another form of deferred giving is a bequest, which is a gift that is distributed through the donor's will. Some donors specify that a portion of their life insurance will be donated to an organization.

Figure 13–4 shows a possible rating system for evaluating major gift prospects. While there are no hard and fast rules here, the simple fact is the organization must have a rating system in place for every donor. Without this information, the fund raiser is operating in the dark. Asking for too much or too little money can have equally negative outcomes. The donor who considers a major gift $500 may be frightened away from the organization that asks for $5,000. At the same time, the donor capable of giving $50,000 may be insulted if asked for only $5,000.

As with any menu, it should be possible for the donor to combine several options. For example, an organization with annual donors who make bequests and give regularly to an endowed fund is in a fortunate position. Offering a selection of donor options is taking the principles of being a customer-driven, marketing-oriented organization to its logical conclusion. The donor programs must be designed to provide the maximum exchange satisfaction for donors who write a check or sign a document giving something to the organization.

Personal contacts Personal contact is the preferred method for cultivating and securing a gift, because fund raising is most effective when people ask other people for their support. The management of public events such as meetings, receptions, lunches, and dinners give the fund raiser the opportunity to keep in direct contact without directly asking for money. Some donors like the social aspects of seeing and being seen at various public functions. Helping them realize their need to be seen probably will pay off later when making the more personal one-on-one solicitation.

In a typical major gifts or capital campaign in which large sums of money are sought, the organization usually engages in a long courtship with the donor. Assume that a museum's donor research targets a local business executive for a gift to the building fund. On paper, this person looks like a good candidate, but without an introduction, the organization might get a firm refusal. If the research indicates that a current member of the board knows the executive, a valuable link exists. If there is no existing contact, an appointment should be made to get things rolling. The first meeting will probably be brief and informational. The board member who knows the executive should attend the meeting to help smooth out the initial communication. A staff member might accompany the

Figure 13-4

Donor Rating Matrix

Donor Ratings

When cultivating a long-term donor you will need to establish a target for the maximum you think is achievable over 5 years.

The factors that may alter this rating system, which is based on 5% of the income or 10% of the net worth, include

* Giving history
* Timing
* Financial stability

Gift Request To be given over 5 years	Minimum income	Minimum Net Assets
$7,500	$30,000	$375,000
$12,500	$50,000	$625,000
$18,750	$75,000	$1,000,000
$25,000	$100,000	$1,250,000
$37,500	$150,000	$1,875,000
$50,000	$200,000	$2,500,000
$62,5000	$250,000	$3,125,000
$125,000	$500,000	$6,250,000
$250,000	$1,000,000	$12,500,000

board member to be introduced and answer questions, but his or her presence is merely functional. A package of information about the organization and a brief outline of how the current fund raising drive is doing probably would be enough for this first visit.

The key goal in making the first contact is for each party to learn more about the other. Follow-up meetings, invitations to various events sponsored by the organization, lunch at a local restaurant, informative notes, and updates by telephone would round out the process. When the fund-raising committee feels that the time is right, the designated contact makes the request. The staff member should not actually ask for the gift. It is unethical for staff members to make such requests because they are paid by the organization. The board member or a volunteer should do the asking.

Communication tools To keep donors informed and aware of your programs and needs, a series of careful planned communications must be part of the cultivation process (see Figure 13–3). For example, newsletters, brochures, flyers, postcards, and even group e-mail can prove useful in keeping your current and potential donors informed. Keeping an active Web site updated also helps deliver news to interested parties faster than print media or letters. In addition, the public relations function of the arts organization must have a plan to ensure news stories or advertisements keep the organization visible in the community. Donors like seeing the organization they support being seen by others as an effective member of the community.

In the News 2

An important tool of the fund raiser is the telephone. However, the issue of how this tool is used is coming under more control.

Colorado Enacts Strict Law on Telephone Fund Raising
Jon Craig

A new Colorado law will require people who solicit money for non-profit organizations over the telephone to disclose numerous details about themselves and the donations they are requesting.

The law, signed last month by Gov. Roy Romer, is believed to be among the most complex charitable telephone-solicitation laws in the nation.

It requires professional fund raisers to disclose the telemarketing company's name, the charity's name and telephone number, and, when appropriate, that a gift will not be tax-deductible. In addition, if they are asked, they must say what percentage of a donation would go to the charity.

The new rules take effect July 1. Patricia Read, executive director of the Colorado Association of Non-profit Organizations, said her group had pressed for passage of the new restrictions. Telemarketing, she said, "is unfortunately subject to the most fraud of almost any area of fund raising."

Even so, not all people who represent charities think the law is a good idea. Some experts on solicitation laws say the Colorado law may violate charities' right to free speech under the Constitution.

"It goes too far," said Errol Copilevitz, a Kansas City, Mo., lawyer who successfully fought a North Carolina solicitation law before the Supreme Court in 1988.

Mr. Copilevitz, who represents many charities and telemarketers, said he was especially uneasy about a requirement that callers must inform prospective donors that they have the legal right to rescind a

pledge within three days of making the commitment.

"Your attention from my message is going to be diverted while I go through this litany of disclosures, and by the time I start telling you about the research we're doing to cure heart disease, you've already hung up on me," he said.

One of the legislative sponsors of the new law, Denver Rep. Gloria Leyba, said she and her colleagues had taken precautions to make sure the law did not violate free-speech rights or other constitutional provisions. For instance, during the drafting of the bill, lawmakers considered putting in a requirement that charities would have to receive at least 50 per cent of the money a telemarketer raised on their behalf. However, the lawmakers dropped that idea because it would be unconstitutional.

Source: Jon Craig, "Colorado Enacts Strict Telephone Fund Raising," *Chronicle of Philanthropy* (May 15, 1997), p. 18.

Telephone solicitations As shown in Figure 13–2, the typical funding pyramid includes many gifts valued at $500 or less. Personal contact is not an effective way to reach all of these donors. One of the most cost-effective alternatives is to make phone calls to as many prospects as possible.

Enthusiastic leadership is a must when motivating the board and other volunteers to ask for money over the telephone. This is especially true because the process of asking people for money can be very discouraging. Fund raisers always tell volunteers, "Don't take that 'no' personally!" However, it is only human nature to feel as if your request was rejected because you did not ask in the right way or you were not convincing enough.

Small organizations normally schedule a week or two each year for telephone fund-raising campaigns. Banks of telephones, eager volunteers, and a little training with a well-written and flexible script can translate into thousands of dollars for an organization. Again, solid research can pay off for the organization. When a caller begins talking with a prospect, an information card or computer screen should help guide the interaction. Potential donors initially are very hesitant about getting a phone call from a stranger, so the first 20 seconds of the conversation usually is scripted to ask questions designed to get the prospect to respond. Assuming that the information about the potential donors is correct, it should be possible to establish what they thought of the last performance they saw or the last exhibit they attended. The key is engaging the person and building to the request in a timely manner. If the caller is able to connect with the prospect, the typical tactic is to ask for a bit more than the donor research indicates. For example, if it is possible that the potential donor might give $150, the caller might be scripted to suggest initially an "investment" of $500. Eventually, an amount with which the donor feels comfortable will be reached, and the "closing" can take place. The logistics of getting the gift information and payment method correct and thanking the donor concludes the process.

Advances in technology have permitted computers to dial automatically and play prerecorded sales messages, but many donors hang up as soon as they realize that someone has invaded their privacy with a request for money. However, the benefit for not-for-profit organizations is a cost savings when they use this technology.

Direct mail　Direct-mail marketing and fund raising is a big business in the United States. Every day, high-speed computer printers merge-print millions of pieces of what most people call "junk mail" with names and addresses purchased from list brokers. Many people never open the handiwork of the direct-mail marketer, but enough people respond to these offers to convince businesses that the cost is worth incurring.

Arts organizations have used the techniques of the direct-mail marketer for years in attempting to build a subscriber or member base. The mailing of a solicitation for funds follows the basic direct-mail principles and traditionally is part of the mix of options used by the development staff.

The outer envelope represents the critical first contact with potential donors. The envelope must communicate a short, strong, and clear message that something of interest is inside. A popular technique uses the word *free* on the envelope with the assumption that people will be curious to see what the offer is. If the fund raiser can get potential donors to open the envelope, the combination of a well-written letter and an informative brochure will bring readers further into the solicitation. Because most people initially scan the text of the letter and brochure, the copy must be written and laid out in such a way as to get the message across in as few words as possible. The response device (the piece returned to the organization) and the reply envelope should provide a fast and easy way of completing the solicitation.

Tracking responses　Direct mail is a long-term investment. Organizations that expect much more than a 1 or 2 percent response rate may be in for a surprise. For example, a 1.5 percent response rate for a 10,000-piece mailing would yield 150 donations. Say the average donation is $25. The first mailing thus yields $3,750. First-class postage, letter, brochure, reply device, and reply envelope cost an average of 60¢ per unit. The first mailing therefore costs $6,000 and but raises only $3,750. However, if you view these 150 donors as a long-term investment, the $2,250 loss eventually will be recouped. Suppose that the arts fund raiser tracks these donors as a target group that responded to a particular campaign. In the next year, a telephone solicitation of these 150 people yields a 40 percent response rate, and the average donation is $75. The organization has gained $4,500 minus the cost of telephone solicitation. Say it costs $150 to get this next $4,500. This leaves the organization ahead by $2,100 on its total investment of $6,150. In the third and fourth years, 50 percent of the remaining donors from the first year's campaign give an average of $125 each. The net yield now increases to $7,635 in donations after subtracting $6,240 in solicitation costs over four years. If carefully monitored and tracked, the organization should be able to create an overall system of periodic direct mail solicitations that yield a regular cash flow.

Note that this simplified example of a direct mail cost analysis is used to illustrate a point. Direct-mail marketers have very comprehensive formulas for calculating campaign costs. For example, the data in this example does not take into account inflation, which is a cost to the campaign. In addition, the cost of raising money is fairly high in this example. Costs of 20¢ or less per dollar raised would be more appropriate. Of course, if just one of those few donors you recruited five years ago makes a major gift to the organization for $250,000 the direct mail costs can become a minor issue.

Special events   Arts organizations usually try to hold at least one event a year as a fund raiser. A group of volunteers coordinates and produces a costume ball, a silent or live auction, a raffle, or a benefit performance. The effort and time required to produce a major event can be overwhelming if the organization lacks the resources to make it happen. The costs of producing an event like a costume ball may run into the tens of thousands of dollars. Careful control of the budget is required, or the event may end up costing the organization more than it earns in donations. However, with a good planning committee and a realistic schedule, it is possible to earn thousands regularly for the organization and provide a memorable experience for donors.

These events can also provide visibility in the community for the organization. Raffles, for example, can be a way of involving the local business community in the arts by persuading business owners to donate goods and services. State and local governments may place restrictions on certain types of events, so it is always a good idea to consult with a lawyer before proceeding.

Corporate Giving

As pointed out earlier in this chapter corporations donated $8.2 billion to charities in 1997. Although this is a substantial amount, it represents less than 6 percent of the $143.5 billion given by all fund donors to charities in 1997. Typically, there is a strong relationship between the economy and corporate giving. In addition, corporations undergo constant changes in ownership as they are bought, sold, and merged. Not-for-profit organizations must adapt to the changing business environment if they intend to capitalize on the available funds. In the best of times, arts and cultural organizations usually are not at the top of the corporate funding priority list, but regular support can be found if fund raisers are willing to make the effort to track down the sources.

Corporate support is based in large part on the concept of *reciprocity*: What will the corporation gain by supporting a performance or an exhibition? A company may have motives for funding a specific event because of its public relations value, marketing potential, or benefits to its employees. The fund-raiser's research must focus on trying to fit the organization into the corporation's donor strategy. The lack of a good strategic fit, as it is called, is the primary reason why support is not given to an organization. Arts organizations must remember that establishing a good strategic match is part of their marketing process. The packaging and emphasis of a proposal may need to be adjusted as the priorities of corporations change.

Corporate support usually is restricted to the immediate community because businesses are concerned about raising their profile in their immediate market. Larger corporations sometimes sponsor performances or major exhibits that have a highly visible national tour program. For the most part, a regional arts group has little chance of attracting national corporate support unless an active branch of the corporation is in the area.

A method once used to raise corporate support in some communities was to develop a United Way-type fund raising campaign for the arts. However, for many not-for-profit organizations, the benefits of a regular funding source were offset by a drop in overall corporate giving. Companies no longer had to give as many grants because they consolidated their giving and reduced their overall commitment of funds. Corporations saw an opportunity to continue to do good but for less.

Potential problems   The most problematic issue related to corporate support is the conditions (some direct, some implied) that may be attached to a gift. For example, a performing arts group or museum may find its corporate support quickly withdrawn at the first sign of controversy. Once withdrawn, the chances of getting this support back may be very limited.

Also the organization may have to take into account ethical considerations before applying for corporate support. For example, seeking funds from companies that produce products thought to be harmful to the environment or people or from companies that have holdings in politically repressive countries could be detrimental to the community perception of the arts organization.

Fund-raising process   The overall planning and research process for corporate fund raising is not greatly different than the one used for individuals or foundations. Corporations that make direct grants are listed in publications such as the *National Guide to Funding in Arts and Culture*. They number slightly more than 300.[9] The Web also may prove useful when seeking information about potential corporate donors. Corporations generally establish foundations to distribute their gifts.

One of the most important steps in this process is the direct contact with an individual in the corporation or business. In this simplified model, if no contact already exists, then a courtship process is undertaken. In many cases, the organization rewrites the proposal before asking for the gift because the initial meeting with the corporate contact made it clear that the original proposal did not address the company's current funding interests. In other cases, contact occurs before the proposal is written.

Whatever the situation, the overall process of corporate fund raising must be integrated within the master plan (see Figure 13–1). The funding manager of a not-for-profit organization should read the business section of the daily paper and follow national trends in the business publications in an effort to stay in tune with the opportunities that may arise.

Foundations

A foundation is defined as a "nonprofit, non-governmental organization with a principal fund or endowment of its own that maintains or aids charitable, educational, religious, or other activities serving the public good, primarily by making grants to other organizations."[10] *The National Guide to Funding in Arts and Culture* lists 3,360 granting organizations. They are distributed as follows:[11]

Independent foundations	2,168
Community foundations	129
Grant-making operating foundations	53
Company-sponsored foundations	707
Corporate giving programs	303

The National Guide is an excellent research source for information about types of grants, amounts granted, purposes, limitations, publications, and application procedures.

As with corporate fund raising, a good match between organization and foundation must exist. Foundations usually fund specific types of activities. For example, the Gap Foundation supports "employee matching gifts, capital campaigns, general purposes, operating budgets" in the San Francisco area. The Autry Foundation gives "primarily for cultural, educational, medical, and youth-related programs" in the Los Angeles area.[12] The fund raiser can investigate the kinds of grants given in the last few years to see if a match can be made.

As always, a clear, concise proposal and ability statement is the first step in the application process. Because many small foundations have little or no staffing, the application procedure may be as simple as a cover letter, a one-page proposal, and a budget. A large foundation may require a proposal of eight to ten pages, and a screening committee may review applications before referring them to a grants committee. Regardless of the length of the proposal, the applicant must state the problem, describe how the organization is qualified to solve the problem, explain the benefits to the community, and outline how the effectiveness of the project will be measured and evaluated. Fund-raising activity remains a person-to-person business, and without the proper introductions, the applying organization is an unknown entity. The greater the depth of involvement of the board in the community, the better are the chances that the organization will be able to make itself a part of the grant-making network that exists in foundation funding.

Government Funding

It is possible to find funding for the arts at all levels of government in the United States. Local arts agencies usually have limited funds, but if an organization is trying to establish a positive record of effectively using grant money, the local level is a good starting point. For example, local agencies often provide funding for outreach programs into the schools. They also may help sponsor programming, assist with advertising to bring in out-of-town audience members, or subsidize ticket discounts to students or seniors. The application procedures usually are simple, and the amount of time and money spent administering the support is minimal.

State arts councils usually have permanent staffs, standard application procedures, formal review panels, and standard evaluation and reporting procedures. They generally offer numerous types of grants, including grants for programming, new works, outreach touring, and individual artists. In many cases, the state agencies parallel the National

Endowment for the Arts. Funding research again is required to achieve the best match between the arts organization and the granting agency.

The National Assembly of Local Arts Agencies (NALAA) and the National Assembly of State Arts Agencies (NASAA), located in Washington, D.C., sponsor annual meetings and offer their members regular workshops on many areas of operation. Because NALAA and NASAA members form the core of agencies that distribute state and federal funds, an arts organization would be wise to cultivate a relationship with these organizations.

The National Endowment for the Arts   As noted in Chapter 4, the National Endowment for the Arts is the major source for funding and recognition in the arts community. The NEA Web site publishes information that gives applicants an overview of the major grant areas. Each program area and division of the NEA publishes detailed guidelines to help applicants through the process.

The 1998 budget for the NEA was approximately $98 million. When adjusted for inflation over the last 15 years, the NEA now has less to give than it did in the late 1970s. Despite the small size of the NEA's budget (compare the NEA's $98 million with the $21.5 billion given by corporations and foundations in 1997),[13] NEA matching grants programs helped stimulate an important partnership between arts organizations and donors. Organizations that received funds from the NEA also benefited from the recognition. Having received a grant added to the legitimacy of the enterprise and, although the NEA never intended it, created a "stamp of approval" for the arts group. Donors assumed that, if a group or an artist had successfully passed through the grant review process, the work must be worthy of merit. As discussed in Chapter 4, the political turmoil that invaded the NEA's operation in the late 1980s and 1990s affected the agency's image and its ability to support the arts in America. While the public's attention was focused on a limited number of controversial grants, thousands of grant requests were being reviewed, processed, and funded.

The peer review process   The core of the NEA granting process is the peer review. A panel of experts are assembled at specific times during the year to review applications. Members of the committee are assigned specific grants to study in detail and discuss at the review process. The time for each presentation is limited, and the competition for support is intense. Each year, the NEA receives thousands of grant applications. The average grant application receives only a few minutes of discussion. Therefore, the proposal must be brief and to the point. The NEA staff reviews the details of the application, but the opening proposal, which is very limited in space, most often is what is read. If the reader's interest is not captured immediately or if the proposal raises more questions than it answers, the request will be pushed to the bottom of the stack. Consulting with the NEA staff may help when researching the kinds of key words, phrases, or concepts that are likely to catch the panelists' attention. At the same time, a brilliant proposal may fail because the organization has no track record, meaning that it has no previous history of having effectively used donated funds.

Applying for NEA funding is not very different from the corporate or foundation process. Establishing contacts within the agency and cultivating relationships with key people will help establish the arts organization as a viable target for funding.

Other government sources   Up to this point, the discussion of grants and the government has focused on the performing arts. The National Endowment for the Humanities also provides grants covering such areas as design, museums, research, music history, and interdisciplinary projects. In fact, thousands of grants are available from the federal government. Many of these grants have criteria that may make it difficult for an arts organization to qualify, but occasionally an opportunity arises that is worth pursuing.

The key to finding government support is research. One helpful source is the *Federal Register*, a thoroughly indexed and cross-referenced publication that lists all federal grant programs. The *Catalog of Federal Domestic Assistance* contains information on government funding programs and is indexed by agency and subject area. The federal government makes extensive use of the Web sites and the Internet to make much of this information available. Patience is required when wading through the myriad of choices, but vast amounts of information about federal programs can prove helpful.

Conclusion

Arts organizations have come to depend on funds from a mixture of donors. Funding levels from individuals, corporations, foundations, and government agencies are subject to changing environments. For example, support for arts and culture changes as the economy improves or declines, as public attitudes about censorship shift, as government support for social services decline, as state arts budgets are slashed, and as companies disappear through mergers. Because the funding arena can be so volatile, arts groups usually are advised to avoid becoming dependent on any one source of funds.

The situation of too many not-for-profit groups chasing too few donations by foundations and corporations probably will not improve in the next few years. In fact, as the demands for private support increase to cover the budget restrictions on government support for needed social and medical services, the actual amounts available to distribute to arts and culture groups may decline significantly. In fact, the privatization movement in government has put additional strains on not-for-profit organizations as local arts and cultural organizations. Funding cuts for activities that do not directly serve the public with services (e.g., sponsoring a Shakespeare Festival with city funding) are becoming more frequent. Self-reliance and reducing the number of people and organizations receiving entitlements has become a high priority in the 1990s. The criteria for what constitutes "public benefit" has been raised, and arts organizations have found it necessary to reframe their message about the benefits they provide the community.

Individual donors find themselves inundated by direct mail appeals and regular telephone solicitations from every conceivable cause. As more organizations learn the tricks of the fund-raising trade, individual donors will be asked to support even more groups. Arts organizations may find a backlash from donors cutting into their major source of support. No doubt the fund raising staffs and the board of directors for many organizations will have to reevaluate their fund-raising strategies in the late 1990s and in to the next century. The trend may be toward more personal appeals in an attempt to form a tighter bond with donors.

Summary

Arts organizations in the United States depend heavily on the support of individuals, foundations, corporations, and the government to achieve their objectives. By tradition, U.S. government involvement in the arts has been minimal.

People give for a variety of reasons based on the concept that they receive intangible benefits in a social exchange with the organization. Giving, which is a person-to-person business, depends on the careful design and integration of the organization's strategic and operational plans. Auditing the organization's readiness to undertake a campaign includes analyzing its mission, objectives, resources, activities, and programs. The fund-raising process requires a marketing orientation directed at donors to be effective.

The case for support is a key element in the organization's overall fund-raising strategy. Support from board and staff members is needed to demonstrate to donors the commitment in the organization. An effective data-gathering and -management system also is needed. Careful control of the costs of raising money and disbursing funds is required for legal reasons.

Campaigns are designed to target funding groups, which include individuals, corporations, foundations, and government agencies. Donor research leads to designing different funding options to fit the needs of different funders. Gift programs are designed to accept current support, deferred giving, and bequests. Personal contact is the most effective way to solicit large gifts from a limited number of wealthy individuals. Telephone and direct mail campaigns are used to reach a wider audience. Corporations and foundations usually are approached based on the strategic fit between the donor's objectives and the organization's needs. Campaigns for government support usually involve meeting program requirements and criteria established by agency staff members.

Key Terms and Concepts

Social exchange model for giving
Funding pyramid
Fund-raising audit
Case for support
Fund-raising data management
Direct and indirect costs
Capital campaign
Annual campaign
Restricted and unrestricted gifts
Deferred gift
Bequest
Direct-mail promotion
Reciprocity
Strategic fit
Foundation

Questions

1. What will be the impact on giving with the change in U.S. demographics over the next 20 years?

2. Do you agree with the concept of expecting staff members to

donate regularly to the arts organization for which they work? Explain why.

3. Do you think it is appropriate for arts organizations to gather personal data on potential donors for future use? What data would be inappropriate to keep? Why?

4. Have you ever been approached to make a gift to an arts organization? What techniques were used to solicit the donation? Did those techniques work? Explain why or why not.

5. Should arts organizations reject donations from corporations because of what the company manufactures or the politicians it supports? Explain why.

6. If an arts organization unknowingly received donations from an individual later found guilty of defrauding people out of their money, should the organization return the gifts for redistribution back to the people who were defrauded? Defend your position.

The following article from 1991 illustrates the impact that the changing government funding can have on an organization.

Case Study

Studio Arena to Seek Funding Sources
Torn Buckam

Cuts in state and city support will force Studio Arena Theatre to seek funds from other sources, a Studio executive said Tuesday.

The regional-theater in Buffalo Place expects to receive $112,000 less in 1991–92 than last year from the City and state, said Raymond Bonnard, producing director.

The bad news includes a 16 percent drop in city aid, to $157,250 from $187,000, and an especially sharp 63 percent reduction in the annual grant from the New York State Council on the Arts, to $46,515 from $128,250.

"Since Erie County's contribution won't be known until December, half-way through the theater's fiscal year, We've been put in a very tenuous situation, financially," Bonnard said.

Although the cuts may appear relatively small, measured against the theater's total budget of $3.2 million, their impact will be disproportionately large, Bonnard contended.

Because of annual increases in inflation and wage rates, the operation always needs more money than the year before—not the same amount or less—to meet expenses, he said.

"This business is extremely labor-intensive. Sixty percent of the budget goes to pay people," Bonnard said.

"When you're involved in a hand-crafted art form, trying to attract the best actors, directors and designers, they simply aren't going to come here for less money than we paid them last year," he said. "We need that $112,000 just to keep up."

Studio Arena already supports itself about as well as can be expected, he said. Earned income, primarily ticket sales, accounts for 70 percent of the budget—more than any of the 20 other regional theaters of comparable size nationally.

"Yes, we could push that figure up to 75 to 80 percent by doing plays that sell more tickets and bring in more income. But the danger in that is that at some point you begin to redefine yourself and start turning into something other than your mission says you should be."

"Our mission is to do plays that have substance and ideas—that challenge the theatergoer. Plays that are entertaining but also illuminating."

The cutback from the state Arts Council caught the theater off guard, even though it was in line with the 66 percent across-the-board reduction in cultural funding proposed by Gov. Cuomo at the beginning of the protracted budget battle in Albany.

Three years ago, the state agency agreed to grant the Studio Arena $142,500 a year for two years. Last year the Studio, recognizing the state constraints, not only agreed to take less in the second year—$128,250—but to accept the same reduced level of funding this year, Bonnard said.

"The advantage of rolling over the grant into a third year, even if it was less money, was that you could at least lock it into your budget," he said.

But the agreement fell victim to budget cutting just the same.

Theater personnel find small consolation that regional theaters in Rochester and Syracuse were stung just as sharply.

Source: Tom Buckam, "Studio Arena to Seek Funding Sources," *Buffalo Evening News* (July 17, 1991). Copyright © 1991 by the Buffalo Evening News. Used with permission.

Case Study Questions

1. What percentage of the $3.2 million operating budget is made up of state and city funds before and after the cuts?

2. What are some of the funding alternatives that Studio Arena might investigate to make up for the projected shortages?

3. As a potential donor, what is your reaction to the idea that doing plays that sell more tickets is not a viable fund raising strategy for Studio Arena? Do you support this idea? Explain why or why not.

4. Based on this article, how well does it appear that Studio Arena planned for changes in the political environment? What are some specific contingency plans that could have been made to prepare for the shortfall in local and state funding?

5. Based on Raymond Bonnard's summary of Studio Arena's mission, are you convinced of the need for support? Explain why or why not.

References

1. Melissa Mince, "History of Nonprofit Organizations: Summary," in *Nonprofit Corporations, Organizations and Associations*, 5th ed., edited by Howard L. Oleck (Englewood Cliffs, NJ: Prentice-Hall, 1988), p. 41.
2. Neil Pendleton, *Fundraising* (Englewood Cliffs, NJ: Prentice-Hall, Spectrum Books, 1981), p. xi.

3. Marilyn Dickey and Domenica Marchetti, "Donations to Charity Rise 7.5%," *Chronicle of Philanthropy* 10, no. 16 (June 4, 1997).
4. Joseph R. Mixer, *Principles of Professional Fundraising* (San Francisco: Jossey-Bass Publishers, 1993), p. 11.
5. Ibid., p. 10-11.
6. James Gregory Lord, *The Raising of Money* (Cleveland: Third Sector Press, 1986), p. 75.
7. Thomas Wolf, *Managing a Nonprofit Organization* (Englewood Cliffs, NJ: Prentice-Hall, 1990), p. 211.
8. Ibid., p. 225.
9. Loren Renz, "Foundation and Corporate Support," *National Guide to Funding in Arts and Culture* (New York: The Foundation Center, 1990), p. vii.
10. Ibid., p. vii.
11. Ibid., p. vii.
12. Ibid., p. 26.
13. Dickey and Marchetti, "Donations to Charity Rise 7.5%."

Additional Resources

Albert Anderson. *Ethics for Fundraisers.* Bloomington: Indiana University Press, 1996.

Mim Carlson. *Winning Grants Step by Step.* San Francisco: Jossey-Bass, 1996.

Joan Flanagan. *Successful Fundraising.* Chicago: Contemporary Books, 1993.

James M. Greenfield. *Fundraising Fundamentals.* New York: John Wiley & Sons, 1994.

14 □□□□□ Integrating Management Styles and Theories

Throughout this book, the stress has been on applying business theory and practice to managing an arts organization. In this chapter, we summarize different styles of management and various strategies for integrating management systems into the operation of an organization. We also review the specific functions of arts management and see how they can be applied to various management styles and systems. The goal of this chapter is to give the reader a model from which to work.

Management Styles

As discussed in Chapter 8, leadership and management styles have a profound impact on the way an organization functions. We also have seen that leadership and management often are different activities. There clearly is a need for leaders who can manage and managers who can lead. Since people usually are not perfect at everything they attempt, it is important for the arts manager to recognize his or her strengths and weaknesses. Leaders have a better opportunity for success if they put together a management team that complements their strengths and compensates their weaknesses.

There are as many different ways to run an organization as there are people in this world. Everyone has a slightly different view of what techniques work best in managing an arts organization. In the interests of developing some practical approaches to management, we examine three basic styles of management that can be used to lead an organization: rational, institutional, and organic. Obviously, many other management styles may be applicable. Flexibility remains the foundation of any style of management. It is important to develop a repertory of responses from which to choose as operational situations change.

Before we focus on three management styles that can help keep an organization operating effectively, let us visit with an arts manager struggling with a dysfunctional work situation. There always is something to learn—even from bad examples.

The Dysfunctional Arts Manager: A Model Rooted in Overextension

No one starts off in management with the goal of becoming a dysfunctional manager. A manager may become dysfunctional as a by-product of an organization with a culture that thrives on functional disorder as its standard operating mode. Organizations usually become dysfunctional either through evolutionary development or when an individual with a strong dysfunctional personality is allowed to take control of the management. Let us trace the development of an organization that becomes dysfunctional or that creates a dysfunctional manager.

Dysfunctional organizations   In Chapter 2, we saw that an organization usually starts up with a small group of extraordinary people willing to spend 18 hours a day doing everything, including marketing, advertising, contracts, schedules, budgets, and stuffing envelopes. Fayol's organizational esprit de corps is seen everywhere. Ambition, optimism, ceaseless energy, and a degree of ignorance about how impossible the job really is— all these elements are mixed together in a flurry of high-speed activity.

The volume of work increases as the number of productions, programs, or exhibits grows each year. Because everyone is so busy working, no one notices the gradual increase in the workload. New tasks and projects are added, staff members groan but accept the added work. The promise of more help and more money is held out as a goal to work toward. However, planning, if it is done at all, is never for more than a few days or a few weeks at a time. Little crises are put aside until they become big enough to disrupt operations. Before long, the problems multiply until the small staff spends all of its time solving one organization-threatening crisis after another. For example, one month the funds in the bank suddenly are insufficient to cover the payroll. "How could this happen?" everyone asks. No one is really certain because the payroll always managed to get done. Someone points out that it is not a payroll problem but a cash flow one. The investigation into the problem leads to the discovery that everyone was so busy last week dealing with a different crisis that no one deposited the box office receipts in the bank.

This example may seem extreme, but unfortunately it is not. Overextended staff members who handle three or four major functional areas often are the norm in arts organizations. The corporate culture may be summed up as follows: "Because you love the arts, you will have the privilege of working long hours at low pay." Arts groups often thrive on having a workforce "addicted" to the organization and the constant adrenaline-producing excitement associated with getting the show or exhibit finished minutes before it opens to the public.

The dysfunctional manager is a product of this organizational system. The stress levels are high, so reason and logic are in short supply. Decisions are made and then quickly reversed because no one thought through the consequences. On any given day, no one knows what really is going on in the organization because of a lack of clearheaded thinking.

One obvious symptom of an organization suffering dysfunctional management is frequent staff turnover. High-energy people burn out quickly in a culture that requires them to sacrifice their private lives. Workaholic managers who drive their staffs to exhaustion assume that everyone is capable of matching their own work level. A newly hired employee is expected to adapt immediately the intense work ethic and to adopt quietly the value system, no matter how unpleasant. The beginning operations-level staff person, with no point of comparison, accepts the required work level as the norm. A staff member with no power to change the work ethic usually opts to resign. The employee who resigns is immediately identified by the remaining staff as someone who "just didn't like to work hard," carrying on the cultural values of the organization.

The dysfunctional manager   An organization also can become dysfunctional when the management team itself is dysfunctional. The cause of this problem is that the manager simply is not suited for the job. In reality, some people were never intended to be managers. You may encounter individuals who may be excessively defensive, aggressive, or passive; verbal abusive; or withdrawn. Unfortunately, the list could go on. Everyone has problems, but the inescapable fact is that the managing process of the organization tends to reflect the personality of the manager.

Unfortunately, a person hired into this situation usually is unaware that there is a problem until a few weeks have passed. After the first few explosions reveal the true personality of the manager and the character of the organization, the new employee has the option of adapting to this dysfunctional culture, trying to change it, or leaving.

How important is it that a manager be able to exhibit a positive personality profile and possess skills and expertise to help further the goals of the organization? It is central to the success or failure of the entire operation! No matter how beautifully crafted the mission statement or how detailed and comprehensive the strategic, marketing, or fundraising plans may be, if the individuals hired as managers cannot work with people in a way that promotes commitment, responsibility, and a sense of enjoyment about the work to be done, then the chances of ever achieving anything more than mediocrity are slim. It is important to remember that an organization is only as good as the people it employs. There is no escaping the fact that organizations can become dysfunctional because of the people who work within them and not always because of outside forces.

Let us now turn to three positive management approaches and contrast them with the dysfunctional and irrational manager. One of these three approaches, depending on the situation, may be more appropriate for effective leadership and management. Keep in mind the lines between one style or another usually are blurry and on any given day a leader or manager may put any one of more of these styles to good use helping the organization succeed. When reviewing the information in Figure 14–1 keep in mind any one, or a combination of all three styles may be used on a given day.

The Analytical Manager: Changing the Culture

Applying an analytical style of management, which is synonymous with leading and managing, to a dysfunctional situation takes persistence by the manager. The first step in the process is to identify those steps that will be most effective in accelerating change where it is needed the most. Some parts of the organization will be impossible to change quickly, and others may be ready to assist with making things different. No rules or guidelines apply universally when trying to change a culture that has grown self-destructive. However, one obvious point to keep in mind is that changes usually are a great deal easier to instigate by moving with the flow of the organization rather than against it. This simply means that changing the attitudes and values of people by cooperation rather than coercion will greatly accelerate the acceptance of the analytical manager's point of view.

One strategy to pursue is to enlist the support of the other senior staff and board members to undertake an organizational assessment and audit modeled after the marketing audit outlined in Chapter 12. The objective is to make board and staff members more aware of how the

Figure 14-1
Management Styles

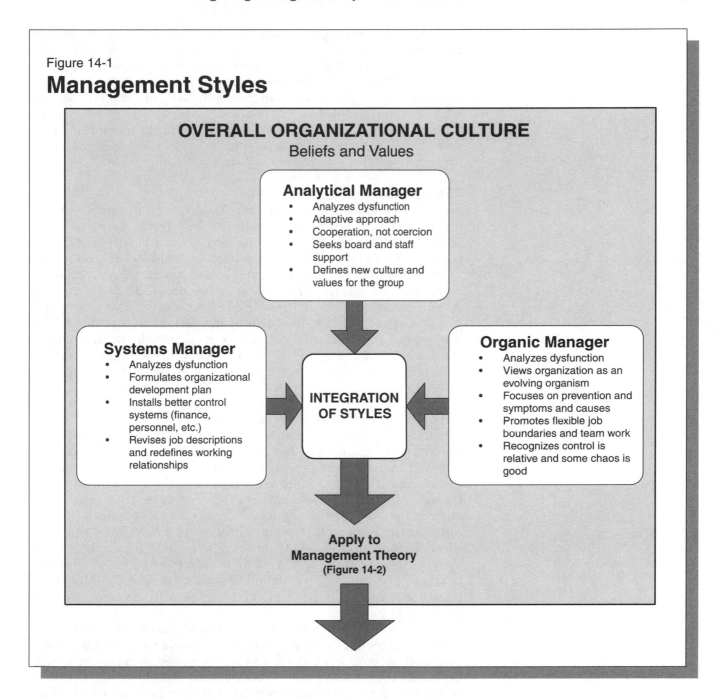

OVERALL ORGANIZATIONAL CULTURE
Beliefs and Values

Analytical Manager
- Analyzes dysfunction
- Adaptive approach
- Cooperation, not coercion
- Seeks board and staff support
- Defines new culture and values for the group

Systems Manager
- Analyzes dysfunction
- Formulates organizational development plan
- Installs better control systems (finance, personnel, etc.)
- Revises job descriptions and redefines working relationships

INTEGRATION OF STYLES

Organic Manager
- Analyzes dysfunction
- Views organization as an evolving organism
- Focuses on prevention and symptoms and causes
- Promotes flexible job boundaries and team work
- Recognizes control is relative and some chaos is good

Apply to Management Theory
(Figure 14-2)

organization behaves and where the values and beliefs need to be changed to make the operation more effective and humane. Making sweeping changes to an organization is a daunting task, especially when that organization is dysfunctional. It can be done, but it may take longer than anticipated. After all, an organization usually takes years to develop a culture of elaborate values and beliefs.

Cultures in conflict were illustrated in numerous examples in this book. For instance, bringing in new artistic leadership is an opportunity for change, but it can lead to counterproductive disruption. Analytical managers understand that rapid change in any organizational system puts a great deal of psychological stress on everyone. Being able to gauge how fast change can be effected is part of the art of managing.

Analytical managers believe that organizations and people learn from their experiences and mature over time. A creative artist and a manager (perhaps the same person), working in cooperation with a board of directors, can use the functions of management to chart a course for the organization that replaces the state of constant crisis and anxiety with controlled growth. Granted, it is not easy to set aside the time for planning and organizing in the midst of the unremitting pressure of daily business, but once a system is in place, the difficulties every organization expects to go through are smoothed out a bit.

The Systems Manager

The systems management style emphasizes organizational development techniques and control systems to help reach the stated objectives. Part of the rise of the systems manager can be attributed to the change from founder-driven arts groups to board-driven arts institutions. The museums, performing arts centers, opera, theater, and dance companies that started off with one or two people 30 or 40 years ago may now employ 50 to 100 people and have multimillion-dollar budgets and extensive office, production, and performance facilities. With this growth and increasing complexity has come the development of the professional arts manager. When a board hires a professional manager, it is usually expects that the organization will adopt a more corporate structure. The change to a more "businesslike" style of operation usually follows a management crisis brought about by a big financial or personnel problem in the organization.

Not everyone greets what could be called the *managerization* of the arts with enthusiasm. For example, some critics say that adding layers of management produces bureaucratic structures that hinder the accomplishment of objectives and add to the operating costs. Although unplanned growth indeed can create such situations, the reality is that most arts organizations tend to function with very limited staff resources; therefore, it is common to give people two, three, or four job titles—any one of which could be a full-time job. What is seen by some as too many managers often is the organization's way of finding a reasonable balance between the number of people required to do the tasks and the organization's stated mission, goals, and objectives.

At another level, the role of the systems manager has grown in response to the increased pressure to produce a balanced budget and the funding community's desire to see its money used responsibly. To cope with the issues of fiscal accountability and increasing organizational complexity, two- and three-headed management structures are finding their way into larger arts organizations.

Regardless of debate about the increasing number of middle- and upper-level managers in arts organizations, the fact remains that what was once an idea in someone's head is now a multimillion-dollar institution in the community. The time and money given by the board of directors, often the most influential people in the community, frequently carry subtle and not so subtle restrictions that can redirect the organization to a safer or less controversial path. A vigilant management and artistic team can work with the board to keep the art alive and challenging. However, given the economic and political pressures, it is not hard to see why many arts institutions begin to engage in forms of self-censorship. If community support for the organization is strong enough, the artistic reasons for performing a particular play or mounting a particular exhibit should outweigh the financial or political pressure placed on the organization.

The Organic Manager

The organic management style recognizes that a changing dynamic exists in organizations and that, like a living organism, the group will grow and change over time. In some ways, the organic manager functions like a doctor who practices preventive medicine. The organic manager works with a dynamic system and focuses on spotting problems that could affect the health of the organization. Intervention is designed to treat the symptoms and the causes. In this case, the tools used to practice this preventive medicine are the theories and practices of management, economics, marketing, and so forth, which have proved to work given specific circumstances.

Organic managers realize that they are working with very distinct groups and that these groups have flexible boundaries of skills and interests that overlap. The ability to give each group a sense of its own importance while, at the same time, promoting communication and understanding is the most important job facing the organization's leaders.

The organic manager also recognizes that there is an element of chaos in any organizational system. However, chaos need not mean that the organization is out of control. In the context of an arts enterprise, chaos is recognized as an element of creative unpredictability. No one is ever sure that a production will really work as planned. Giving artists the freedom to experiment carries with it risks that an organic manager recognizes. The organic manager makes allowances for the different levels of structure required for the various parts of the organization. The accounting department has rules and regulations restricting what can be done, but directors, choreographers, and designers are given more freedom to explore alternative solutions. Recognizing the differences in the way subunits need to operate does not mean abdicating control. The latitude given to creative artists still fits within the overall control system that everyone agrees is necessary.

Management Theories

Having established a management style, which may include a combination of analytical systems and organic techniques, the manager can turn to adapting various management theories to arrive at an overall operating approach to the organization (see Figure 14–2).

Scientific Management

Many of the fiscal and production aspects of an arts organization can benefit from the application of quantitative procedures and ongoing statistical analysis borrowed from the scientific theories of management. Gains in productivity could be realized if constant monitoring of routine procedures is a part of the organization's culture. Is there a more effective way to go about the process of constructing, storing, or rigging scenery? Can money be saved if a rehearsal sequence is altered? Is the method used to enter sales data producing the timely information management needs to quickly spot financial problems? Is the procedure for processing an order organized to reduce the number of steps required? Nearly all of the tracking of responses to mailings, donation requests, marketing, and sales campaigns relies heavily on techniques related to

Figure 14-2

Integration of Management Styles with Theories

MANAGEMENT STYLES

from Figure 14-1

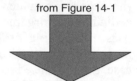

CONTINGENCY OPERATING SYSTEM

Scientific Management Theory

Work Process Analysis: Is work being done most efficiently with resources available?

Quantitative Analysis: Is data gathering system providing information needed to make informed decisions?

Human Relations Theory

Value of Employees: How does the organization value and reward job performance?

Performance Standards: Establish system based on different needs of varied work groups: staff, hourly, contracted, guest artists, board, volunteers

Open System Model

Input: How does external environments and internal information systems shape the organization?

Transformation Process: How are the resources and inputs transformed to deliver the events produced by the organization?

Output: How well does the organization fulfill its stated mission, goals and objectives?

Management of the organization

scientific management. As we saw in Chapters 9 and 11, an organization's MIS and FMIS require the vigorous application of quantitative systems if the organization is to stay informed about its fiscal health.

One clear signal that it is appropriate to undertake a more scientific approach to aspects of the operation is when you hear the phrase, "But we have always done it that way around here." There may be good reasons why certain procedures are accomplished in specific ways, but nearly everything that is done routinely usually can be done more efficiently if given some thought.

Human relations　As we saw in Chapters 3 and 8, the human relations approach to management grew out of McGregor's Theory X and Theory Y, Maslow's hierarchy of needs, behaviorist theory, and other psychological approaches to the workplace. Because the product of a performing arts organization is the work of people, there is a natural fit between human resource management and an arts organization. The arts manager must realize that each employee group has its own set of behaviors and expectations about the work of the organization. For example, the stagehands working on a show will have a very different perspective about their job and their place in the organization than that of fund raising assistants. Both support jobs are needed to make the show work, but employees in each category need different types of recognition and rewards for their contributions to the organization.

Developing performance standards and an appraisal system that recognizes the similarities and differences in employee groups while keeping employees focused on the defined objectives requires a significant commitment of the manager's time. Given the dynamics of an arts organization, once-a-year job reviews simply will not monitor adequately the work output of employees. Daily, weekly, or monthly reviews of employee performance may be more appropriate, depending on the type of work being done.

Attention must also be paid to how effectively the organization's communication and management information systems are working. Information often is equated with power. Those who have the information have power over those who do not. However, this is a very destructive approach to information management. As we saw in Chapter 6, all organizations have formal and informal structures and communication systems. If any employee group is excluded from the communication system, the risk of rumors and the harmful distortion of information increases in great leaps. No employee communication system is perfect, but it makes little sense to establish communication approaches guaranteed to alienate people.

The Open System

The open system and the ability to adjust to changing circumstances were stressed in many chapters in this text. Input from clients, audience, staff, and so on is combined with input from the external environments—economic, political and legal, cultural and social, demographic, technological, and educational—to produce an organization that constantly changes and adjusts to the world around it. The open system approach to management does not mean that the organization's mission undergoes constant change. Rather, the open system allows the organization to capitalize on opportunities that support its mission while minimizing the impact of threats to the enterprise. For example, new digital video technology may provide additional cash flow opportunities for the arts by opening up new markets for distribution of their product and by creating new viewing audiences. At the same time, an adverse tax ruling by the IRS or a proposed federal law that affects labor practices can be addressed through active participation in the political system.

The Contingency System: An Integrating Approach

The approaches and theories reviewed thus far all are directed at finding a way to integrate the various styles and theories of management into a workable system. Combinations of analytical, systems, and organic management techniques applied to theories of scientific management, human relations, and the open system can help a manager achieve results when carrying out the functions of management.

One model that meshes these styles and theories is shown in Figure 14–2. The integration of these styles and theories into what is called a *contingency system* holds much promise. The important point to remember with this system is that, depending on the circumstances and the nature of the problem, the manager can pick and choose options, combining some portion of each approach. Sometimes, it is a human resource problem; at other times, it is a quantitative problem; and on still other occasions, the problem relates back to a change in one or more of the environments or input groups. Each individual will feel comfortable with different applications of a contingency system; however, the central point is that a manager must actively choose the particular combination of styles and theories that will best solve the organization's problems.

Let us review the functional areas of management from the perspective of applying the contingency system of management.

The Management Functions

The center of the arts organization's operational system is found in the functions listed in this section. The goal of the entire organization should be to take the contingency system, which integrates management styles and theories, and apply it to the operational areas in ways that achieve the organization's stated goals and objectives.

Planning and Development

Looking toward the future is a major responsibility of a manager in any organization. As we saw in Chapter 5, the ability to plan requires no special genius. The key ingredients are self-discipline and an established process. Of course, the underlying culture of the organization must value looking ahead and should stress the involvement of the board and all levels of staff in the process. Every action that an organization takes must relate to the overall master plan. If it does not, human and other resources will be misdirected and ultimately wasted.

Types of plans   All managers, including overextended managers, engage in short-term and crisis planning. Problems such as cash flow difficulties, a show that might have to be canceled, a tour cut short because presenters backed out at the last minute, a work of art damaged at an exhibit, or the death of a member of the cast are part of the business. Managers with a methodology in place for problem solving quickly identify the source of the difficulty, generate alternatives, and implement and evaluate decisions before a crisis develops that threatens the operation of the organization. Written outlines and procedures to follow when a crisis does strike can help the organization keep its balance.

Intermediate-range planning (one to five years) is integral to the program development and fund-raising activities of an arts group. Launching any fund-raising campaign requires coordinated planning to organize resources and people in cost-effective ways. The case must be strong, and the reasons for giving must be clear to potential donors. The need for the funds must relate directly to the organization's strategic planning.

Long-range strategic planning and development (five to ten years), although always subject to revision, are important processes in helping to shape the organization's future. Long-term planning is a serious business, but the enjoyable and creative side of the process should not be overlooked. "What if" discussions among the board, the artists, and the staff can lead to new ideas and directions. In fact, planning is a break from the routine of day-to-day work, and it should be a strong selling point for potential board members. After all, would you rather be on a board of directors that was actively engaged in charting the future of the organization or would you prefer to sit through yet another report detailing fund balance transfers?

Marketing and Public Relations

Arts organizations are businesses that must function in the highly competitive entertainment industry. Effective marketing and positive public relations can help any enterprise target and inform people of goods and services designed to meet their wants and needs. The key to success, especially given the very limited resources that most arts groups have to work with, lies with making sure that you are talking to the right people.

The universe of goods and services seems to be expanding as thousands of new products come on the market every month, making the task of keeping an arts organization visible even more exacting. Therefore, expanded press and media relations must be a central part of the organization's strategic plan if the organization is to command any attention.

As we saw in Chapter 12, marketing is an organizational orientation that places the consumer at the beginning of the process. To be truly customer driven is seen as an ideal in establishing a long-term product-consumer relationship. However, many arts organizations equate being "customer driven" with lower artistic standards and pandering to the public. They therefore engage in what is more accurately described as a "selling orientation" toward the public. The selling approach assumes that if consumers are made aware of the product, they will buy it. In more extreme cases, organizations adopt a product orientation, which assumes that because the product is so inherently good, people will want to buy it.

Marketing strategies   Chapter 12 pointed out that the adoption of a marketing orientation for an arts organization requires a careful analysis of the four Ps (product, price, promotion, and place) and, at the same time, an understanding of the limits of marketing. For example, no marketing campaign suddenly will create an arts audience by changing the well-established behavior of masses of people overnight. As we have seen, the audience for high-culture events is a by-product of the education system, especially at the college and university levels. Arts marketers interested in building a long-term purchase and donation relationship with consumers would assemble demographic and psychographic profiles of the community, and a distribution of neighborhoods by spending type (e.g., money and furs, pools and patios) in an effort to piece together the most effective campaign that the available resources permit. The objective is to get inside the consumer's head to find out what combination of the four Ps will lead to the exchange process: money in exchange for the arts experience.

Of course, marketing strategies need not be targeted to only a limited segment of the population. Marketing to reach a diverse audience is important and will become critical as the demographic composition of America continues to change. The key to reaching people lies with how and what you communicate about the product to the public. Reaching new audiences, especially members of minority groups, depends on the mix of programs and community outreach, the right price, and access to the facility.

It must be stressed again that all of the innovative marketing strategies in the world cannot create an arts consumer overnight. Marketing is a long-term investment of the organization's resources. Results should be measured over three- to five-year periods of time not just one season.

Finally, it is important to remember that marketing and fund raising share the similar goal of establishing an exchange relationship with audience members and donors. The progression from single ticket buyer to subscriber or member and finally to long-term donor dictates an integrated plan under the general heading of development.

Personnel Management: Staff, Labor, and Board Relations

Even when the manager adopts a human resource management strategy that takes into account the various attitudes and values of the different work groups within the organization, being able to keep employees happy and productive still is an enormous challenge. Establishing working conditions that support the creative process and encourage artists, the board, and staff members is one of the manager's primary objectives. This would seem to be self-evident, but judging by the stories of performers, designers, staff members, and technicians about the abuses of management—which also includes directors, conductors, and choreographers—it is a miracle that strife is not more prevalent in arts organizations.

Unions   The abusive past practices of management were a primary reason for the establishment of unions in the arts. Although managers and unions may never see eye-to-eye about how the organization operates, it remains management's job to establish the criteria for performance. For the arts manager, defining acceptable practices is at the heart of the relationship with the union because, when both sides sit down to negotiate a contract, the odds are very high that labor and management will not agree about levels of compensation, benefits, and work rules. The arts manager who does not understand how the backstage really works in a theater, concert hall, or museum will at a huge disadvantage when it comes time to evaluate the rules written into a contract. A lack of appreciation for the work environment could cost the organization thousands of dollars every time a show is performed or an event takes place. In addition, an arts manager must remember that a union is also a complex organization and therefore subject to the same external and internal forces that shape the arts group. Understanding the perspective of union members and the union organization can make the arts manager's job a little easier.

Board of directors   Another group that is part of the overall mix of human resources in the arts is the board of directors. Managing relations with the board is just as important to senior- and middle-level staff members as a successful contract negotiation with a union. The board, which could be made up of as few as 8 or more than 50 people, has its power blocs, hard workers, and deadwood, just like any other organization. A powerful finance committee, for example, could prevent a manager from implementing new programs by not approving a budget. A board personnel committee could hold up a key appointment or lobby for a candidate of the board's choosing. Approval of a season might be held up if the board has doubts about the works selected.

For the arts manager, a clear picture of the scope of the board's power and responsibility is of primary importance if the organization is to function effectively. In numerous case studies in this book, we have seen board actions both strengthen and undermine arts groups. There never seems to be a shortage of stories about the communication gap between artistic directors and the board. The case study in this chapter provides a good example of board-staff challenges.

Personnel management   Meanwhile, as organizations mature, issues of salaries, staff training, and renewal will become more important. Finding new challenges, revising job descriptions, reorganizing departments utilizing volunteers, and combining or separating jobs all should become part of the overall operation of the personnel area.

When adding up all of the work required managing the personnel functions of an arts organization, artistic directors or museum directors might wonder when they will have time to direct a production or engage in scholarly research. In reality, there is no time. Upper-level managers, like artistic directors who involve themselves in production, find that, more often than not, one or more functional areas are left unattended. What strategy can an artistic director use to resolve this conflict? One obvious approach has been to split the job into different positions based on operations and product development. This explains why more organizations are creating two or three upper-level management positions to supervise the fiscal, planning, and operational aspects of the arts enterprise. The trade-off for some artistic directors is that they must share their power with others. At some future date, should conflict arise with the board, artistic directors might find one of their operational peers undermining their credibility and forming a power bloc against them.

Fiscal Management

The area of fiscal planning and control also is at the core of the arts organization. A large portion of a manager's time probably will be spent on this area, often at the expense of such equally important areas as planning, programming, and staff development. Financial management is at the center of so much attention because expectations about the amount of money that can be generated through sales and donations often are unrealistic. At the same time, prices, labor, and operating costs continue to escalate higher than anticipated. The combination of these two elements establishes a perpetual deficit hanging over many organizations.

In *The Quiet Crisis in the Arts*, McDaniel and Thorn note that arts organizations are in a state of constant debt crisis, which produces an unbelievable amount of personal stress on the staff.[1] The cycle of over-spending followed by painful budget cutting takes its toll on people. When artistic directors speak of maintaining quality even in the face of budget cuts of tens of thousands of dollars, people know that it simply is untrue. If you cut the budget, you reduce quality. The expectation that the performers, designers, technicians, museum preparators, and others will somehow be able to create the same quality product with fewer rehearsals, less money for resources, and so forth is total nonsense. The assumption seems to be, "If we say often enough that we are not going to lose quality by cutting budgets, then maybe everyone will begin to believe it." Managing and leading by fiscal self-delusion is hardly the most effective way to build board and staff confidence. As a matter of fact, a board member asked to raise yet another million dollars might ask, "Well, if we can do the same quality with a million dollar budget cut, why did we go a million dollars in debt in the first place?" The answer usually comes back, "Because we are dedicated to pursuing excellence in the arts." The more accurate answer would be, "Because we didn't know how to effectively manage the human and production resources we had available to us." Needless to say, the latter reason usually is not a discussion item for staff and board meetings.

Strategies   A few fiscal management strategies are likely to keep the organization solvent and the board confident. They include the following:

- Realistic budget planning procedures for revenue first, then expenses,
- Organizational attitudes and values that stress that budgets are not to be exceeded,
- Very tight control and oversight systems for expenditures,
- A clear picture of the cash flow needs of the organization,
- A system for accounts payable activity that pays no bill before its time except when there is a discount for early payment,
- A very aggressive "asset management program" that involves investment in a wide range of financial instruments.

Government Relations
As we learned in Chapter 4, government relations extend from the federal to the local level. A manager's involvement in the political arena usually is fairly limited. However, as we have seen in the last decade, without the support of the people who make the laws and sit on the appropriations committees, arts organizations will suffer. Arts groups must earn the support of elected officials at all levels of government. Support is not given just because the arts organizations and artists think their enterprise is nobler than other agencies established for a public good.

The first step for successfully interacting with the government system is education. The arts manager must learn how the various local, state, and federal systems work. The second step involves learning about the power brokers and the issues close to them and their constituents. The third step requires the arts manager to visit the various representatives in an effort to become visible. The fourth step involves making the newfound visibility mean something by updating the representatives about the organization's important activities and the positive impact of the arts on the community.

For a weary arts manager trying to cover all of the management functions described in this section, the political system, with its complex subculture, is not always the highest priority. If the arts manager is too busy to have lunch with the local director of cultural affairs or to go to a candidate's fund-raising dinner, there should be no surprise when politicians do not spring to the rescue when the arts group has a budget crisis or some other problem.

Conclusion

The goal of developing an integrated approach to management styles and theories is to help the organization succeed at whatever it attempts. As we have seen, managing is an intensely personal process. The theories may provide the overall structure, but the effectiveness of any management system ultimately depends on the people who are doing the managing. The ability to establish an overall work environment where people can express a point of view without fearing for their jobs or where they can make suggestions that will be heard often is overlooked when it comes to designing an organization. Of course, people who work in any organization want to earn enough money to live comfortably, and they want to have the support of health benefits should they have an accident or become ill, but on a day-to-day basis, people also have an intense desire to believe that their work is making a worthwhile contribution and that their effort is being recognized in some way. Therefore, a manager always must remember that it is the people who are important to the organization not just the product. Treating people with respect and recognizing their daily contribution to the enterprise are key ingredients in successful organizations.

To integrate management styles and theories, managers also must know their own strengths and weaknesses. Undertaking a personal inventory helps a manager to see more clearly the things the organization does well and identify areas that need improvement. The advantage of using this approach is that it keeps the manager and the organization renewed. It also is important for the manager to reap a personal satisfaction when it comes time to evaluate how well things are working. Success is a great motivating force, especially when it is widely recognized throughout an organization.

Questions

1. Based on your own experiences, can you cite examples of situations in which analytical, systems, or organic management styles were used to solve a problem effectively?

2. With proven approaches to managing, such as scientific and human relations management, and organizational models, such as the open system, to help guide operations, why do so many arts groups have trouble with their management structures?

3. Use any of the case studies in this text to provide examples of the effective use of the following functional areas:
   - Planning and development,
   - Marketing and public relations,
   - Personnel management,
   - Fiscal management,
   - Government relations.

Case Study

A Dramatic Disagreement: Did the Rep Have to Die?
Yes, says the board; no way, says the staff.
Barry Johnson

Most of the facts involved in the January 22 decision to close the doors at Portland Repertory Theatre aren't in dispute.

The company was carrying a sizable debt, and cash-flow problems were so acute that it was going to miss at least one payroll.

But did the theater need to die? On that crucial point, the staff and board of Portland's second-largest theater company are completely at odds.

And local actors who have been part of artistic director Dennis Bigelow's splendid unofficial company are outraged at the board's decision.

"I think that these people just plain wanted out," said David Meyers, one of the actors in the Rep's production of "Old Wicked Songs" that was closed down by the board in the middle of its run.

"They were just tired of playing with it and decided to kill it," he continued. "They killed a vital organization for their convenience."

Board members such as Bill Coniff have a different view: "We had no choice," Coniff said. "We held it off as long as we could."

The Rep's death leaves a gaping hole in Portland's arts scene. During the past three years under Bigelow, the Rep has been the home of some of the best theater in town—such productions as "Three Tall Women," "Two Trains Running" and "Arcadia." And it's been an important home for many of the city's best actors, many of whom may not be able to stay here without the work the Rep provided.

But no matter who is right, the essential fact is that Portland Repertory Theatre is gone.

What went wrong behind the scenes while the company was moving from success to success onstage?

The Rep's troubles didn't start yesterday. It had been struggling with a large deficit long before Bigelow was named artistic director three years ago—nearly $500,000 for a nonprofit that brought in little more than $1 million in its best years.

And the deficit had grown in the two years before Bigelow arrived while the company, under Geoffrey Sherman's leadership, had anticipated to upgrade itself and become a player in the regional theater world. When Sherman left to become artistic director of Meadow Brook Theatre in Michigan, the board had serious discussions about closing the theater.

But it decided to carry on, choosing Bigelow to help it put its financial and artistic house in order.

Bigelow actually began to shrink the deficit. But a double whammy brought his financial juggling to a halt in October. The company owed significant sums of money to both its bank, U.S. Bank, and its landlord, the World Trade Center. It was broke, it couldn't borrow money, and the new season's expenses were about to pile up in earnest.

Bigelow went public with his plight, telling *The Oregonian* that if a significant rescue attempt wasn't mounted the theater would have to close.

The Regional Arts and Culture Council and the Northwest Business Committee for the Arts responded by hiring well-regarded arts consultant George Thorn.

Thorn's conclusions were surprisingly optimistic. The company had already taken major steps to cut its expenses, trimming staff and moving to smaller, cheaper quarters. It had just finished its fiscal year with a small surplus. Its artistic achievements had just been recognized with the local Drammy Award for best show of the year for its production of "Arcadia." Thorn thought that if the company could start an aggressive fund-raising campaign to help it through its cash-flow difficulties, its long-term prospects were good.

Good Signs

Sure enough, when the staff went to its subscribers with a plea for money, they responded surprisingly well. Since October, the Rep had raised more than $170,000, much of it in small contributions from subscribers.

"I think it's significant that our Community stepped forward for us, and for the first time we didn't borrow money in October, November or December," Bigelow said. The Rep had frequently used its line of credit with U.S. Bank to get through those high expense, low-income months. Traditionally, the company was flush with cash in the spring, when its subscribers signed on for the next year. Last year's receipts for those months were more than $280,000, Bigelow said.

So, the game was to get through the lean months until the spring's cash infusion.

Living today on tomorrow's receipts can be a dangerous sport. The subscribers, after all, were paying for shows they wouldn't see until next year. Allen Nause, artistic director of Artists Repertory Theatre, the city's third-largest theater, said his company tries never to use its subscription income on anything but expenses for the upcoming season. But it's still a common practice. Artists Rep, known for its conservative financial philosophy, has done it in bad years. And it's simply a fact of life for many other arts organizations with subscription seasons to sell.

"In this day and age, when arts organizations aren't carrying huge cash reserves, there's always the need to finance your work from a cash-flow standpoint," said Cynthia M. Fuhrman, director of public relations and marketing at the city's biggest theater, Portland Center Stage. "It's not just theaters; it's symphonies, operas and ballets, too."

That's why subscription renewal campaigns for the next season start an early.

January Slump

Money from the Rep's contributions dried up in January. And although both "Molly Sweeny" and "Putting It Together," the company's fall and Christmas shows, were critical hits and did reasonably well at the box office, they didn't meet the Rep's projections. Bigelow and board members say the box office was hurt because the company didn't have enough money to advertise them well.

Last season, the company used a Meyers Memorial Trust grant quite successfully to boost single-ticket sales. Its "Arcadia" did about $70,000 worth of single-ticket sales. The advertising money wasn't available for this season.

"We faced the immediate cash flow crisis of not being able to meet payroll," Bigelow said. "It caught the staff a little off guard when we missed payroll, but to a person they were willing to work to make the season happen. Everyone knew we were about to mail next season's renewal form."

After that, things moved fast. The board met January 20 and 22 to deal with the problem of missing the payroll. At the first meeting, the board decided to consult a bankruptcy attorney. At the second, it voted to close the theater's doors.

Board President Avery Loschen said the board looked at the staff's projections of revenues and expenses as well as cash flow. Board members estimated the percentage of outstanding grants that were likely to come through. And they came to a stark conclusion "It was not prudent for us to accept donations or start a subscription campaign if we didn't believe we could mount a new season. And we don't believe we could have mounted a new season. Given the numbers we were given by the staff, anybody who would have made the decision to go forward would not have been making a prudent business decision."

Another Interpretation

The staff has a completely different assessment. It argued that the situation wasn't as dire as the board made it sound and that the board did a dismal job of raising money.

"They are confusing cash flow, the immediate problem, with end-of-the-year performance," said Michelle Schneiter, the company's director of development. "Our projections all showed we were going to do $30,000 better than last year, which was our first season in the black.

Schneiter said the company had received positive signals on two pending grants, one for $50,000 and another for $10,000. News from the foundations was expected by the end of January or early February, she said.

"I can tell you in the past we've been led to believe we were going to get grants and they didn't come through" Loschen responded. "Anyway, the money wasn't enough to solve the problems."

The staff, Schneiter said, was hoping board members would solve the immediate cash-flow problem by lending the company money to meet payroll. Then the company would use income from season subscriptions to repay the board.

But Schneiter's critique of the board didn't stop there. "January was a challenge, and we really needed the board to fund raise. They just didn't, " she said.

Since we went public in mid-October, they raised very little money, less than 10 grand. That was pretty frustrating. I chalk that up to poor leadership on the board."

Board President Loschen disagreed. "Many, many of those checks were solicited by board members during that urgent campaign," he said.

Thorn's report on the company had suggested that expanding the company's circle of significant donors, traditionally a function of the board, was crucial to its success.

"Generally, we did not have enough contacts to broaden our base of funders," Bigelow said. "That was going to be the key to the Rep's future." He said only 1 of 19 board members was doing a good job in this area, though the board did raise $40,000, including one $10,000 gift, from among its members before it went public with its problems in October.

Ask Schneiter, should the Rep have closed its doors, and the here response is succinct. "Yes, we did have to close, because the board didn't want to fund raise. *Should* it have closed? No."

From the Outside

It's difficult to sort out this profound disagreement between staff and board. Both sides agree that the company had a large deficit and severe cash-flow problems. They even agree that substantive steps had been taken to correct the problems.

But the board decided those steps were not enough. "We kept hoping an angel would appear, but it never happened," Coniff said.

Bill Bulick, executive director of the Regional Arts and Culture Council and a longtime audience member of Portland Rep, followed the company closely the past few months.

"There was a rallying around the company," he said. "Money came in, and it seemed there was a possibility to dig the company out of its cash-flow crisis and its deficit. The board had to be aware of the heavy lifting this would involve and didn't think it was up to it."

But the larger community is also complicit, he said. "It always seems like there should be more resources than there are out there because this community says it cares about having these vital, creative people in its midst."

Aftermath

For the actors who frequently worked at Portland Center Stage, the closing of the company is disastrous. As one of two full Equity companies in town (Artists Repertory Theatre recently joined this small group, but it is operating under special rules for the next three years), Portland Rep was an important source of employment for the city's best actors.

Actors David Meyers and Sharonlee McLean are maintaining a wait-and-see attitude. McLean has started regular gatherings of actors to talk about what happened and begin to think shout starting a new theater along the lines of Portland Rep. But just about everyone in the theater community worries about what might happen to the scene here.

During the past few years, the number of talented, accomplished actors in Portland has increased dramatically. Portland Rep, using locally based actors for nearly all its shows, was one of the major reasons for this growth. Without the Rep, those actors have far fewer chances to work—and actors from other cities one less reason for coming.

For audiences, the niche the Rep filled, bringing recent American plays to Portland for sharp, professional productions, is empty. It's difficult to imagine the fall season this year without the powerful performances of Gretchen Corbett, David Ivers and Wayne Ballantyne in Brian Friel's delicate "Molly Sweeney." In thinking about theater in Portland without experiences like this one, the magnitude of the loss of Portland Repertory Theatre begins to sink home.

Sources: Barry Johnson, "A Dramatic Disagreement: Did the Rep Have to Die?" *Sunday Oregonian*. Copyright © 1998 by The Sunday Oregonian. Used with permission.

Case Study Questions

1. Identify and summarize the major differences between the board and the staff over the closing of the theater.

2. Based on the facts as they are stated in this article do you believe the board was correct in taking the action it did? Why or why not?

3. What would be a better business practice than paying for current year expenses with the next season subscription sales? What suggestions do you have for this or any arts organization about managing cash flow?

4. The article stresses the importance of the board fundraising function. However, it would appear that the $500,000 deficit played a factor in bringing the company to a close. What overall leadership and management styles would you suggest could have been adopted by the Portland Rep to possibly have averted this closing?

Reference

1. Nello McDaniel and George Thorn, *Workpapers: A Special Report—The Quiet Crisis in the Arts* (New York: ARTS Action Issues, 1991).

Final Thoughts

15
□ □ □ □

In the previous chapter, we discussed the integration of theory and practice with specific styles of management. It seems appropriate to end this text with a brief discussion of the future. When it comes to actually making an organization work, the pressing demands of the day-to-day routine seem to devour every available minute. There never seems to be enough hours in the day to put aside time for the future.

As we have seen throughout this book, middle- and upper-level managers always look beyond the immediate future. The planning process can be viewed in much the same way that an artist views a rehearsal: as an opportunity to refine and perfect the work before an actual performance. Most performing artists always find room for improvement in their work, even after what many people would call a brilliant performance. The arts manager must adopt this attitude about planning: It never ends, and there always is room for improvement. If, as the saying goes, the way to Carnegie Hall is through practice, then the way to become a first-rate arts organization is through the equivalent of constant planning.

This last chapter focuses on the future. When venturing into this territory, there are no right answers—except in hindsight. Keeping that in mind, we look at current trends and possible future directions that point toward growth. We examine some of the key economic realities facing arts groups.

Current Trends and Future Directions

One could find optimistic and pessimistic views on nearly every aspect of an arts organization's operation. The most troubling area is the fiscal health of the arts. Despite what appears to be a great deal of grassroots support for the arts in most communities, competition for the entertainment dollar continues to increase each year. About the only thing that it is safe to say about today's arts organizations is that they will be more expensive to operate tomorrow. Finding the resources to keep the doors open will require continuous effort on the part of the arts manager.

The financial health of the organization is linked directly to the willingness of donors, patrons, members, or ticket buyers to support the programming of the organization. Support, as we have seen, is related to how well you communicate your needs and how well the programs you present satisfy the exchange process. If people like the shows you do or the exhibits you present and they have a positive image of the quality of your organization, the chances for building long-term support are increased significantly. Organizational survival depends on developing a loyal and supportive audience because, to put it bluntly, they are a stable cash flow. In addition, it is a fact that only a limited number of people have the income, education, motivation, and time to spend their discretionary income on tickets and donations to your organization.

Realistically, America probably will not undergo a cultural renaissance any time soon. Like it or not, the commercial mass entertainment media sets the context in which the fine and performing arts must function and compete. Thousands of people will not be spontaneously turning off their television sets and choosing to become subscribers and patrons of the arts any time soon. Therefore, the universe of potential audience members is limited. Luckily, the artists driven to create and share their creations with the public do not let the challenge of finding an audience become their first priority. If they did, they might abandon their worthwhile efforts. Our job as arts managers is helping the artist find that audience, and as you have seen from this text, it requires as much creativity, intelligence, passion, and commitment as the artist possesses.

The Future Is Always Uncertain

The future is always uncertain, and predicting what things will be like 5, 10, or 20 years from now really is nothing more than a mental exercise. We can spot trends and track them, but that is about it. Within this uncertain future, we would classify some people as pessimists, who describe the proverbial cup filled to 50 percent capacity as half empty, and others as optimists, who call it half filled. For an arts manager facing cutbacks in funding support on many fronts, limited corporate support as companies focus on competing worldwide, increasing insurance costs, spiraling production and labor costs, an aging audience, and very low growth in discretionary income, it is hard to see a rosy future.

The statistics clearly indicate that, since the 1960s, thousands of new arts institutions have been created all across the United States. Regional theater, opera, and dance companies; music groups of all sizes; performing arts complexes; university arts programs; and numerous museums now exist in communities with no past history of arts patronage. Millions of people subscribe, have memberships, or regularly buy tickets to events that employ tens of thousands of artists and support personnel. By every account, the cup looks more than half filled. Why, then, is there pessimism?

The efforts of the last 30 years—which have produced significant funding increases from government, foundations, and corporations—are only closing the income gap enough to delay the inevitable financial collapse of many not-for-profit organizations. In many cases, it appears that the increased funding and ticket sales associated with the baby boom audience helped fuel growth beyond the long-term abilities of private and public support. Therefore, the condition seems to be one of too many groups seeking too few funds, and as the market system theory predicts, some organizations will have to drop out of the market to restore equilibrium.

Modest to No Growth?

For the larger, well-established arts organizations, rapid growth is a thing of the past in some parts of the United States. Arts groups in the South and West will have the opportunity to capture new audiences as those regions grow. In the Northeast and Central regions of the country, the population loss slowed in the early 1990s, but it is unrealistic to think that the millions who moved away will be back any time soon. The continuing shift to a global economy and the need to keep labor costs as low as possible may further accelerate the exodus from many of the older cities in the East and Midwest.

The NEA study on the baby boom attendance patterns discussed in Chapter 12 also may have an impact on future growth in the arts audience. The finding that the percentage of baby boomers attending the fine and performing arts was lower than previous generations presents a challenge arts managers cannot ignore. It would be foolish to predict a cataclysmic decline in arts attendance in the next 30 years. Change typically creeps up on organization until it accumulates to the point that a crisis is reached. However, it is safe to say the effort and cost to maintain, and incrementally increase, the current numbers of subscribers, patrons, or members at a rate that corresponds to the demands of the arts workers for increased pay and benefits will be enormous.

The pressures felt by the not-for-profit arts manager to keep people coming to the shows and exhibits are not any less than in the commercial entertainment industry. The issue of how much people will pay to be entertained and what appeals to the public are central to the Broadway stage, touring events, pop concerts, theme parks, and the like. For example, by the late 1990s, the $60 to $75 theater ticket was common on Broadway. Likewise the half-priced ticket booth in Time Square continues to do a booming business. The participation of the Disney Corporation on Broadway has brought renovation to theaters and a profitable extension to the product life cycle of movies and merchandise related to *The Lion King* and *Beauty and the Beast*, for example.

Ultimately, the success of the profit and not-for-profit arts and entertainment sectors will depend on the product and the appeal of that product to very defined target markets. One can only assume that the search for the artistic product will be relentless and the level of marketing and advertising will escalate. Keeping the fine and performing arts visible in this very competitive entertainment environment will only continue to increase in difficulty.

Arts Facilities and Social Engineering

The process of creating or renovating performing arts centers in downtown areas in large cities, despite population losses, has helped lead to an economic revival in some communities and has provided homes for many of the newly created performing arts companies and visual arts organizations. The concept of arts centers surrounded by apartments, condominiums, and shopping malls is appealing because it can lead to a critical mass of economic development and expansion. For example, if enough people shop and use the services of the stores and the arts groups, a self-sustaining microeconomic system could be developed within the community. In reality, however, the loans used to start up these new buildings and businesses must be paid and operating costs continue to rise. The cash flow required to keep these businesses alive may prove insufficient unless enough people can be enticed to resettle in central city areas. Noontime shoppers will not generate enough economic development to support the entire system. Meanwhile, the arts group may be left with a lot of new, expensive overhead in the form of a building that absorbs hard-earned dollars.

The development of the arts complex and the commerce to support it, in many ways, is an attempt at a type of social engineering. However, if the rest of the society and its leaders are not capable of creating a system of government and control that solves fundamental problems like poverty, racism, and crime, we should not be surprised to find that these arts centers turn into ghost towns on the evenings when no performances are scheduled. When coupled with a constant barrage of stories in the media about the murder and mayhem in the streets, it is little wonder that the vast majority of the people who attend the arts live far away from the cities.

Until other serious social problems are solved, the urban arts center will require heavy subsidies in combination with substantial private giving if it is to survive. It remains to be seen how cities strapped for resources will be able to afford politically to support these expensive operations as city services continue to decline. The search for funds to create an operating endowment will probably be a high priority for several major arts organizations during the remainder of this decade.

Conclusion

Trying to predict glory or gloom for the fine and performing arts in the United States is a risky business. The variables seem almost infinite. The external environments, the audiences, and the always-changing interests of artists make for a dynamic mix. Looking to the past will not prove a useful method for predicting the future of the arts, because there are no similar combinations of circumstances to use as guides. Far more arts organizations of all sizes are distributed across the United States today than ever before. Although many of these organizations spring into existence overnight and go out of business just as fast, a substantial number have been established in the last 20 years. Why? One answer lies with the greater number of people who have attained some knowledge in or experience with the arts through their education. If the number of people earning college degrees continues to increase faster than the growth in population, the established arts organizations and many new groups may flourish in the next 20 years. At the same time, rising education costs and dwindling financial support for students may undermine this trend. It is hard to believe that, with the United States facing increasing global competition, the political system will fail to find the resources to educate its people to the level required to stay competitive.

The Partnership: Artist and Manager

Running an arts organization never was and never will be easy. Although arts organizations can benefit from applying management theory and practice to become better organized and more efficient, still no single element guarantees survival. Getting better at doing well is an ambitious goal that any arts manager should be proud to work toward. To achieve that goal, an arts manager should be prepared to borrow any techniques that work from business, government, educational institutions, or other not-for-profit organizations. Successfully integrating these different approaches to effectively manage an organization requires as much creativity as any visual or performing artist. Forging a successful partnership of manager and artist therefore is predicated on each party recognizing the other's creative contribution to one goal: creating a world in which life is enriched by the accomplishments of both parties.

A Final Question

What are *your* predictions about how the arts will fare in the United States during the next 10 to 20 years? Will there be growth or shrinkage? Will demographic shifts and changing cultural values change attendance patterns at arts events? Will the political system help or hinder the arts?

Index